The Vetting of Wisdom

The Vetting of Wisdom

*Joan Montgomery and
the fight for PLC*

KIM RUBENSTEIN

Copyright © Kim Rubenstein
First published 2021
Franklin Street Press

All rights reserved. No part of this publication may be reproduced, distributed, or transmitted in any form or by any means, including photocopying, recording, or other electronic or mechanical methods, without the prior written permission of the publisher, except in the case of brief quotations embodied in critical reviews and certain other non-commercial uses permitted by copyright law.

ISBN 978-0-6488998-0-8 (paperback)

 A catalogue record for this book is available from the National Library of Australia

Book and cover design: Peter Fullerton

We all have things for which we are especially grateful, we also know that there are particular things in which we could do better,
— we could be more tolerant and less ready to condemn
— we could be more aware of others' difficulties
— more ready to share our time and talents.

For a few moments, let us think quietly of
— those things for which we are especially thankful
— the things in which we resolve to do better.

Joan Montgomery
Beginning of Term Assembly
25 May 1982

Contents

Acknowledgments ix
Foreword xvii

1	Jeopardy	1
2	*Loch Long*	11
3	PLC Girls	25
4	A Church in Hawthorn	51
5	Coronation	65
6	Excommunicated	93
7	Clyde	111
8	PLC Principal	127
9	Ruined	159
10	Miss Montgomery	187
11	A 12 to 5 Carve Up	215
12	Church Tightens PLC Hold	235
13	I'll Have To Ask Mr Bradshaw	263
14	Outcry	287
15	Fight the Good Fight	307
16	The Final Year	341

Afterword 357
Notes to Chapters 373
Index 385

Acknowledgments

To produce a biography is to owe thanks to many people, particularly when it has taken so long in the writing. Begun when a young lawyer back from studying overseas and looking for an intellectual diversion while planning to resume my junior position in a large law firm, I was not to know then of the extended journey ahead of me. The prospect of further overseas study was soon ahead but not to begin immediately. So, to keep myself stimulated, I approached Joan Montgomery to write her biography. She was a reluctant starter but a starter nonetheless and I took full advantage of the half-opened door. Well, it may have begun that way but as the years rolled by her cooperation was total. She was ever modest and never thrust herself forward, but she was always there to assist me. We met regularly, there were many interviews over many hours and she gave me ready access to diaries, letters, documents and photographs, many of which she entrusted to my keeping. She read the numerous drafts, noted corrections and sometimes disagreed graciously with the content, context and interpretation of my accounts. She was never insistent, however, and always made clear that it was *my* book. She was always forgiving of my shifting finishing dates as the project meandered over the years, squeezed around raising a family and full-time work. Once or twice, she may have reminded me that she was unlikely to live forever. I didn't believe her. I hope I expressed my thanks and appreciation along the way and now that the book is finished, I have the opportunity to do so fulsomely and publicly and with a huge dose of relief that I made it to the finish line before she did. For although she is indeed immortal, her immortality is not expected to last forever.

After Joan my thanks go to those of whom Joan's story involved a large slice of their own story, those with whom she taught and travelled — including Jean Ford; those with whom she allied, in particular, Ray and Joan Northrop, Alex Chernov, Robert Anderson, Mary Murdoch and Pam Royle and those with whom she "battled" including Brian Bayston (who sadly died as this book went to press), a formidable opponent, though less unremitting than his mentor Max Bradshaw (the chief protagonist in the *Fight for PLC*) but who, unfortunately, had died before I set out upon this project.

Indeed, so many people gave generously of their time and I interviewed at length the following (in alphabetical order): Reverend Robert Anderson, Brian Bayston, Sophie Borland, Frances Boyd, Elizabeth Butt, Max Charlesworth, Diana Cherry, Alex Chernov, Jan Douglas, Jean Ford, Joyce Gibbons, Lesley Grant, Judy Gregory, John Habersberger, Christina Hindhaugh, David Hodges, Joan Kent, Kathleen McCredie, William Mackay (Edinburgh, 2005), Ewen McRae, Dr Olive Mence (née Wykes), Dame Elisabeth Murdoch, Mary Murdoch, Joan Northrop, Ray Northrop, Ted Pearsons, Jenny Pring, Judy Rayson, Alison Rechner, Russell Rechner, Hazel Rowley, Pam Royle, Pat Smith, Ev Tindale, Deborah Seifert, Marsha Watson and Constance Wood. I fear that my record keeping over such a long period of time may mean I have not acknowledged everyone I interviewed and my absence of direct thanks does not reflect an absence of gratitude for time spent with me. Sadly, a number of those thanked have since died and I regret they did not get to sample the effort built on their contributions nor to parry, qualify or defend any mistakes, misinterpretations or injustices that they might have felt redound against them personally or their cause.

I also wish to thank Pam Royle and Ray Northrop and Mary

Acknowledgments

Murdoch (and their families) for entrusting me with their respective archives of that tumultuous period of their lives and to thank also the many other individuals who sent me material.

Hazel Rowley and David Marr were encouraging at the outset of this project and I was inspired by their own accomplishments in the field of biography. Melanie Guile, who wrote the Clyde school history, was generous in our discussions as was Sarah Martin, Davis McCaughey's biographer. My friend, Michelle Schwarz, who wrote books about David Hookes and Geoff Clark was an early enthusiast as was Carolyn Strange, the biographer of Griffith Taylor. Carolyn made the connections between my approach to writing the book and my 'presbyterian education' as did my friend and now colleague Chris Wallace, biographer of Germaine Greer, John Hewson and Donald Bradman. I thank Frank Moorhouse for introducing me to Chris and to both of them for the many hours over many years discussing this book with me and I thank them all for their wisdom around writing about other people.

Professor Stuart Macintyre, first a teacher and then colleague during my University of Melbourne days, recommended I meet with Dr Jim Mitchell, the distinguished author of that fine book *A Deepening Roar: Scotch College, Melbourne, 1851-2001*. I already knew Jim from his time as my sensitive history tutor during my undergraduate Arts/Law student years. It was lovely to reconnect with Jim who continued as a great encourager and brought his period knowledge and well-trained eye to my manuscript catching errors and culling howlers. His help was invaluable, as was that of Dr Peter Fullerton who voluntarily brought his sharp publishing head to the manuscript intent on supporting the book's research and writing with "small design elements that most readers won't especially notice but which together announce the book as one to be taken seriously." I hope indeed that is the case but, if not, Peter did all he could to prevent it. Joan Montgomery, Alex Chernov, Norman Pritchard, and

Leigh Rubenstein also hunted the manuscript for ways to improve it and I thank them all for spotting errors and suggesting enhancements.

Joan's sisters Margaret, Elizabeth and Helen gave generously of their time and were invaluable contributors to the well of memory that these projects draw upon. It is of great regret to me that none of them lived long enough to see its completion. I also thank Joan's nieces and nephews, a band of enlivened players who enriched Joan's life and she theirs and who occasionally flicker from within these pages, notably bath time at Clyde.

I wrote this book over 28 years as a full-time academic—first at the University of Melbourne, then at the Australian National University and now, at the University of Canberra. My colleagues at each workplace were enthusiastic supporters of my 'extracurricular' activity. I also spent various sabbaticals working on the project—first at the University of Melbourne at the Australian Centre in 2003, supported by its then director Professor Kate Darian-Smith. All members of the Centre helped me move the project from a collection of interviews to the very beginnings of a book. Then, in 2005, Dame Elisabeth Murdoch—a Clyde alumna who had been involved in employing Joan as Clyde Principal—whom I had interviewed in 1993 made a generous donation to the University of Melbourne to 'buy out' my teaching for the year so that I could work solidly on the book. While taking another 15 or so years to complete, the book began in earnest then and I am sorry she did not see its completion, but I am grateful for her trust that I would finish it. Melbourne Law School, and in particular my Dean, Professor Michael Crommelin, who knew Joan from their respective holiday homes in Shoreham and from Joan's continued involvement with and contribution to the University of Melbourne, was a great support in enabling that arrangement to occur.

When I moved to the Law School at the Australian National University, my first sabbatical in 2009 was spent at the ANU

Acknowledgments

Humanities Research Centre and during that time I benefitted from the collegiality of that environment. I presented on the project, both to the Centre and also at the National Library of Australia's *Winter Tales* series hosted by the Australian Women's Archive project. I am also grateful to Professor Melanie Nolan and the National Centre of Biography at ANU for enabling me later to participate in their biography workshops and hosting my presentation on this book during one of their wonderful sessions. I managed to finish my first full draft of the book during another later sabbatical from the ANU Law School and its Dean, the late and great Professor Michael Coper, a dear friend, still sorely missed, was an enthusiastic supporter of the project, and indeed all my work!

I am most grateful to PLC, both as the school providing me such a rich and wholistic education, but also to Elizabeth Ward who was the school's Principal in 2005 when I spent the year working on the book. She recommended I reach out to the current Council, and this resulted in my meeting Brian Bayston. Jane Dyer at PLC's Archives and Julie Schroeder from the school's Development Office have been extremely responsive to many of my queries over many years, and the PLC Old Collegians' Association has had many Presidents and members who have shown great support—both financially in supporting the transcription of many of my interviews in the earlier days, (raising funds at a special Lyceum Club Old Collegians' lunch in 1996) and in-kind support of various measures, including many Old Collegians who wrote to me with their own stories and memories of Joan, and former teachers who contacted me and spoke to me at a special Lampas Society (former teachers and friends of PLC) dinner that I spoke to about the book. I thank everyone for sharing stories and I hope I have been able to weave them to your satisfaction into this book. I have stayed in touch with many of my own PLC friends from our 1982 HSC cohort and thank in particular Fiona Snape, Sara Gipton and Sancia Robinson for their 40 years (even more as Sara was one of my first grade 4 friends at PLC) of friendship—Sancia and I particularly miss Dale Langley who would have been so happy to know I finished this book.

I owe a great deal to my much-loved parents Sue and Leigh Rubenstein for sending me to PLC, supporting and cheering me on and for the exhausting years spent in anticipation of this book. I don't know how many times they had to parry inquiries from their friends on when their daughter's biography of her school Principal would eventually hit the streets.

Thank you again to my beautiful mother who years ago transcribed Joan Montgomery's more than 200 letters sent to her three sisters and their and her guardian cousin during Joan's two stints abroad 1952-54 and 1958-60. Sue set to work many years ago with the urgency she devotes to all of her tasks and thinking that I would swoop on her output in far faster fashion than turned out to be the case.

To Sue and Leigh, I hope that the finished product brings them some residue of the *nachas* owing to such deserving Jewish parents.

My sister Elana trained her practised design skills on the book cover and I thank her for her feedback and support as a sister and someone who shared with me those very charmed PLC years.

I note particularly Mark Baker, the distinguished author and journalist who also happens to be a brilliant editor—such a stylist and wordsmith—who brought his great talents to the production of a far crisper manuscript. I thank him for each one of his many improvements and his encouragement for us to call upon the redoubtable indexing services of Rachel Salmond, who held off her well-deserved retirement for one last book. Apparently, it was the nod to PLC old girl Ethel Richardson in the title that did it.

I met my husband Garry Sturgess, thanks to various forces for which I am eternally grateful, in May 1994, within a year of

Acknowledgments

starting my regular meetings interviewing Joan. My 'project' has been part of our blessed life together, and he has always been a wise counsel on this and all of my and our life decisions. In addition, for this book, he has taken on a more dedicated role, being the first editor of my full draft, reining in what was originally more than 200,000 words into something that Mark Baker could properly work with. Since then, Garry has become the publisher of this book through Franklin Street Press and he has also incorporated the telling of Joan's story into his wonderful new website *insidelives.org*

And last but never least, let me thank our two cherished children Cohava (22) and Eliezer (20) for their unfailing enthusiasm for this book. They do not seem to lament that the shadow of this book has fallen across the full measure of their lives. They assure me that for them it has not been *The Vetting of Wisdom* but rather it has returned to its original handle and brought with it *The Getting of Wisdom*. I truly hope so, Joan's life certainly merits that return.

K.R.
Canberra
2021

Foreword

The inspiration to write about Joan Montgomery and the Presbyterian Ladies' College came in the late Australian spring of 1992 when I was working in Washington, D.C., after studying law at Harvard. Joan had been a major encourager of my postgraduate study and was always a reliable and supportive referee. When the first scholarship I applied for went to someone else, it was Joan who gave me solace and taught me an important lesson. "As one door closes, another opens," she told me. Joan and PLC, where I had been a student from 1974 to 1982, had given me the confidence and the freedom that enabled me to be on the loose that spring in the American capital and viewing the *First Ladies: Political Role and Public Image* exhibition at the Smithsonian National Museum of American History.

The *First Ladies* exhibition of campaign memorabilia, restored gowns and other personal items together with hundreds of illustrations and photographs[1] fascinated me. I was especially drawn to Eleanor Roosevelt. I knew little about her and only later learnt that she was born a Roosevelt and was Franklin's cousin.[2] It was shortly before Hillary Clinton became First Lady and acknowledged Eleanor as a mentor, once again popularising her memory. As I listened to a recording of Eleanor's radio address to the nation on the eve of the US entering World War II, goose bumps swept my body. What an inspiration! I went straight to the bookshops to learn more and found the just-released biography of Eleanor by Blanche Wiesen Cook.[3] In that book were the seeds of this book.

Vetting of Wisdom

I learnt that Eleanor was greatly influenced by her teacher, Marie Souvestre, who introduced her to an "alternative way of being—assertive, independent and bold."[4] Souvestre was the Principal of Allenswood, the English school Eleanor attended at the age of 15 after both her parents died, a story much like Joan's. Unlike other finishing schools of the period, it "took the education of women seriously at a time when they were denied access to the great halls of learning. Feminist and progressive, Allenswood and its predecessor, Les Ruches, were responsible for the education of several generations of outstanding and notable women."[5]

Any graduate of PLC Melbourne would immediately identify, as I did, with Allenswood. As Katherine Fitzpatrick writes of PLC's origins, "the struggle for the higher education of women began in England."[6] And so my recognition of Marie Souvestre's school makes even more sense. When Eleanor set off for Allenswood in 1899, PLC was already 24 years old. More than 120 years on, PLC could easily make the same claim as Allenswood of having produced generations of outstanding and notable women with Joan Montgomery undoubtedly among them. Indeed, she may well top that list by herself producing more than a generation of graduates during her time as head.

Joan's first year as a student at PLC, in 1938, coincided with the first year of the first woman Principal, Miss Mary Neilson—a clear affirmation of the school's underlying belief in women being entitled to do anything. Perhaps more significantly, as Fitzpatrick explains, when Joan Montgomery herself became Principal, in February 1969, she came to the position never having known the days when PLC had a male head. She was to build upon those strong underpinnings of the school in ways that she may not have articulated herself as "feminist" but which were entirely consistent with a world in which women viewed their right to full participation as intrinsic and unquestionable. Or as the singer Kathleen Hanna claims—feminism isn't something that you are; it's something that you do.

Foreword

It was Joan Montgomery as Principal, not schoolgirl, who came into my mind as I read about Marie Souvestre and Eleanor Roosevelt. It wasn't even Joan Montgomery but it was "Miss Montgomery" — pronounced Mont-gum-ery in the way of her Scottish forebears — who I thought of. It took me a long time before I could refer to her by her given name; having always called her Miss Montgomery at school and for a long time after.

Towards the end of my own fifth form year at PLC — Year 11 — I was elected by my peers to become School Captain the following year. Judy Bush was elected Deputy Captain. Every morning we would meet with Miss Montgomery in her office for five minutes before the school day began. Each Monday, after our meeting, we would join her on stage for the assembly, during which she would give her address to the students and staff. Before becoming School Captain, my relationship with her was like other students, listening to her morning assemblies and passing her in the corridor, appreciating that she knew my name and all of our names. The respect I held for her and the pedestal upon which she sat for many of us meant that when I had received the phone call from her one evening to tell me I had been elected School Captain, it left me almost speechless. I sat up the entire night, talking with my very proud mum, unable to sleep. When I came to meet her for the first time after that phone call I stumbled over my words, which shook my self-image as an accomplished debater.

Over the course of my final year at PLC, my respect and admiration for Miss Montgomery grew. When I left school, I stayed in contact with her. She invited me back to address the students on my return from a year in Israel between my final year of school and the start of my university studies. It was during that year, 1984, that the controversy over her term as Principal at PLC arose forcefully in the public domain when the PLC School Council announced that it would not renew her contract at the end of 1985, after she turned 60. Her status as Principal had been uncertain since the Presbyterian Church split in 1974, but like many I was unaware of the explosive private meeting on 7 May 1980 where an attempt had been made to secure her resignation with the offer of a golden handshake. None of her discussions with me or other students ever touched upon it. But perhaps there was enough in the discussion outside the school for me to have a slight quiver in my voice when I spoke at the annual Speech Night at the Melbourne Concert Hall in December 1982. I said my role as School Captain had been made even more enjoyable because of the opportunity to work with Miss Montgomery: "Her willingness to listen to people's suggestions and her commitment to work for a particular ideal has been of great influence on my outlook on both school and life. Our daily morning meetings gave us an insight into the truly busy life she leads, and my memories of Miss Montgomery will always be fond ones, for her mark on PLC is one that will always be appreciated, by those who recognise the excellence of this school." At the end of that sentence, I had to stop and wait for the applause for Joan to subside. On giving me a gift at the end of the year, my admiration grew greater still when she generously wrote: "Just a small reminder of those interrupted, disorganised morning meetings I enjoyed with you and Judy. You completed an outstanding year when you spoke so excellently at Speech Night – we all basked in reflected glory!"

Despite that special experience of working closely with her over my final school year, my reading of Wiesen Cook's book in Washington, D.C., made me ponder how little I really knew about Joan Montgomery's life—at PLC and beyond. I also reflected on how little was known about this woman who had been of such significance to women's education, when I read the following paragraph in Cook's introduction: "We have tended to constrict the range of historical inquiry about women, failing even to ask life's most elemental questions. We have been encouraged to disregard the essential mysteries of a woman's life: What is energy—to write, to organise, to love? How do we acquire courage, develop vision, sustain power, create style?"[7]

What had influenced Joan Montgomery to become a school

principal, to be so committed to excellence in women's education? How had she come to command such respect and admiration from those who worked with her? Where did her courage spring from? How did she develop her vision? How did she sustain power and create her particular style?

While pondering these questions in Washington, D.C., I ventured up Connecticut Avenue to the Politics and Prose Bookstore to listen to expatriate Australian Jill Kerr Conway speak about her book *Written by Herself: Autobiographies of American Women: An Anthology*.[8] The book says the selected autobiographies "all claim our attention because of the powerful motivations which led these writers to cast aside the convention of female 'modesty' and set them to telling the world about their lives."[9]

This very same modesty dictated Joan's response when I first raised the possibility in January 1993 of writing her biography. Recently returned from the US, with Wiesen Cook's and Kerr Conway's books under my belt, I wanted answers to those questions on courage, vision, power and style.

"But my life is so ordinary" she protested. But as we talked and I persisted, Joan reflected, "I suppose that nothing has been written about the whole PLC and Presbyterian Church experience, and I do think that is an important story to be recorded".

To satisfy her modesty, we began talking about it as a PLC project, a PLC story, which of course she had been a part of for 17 years as Principal, not to mention her school days. And as I began to interview her regularly, we spent more and more time on her life, her family, her mentors, her friends, her travels (in particular her two extended trips to England in the 1950s), the books that had been of influence, her life unmarried and, integrally connected to that, her life as Principal. I also met many others who shared their stories about Joan.

The journey has spanned more than 25 years. I point out, to my mother in particular, who was especially keen that I should finish the book started all those years ago, that writing Joan's biography was not my day job. It has been squeezed in and around a life of full-time work that included raising a family of my own and years of weekly commutes between Canberra and Melbourne.

But I confess that at least part of the biography's long gestation has been due to my not wanting to bring to an end the truly enjoyable and richly appreciated connection I have had with Joan over all these years of interviewing, discussing, reliving and researching. I hope the result does justice to the remarkable life of Joan Montgomery, now in her 97th year, as sharp as ever and, up until the arrival of Covid, still driving and travelling internationally.

1

Jeopardy

Wednesday 7 May 1980. It's a mild late autumn day in Melbourne but in the inner eastern suburb of Burwood a storm is about to break, one that has been gathering for more than a decade. It arrives at 1.45 p.m., announced by the heavy stride of Frederick Maxwell Bradshaw down the long corridor from the main entrance of Presbyterian Ladies' College towards the office of the Principal.

Max Bradshaw is a man, in his own conviction, on a mission from God. His critics, whose ranks are about to swell, paint him as a calculating and ruthless zealot. Those close to him revere a devout layman with, as one will say, "a steadfast industry in doing good with the skills which God had given him."[1]

A few months shy of his 70th birthday, Bradshaw is thick-set, short of breath and has failing eyesight. Yet he still cuts a formidable figure. He is a leading barrister, a legal text-book writer, a historian and soon to be vice chair of the Scotch College Council. More than this, he is one of the most powerful men in the Presbyterian Church of Australia, and one of its most driven advocates of doctrinal orthodoxy. Appointed the Church's Procurator, or chief legal officer, in 1959, he drafted the 1953 Act of Parliament which enabled the union of the three congregations of the Free Presbyterian Church of Victoria. That, however, would prove the limit of his appetite for church union.

On this day, on a mission to impose his legal and moral will on the future of one of Australia's most celebrated girls' schools, Bradshaw is flanked by the younger, taller and fitter figure of the

Very Reverend Ted Pearsons. At 43, Pearsons is Clerk of the General Assembly of the Presbyterian Church of Victoria, a position he will hold for a record 32 years. He is also in awe of Bradshaw, his mentor. "I was more like a son to him," Pearsons would say.[2]

The two men reach the office, a floor above the school tuck shop, at 1.50pm and are promptly ushered in by the secretary. The Principal, Joan Montgomery, has been awaiting this moment for several years.

After 11 years as head of PLC, the school she first attended as a student in the 1930s, Joan Mitchell Montgomery enjoys a reputation as one of Australia's eminent educators. She is president of the Association of Heads of Independent Girls' Schools of Australia and will drive its merger with the equivalent association of independent headmasters. She is an Officer of the Order of the British Empire and will become a Member of the Order of Australia for her services to education. And, most of all, she is loved and revered by generations of students and parents as an exemplary leader and a warm and compassionate woman.

For the meeting with Bradshaw and Pearsons, Montgomery is joined by her deputies, Evelyn Tindale and Jan Douglas. All three will later file separate notes of the conversation.[3]

The formalities of arrival complete, Bradshaw begins with what he calls a proposition for Joan Montgomery but what effectively is a notice of her dismissal: "Given your (employment) agreement has five years to run, we suggest you seek independent legal advice on your agreement with the Trusts Corporation of the Presbyterian Church of Victoria."

Joan will respond calmly but firmly that her advice is clear: her employment contract transcends the upheaval that has riven the Presbyterian community and stands. But the end of her tenure as PLC Principal and her outstanding career is now only a matter of time.

Six years earlier, on 1 May 1974, the Presbyterian General Assembly had voted to unite with the Methodist Church of

Australasia and the Congregational Union of Australia and merge their congregations and assets. The new Uniting Church in Australia, with more than one million adherents, would become the third largest Christian denomination behind the Catholic and Anglican churches and Australia's largest non-government provider of community and health services.

But not everyone was united. A number of Methodist and Congregational communities would oppose church union and it would cleave the Presbyterian Church in two, with a third of their number resolving to remain as Continuing Presbyterians.

The Presbyterian schism was confirmed when a substantial number of the clergy and laity walked out of the 1 May meeting at the Assembly Hall at 156-160 Collins Street in Melbourne and headed around the corner to reconvene at 46 Russell Street. Among the leaders of the walkout were Max Bradshaw and Ted Pearsons.

These dramatic events would have echoes of the great "Disruption of 1843" which saw the General Assembly of the Church of Scotland split. As Max Bradshaw himself had recounted when addressing the Diocese of Melbourne's Church of England Historical Society in August 1965: "Four hundred of Scotland's leading ministers, led by the Moderator of the General Assembly, Professor Welsh, walked out of the General Assembly and constituted themselves the General Assembly of the Free Church of Scotland."[4]

Protesting the State's encroachment on Church independence in appointing ministers to vacant posts, another account by Church historian Alan Rodger records them walking from St. Andrews Church in Edinburgh, "(a)long George Street … down Hanover Street and on to the Tanfield Hall in Canonmills, through crowds mostly waving and cheering but just occasionally hissing. When they arrived at the hall at about a quarter to four, many more ministers and elders were waiting for them."[5]

There would be no cheering or hissing crowds when Bradshaw and his brethren marched out of Assembly Hall in Melbourne, but their passion and indignation was equal to that of their Scottish predecessors. Meeting later in Camberwell, the splinter group constituted itself as a Continuing Assembly in defiance of the decision by an overwhelming majority of Presbyterians to unite. Therefore, until the Uniting Church came into being on 22 June 1977, there were effectively two Presbyterian Assemblies.

Bradshaw had been the leading and most effective opponent of church union from the outset. While ultimately unsuccessful in stopping it, he now brought his customary zeal to securing whatever spoils remained for the vanquished. On the day of the decision to unite, the Presbyterian Assembly set up a Property Commission to determine the fate of Church schools—those to remain Presbyterian and those to become the property of the Uniting Church.

Vast power and abiding controversy smouldered in the determinations of the Property Commission, of which Max Bradshaw was an influential member. Upon its deliberations, Ballarat and Clarendon College, The Geelong College, Haileybury College, Hamilton and Alexandra College, Morongo Girls' College, Penleigh and Essendon Grammar School and St Leonard's College, all became property of the Uniting Church in Australia.

Manifestly, the weight of numbers went to the Uniting Church with all but two schools going to the Continuing Presbyterians. But those two schools, Presbyterian Ladies' College and Scotch College, arguably the jewels in the crown, and one of them with singular stature as an educator of young women, were to remain associated with the Presbyterian Church.

Presbyterian Ladies' College had been founded in 1875 in East Melbourne with an initial enrolment of sixty students. Among the first girls to enrol were Catherine Deakin, sister of later Prime Minister Alfred Deakin and Helen Mitchell who would be one of the world's most famous women, opera singer Dame Nellie Melba. When the University of Melbourne first opened to women scholars in 1881, many were former students of PLC. They included

Constance Ellis, who was the first woman to receive the degree of Doctor of Medicine; Flos Greig, the first woman to be admitted to legal practice in Victoria; Ethel Godfrey, one of the first woman dentists in Victoria; and Vida Goldstein, suffragette and the first woman to stand for election to the Australian Federal Parliament.

Not surprisingly, several court cases attacked the Property Commission—its membership and, moreover, its claim to a wisdom even greater than that of Solomon, with splits affecting thousands of young lives. In 1975, the first two cases centred on Max Bradshaw's appointment to the Commission. More pointedly, in 1977, the PLC and Scotch school communities challenged the legality of the Property Commission's pronouncement that PLC and Scotch would remain the property of the Continuing Presbyterians.

While the case was not heard in the courts until 1979, from its initiation onwards rumours abounded around Joan Montgomery's position as Principal of PLC. But those rumours would not take tangible form until Max Bradshaw and Ted Pearsons came calling in May 1980.

After declaring that Montgomery should seek independent legal advice on the status of her employment contract, Bradshaw pressed on: "We are here representing the Presbyterian Church and while we can't speak on behalf of the [school] Council it is just as well for you to be prepared for the first meeting where your agreement will be discussed. The existing contracts are not taken over by the new company where they are of a personal nature. Company law prohibits this. Assets and liabilities certainly, but not agreements of a personal nature."

"My legal advice differs," Montgomery rejoined, calm by nature and immunised from bluff by Ray Northrop, Federal Court judge and chairman of the former PLC Council. Northrop, steeped in the ramifications of the church split and its impact on PLC, was a stalwart of legal advice and, with his wife Joan Northrop, personal support to Joan. Bolstering his advice was Mallesons, a leading law firm retained by the old Council.

"I believe that all existing contracts and agreements, the Principal and the Staff are to be taken over," Montgomery noted.

"Not the case," said Bradshaw, shaking his head, before adding with feigned courtesy, "In view of rumours that you would resign if the Presbyterian Church took over, we thought you would like to be forewarned."

"I, too, have heard those rumours, among others," Montgomery countered. "I have never made such a statement and I have no intention of resigning. I appreciate the right of the Council to dismiss me."

Bradshaw met her head on: "The new Council will have the right not to have the Principal on the premises given the personal nature of the agreement."

"Quite so," said Pearsons, in the style of a junior partner but with something of his own to add. "By way of amplification, the Principal plus the staff and groundsmen for that matter are personal agreements and are not covered by Company law."

Montgomery could see there was little point in carrying on. "This discussion is hypothetical in view of the fact that the first Council has not convened," she reminded the visitors.

"True," said Bradshaw, "but from the Presbyterian Church angle it is as well for you to be aware of the situation and prepared, as your agreement will be discussed at the first Council meeting. I am a member of Council, you know."

With this cudgel he changed tack, acknowledging, "as your contract has some five years to run, the Church would feel bound to make an adequate, indeed a not ungenerous settlement."

"A golden handshake?" Montgomery replied. "Better than a silver one," Bradshaw quipped, well amused with himself.

To this point, the Deputy Principals had sat mostly silent but with rising alarm as the threat to their beloved leader crystallised. Ev Tindale, an alert, athletic woman who taught both Physical Education and Modern History, was seldom stunned but this encounter had taken her aback as the threat to the school they all cherished was laid out. Finally, she interjected, "Surely a school's Principal is an 'asset' of the school and is therefore passed over with other 'assets.' The personal nature of the agreement is not relevant?"

"Quite relevant," Bradshaw and Pearsons responded in unison. "There are thousands of cases of precedent where companies are taken over without staff," Bradshaw added, confidently.

"Imagine what the staff would think if they could hear this conversation," Montgomery reflected out aloud.

"Oh, no cause for concern," Bradshaw responded. "Only the Principal is involved."

But, for all concerned, this was more than a word game or a legal manoeuvre — there were, indeed, several principles involved. And these would play out in one of the most furious battles over a school's direction and purpose in Australia's history.

But for now, in Montgomery's mind, it was time to wind up the meeting. She returned to the point in the circle she had opened earlier: "All of this is hypothetical, there is no point continuing this discussion until such time as Council indicates that my services will no longer be required."

Bradshaw too was stuck at the beginning. "It is as well to be prepared so a new situation may be met before it arises," he reiterated.

Appealing for mutual respect, Jan Douglas then spoke what both of her colleagues were thinking. "The ramifications of all this are enormous, far beyond the staff level — what of parents and the education of the girls? The reputation of the whole school is at stake!"

"We are mindful of this," said Pearsons. But was he mindful of the repercussions of firing a Principal so aligned with the history of the school and so emblematic of its place as a pioneer and bastion of women's education?

Ev Tindale now spoke again. "As a member of staff and a Vice

Principal, if the Council decided not to continue Miss Montgomery's contract I, for one, would not wish to remain and a large proportion of the staff would think likewise."

Jan Douglas then further intervened, warning of the fallout with other school stakeholders. "Not only the staff but the parent body of the school would respond," she added.

"The Council would be aware of these facts and consider them when making their decision," Bradshaw acknowledged.

And there the conversation came to a halt. There was an exchange of glances, tea was offered and refused, as another appointment pressed, and, with that, the visitors departed at 2.10pm.

......

Wind back to 1939. Joan Montgomery, aged 14 and a student at PLC's then East Melbourne campus is sitting in the classroom near the clock, off the main corridor that runs from the library to the tuck shop.

As the winter aromas of pies, pasties and sausage rolls waft into the room, Joan is sitting in one of Miss Annie Rentoul's Latin classes. Slight and frail, Miss Rentoul has taught Latin at PLC since before World War I. The exigencies of yet another war have pressed her from recent retirement into the classroom once more. The finest scholar of her day, shattering the boys' monopoly on the Classics Exhibition in her matriculation year of 1902, she is no match for Joan and her cheeky student coterie. Despite more than 20 years of teaching, it would be said that she "lacked the capacity to impose her will on others".[6]

For Joan, Latin is not the issue. It is grappling with the peer challenge of leaving the room without being seen. Dared before, she once hid under her desk for an entire lesson, pushing Miss Rentoul to ask: "How are you feeling Joan? Were you unwell yesterday?"

"Oh, but Miss Rentoul, I was here."

"Really? I was sure you hadn't been, Joan."

Jeopardy

"But Miss Rentoul, how then am I able to recite the entire contents of yesterday's class?"

With Miss Rentoul's attention always on those in the front row, Joan again crouched under her desk near the back of the room, and then eased her way out of the room. Almost down the steps and heading towards Albert Street, she froze at the sight of the brown, highly-polished, laced-up shoes fast approaching. They belonged to the much-admired Vice Principal, Miss Helen Hailes, coming from her office at the top of the very path Joan was hoping to reach.

Miss Hailes had begun teaching at PLC in 1913, the same year as Miss Rentoul. But she was of entirely different stock. While Miss Rentoul might have been described as a "fit inhabitant of the land of faery",[7] Miss Hailes certainly was not. "Mother Earth was her element and strong common-sense her sign manual."[8]

"Stand up and return to your classroom," she ordered, as Joan straightened from her crouched position, "Your position at PLC is in jeopardy!"

Unsure what Miss Hailes meant, that evening at the family home above the Bank of Australasia her father managed in Middle Brighton, Joan puzzled through the dictionary, searching through the letter i. Her father suggested she try j.

"In Jeopardy!", an ominous threat for a schoolgirl prank. But the words will lay a dormant memory until some 40 years later when she will collide head on with the forces that threaten to jeopardise her life's great work.

2

LOCH LONG

Joan Montgomery's story really begins on 6 October 1877 when 55-year-old joiner Hugh Montgomery and his sons Robert and Hugh Jnr set sail from Glasgow aboard the three-masted clipper ship the *Loch Long*. Launched just a year earlier, the 1261-ton iron-hulled vessel was one of the fastest of the hundreds of sailing ships of her era that carried emigrants and manufactures to the colonies of Australia, returning laden with wool and grain. The voyage of the Montgomery men and their 32 fellow passengers took 120 days. Save for the usual periods of heavy seas and seasickness, the passage was uneventful, punctuated by Sunday services of worship to which all aboard were summoned by the ship's bell. But the perils of ocean travel in the 19th century would have been ever present. The luck of the *Loch Long* ran out in April 1903 when she was lost with all hands near the Chatham Islands, south east of the New Zealand mainland, homeward bound with a cargo of nickel ore from New Caledonia.

Both Robert, 29, and Hugh Jnr, 21 (Joan's grandfather), had worked as clerks in Scotland. The men's excited anticipation of starting a new life on the other side of the world would have been tempered by thoughts of those they left behind. Hugh Montgomery had been a widower since the death of his wife, Helen Thompson, the year before. And he farewelled three adult daughters in Scotland — Ann Craig, 32, Mary Mitchell, 26, and Helen, 23.

The *Loch Long* arrived in Melbourne just after New Year, on 3 January 1878. The gold rushes of the 1850s had radically transformed the city from the raw town Max Bradshaw depicted in his history *Scottish Seceders in Victoria*—a city without gas or water supply and with "tree stumps ... only just disappearing from its principal streets."[1] Melbourne was now one of the richest and most admired cities in the world, resplendent with grand public buildings, private mansions and extensive parklands.

In 1878 the first telephones were installed in Melbourne and construction of the Ghan railway line began in South Australia. That Easter, the Stawell Gift was run for the first time and, a year earlier, the first cricket Tests had been played against a touring English team, with the Australians and visitors winning one each. In November, Ned Kelly and his gang locked 22 people in a storehouse on a sheep station near Euroa before robbing the local bank the next day.

Soon after their arrival, the Montgomerys moved to Tasmania, settling in the hamlet of Forth, near Deloraine. Hugh Jnr went into banking—training in Melbourne and later New Zealand—while Robert stayed in Tasmania as a shopkeeper (Robert Montgomery & Co.) in the village of Don, on the outskirts of Devonport.

Hugh Jnr's banking career began when he applied to the Bank of Australasia on 11 March 1878 for a Supernumerary Officer's position, stating his previous occupation as a clerk in the City of Glasgow from 1 July 1873 until his departure for Australia. The bank archives document his progression, starting in March 1878 without a salary and by 13 May becoming a clerk on an annual salary of 110 pounds. Family lore has him spending his first pay packet on a book of poetry by James Montgomery, the Scottish-born hymn writer, editor and humanitarian.

With yearly pay increases and a promotion to Ledger-Keeper, by October 1880 Hugh Jnr's salary had risen to 155 pounds. A year later he was made a "New" Teller and transferred to Christchurch in New Zealand with a salary of 190 pounds.

Soon after moving to New Zealand, Hugh met Frances Isobel Mitchell, who at 19 was ten years his junior. They married in 1885.

Two years later, on 14 October 1887, Joan's father William Mitchell Montgomery was born. The young family lived in Christchurch until October 1894, although Hugh had stints relieving in bank branches in Manaia, Hawera, Patea and Wanganui.

By April 1888, Hugh's salary had increased to 220 pounds per annum, slowly rising to 260 pounds by 1894. That July, a concerned bank superintendent would record hearing with regret that Hugh was ill and "willingly accord[s] him two months' sick leave." While the nature of the illness is unclear, a dispatch sent from Melbourne 20 days later reported a doctor's advice that it was necessary for Hugh "to live in a warmer climate" and advised that "he has been offered and has accepted the management of Mooroopna Branch".

Mooroopna, a country town 181 kms north of Melbourne, on the Goulburn River, would be the Montgomery family home for the next two decades. By the time of Australia's Federation in 1901, young William was attending Mooroopna State School. He later spent two years as a boarder at Scotch College in Melbourne, between April 1902 and December 1903. It would be the family's first link with Presbyterian Church schools in Australia, although in common with many Scottish immigrants, the bond with Presbyterianism was already strong.

After undertaking a six-month course at Bradshaw's Business College, beside Princes Bridge on the site of the present-day Southbank complex, William literally followed his father's footsteps into the bank. He joined the staff of the Mooroopna branch where Hugh Snr was manager on a salary of 100 pounds a year. After beginning as a Supernumerary, by August William was appointed as a Clerk across the river at the Shepparton Branch. His later transfer to the Katamatite Branch, 45 kilometres north east of Shepparton, was cause for a Shepparton paper to regret the departure of "the busy and energetic member" of the local golf club which hosted him an impromptu farewell with "singing, dancing and other congenial amusements." After a good supper, the president, Mr Dundas Simson, "in a short and pithy speech, made a presentation ... of a pair of very pretty sleeve links inscribed with William's initials."

In 1910, William moved to Sydney and, soon after, was appointed Clerk at the Ballina Branch, in northern New South Wales. In August 1914, as war broke out in Europe, he returned to Sydney. Over the following year he would receive a 5 percent pay bonus on account of his unspecified work supporting the war effort. In 1916, he moved back to Melbourne and was appointed to the staff of the Collingwood Branch. Soon the war that was claiming the lives of so many young men would transform his.

On 4 August 1917, William Mitchell Montgomery enlisted with the First AIF, at the recruitment centre in the inner Melbourne suburb of Fitzroy. Lingering weakness from a childhood bout of rheumatic fever had delayed his acceptance by the army but now he was assigned to the 21st Battalion. He listed as next-of-kin his mother Frances, of 345 Upper Heidelberg Road, Ivanhoe. Hugh Montgomery retired from the bank on his 60th birthday and he and Frances had moved back to Melbourne. William's attestation form would record that he was three months away from his 30th birthday and stood 5 foot 6 and a half inches with sallow complexion, brown eyes and dark brown hair. Private Montgomery (No. 6847A) embarked from Port Melbourne aboard HMAT Nestor with the battalion's 20th Reinforcements on 21 November 1917.

While the war had less than a year to run, it would inflict a heavy toll on the young bank clerk. Although he survived, his health would be impaired for the rest of his life. After further training in Egypt, he arrived in France in time for the murderous 100-day German Spring Offensive between March and July. On 23 July, soon after the 21st Battalion took part in the stunning Australian victory in the Battle of Hamel, "the whole sky burned"[2] for William after he was seriously wounded in a gas attack. His recuperation would take two months but just a few days after returning to his unit he was again wounded, on 5 October 1918, during a battle at Estrees, north of Hamel.

Loch Long

William would recount the moment in the diary he had kept since embarking from Melbourne: "We waited impatiently for the barrage to lift and were soon moving up behind it again. Another 20 yards and I felt a kick in my right arm and it became limp as a rag with no power in the hand ... the shells were coming over thicker and faster now so looked around for a better shelter. A short distance ahead there was a light railway on each side of which ran a gutter about 13 inches deep. Made for this and, burying my nose well down, waited for a lull in the proceedings. Stuck my rifle into the ground, butt up—the wounded signal—in case I should fade right out."

The gunshot wound to the right forearm would effectively end William's war. When the Armistice was declared on 11 November 1918, he was still convalescing in the Norfolk War Hospital in England. He returned to Australia in mid-1919. The wartime injuries meant William suffered regular chest complaints over the years that followed and his beloved golf and tennis were limited to his left hand.

Soon after returning from the war, William met Beryl Harvey, who worked in the National Bank typing pool from 1915 to 1922. They were married at the Free Presbyterian Church in East St Kilda on 10 June 1922.

Beryl Rankin Harvey, five years younger than William, was born on 19 September 1892. Her parents, William Harvey and Eleanor Kimpton lived in Boort, a small town in the Mallee region, 252 km north-west of Melbourne. Like his new son-in-law, William Harvey was a banker, employed by the Commercial Bank before moving to the National Bank. The fifth in a family of 16 children, his life bristled with community. He was treasurer of the local Presbyterian Church and Secretary of the Boort branch of the Australian Natives Association. But on 6 December 1892, shortly before his and Eleanor's second wedding anniversary, William died suddenly. Beryl was not yet two months old. The shock of his sudden death at the age of 26 was captured by the Boort newspaper which reported a "deep gloom ... cast over the community on Tuesday afternoon when it became known that Mr W.B. Harvey, the well-known and popular young accountant in the National Bank, had expired from apoplexy." William's body was brought to Melbourne where he was buried beside Eleanor's brother, who had died of typhoid at the age of 19 and was the first to be buried in the Kimpton family plot in the Melbourne General Cemetery. In 1896, when Beryl was four, Eleanor remarried. Anton Reinhardt Frederick August Meyer was a German cabinet-maker with a shop in Franklin Street, Melbourne.

Joan Mitchell Montgomery was born on Monday 6 July 1925 at 5 Queens Road, South Melbourne, William Montgomery and Beryl's first child. She spent her first seventeen months in Hawthorn before the family moved to Bright in the alpine country of north eastern Victoria, in December 1926. Added to William's salary as the newly appointed bank manager was a 25-pound allowance for a horse. But it would be the car that Joan remembered, "a big old open-type Dodge; later he had the first sedan in the district. Father was amused to be asked to drive a bride to her wedding."

Joan's childhood years in Bright were a rich and joyful time. The town had two banks and two hotels. The Bank of Australasia, where the Montgomerys also lived, was on the corner of Anderson and Gavan Streets. Joan went to the local primary school but her clearest memories are of visiting William's parents, Grandpa Hugh and Grandma Frances in the Melbourne suburb of Ivanhoe. No more than four or five years old, she would depart at 5am aboard the rattling, steam-driven train, with a large card hanging around her neck announcing details of her name, address and destination. Put in the charge of the guard for the day-long journey, "there always seemed to be some lady travelling to Melbourne" in whose care Joan was also entrusted. Carrying cut sandwiches in her lunch box, she longed to buy a meat pie from the Seymour station refreshment room.

As the first daughter of an only child, Joan was a favourite of her grandmother, who was known as Granny Fanny. During her visits to 345 Upper Heidelberg Road, Ivanhoe, Joan remembers Frances trimming the cypress hedge that bordered the house. "Granny was definitely the matriarch," she would recall. Frances had two sisters—Matty (Matilda) and Jinny (either Jennifer or Genevieve), who was spoken of in hushed tones because she was divorced. Grandpa Hugh is remembered from these holiday visits as a kindly gentleman. Joan recalls the house had "a big Aladdin lamp, fuelled by petrol … and hissing away [throwing a] very good light."

On the night of 27 April 1929, shortly before her fourth birthday, Joan was eating a poached egg for dinner at home in Bright when Sister Kneebone, a maternity nurse and long-time family friend, came into the room and announced, "You have got a little sister!" Disappointed, Joan retorted, "I wanted a little brother!" Her reaction was similar 19 months later, on 7 November 1930, when another sister, Margaret, was born and Joan was again packed off to Melbourne to stay in Ivanhoe with her grandparents. On a later trip, Elizabeth remembers Frances quietly reprimanding Joan on leaving, "You haven't been the nice little girl that usually comes to stay with us."

The coming of younger siblings brought its own dynamic. Joan was more than three years older than Elizabeth who was a shy girl in contrast to Joan's confident self-sufficiency, and they had different interests. After Margaret arrived, she and Elizabeth soon developed an inseparable bond. They did everything together, and "I was on the outer," Joan reflects, although with no memory of being unhappy. Joan had a flinty independence and strength of spirit which the arrival of her siblings merely affirmed. She was unusually forthright from a young age. At her 4th or 5th birthday party in Bright a neighbour, Miss Roberts, brought an imported Royal Doulton children's tea set inscribed with nursery rhymes. On being presented with it, Joan told Miss Roberts she could take the tea set home: "We have enough cups in our house."

While Beryl was Anglican and William Presbyterian, the family attended the Presbyterian church on the hill in Bright, forever enlivened in Joan's mind by the thrill of a cow wandering in during a service. In the Scots tradition, the Sabbath was strictly kept and domestic chores, even cleaning shoes, forbidden. After church, there was a traditional Sunday roast followed by an afternoon drive in an age notably free of traffic. Beyond church, Joan remembers family tobogganing and, as William was a keen angler, they would fish in the Buckland River and take picnics.

In January 1933, William was appointed manager of the branch at Numurkah, about 180 kms west of Bright. Once again, the family would live on the bank premises, this time on Melville Street in the town's centre. Joan had a room of her own, while Margaret and Elizabeth shared, a piece of cotton strung down the middle of the room from the dresser to delineate the messy from the tidy.

Since 1882, the Numurkah Agricultural Show had been held every spring across Broken Creek from the town centre. It was a highlight of town life and the Montgomerys joined the pitch for various prizes. Beryl did well with her lamingtons and gingerbread, while Joan competed in handwriting and elocution events. Her lettering was remarkable for its attention to detail, a quality that endured throughout her life. All her letters, including the hundreds sent home during her later travels overseas, were meticulously written. Her speech too showed a commitment to order and precise delivery. No doubt her elocution teacher Mrs Trott helped here, as did her father. "Dad was very particular about language," Margaret would recall. "I remember referring to a 'hankie' and father said: 'Margaret, the word is handkerchief, with a D '!"

Numurkah had Presbyterian, Anglican, Wesleyan and Catholic churches. The Montgomerys joined St. Andrew's Presbyterian Church, established in 1882. In the Communicants' Roll Book, "Mr and Mrs Montgomery," are listed at their residence "Bank of Australasia." There was only one communion in April in 1933 and the Montgomerys were not ticked. From 1934 through

1936 they were recorded as present under six separate communions, although Beryl is not recorded joining the last, on 2 August 1936. The birth three months earlier of another daughter, Helen, could well explain the absence.

Despite its strong church-going habit, Numurkah, like so many communities across Australia at that time, was infected by sectarianism. One of Joan's earliest memories of difference was her Numurkah Primary School classmates taunting children attending St. Joseph's, the local Catholic school, with variants of, "Catholic dogs, sitting on logs, eating gizzards out of frogs." It was, she would later reflect, "dreadful." The targets of such taunts would almost certainly have included Max Charlesworth, later the eminent philosopher and Melbourne University professor, who was a pupil at St. Joseph's on Tocumwal Road about a 15-minute walk from Numurkah Primary on Quinn Street. Joan knew Max, who was six months younger than her, as the son of an articled clerk at the local law firm Morrison & Teare.

Position and social status also figured in the workings of the town, often drawing together people that sectarian prejudices might otherwise have separated. Being the child of a professional placed you in a certain milieu or class. Both Joan and Max's parents would have met through their status in the town. Max's father, for instance, had a group of men he invited regularly to play solo – including William, as the bank manager, Father Rohan, Dr Parker, one of the two doctors in town who was also the Montgomery family doctor, Dr Thomas, his counterpart, and no doubt the owners of the *Numurkah Leader* newspaper, the Morris brothers.

While solo was played at the Charlesworths', Beryl Montgomery had her regular bridge group. Max's mother, Mabel Charlesworth, was one of the group that also included Mrs B.E. Hall; the Bitcons, owners of the General Store; Meredith Dibbs, the wife of another bank manager; Mrs A.M. Coxon, wife of the Numurkah garage owner; Elspeth Parker, wife of Dr Parker; and Hilda Morieson, the dentist's wife. And there were many others, their names all inscribed in the book *In Search of Ireland* by H.V. Morton (then in its 11th edition, 1936) given to Beryl from the women of Numurkah on her return to Melbourne in 1937. The social handle 'wife of' is partially reminiscent of earlier times not quite outlived. Some of the inscribed names came through Beryl's involvement with the Red Cross and playing golf.

Both Joan and Max's fathers were members of the local Freemasons paternity, which brought together the professionals and the wealthy farmers of the district, although neither Joan nor Max knew much about its secret lore.

Joan's childhood in Bright and Numurkah bridged the Great Depression years so well captured in Frank Huelin's and Alan Marshall's classic accounts *Keep Moving*[3] and *How Beautiful Are Thy Feet*.[4] She recalls the steady stream of swagmen seeking work, wood chopping, odd jobs, anything they could find to survive. Max Charlesworth would remember sudden deaths in Numurkah, euphemistically attributed to accidents with guns but which were really triggered by a reversal of fortune leading to ultimate despair. For Charlesworth's father, fear of another depression cast a long shadow. As a bank manager in country Victoria, William Montgomery was acutely aware of the savage impact of the Depression. He took a 10% pay cut, as was the common lot of Bank of Australasia managers. Joan, however, was largely cocooned from the harsher impacts of the economic crisis.

The homogeneity of the town was further fortified as there was little immigration to Australia in the depression years. Australia's population in 1933 was 6,629,839 and in Victoria it was 1,820,261. In 1934, the Federal Government responded to pressure and reduced the landing tax for non-British Europeans with relatives in Australia. When Joan turned nine and began elocution classes, the Dictation Test was used by government authorities to prevent the left-wing Czech-Jewish writer Egon Kisch from landing in Australia. In an otherwise unified community, distinctions between Protestants and Catholics formed Joan's main brush with difference. She does recall one Chinese man who ran the Numurkah laundry, starching gentlemen's collars. There was no Indigenous presence anywhere in the community. "We seemed to pray for everyone, but not Aborigines," Charlesworth would say, although his father most likely had Aboriginal clients, as there was a large settlement in Robinvale in the Murray Valley, home of the Latje Latje tribe.

One of the most famous local characters of the era was the redoubtable Catherine (Katie) Walsh, a dairy farmer who added eccentricity, colour and fright to Numurkah. Joan recalls her as a scary figure with questionable hygiene. On one of her visits to the bank she was invited to tea in the kitchen and Joan noticed her boots and her strong smell. Beryl chose not to shop at the store that purchased Katie Walsh's milk. William Henry Bossence's 1979 book *Numurkah* describes her with literary flair as "the wildest ... Walsh daughter" of Michael and Mary Walsh, a "flighty and unrestrained" figure following "mobs of sheep as they grazed their way along the public roads."[5] William Montgomery, who valued properties as one of his responsibilities, had assessed the 300 acres at Walsh's Bridge, named after Katie's parents, and another 100 acres of reserve. The valuations were often incorporated into family drives and Joan recalls waiting in the car one day while William went into Katie's house. There was a couch on the veranda and cows appeared to be roaming about in squalor. Max Charlesworth would also remember Katie as his father accepted in-kind payments for legal work dealing with cattle thieves who had struck at the Walsh property.

Katie Walsh died aged 75 on 20 November 1957 and Joan recalls the reports of a significant estate and a legal scrap over its distribution. Walsh had spent her last year in the Numurkah District Hospital peeved at the regular baths and the otherwise undesirable attention she received. She struck back by seeking to change her will, no longer bequeathing her property to the hospital but rather leaving it to church charities. The new will was witnessed by a Mr Jack Martin and the then manager of the Bank of

Australasia (one of Joan's father's successors), Mr Frank Whitelaw. "Martin signed at once but Whitelaw took the document with him so that he could add the bank's stamp." The delay invalidated the will as the probate officers noticed the two witness signatures were written with different inks. Foiled beyond the grave, Katie's legacy continued to go to the Numurkah Hospital that, together with a government grant, added the Catherine Walsh Wing and so doubled the hospital's size.

Merle Allen who lived a few miles out of town was Joan's closest friend at the time and Joan often spent her weekends with the Allens. They were strong Methodists and Joan remembers signing a Rechabite certificate Merle had given her which she proudly displayed upon her return home from the weekend. As well as regular churchgoing, there were frequent family outings including fishing trips to the nearby Murray River. It was an era of greater formality in parent-child relationships. In the Montgomery home, the children ate earlier than their parents with their maid Lizzie Lynch, a kindly person who lived with them. Later, Lizzie married a widower with 13 children which, Joan would observe, reflects "badly upon us if that was her escape." But eating with Lizzie "was quite normal in those days—with 4 children." The special Sunday family meals in the dining room were another highlight.

Joan's interests in those years often revolved around sport. She played rounders and basketball at school and for her 9th birthday was given a basketball ring to practise her goal throwing. She remembers admiring a tennis racket in a shop window costing 32 shillings and 6 pence. But her greatest sporting desire was owning a bicycle just like Ken Hall, the son of the State Savings Bank manager who lived across the road. Knowing of her father's keen interest in her schooling, Joan formulated a proposal. "If I were to come first, second or third in my class over the next five years at school, do you think I could have a bike?" she asked her father. "Yes, I suppose you could," William replied. Not mentioned again, the conversation stayed with her throughout the days in Numurkah. Bikes had a singular allure. On the day of Helen's birth in 1936, when Joan was seven, she was allowed to hire a bicycle and went out for the day with Ken Hall and a picnic lunch. "When I came back, I was told I had a little sister," she recalls.

Beyond sport and family outings, reading was a constant and critical shaping influence upon Joan. Life in country Victoria increased the attraction of certain books, in particular Mary Grant Bruce's children's classic *A Little Bush Maid* and Bruce's other Billabong books published between 1910 and 1942. Covering the fundamentals of "families, friendships and feelings", the books' 12-year-old central character, Norah Linton, appealed to similarly aged and free-spirited girls like Joan. Norah lived "on a big station in the north of Victoria — so large that you could almost, in her own phrase, 'ride all day and never see any one you didn't want to see,' which was a great advantage in Norah's eyes." Like Norah, Joan was bored by little girls who prattled of dolls, loved to skip, to dress up and "play ladies".

Books enveloped Joan's early life and her sister's memories of the time also focus on Joan's love of reading. Perhaps the kindred name of Canadian author Lucy Maud Montgomery deepened Joan's interest in her series of novels best known by the first of them, *Anne of Green Gables*. Beyond reading, there was radio and, most memorably, Dr Mac, the evergreen Macquarie Network series about the life of a Scottish doctor in country-town Australia. "It's not in the big cities that the heart of Australia lies," says Dr Robert McIntyre, played by the much-loved character actor Lou Vernon, in one of the 15-minute episodes. "It's way out in the country where life is hard, where the sun and the elements are ruthless opponents, where men wrestle to make a country great and become great because of their tussling. There lies the heart of this country and I like to get at the heart of things."

Like Norah from *A Little Bush Maid*, Joan had a strong relationship with her father but she was not afraid to test it. Her sisters recall her willingness to stand up to him. "We'd be upstairs and we could hear Joan listening to Dr Mac and father ascending the stairs from the bank and demanding, 'Turn that off'," Margaret recalls. As he returned downstairs, Joan would turn the radio on again. William would return, cautioning her, "If you turn that on again, you'll get the strap!" Not one to resist a challenge, indeed a dare, naturally she would turn the radio on again. "Father had this strap, called a strop, to sharpen razors," said Margaret, "and she would get it around the legs. She'd get a couple of hits on the back of her legs and she'd be so defiant; biting her lip, she wouldn't cry."

"That didn't hurt!" Elizabeth recalls her saying

While Joan had an independent spirit, particularly in dealings with her father, there was still a strong respect for parents: "You obeyed your parents — there was a different emphasis — behaviour was more prescribed. As well-brought-up children, you would only speak when spoken to and you were expected to stand up when an adult came into the room."

It was during their time in Numurkah that Frances Montgomery died, around the aged of 70. Joan was 10 and remembers the moment clearly. Sent to bed early for being naughty, her punishment ended abruptly at 7pm after the telephone call relaying the news. "I don't remember finding out how she died, we didn't ask questions like that."

3

PLC Girls

In December 1936, William was appointed manager of the bank's Middle Brighton branch. The Montgomerys, now a family of six—William, 49, Beryl, 44, and their four girls Joan, 11, Elizabeth, 7, Margaret, 5 and Helen, just seven months—moved to their new home above the bank, on the corner of Church and Carpenter Streets. For Joan, the move to Melbourne was tied to the thrill of receiving at last her "beautiful" new Malvern Star bike, courtesy of the pact she had entered with her father five years earlier to come first, second or third in her class throughout her primary years.

The bike would be a godsend, arriving ahead of Australia's worst outbreak of polio in 1937. It was not a new threat, as Joan McMeeken would write: "For more than half a century, through to the 1950s, Australians were periodically terrified by recurrent epidemics of polio that could potentially leave its victims paralysed, sometimes permanently."[1] The hard-earned Malvern Star kept Joan away from the risks of other children. Instead of travelling to PLC on public transport, she rode her bike each day to St Leonard's Church Hall, at Brighton Beach, the temporary home of Hampton High School's Year 7 while their school was undergoing alterations. But contracting polio was an ever-lurking danger, brought home to the Montgomerys when, as a young man, Max Charlesworth spent time in a sanitorium on the Mornington Peninsula recovering from it.

Being in fresh air was encouraged and much of Joan's time was spent playing tennis or cricket. Depending on the weather, her sisters had lessons on the nearby beach. The bike is also remembered for pulling Helen's push-cart. When asked to take Helen for a walk, Joan would tie the bike and cart together with a piece of rope and head-off, Helen screaming with delight. "That went on until a friend of mother's saw us," Joan recalls.

The joys of biking and sport were augmented by Joan's keenness for stamp collecting and, in Brighton, she added silk worming to her range of interests. William helped by making her an effective little machine for winding silk from the cocoons. The move to Brighton brought Beryl's mother, Nana Eleanor Kimpton, into more frequent contact and she often came to lunch and dinner. Disappearing after dinner with a book became tricky as Nana would volunteer to wash up and would soon declare: "Come along Joan, there are the dishes to be dried—there was no escape." Brighton also meant moving to a new Presbyterian church, St Cuthbert's, where Joan was confirmed by the Reverend Karl Forster.

As an old Scotch College boy, who had built a house in Kembla Street, Hawthorn, "a stone's throw' from Scotch", the arrival of four daughters may have been a disappointment to William. But Presbyterian Ladies' College stepped straight into the Montgomerys' long-term planning. There had been early talk of Joan beginning at Stratherne, also in Hawthorn, a feeder school to PLC. William's rural postings, however, precluded that step. Instead, after the year at Hampton High School, Joan's lifelong link to PLC began on Tuesday 8 February 1938 when she set off for her first day at the school.

Too far to ride and with the polio epidemic of 1937 less in mind, Joan's daily commute to PLC started with a train trip from Middle Brighton to Flinders Street. From there, it was a walk to Collins Street to catch the tram turning into Victoria Parade or a walk from Flinders Street to the Fitzroy Gardens and through the gardens to the Albert Street entrance of the school. Almost 70 years later, a former PLC girl living in Germany would remember Joan, a few years her junior, joining the train in Middle Brighton, with neat plaits and "fitting perfectly into class and sport."[2]

Joan's first day was also the first day as Principal for Scotswoman Mary Neilson. It was an historic day recorded in the May 1938 school magazine *Patchwork* as being "the first time since the College was founded, in February 1875, a woman holds the office of Principal." Joan, indeed, "never knew the days when the College had a male head"[3] until her own departure from the role 47 years later. The message that came with Miss Neilson's arrival was clear to all the girls: women can be heads of schools, and more. This subliminal feminist concept which permeated the school throughout the subsequent years, led some to say that PLC girls had a certain way about them — a confident, independent, strong, determined, "not-to-be-messed-with" identity as women[4] — qualities that Joan absorbed and embodied throughout her life.

The seeds of the new PLC identity were sown in less confident times, when girls' education — scarce as it was, with only thirteen girls' secondary schools in the whole of England — languished in crisis. It took the English Schools Inquiry Commission[5] to disclose in its 20-volume report in 1868 a vivid and distressing picture of English middle-class girls schooling: "Want of thoroughness and foundation; want of system; slovenliness and showy superficiality; inattention to rudiments; undue time given to accomplishments, and those not taught intelligently or in any scientific manner; want of organisation."[6]

The report reverberated throughout England and internationally. The ripple-effect touched Allenswood, the school Eleanor Roosevelt attended in 1899, and there is clear evidence the "foundation of PLC is a direct consequence of the movement for the higher education of women in the United Kingdom."[7]

But the report itself sprung from earlier trail-blazing educators and practitioners of reform. Frances Mary Buss (1827-94) and Dorothea Beale (1831-1906) were pioneers in the field and became famous as the leaders of the reformed educational movement. The

Encyclopedia Britannica includes them as among 100 Women Trailblazers, "extraordinary women who dared to bring gender equality ... to the forefront." In particular, the editors note how "their widespread reputations for single-minded dedication to the cause of female education' inspired the verse: 'Miss Buss and Miss Beale Cupid's darts do not feel How unlike us Miss Beale and Miss Buss'."[8]

Frances Buss had been teaching with her mother from a young age and was an early attender of evening classes at the new Queen's College for Ladies in 1848. Importantly, she founded the model North London Collegiate School for Ladies. In 1864, she gave evidence before the Schools Inquiry Commission and its report singled out her school for exceptional commendation. Indeed, her pioneering work put the education of girls on a proper intellectual footing and was given further impetus in 1871 when the Brewers' and Clothworkers' Companies rehoused her North London Collegiate School and also funded the establishment of a Camden Lower School for Girls. Buss and Dorothea Beale, the Principal of Cheltenham Ladies College and a founder of St Hilda's College, Oxford, played an active part in promoting the success of the Girls' Public Day School Company, encouraging the connection of the girls' schools with the university standard by examinations, working for the establishment of women's colleges and improving the training of teachers. Beale was also one of the first to attend lectures at the newly opened Queen's College for Ladies, London. Under her principalship, Cheltenham Ladies College, which had opened in 1854, became one of Britain's great girls' schools and played an important role in shaping a revolutionary new attitude to the higher education of women. Buss founded the Association of Headmistresses in 1874 becoming its first president (1874–94) and Beale succeeded her in the post.[9]

Both women would have recognised the need for male champions as essential to achieve change and it is likely they read and felt supported by J.S. Mill's classic, *On the Subjection of Women*.[10]

It was published in 1869, the very year when the Presbyterian Church of Victoria directed its Education Committee to "ascertain the practicability of a ladies' College in connection with the Church."[11] Mill's essay fixed on his realisation "constantly growing stronger by the progress of reflection and experience of life: that the principle which regulates the existing social relations between the two sexes—the legal subordination of one sex to the other—is wrong in itself, and now one of the chief hindrances to human improvement; and that it ought to be replaced by the principle of perfect equality, admitting no power or privilege on the one side, nor disability on the other."[12]

Also published in 1869 was British feminist Josephine Butler's *Woman's Work and Woman's Culture: A Series of Essays*.[13] More than 150 years later, unsettling similarities remain. Butler protests, "against the questions treated herein being regarded as exclusively 'women's questions.' Or the cause advocated as the cause solely of women. It has long been my conviction that the cause we advocate, though primarily and more immediately the cause of women is secondarily, in a yet graver and more weighty sense, the cause of men."[14]

The coincident timing of Mill's essay and Butler's collection, encouraged Butler to disclaim Mill's influence in her introduction: "The Essays, including the introductory remarks, were all written before Mr J. S. Mill's book The Subjection of Women appeared … In some of them the same lines of thought are pursued more in detail which are opened up in Mr Mill's book, and a measure of agreement will be found with the general principles announced by him." And she records for posterity: "As the effect of independent enforcement would be impaired if plagiarism were suspected, I think it desirable to say on our first page, that the case is as I have stated it."[15] So, she had not copied Mill. Male champions are one thing and encouraged, male opinion as wholly original and oracular another.

The only part of Butler's collection that did involve revisions, after Mill's book appeared, is referred to in a footnote as "the latter part of the Essay on the Education of Girls; those pages were kept back until after the 14th June 1869, when the Endowed Schools Bill was considered before a Committee of the House of Commons."[16] That chapter by Elizabeth C Wolstenholme on The Education of Girls, its Present and its Future[17] is especially relevant to PLC's history. In it, she argues, "as a matter of soundest national policy and a means of the highest social well-being, it is imperative that Englishwomen should be as well instructed as Englishmen."[18] Her chapter was most likely read by another of the book's contributors, Charles H. Pearson, himself to figure largely and controversially in the history of PLC.

Pearson wrote *On Some Historical Aspects of Family Life* with a swingeing critique of "legal relations of husband and wife (as) a relic of primitive times."[19] This was not an attack on connubial living but on legally enshrined male dominance such that, "English domesticity has few worse enemies than the law which vests the husband with the control of his wife's property and earnings."[20] Women's education was thus a threat to male power and means of liberation from it. Pearson rallied to the opportunities enabled by a century of change and of harnessing that change to Wolstenholme's challenge, the equal education of women. That same year, Pearson's commitment and the views expressed in the edited collection would find practical expression some ten thousand miles away in Australia.

In 1869, when the General Assembly of the Presbyterian Church of Victoria referred to its Education Committee the suggestion that the Church provide secondary education for girls, the committee moved swiftly. It set up a special Committee on the Ladies' College that presented its first report seven days later, on 17 November 1869. Thereafter progress slowed and it was not until 1875 that PLC was established in East Melbourne. Importantly, for the latter part of Joan's story, the Church made clear its intention to, "assume only a limited financial responsibility for the Ladies' College. It would provide the site, build the school and a residence for the Principal, and give the advice and backing of the Church, but the school was to be self-supporting. The Principal was to conduct the school as a private enterprise, paying the teachers and other staff and gaining his livelihood from the pupils' fees. His appointment was to be for five years, subject to renewal."[21]

George Tait, a thirty-year-old Presbyterian minister, was the school's first Principal. To better manage the school as a private enterprise, he created the position of Headmaster with responsibility for the curriculum and offered the role to Charles Pearson, who had earlier contributed a chapter to Butler's collection. With a great sense of "triumph," Tait's 21 November 1874 notice in the *Argus* extolled Pearson's appointment and credentials—MA, late Fellow of Oriel College, Oxford, and sometime Professor of Modern History at King's College, London. When it came to advertising PLC's opening on 15 February 1875 in the pages of the *Age*, Tait saw "the glittering lure of the name and qualifications of the Headmaster"[22] as a major drawcard.

Four days before PLC opened, Pearson delivered his inaugural lecture on "The Higher Culture of Women." It mirrored his chapter "On Some Historical Aspects of Family Life" and noted the "social changes that had taken place within a century and their inescapable effects on the lives of women."[23] A copy of the lecture, with underlinings and ticks in the margins, is in Joan Montgomery's papers and one finds in Pearson's address a champion of the female cause. Sweeping social change favoured "teaching (women) more, not of teaching less, of making the training more intellectual, not more industrial."

Historian Kathleen Fitzpatrick would link the birth of PLC to cosmic augury: "(D)uring the weekend after [Pearson's] inaugural lecture a comet, the traditional portent of notable coming events, appeared in the sky over Melbourne, and on Monday 15 February 1875 PLC was born."[24] Fitzpatrick's artistic licence matched the facts. On that day, PLC Melbourne became the first Australian school to offer an education for girls equivalent to that provided by the leading colonial boys' schools.[25] While change was afoot, it was a leap ahead of its time. Women were entitled to take the matriculation examination, yet they were unable to enter university until 1881 when PLC graduates became the first women to attend Melbourne University.

Both the Church and Pearson as Headmaster were delighted with the first year. The success of the College exceeded all expectations, the numbers rising from 60 students in the first term to 170 in the fourth.[26] While only one College student passed the November matriculation that first year (Alfred Deakin's sister Catherine, who subsequently became a member of Pearson's staff),[27] in the third year the numbers had jumped to six and the College decisively led the field of institutions sending up girls for the examination.[28]

But nothing roils, divides and damages a school and its community more than a controversy centred on its head. As it turned out, Pearson's term as Headmaster was brief, finishing in a blaze of publicity not unlike that which would engulf Joan Montgomery a century later, but in quite different circumstances. Unlike Joan, Pearson openly coaxed and courted his demise.

By the end of his second year as Headmaster, Pearson burnished his political debut with an address on 11 December 1876 on "The History of Taxation in England and its bearing upon Taxation in Victoria." His biographer, John Tregenza, notes it was not "a strictly political occasion, for this was merely the first in a series of summer lectures to be delivered in the Emerald Hill Mechanics' Institute, and the large audience must have had an interesting time trying to take the lecturer's measure as a potential politician."[29] However, the content was radical for Victoria at the time, calling for a land tax "because it was undesirable in any country that a few wealthy proprietors should monopolize the soil." Its political potential was immediately recognized by John Gavan Duffy MLA "who deliberately voiced the question that must have been in everybody's mind, by remarking amidst hearty applause, that he 'only wishes that the Professor could reiterate his admirably-expressed opinions in Parliament'."[30]

"The reverberations of the address were still being felt nine days later when the annual prize-giving took place at PLC."[31] That morning, Sir Samuel Wilson, the second greatest landowner in Victoria and a recent donor of 30,000 pounds to the University of Melbourne for the building of a great hall, attacked Pearson's position in a letter to the *Argus*.[32] Palpable tension filled the room during the afternoon's prize-giving ceremony as the politicians most likely to suffer from what Pearson proposed, Sir James McCulloch and Mr James McBain, sat on the platform both slated to talk. But with admirable restraint, no one referred to the events outside the school and Pearson's second school year came to a successful conclusion. The mingling of politics and the head-mastership was, nonetheless, heading for trouble. It came on 19 February at a public meeting called by the National Reform League at Melbourne's Princess Theatre to "advocate protection and a Land Tax." With elections imminent, several thousand "eager and orderly listeners"[33] were present to witness Pearson on the platform moving a motion to introduce a land tax. As Tregenza records, "the reaction of the conservatively inclined Melbourne Punch to Pearson's speech was swift and unscrupulous. 'I wonder,' wrote a columnist, 'What the parents of the young ladies in the Presbyterian College, most of whom belong to the criminal classes—by which I mean the classes which have committed the capital offence of acquiring property—think of Professor Pearson's alliance with the Communists?'"[34]

The Reverend Tait was alarmed, interviewing Pearson at length the following week.[35] Pearson offered to give up politics but Tait sought and received his resignation effective July 1877 and reported in the *Age* in February 1877.[36] The news unleashed a public storm. The headmasters of Melbourne Grammar, Hawthorn Grammar, Scotch College and Wesley College, and the professors of Classics, Natural Sciences, Engineering, Law and History at

Vetting of Wisdom

Melbourne University wrote a joint letter published in the *Age* on 20 March 1877 urging Pearson to reconsider his resignation and ignore the push that had forced his hand: "We know, as few except your pupils and their parents know, the extent of the loss which education will suffer deprived of your earnest zeal and eminent attainments. We would fain express a hope that this calamity may be averted."[37]

The public outcry forced Tait to blink, if only tactically. He offered Pearson a new, "though much less generous contract on the old condition that he gave up politics." Martin Howy Irving, the distinguished head of Hawthorn Grammar, was unimpressed. It made him think that Tait "was glad of a chance to get rid of a Head Master who took too large a share of his profits".[38] As for Pearson, he was now far too committed to a political career and to his election committee in the Victorian seat of Boroondara to enter into such a contract.

Staff and students were devastated. There was great sadness as they presented Pearson with a farewell gift, a silver claret jug and goblets. Professor Barton read an address signed by all the teachers: "We have felt it an honour to be associated with you in our common work and we shall endeavour in the future to show by the quality of our teaching that your influence has not been lost."[39]

From its first days, then, PLC, through Pearson, had imbued in its students and female staff the confidence in their ability to study and teach on equal terms with men, and, in the wider community, to play an equally creative role in social reform and improvement. It was a legacy that Joan Montgomery would later take up as a graduate of PLC and then as the school's Principal some 92 years after Pearson's resignation.

But first she must endure PLC's lowers, middles and uppers, starting with Class IVb and Miss Washington, her first form mistress: "Good morning girls—take out your grey books and answer these questions." The new routine came as a shock to Joan who had spent 1937 at St Leonard's Church Hall Annexe mostly outdoors playing cricket with a rubbish bin wicket. As a result, she repeated the year, starting PLC in the Lowers (year 7) with the gauntlet of Middles (year 8), Uppers (Year 9), Intermediate (year 10), Leaving – Pass (Year 11) and Leaving – Honours (Year 12) (the final year being for those interested in tertiary education) still to run. Nonetheless, within the first few weeks, her peers elected Joan as a class captain.

Another class captain, Fay Miscamble, shared Joan's mischievous spirit and they became great friends. Fay lived with her grandparents as her mother had died. It was amusing shopping with Fay after school at Myer's (the Myer Emporium) or Buckley's (Buckley & Nunn), putting things on her grandparents' account. "That can go on the Miscamble account," Fay would explain, beginning the familiar routine: "Is it the Miss Campbell account?" "No!", she would reply, "Not Miss Campbell, the Miscamble account!" Joan's contact with Fay ended when Fay developed TB and was whisked to a sanatorium in the outer eastern suburbs.

Life at PLC in the 1930s was packed with extra extra-curricular activities — from editing and producing the school magazine *Patchwork* to participating in the Camera Club, the Crusader Union, the Critic's Club, the Dramatic Society, the League of Nations, the Literary and Scientific Society, the Music Club, the Stamp Exchange Club, the Language Club and the Student Christian Movement.

Aside from her love of reading, Joan's main extra-curricular interests were her passion for baseball in summer and tennis and basketball in winter, sports she played before and after school and on weekends. Joan and Elizabeth would time their train trips in and out of Middle Brighton according to Joan's sporting commitments. But their keenness to catch the 7.16am train was too much for their father: "You cannot catch a train before 7.30am in the morning."

Early starts for sport was one thing but her early morning violin lessons of a Saturday in those first years at PLC were another. Here the long, cold walk to her lesson from North Brighton station would be an abiding memory. Her teacher was a violinist with the

Melbourne Symphony Orchestra, part of a notable father and son team, Franz and Frank Schieblich, both of whom are recorded in the MSO's commemorative history book.[40] It was Frank, the son, who taught Joan. He was then probably in his 30s and a photograph from 1954 in the MSO history shows him as a friendly, round-faced man with a genuine smile.[41] He was often still in his dressing gown when Joan arrived for her lesson, much to his mother's disapproval. Miss Schieblich, a formidable musician in her own right,[42] is remembered by Joan as "a small apple-cheeked German lady."

William Montgomery probably knew someone who put them on to the Schieblichs, given his own love of music. His father Hugh played the violin and the family would often sing hymns on a Sunday night around the piano played by Beryl with William accompanying her. "I must have been a great disappointment to him," Joan reflects, as she much preferred listening to radio hits, among them Glenn Miller and his orchestra's "In The Mood"; Ella Fitzgerald's "A-Tisket, A-Tasket" and "This Time it's Real"; and, of course, Judy Garland's "Somewhere Over The Rainbow".

Whether it was Frank Schieblich's sleeping-in episodes or maybe just the convenience, William decided Joan should learn at PLC with Miss Nottman as her new violin teacher. Joan persevered for three or four years and played in the school orchestra with Miss McConchie as the director of music and the girls required to wear organza dresses with velvet sashes. Timing was not a strength. "Dad tried to improve Joan on issues of time and reliability, but to no avail," Margaret recalls. "When we were at Brighton, Joan would come home from PLC ... and Dad would say, 'Joan, have you got your violin', and she would say, 'Hmm ... oh, I think I have left it on the train'." While Margaret claims it was a weekly occurrence, Joan thinks it only happened three or four times over several years. Either way, she became a friend of the station master at Sandringham when she had to catch the train to retrieve her violin from the terminus.

PLC opened Joan's mind to the world beyond Australia. In

April 1938, *Patchwork* reported on Miss Gedge's recent arrival from teaching in Eastern Europe and her lecture on Romania: "Still recovering from the effects of the Great War, and even now, the blasted and broken trees standing bare against the skyline are a grim reminder of the horrors of wartime." The first Jewish person Joan met was at PLC. It followed the Australian government's decision in 1938 to accept 15,000 Jewish refugees from Nazism over three years. Only 7,500 reached Australia, however, before war broke out and immigration ceased in September 1939 with the outbreak of World War II.

The world of newspapers also stretched Joan's horizons, helped by a visit to PLC by the *Age* newspaper's Mr Hardiman on 3 March 1938. He explained "how the news was collected from all parts of the world, re-written, set up and spaced," passing around galley proofs as he did so. He gave the school a subscription to the paper and from then on the *Age* was on display each day in the school library. Joan always loved reading the newspaper and at home she was often consumed, kneeling on the floor reading with the paper spread out across the carpet.

At Joan's first speech night, Miss Neilson encapsulated the school's values: "To train young people who will be self-disciplined, reliable, unselfish, and public-spirited.[43] We cannot make every girl into a brilliant scholar, but the school and home together ought to make every girl into a good citizen." To William, whose watchwords were self-discipline and reliability, Miss Neilson's address struck a chord. But they were not, as yet, Joan's strong points, her travel independently to and from school aside. She was more immediately excited by the end of term trip to Hillier's on the corner of Collins and Swanston Street for a chocolate milk shake.

Driven by her desire for the Malvern Star bike, Joan had been a strong primary school student. But her first year at PLC was all too easy and the decision to repeat year 7 had been a mistake. So, in 1939 Joan jumped into Uppers—Year 9. It made no difference to her popularity with her peers and, together with Dorothy Olorenshaw and Adele Rothberg, she was again elected class captain. It was a year of gathering storms internationally and shocks at home, beginning on 7 April 1939 with the death of Joseph Lyons, the first Australian Prime Minister to die in office. *Patchwork* reported on the school's short service honouring the death of "a poor man's son" who "had to earn his living early, but he decided to become a teacher and kept on studying until he had achieved his object."

The outbreak of the war in September made for brooding and uncertain times. Miss Neilson was determined to shield her students, pleading with parents in her 12 December 1939 Speech Night address: "Wherever it is at all possible, the child should not suffer ... The war may deprive your daughter of much that you value; but her education cannot be taken."

For Joan, it had been another year of merriment, including her escape from Miss Rentoul's Latin class. But now she was paying for it and it was not a Speech Night she enjoyed. She had just gone home with a report which she recalls saying: "It is with great regret that we have decided Joan may no longer hold office in this school." Worse, skipping a year had little impact upon her schoolwork and, rather than going on with her classmates, she was headed for another year of Intermediate. She celebrated the end of year in the usual way, going to Hillier's and a film, but burning a hole in her pocket was the unsealed school report. She didn't look at it, though she would have loved to, as you did not look at anything addressed to your parents, sealed or unsealed.

Joan didn't dislike schoolwork. It was more that she was often distracted, like leaving her violin on the train or Friday afternoon rehearsals playing 3rd violin in the school orchestra. A classmate Joan Kent (Battersby) recalls Miss McConchie looking around and asking: "Is Joan Montgomery coming?"

"I think it is tennis, or I think it is baseball," came the reply.

It was not that she didn't like her studies and music, it was just that she liked other things more. Sport was the priority. Joan played short stop in baseball and "she had [a] lovely throw from short stop back to base."[44] A photograph of combined sports teams in the December edition of *Patchwork* in 1940 shows Joan sitting on the far right of the front row, smiling and carefree—secure in her place as a member of the baseball team.

Sport and reading were her great passions. A book review of *Gone with the Wind* in the 1940 *Patchwork* portrayed a "book of true-life, peopled by characters of intense and gripping reality, moving through a period of history made vivid by the pen of an artist".[45] This encouraged Joan to borrow the book from her local library. At home she covered it in brown paper, worried her parents would think it too advanced for her class of Vc where she had rebounded to once again be one of the class captains. But the subterfuge was in vain: "I used to read under the bed clothes. I thought nobody knew, but everyone did. It was very risqué … sex … it was almost banned. One morning I remember Mother saying, 'don't forget to take your book back.' I said, 'which one?'—'Gone with the Wind,' she said; 'it's under your bed'."

In the same issue of *Patchwork*, Olive Battersby (VIb), had written "The War", her perspective sharpened beyond that of her classmates having recently arrived from England with her younger sister Joan and two brothers, Charles and John. Olive and her family later moved to Brighton and lived on the Esplanade within a ten-minute walk of the Montgomerys. On first arriving in Melbourne, while staying at Clarendon House, beside the Fitzroy Gardens in in East Melbourne, Mr Battersby saw a long line of girls streaming in pairs past the gardens and down Collins Street to Scots' Church. Thinking they were heading for school and needing one for his daughter, he followed them to see which one they attended. A cameo of what he saw is captured by Leila Shaw, a boarder at PLC during the war years, in *The Way We Were*: "Dressed in school uniforms we walked in pairs, crocodile style, in a long file across Fitzroy Gardens and along Collins Street to Scots' Church every Sunday. We chattered together and admired the shop windows as

Vetting of Wisdom

we passed along the street. We also admired the many American servicemen in their smart tailored uniforms."[46]

When the Scots' Church service was over, Mr Battersby followed the crocodile line back to PLC in Albert Street. The next morning, with Olive on one arm and his younger daughter Joan on the other, he went to see Miss Neilson, and the girls were enrolled at PLC. Joan Battersby remembers Miss Neilson's Scottish "brogue" saying the girls would start on 6 February, to which Mr Battersby responded: "No they won't, they will start tomorrow!" It was around December and he was thinking about the English school year. So the Battersby girls went to school for the final 10 days of the year, without the school uniform and being teased by some girls for only having the school tie.

Patchwork was cut back to two editions a year for the duration of the war and other aspects of school life were impacted. Wartime certificates, designed by girls in the Art School, replaced end-of-year book prizes. Miss Neilson told her 12 December 1940 Speech Night audience that the savings would be used for patriotic purposes, namely the education of an English girl at PLC. Rationing of tea and sugar began in 1942, followed by butter in 1943 and meat in 1944. Joan's sister Margaret portioned her butter ration and William would mix the butter with milk in her "Mary-Had-a-Little-Lamb" saucer and cup, so that it lasted the full week. On Sundays, the family walked home from Church hastened by the thought of the roast dinner awaiting them to be followed by a desert of tinned peaches topped with whipped cream. Margaret remembers asking for special food hampers for her birthday and keeping the box of Kraft cheese under her bed as a way of rationing the pleasure.

The Battersbys' move to Brighton began a close union with the Montgomery girls. Olive, a year older than Joan, was Joan's friend, while Joan Battersby was the same age as Elizabeth. The Battersby girls would pass the bank on their way to Middle Brighton station and all four girls would travel together by train to and from PLC. Much of their time outside school was spent on the beach and "no-one could have been more hospitable than Mrs Battersby. She lived for her family, and their friends were so generously welcomed that No 144 The Esplanade was like a second home"[47] to Joan. The bank only had a small garden, whereas the Battersbys had a large one shared with the other three neighbouring maisonettes. With the beach opposite, it was the perfect place to play.

Olive was two years ahead of Joan and a school prefect in 1941. Joan was in Class V the equivalent of Year 10 today. The repeated Intermediate year marked a significant change in Joan's approach to her schooling. She bubbled with her usual enthusiasm but did so with more of a focus on her school environment. Part of her efforts centred on refurbishing her form room near the tuck shop, part of the original PLC building that was once the schoolroom of Dame Nellie Melba. As she recounted in the May edition of *Patchwork*, the work began on a Saturday morning when a group of girls descended on the school and emerged from the cloakroom in a weird variety of dress. One wore "startling striped apparel" resembling "the coat of a … wildcat species." Another "a more sombre neck-to-ankles garment". Others displayed "their shapely limbs while clad in brief shorts or playsuits."

> There was one horrible moment when an ardent worker discovered that the kalsomine intended for the wall was slowly trickling down the spinal column of her form-mistress who happened to be passing below. It was also disconcerting to find that when one dealt a particularly vicious blow to an obstinate piece of wallpaper the surrounding wall invariably crumbled away, giving the impression of a heavily-bombed area. Frequent short rests were found necessary for refreshment or for the removal of kalsomine from one's eyes, ears and mouth. At the end of the morning the room did not present a very comfortable appearance, its walls being in various

stages of scraping, sand papering or scrubbing, with the desks and lockers coated by a thick layer of grit and dust, and the floors covered with an ankle-deep collection of wallpaper, putty and kalsomine. After a fortnight's hard work there emerged a very much improved form room, with fresh cream-coloured walls and newly oiled chairs and tables.[48]

A collection of small photographs kept for years in a black deed box captures Joan and her contemporaries at the end of 1941. As well as Olive Battersby there is Jean Craven — on whose court Joan and her friends played tennis for many years — wearing a prefect's badge and smiling directly into the camera; Elaine Chenoweth, the Head Prefect, smiling too and holding her own camera; and Margaret McColl, Joan's predecessor as captain of the baseball team and of Leven House, wearing the PLC sports uniform a white, short-sleeved blouse, grey woollen shorts with four box pleats and lined with grey woollen pants with elastic round the legs: "Even if we did Catherine Wheels on the lawn we could never look indecent!"[49] In another shot, Joan holds the same sports uniform, carefully boxed and folded. It was taken in 1939, the year the new rig was introduced. Joan has long plaits, a PLC bag over her right shoulder and stands with Marjorie Cunningham who is holding a baseball bat. Marjorie and Joan were chosen to model the new sports uniform and the photo shows some of the East Melbourne grounds, with the colonnaded arched-way sprawling in the background.

One more snap, with a Kodak postcard imprint on the back, shows Judy Cowling who shared a bout of chicken pox with Joan and whose mother took both girls up to Yarra Glen while they were contagious. They played tennis together and Judy's father was manager at Kooyong Club. The photo is out of focus and has a hazy, dreamy feel to it. As she recalls the moment, Joan remarks: "She was attractive."

Was it common for girls to have crushes? "Oh yes, it was absolutely normal, but no longer." Why? "I think everything is more liberal these days. We had very little to do with boys … I had no brothers and I really in a way would have been better in a co-ed school, although it didn't seem to harm Margaret – she was always in demand. But I was fairly shy and my mother would have pushed me off socially but she wasn't around … Oh yes, it was quite normal; even if you didn't feel strongly about a crush you had to let people think you did. It was just a schoolgirl thing to do." And what would a girl who was the subject of a crush do about the attention? "Mainly ignore it and act as if it wasn't there. Giving encouragement was not the done thing."

Loyal friendships with women become important and nurturing in Joan's life, as a student and beyond. In *The Social Sex: A History of Female Friendship*, Marilyn Yallom and Theresa Donovan Brown identify girls' schools where "adolescent crushes could develop into lifelong friendships that continued even after one or both of the women had married. Society not only accepted the sentimental intimacy of two women, but actually promoted it as a feminine ideal. While men had their work, clubs, or taverns — depending on their class — what better pastime for a woman than to share the loving company of her best friend?"[50]

The strong male figure in Joan's world was her father who was committed to the education of his children. He was not the focus of Miss Neilson's 1941 Speech Night lament "that wartime conditions had attracted many girls away from the maturer school years," adding "parents who allow their daughters time to become thoughtful and educated young women are performing a patriotic duty." And while Joan may have been made to repeat the year, having achieved her Intermediate certificate there was no doubt she would be back in 1942 for her Leaving and Matriculation year. But first, there was the joyous stretch of summer ahead. Only one obstacle stood in her path of spending it on the beach with the Battersbys. The wartime air raid shelter at the base of the bank property in Brighton had to be drained of water and it was Joan's task to do it: "Everything drained into it; we would have died of drowning if there had been any bombing."

In early 1942—Joan's Year 11, her Leaving year—rumours swirled that the school was about to be evacuated from East Melbourne. *Patchwork* reported a "strained and uncertain" atmosphere. Joan recalls each student having a small rucksack with a pair of jodhpurs, a few cotton shirts and a quantity of pants and socks: "We were allowed two blocks of chocolate and raisins; my chocolate never lasted long." To Joan, it promised excitement and adventure before she discovered she would be evacuated with her sisters! Finally, Miss Neilson announced at the Parents' Association annual meeting: "Plans for evacuation to the country had been altered due to unforeseen difficulties and that preparations were being made to move the school as a unit from East Melbourne to Burwood, if such a step should prove necessary."[51]

Miss Neilson used the wartime challenges to emphasise qualities relevant to school life. PLC girls might not be required to "show the supreme courage and loyalty demanded from the Fighting Forces" but were nevertheless encouraged to show courage and loyalty "when it is required of us."[52] With relatives in the UK and Singapore, Miss Neilson became good friends with the Battersbys who well knew the anxiety of having family elsewhere. That sense of kinship made her a frequent visitor to the Battersby home. On returning from one such visit, Miss Neilson stopped by the Montgomerys' in Church Street to inquire about Beryl's health, perhaps sensing the Montgomerys' imminent need of those qualities of courage and loyalty.

According to Margaret and Elizabeth, Beryl was never well after Helen's birth in 1936 and often in bed. "She would get terrible migraines," Elizabeth recalls. "I would see her going to the bathroom literally holding on to the wall." Margaret remembers Beryl struggling with sickness and of housekeepers playing an ever-increasing role.

In the autumn of 1942, Joan and Olive Battersby attended evening first-aid classes at Firbank Grammar School in Brighton. On the night of 13 April Joan arrived home to find an ambulance outside the house. While William was hosting a special function in the bank downstairs, Beryl had suffered a massive stroke. Dr Parker, their doctor from Numurkah days who was now based in nearby Sandringham, was summoned. His arrival was delayed as he thought the call had been for another patient named Montgomery in Sandringham and he had gone to the wrong address. But in the end, it made no difference as there was nothing he could do. Beryl was dead within four hours from the cerebral haemorrhage. She was just 49.

Beryl was cremated at the Springvale crematorium following a service at St. Cuthbert's. As was the custom, the girls did not attend the funeral. Margaret, however, credits her father with doing "something very advanced, allowing us to see our mother's body and farewell her."

William, now widowed with four daughters to care for—Joan 16, Elizabeth 12, Margaret 11 and Helen 5—assumed the role of sole parent with fortitude and stoicism. Some weeks after Beryl's death, Anne Roberts Montgomery, William's first cousin, moved into the Brighton home to help care for the children. Anne's own life had been beset by tragedy. Her mother, Annie, had died of TB at the age of 35, her father, Robert, had passed away in 1918 and, soon after that, her fiancé had died when crossing The Great Australian Bight shortly after the First World War. She would continue to wear his engagement ring for the rest of her life. Tragically, there was more grief ahead as within two years of Beryl's death, Anne would become a surrogate for both parents.

Beryl's death ruptured Joan's world, yet school remained secure and certain, even if the times were uncertain. To help the war effort, Joan and her fellow students filled their spare moments making camouflage nets at school. Sport was a continuing endeavour—tennis and baseball, with Joan appointed team vice-captain. Joan was also elected House Captain for Leven and, in third term, class captain of VIb.

As Joan's form mistress in 1942, Nora 'Jo' Wilkinson, emerged as an important force in her school life, an influence Wilkinson exerted over many PLC girls. Trained at the University of Otago, Kathleen Fitzpatrick calls her "the most remarkable teacher of geography that PLC ever had. In her day, the Exhibition in Leaving Honours Geography came to be regarded as the property of PLC."[53] Wilkinson was almost too good a teacher, according to Fitzpatrick, as under the spell of her classes some Old Collegians studied geography at the expense of other subjects for which they were better suited. Another complication was the University of Melbourne's lack of a geography department. So Miss Wilkinson's protégés were redirected to Economic Geography, the University's closest equivalent. Stimulated and stymied, many of them later went on to do further geography studies overseas, including Joan Battersby and Joan Montgomery. Joan Battersby followed in Wilkinson's footsteps as a geography teacher.

Miss Wilkinson and Miss Aitken, the senior history teacher, devised a course that taught Leaving Geography and History as an integrated discipline. Now commonplace, it was then a bold and original concept.[54] It was typical of Miss Wilkinson's forward thinking, as was her suggestion that boys and girls from local high schools should be invited to PLC to attend discussions about current affairs and be allowed to use the library for that purpose.[55] It was Miss Wilkinson who organised the excursion to the National Gallery on 30 September 1942 to "inspect a collection of documental records and plans, relating to the development of Melbourne during the last hundred years" that Joan reported on in the December 1942 *Patchwork*.[56] The report included references to many notable documents including Batman's Deeds and Hoddle's diary.

Miss Wilkinson understood Joan. During that period, 'Bible memory work' was the norm at PLC, with girls mandated each term to learn a psalm or New Testament passage. It was learnt parrot-like, punctuation included. In Term 2 in Year 11, Joan and several of her friends balked at this. As a form of protest, they opened their bibles in front of them on the desk for everyone to see. Joan wouldn't cheat, but neither did she learn it properly, either. She made almost one hundred mistakes. Miss Nora Wilkinson was administering the test and took her aside;

"You seem to have trouble memorizing?"

"Oh yes, I do" Joan replied.

"But you don't have trouble with English context questions," Wilkinson responded. "Well there is no use making you learn something else, if you have such trouble memorizing, perhaps an essay would be more suitable?"

Joan enjoyed writing essays and chose the prophet Amos who, not being from a school of prophets, claimed therefore to be a real prophet: "I am not a prophet nor a son of a prophet."(7:14) But she was less happy with Miss Wilkinson's parting words—"It will be sent to a Minister for correction."

As her form teacher in 1942, Miss Wilkinson was closely connected to Joan at the time of her mother's death. Joan remembers coming to school for the first time after the death and Miss Wilkinson being very matter-of-fact, asking who was looking after her. "Oh yes," she said on hearing about Aunt Anne and work proceeded. Clever and practical, in the same way she gave Joan the essay to write in response to her protest against rote learning in Bible memory work.

By the end of 1942, her Leaving and Honours year, Joan was well and truly back on track academically, ready to take on her final year of school. Winning the Bible essay prize in 1942 was a precursor to the following year, which saw Joan winning another War Savings Certificate and the Christina Stirling Prize for Bible. Indeed, her final year was to be a sterling year in many ways.

Joan was one of 18 school prefects in her final year with Alison Hutchinson Head Prefect. The prefects had a significant role in the daily life of the school. A fellow prefect, Lexie Luly, wrote that prefects would stand at the "Albert Street or Victoria Parade gate to check if every home-going girl was properly dressed with hat on straight, blazer buttoned up and wearing gloves ... Each morning two prefects joined the procession of staff and the Principal from the back of the Hall and up onto the platform to announce the Hymn or to read a passage from the Bible ... it was a frightening experience ... raising one's voice in front of a large audience. There were no microphones in those days. Prefect duties included standing in the aisles before Assembly to stop the talkers as there must be absolute silence before a religious service. Lunchtime duty was another thing. Two prefects had to 'stroll' up and down the main corridor and around the lawn showing their presence."[57]

During 1943 Joan's form mistress and English teacher, Margaret Begg, died from cancer. She was replaced by Miss Burrage and Mrs Brown respectively. In light of her own mother's death the previous year, Miss Begg's death might have struck Joan hard, yet she responds without sentiment: "No, teachers were more remote."

Joan's final school report for 3rd term in 1943, bears out her enthusiasm for school with no absent days recorded and a report that praises her for doing "well as School Prefect, Club Member and as Captain of the Baseball Team." Miss Burrage would write: "Joan's general ability and effort may be judged from ... the Harris Prize for Sports and Studies. She has done good work in all subjects except Biology, to which she could not give sufficient time, and shares the Bible prize." Miss Neilson added two lines of her own: "We are sorry to lose Joan and wish her success and happiness in her future career—MN." Joan sat her external examinations "covered in spots" after a bout of German Measles. Her results were solid but not outstanding. She received a third-class honour for English and passes in Geography and British History.

At Joan's final speech night at the Melbourne Town Hall, the Moderator General of Australia, Robert Wilson Macaulay, was the guest speaker. "Character," he declared, "was not taught in a school lesson but could be gained only by working towards a high ideal with faith in success and in God."[58] Dr Macaulay was also responsible for handing Joan the Harris Prize for Sports and Studies, the Christina Stirling Prize for Bible (Aequalis) and the Runner-Up School Tennis Champion Prize.

William Montgomery was glowing, proud of Joan for winning the Harris Prize and for having grown from mischievous young student to a school prefect — demonstrating the reliability and trustworthiness he expected. The next morning, William drove Joan to Spencer Street Station — a rare treat at a time of petrol rationing — where she set off to go fruit picking on a small orchard out from Merrigum, near Kyabram, with a group of friends including Olive Battersby. His words of farewell would be the last she would hear him speak.

Later that day, William collapsed and was taken to hospital. Joan knew nothing until she received a letter from cousin Anne a few days later, "saying that he had a mild stroke and was in the hospital, you know, no cause for alarm, don't come home. And then after perhaps 10 days, I got a phone call saying that he had had another stroke and that I should come home."

By the time Joan reached her father's bedside, there was no interaction. William died on 29 January 1944. His death certificate lists the cerebral haemorrhage having occurred six weeks prior to his death and records his decade-long struggle with arteriosclerosis. Two years after certifying Beryl Montgomery's death, the unhappy Dr. Parker also certified the death of her husband. At the age of 18, Joan was now without both parents, as were sisters Elizabeth, 14, Margaret, 13, and Helen, just 7 years old.

William's funeral, on Monday 31 January 1944, a public holiday, was a large one as he had had a wide social circle as a returned soldier, a senior bank manager, a Freemason and an inveterate joiner. As the oldest child and with the younger children again not in attendance, Joan was the chief mourner, with her guardian cousin Anne.

Feeling the need to stay in Melbourne to assist with her sisters,

Joan was determined to go on to university. Steeped in patriarchy, the trustees of her father's estate were not entirely convinced and sought professional endorsement of Joan's choice. It came from Miss Neilson, an enthusiastic advocate of university education for women and the principal of the first Melbourne girls' school to provide women entrants. So, within weeks of William's death, Joan began life as a student at the University of Melbourne, an association that would continue, with breaks, for almost 50 years.

4

A Church in Hawthorn

In 1923, two years before Joan was born, William and Beryl Montgomery built a house on the corner of Illawarra Road and Kembla Street in Hawthorn. Araluen—an Aboriginal word meaning place of water lilies—was planned as a permanent family home but would be that for just the few years before William's appointment as manager of the bank branch in Bright. In choosing the site, within walking distance of Scotch College, William, an old boy of Scotch, surely anticipated the arrival of a son or sons to follow in his footsteps. But that was not to be.

After the young family moved to Bright, the large red brick house with the return verandah at No. 7 Kembla Street was rented to three unmarried sisters, the Misses Galloway, who would remain in residence for almost two decades. After William's death, Anne and the Montgomery girls could no longer stay at the bank premises in Middle Brighton, despite the bank allowing generous leeway on their departure.

The logical move back to Kembla Street was complicated by the fact that the Galloways had been paying "peppercorn" rent and had no desire to end their protected tenancy, especially during the difficult days of wartime when rental accommodation was limited and expensive. At that time, tenants could not be evicted unless a similar property, at no greater expense, was found.

Initially, Margaret and Elizabeth went to stay with Great Aunt May in Fairfield, and Anne, Joan and Helen rented a house in Brighton. A house was then found in Moreland Road, Moreland, where they could all be together again. But as time moved on and the Galloways still hadn't found a suitable new home, the Montgomerys moved in with them. Elizabeth remembers: "The solicitor said we had to move in because ... they had already knocked back more than one house because it had no fireplace. So, it looked as if they would never leave unless forced!" It would not be a happy cohabitation.

A wide central hallway divided the front of the house with living and bedrooms on either side, many with stained glass windows and fireplaces. Initially, while the Galloways continued to scout for new lodgings, the girls were accommodated in a sleepout which was located past the vestibule.

The house had only one bathroom, which created immediate problems given there were now eight residents. On weekday mornings, the girls needed to get ready for school but the Galloways kept the bathroom door shut as they followed each other in and out, without a break, readying themselves for work. Georgina Galloway, a teacher at Stratherne, made it particularly difficult as she liked to shower early. This was all Joan needed to rouse her mischievous streak. When the coast was clear, she would enter the bathroom through the window to secure it for the Montgomerys.

Elizabeth remembers Joan dropping through the slightly ajar bathroom window a toy mouse on a piece of black string. Georgina Galloway shrieked and rushed for a straw broom to thrash at the mouse. It was Anne who had to deal with the aftermath when Georgina discovered the truth. In the meantime, the Montgomery girls had gained early entrance to the bathroom. Such incidents helped speed the eventual departure of the Misses Galloway.

At Hawthorn, Anne Montgomery's role in the lives of her young cousins—and her self-sacrifice—came into sharper focus. Now more a surrogate parent than the housekeeper of her first months with the family, Anne provided a loving and supportive environment in which the girls could grow and flourish. Although there would be some lingering resentment that however caring and supportive Anne was, she could never replace Beryl or William.

Later, with only Elizabeth and Helen at home, Anne did some part-time bookkeeping for a local real estate agent. She had a close friend, Irene, a remarried young mother with several small children, known as "Bob". Each night the two women would chat on the phone. "It must have kept her sane," Elizabeth reflects. Later in their lives, all of the Montgomery girls would acknowledge their great love for Anne — and the debt they owed her.

The move to Hawthorn would draw Joan Montgomery firmly into the orbit of the man who would loom large in and eventually eclipse her distinguished career. Their first unhappy encounters would be as members of the congregation of the Hawthorn Presbyterian Church but ultimately their conflict would turn on no less than the fate of one of Australia's finest schools, Presbyterian Ladies' College.

Frederick Maxwell Bradshaw, an only child, was born at the family home *Burnside*, 62 Riversdale Road, Hawthorn, on the corner of Riversdale Road and Fordholm Road. When the Montgomery girls moved to Kembla Street, about a kilometre away, Max Bradshaw was 34, almost 15 years older than Joan, and already set for a distinguished career in the law. An old boy of Scotch College, he had graduated from Melbourne University with masters degrees in law and arts and was serving his articles with the firm of Krcrouse, Oldham & Bloomfield. He would sign the Bar Roll in 1936. Bradshaw also was already a prominent figure in the congregation of the Hawthorn church — a position that would propel him into a leading role in the affairs of the Presbyterian Church at a State and national level.

His younger friend and mentee Brian Bayston, a fellow

lawyer and devout Presbyterian, would evoke Psalm 26:8 to describe Bradshaw's spiritual connection with the suburb of his birth: "A house in Hawthorn is where he lived his life; a school in Hawthorn moulded him, and he sought to mould it; a church in Hawthorn was the house for him in which God's honour dwelt." And the church at 573 Glenferrie Road was also the place where Max Bradshaw would seek to impose his zealous perspective on his fellow parishioners and the wider community. He was appointed a manager in 1936, an Elder in 1941 and Session Clerk—the most senior lay role in a congregation—in 1945. "These were the days when you wore your Sunday best to church," Bayston explains. "On the occasions when the Sacrament of the Lord's Supper (communion) was observed, Max wore morning suit. When an infant was baptised, Max led the parents with their child into the church. Public worship was an occasion to be observed with due solemnity."[1]

When he became leader of the Hawthorn Young Men's Bible Class in 1951, absenteeism was not tolerated. Bayston says Bradshaw would appoint a delegation to find the truant and "figuratively ... beat him up". And he would lead by devout example: "When Max led in prayer, there was no pietistic language, but a sense of awe matched by a certainty of audience at the throne of grace through the merits of Jesus Christ. Max taught us to sing the psalms unaccompanied, save by a tuning fork, and took us on excursions to churches where the psalms only were used in the public worship of God."[2]

Anne and the Montgomery girls joined the Hawthorn congregation soon after they moved into Kembla Street. The church's Session minutes record Anne and Joan's transfer to Hawthorn from Brighton on 7 December 1944 and show Margaret and Elizabeth's admission to communicant membership on 28 July 1946 when they received their first communion. Church was an important factor in their lives with Margaret involved with the youth group, the Presbyterian Fellowship Association, and teaching Sunday school. Joan, while a regular churchgoer, wasn't involved in Sunday school teaching.

Bradshaw's commitment to his church and its history and traditions is reflected in his authorship of *Rural Village to Urban Surge: A History of the Presbyterian Congregation at Hawthorn, Victoria* published in 1964 to commemorate the church's centenary.[3] The Reverend Robert Swanton, who had been the congregation's minister since 1940, wrote in the book's foreword of Bradshaw's close connection to the Hawthorn Church for nearly half its life and of his "marked devotion and competence." These qualities would shape the future direction of the Presbyterian Church, for Bradshaw's conservatism would drive his uncompromising approach to the Presbyterian response to the move to union. Swanton, tied both to the Congregation and to the strength of Max's personality and theology since his late twenties, concluded his foreword by looking back to the founders of the Hawthorn Church: "Convinced and informed upholders of the Standards of the Church, who imparted a character to the Congregation, which has continued through succeeding generations. In our day of fast change, a true sense of destiny can only arise from a genuine appreciation of our heritage. 'Look unto the rock whence ye are hewn, and to the hole of the pit whence ye are digged'."[4]

The beat of the times and the pressures brewing in the congregation during the period the Montgomery family was part of it is reflected in the final chapter when Bradshaw surveys "the contemporary scene" and observes: "The war years were difficult. There was the dislocation of ordinary community life; there was sadness in a number of homes; blackout restrictions curtailed church activities. For quite a time the evening service was held in the school hall, from which the emission of light could be more readily checked than from the church."

For the Montgomery sisters, Robert Swanton was perhaps too young to help salve the sadness in people's homes at the time

Vetting of Wisdom

and certainly his visits to Kembla Street were a strain. An emissary of a church run and ministered by men, Swanton, socially awkward anyway, and Max, cerebral, orthodox and unremitting, were alien envoys to the world of young women the Montgomerys represented. As Brian Bayston would write: "Max and Robert were both bachelors, and I am sure that this was a hindrance to the effectiveness of the congregation."[5]

Empathising with youthful female congregants was but one of the challenges facing the church though the war and its aftermath—indeed, the peace brought added pressures. There was the lure of the new suburbs and "the great exodus of young married couples to outer suburbs" evident even before the war. But post war: "It became practically axiomatic that they would thus go. What is more, many of the older and well-established families did the same thing. Up to the early 50s, the minister and the congregation had to face the depressing spectacle of a steadily diminishing membership each year."[6]

By the time the Montgomerys joined the Hawthorn church in December 1944, the Session already had determined to reduce the number of communion services from four to three times a year. Bradshaw explained it as a reversion "to the original decision of the Session on frequency of communion adopted in November 1871."[7] Communion attendance would become a Gordian knot of future strife in Joan's relationship with Max Bradshaw—a conflict that would presage the battle royal that ended her career.

......

Joan's university studies began shortly after her father's death and the move to Hawthorn. Over the following four years she studied for a Bachelor of Arts with subjects including English, French, British History, Economic History, Economic Geography, Philosophy 1 and Psychology 1. Much like school, her academic studies were squeezed around a busy sporting calendar. Indeed, her degree would take an extra year as she failed the French 1A compulsory subject in her first year in 1944 and had to repeat it in 1947. (She then went on to a Diploma of Education (1948) and a Bachelor of Education, conferred on 24 March 1956.)

When Joan began her university studies, many of the students were returned servicemen. Among them was David Hodges, who had been in army "recruitment at Royal Melbourne Park." Joan already knew David as a family friend of Jean Craven and as one of a group who played tennis on the Craven's court in Howard Avenue, East Malvern. David and Jean's mothers were "PLC born and bred, established is probably the right word," Hodges reflects.[8] Joan was different. She didn't have that background or exclusive or elitist bearing. He remembers her as "sporty", "free-spirited" but "serious" all the same. Hodges was studying Arts and Education and Theology after telling the Army Education Unit that he wanted to teach. It was in English and History classes that he caught up with Joan, often joined by Stan Kurrle, another university contemporary. Joan and David spent time together outside university, especially on the squash court and there was one occasion when she accompanied him to a wedding. It wasn't a warm invitation, Joan recalls. Nonetheless, the friendships with David and Stan endured. Stan would become Head of Caulfield Grammar and then Kings School in Sydney, and David became closely connected through the Presbyterian saga that lay ahead.

Summer breaks from university began for Joan with a three-week pre-Christmas stint fruit picking in north central Victoria and later working at the Hawthorn fruit preserving company Fowlers Vacola, long a source of holiday work for school and university students. During and after the war, "large advertisements for women and girls to work at Fowlers Vacola ... filled the local press."[9] The work was far from glamorous. During wartime, Joan recalls women from non-essential industries, such as milliners, turning up in high-heeled shoes and makeup and being transformed by the menial work. For Joan, that was often the onion belt: "The moment I walked through the door (at home) I was told to get into the shower to get rid of the smell." Then, there was the grubbing belt: "Sitting with a knife attached by a string to my waist and taking the grubs out of the tomatoes and throwing the grubs into cake tins, probably about 15 inches long and 6 inches wide. The knife was tied to our waists because if it dropped onto the grubbing belt it would wreck the machines."

Joan's work at Fowlers took place under the practised eye of a Mrs Cridge who lived across the road from the factory on Burwood Road. On one occasion, the men needed help with the bottling. Mrs Cridge looked towards the girls on the belts and said: "Joan will be safe." Joan reflects, "That's how respectable I must have been!"

Joan also had a casual job at Tim Fitchett toys: "It was rather dull, assembling little plastic rocking horses a few inches high. There were two halves and a little mould; you put the bottom half into the mould, and you put the top on and pressed the handles. I think I also used to count marbles into little bags too." The factory jobs were an eye opener for Joan. While not "PLC born and bred" she had nevertheless lived a comfortable life as a banker's daughter.

Joan's career in education began in July 1948 during her Dip. Ed. year when she set off for a three-week teaching round at Frensham, a well-regarded boarding school at Mittagong in the Southern Highlands of New South Wales. "That was seen as one of the 'plum' schools," Joan reflects. Frensham's Principal, Phyllis Bryant, was then overseas and her deputy, Phyllis Clubbe, one of the school's founders with Winifred West, was in charge. Clubbe is also remembered, along with her sister, for introducing hockey to Australia and, more ephemerally, for her big car and big dogs. "Between her 'funny' bursts she's so essentially kind and helpful," Joan would write to her sister Elizabeth after arriving at Frensham.

Winifred West was still teaching an Upper Sixth Divinity class and Joan was invited to join the class discussion. While Joan "could think of no more hellish experience than teaching if you didn't enjoy it," Frensham was a turning point as she began to regard teaching as not just enjoyable but also great fun. Her attitude and aptitude must have impressed those around her as Phyllis Clubbe offered her a job for the following year. The offer involved teaching some English. While Joan's love always was geography, she accepted nonetheless.

The move to Frensham marked a new stage in Joan's life. Anne, at home in Hawthorn, also confronted a new scenario with Joan living away, Margaret beginning her nursing course at the Royal Melbourne Hospital and Elizabeth doing her final year of kindergarten training. Helen was 12 and at PLC when Joan set off in January 1949.

Winifred West was in her late 60s in 1949. Both she and Phyllis Bryant, the Headmistress during Joan's time at Frensham, became important role models. West was a powerhouse, viewed by Joan as "a woman of great vision and ideas." Her biographer Priscilla Kennedy writes: "All her life Winifred had the kind of faith—God, in other people, and in herself—that could move mountains of faint hearts, weak wills and scepticism."[10]

Inspired by the thought of a country boarding school for girls "to develop to the full the capacity of every girl and help her to become a useful and gracious woman," West leased a house with several bathrooms close to the station at Mittagong. The arrival "on a fine clear day in 1913" of "a most important little party that would alter the outlook of a great number of people of NSW" is described in detail by a junior assistant at the station, G.W. Handley. Miss West was "a distinguished looking lady with a lovely voice", Miss Clubbe, "small in stature" and "rather a Mannish type". There were just three staff and five students.[11] West had started with only the name Frensham (after her birthplace in Surrey), the nucleus of a staff and enough money for a very modest beginning.¹² Now she had the building and by 1925 there were 139 students.

When West retired from Frensham in 1938, 25 years after founding the school, she stressed the need for change: "Last year I spoke of change as being an essential part of life. There is in all life a movement and rhythm — the beat of the heart, the ebb and flow of the tide, the circling of the planets — and I think we often make mistakes because we ignore this fact, and plan and act in a mechanical way, as though we were detached beings and not part of this moving life, and so our actions cut across the swing of events … There is a time to end as well as a time to begin."¹³ Later, in the same spirit, Joan would regularly evoke Ecclesiastes 3:1-11 at her PLC assemblies: "To everything there is a season, and a time to every purpose under the heaven."

While Winifred was no longer Headmistress in 1949, she was still a significant part of the community at Mittagong having started a craft centre called Sturt, primarily for students who left the public school at 14. Sturt later became part of the Winifred West Schools Limited that also includes Gib Gate, the primary school. Sturt focused on carpentry, pottery and handcrafts, especially spinning and weaving. Although preoccupied with Sturt, West chaired the Frensham School Council and remained a presence around the school community. In Joan's experience, she never missed an opportunity to educate: "I was at Frensham one day and admitted to Miss West that I hadn't read anything of Albert Schweitzer. She was shocked and, of course, if Miss West was shocked, she promptly did something about it. And she said, well take this and read it straight away. No nonsense!"

West had a keen wit and a talent for producing "an ear-splitting whistle through two fingers stuck in her mouth"¹⁴ — both qualities that would have appealed to Joan who had a sharp tongue of her own and an ear to what might claim people's attention on the hockey field. Miss Bryant followed West as Principal and, during this time, Joan would sometimes take assemblies when Bryant had a free day. On such occasions West and others saw in Joan a future Principal in the making.

In 1952, after completing her three years teaching at Frensham, Joan wrote to her sister Elizabeth after learning she had recently visited the school.

> I was interested to hear that "in a way you felt sorry for Miss W?" I can understand that completely — in fact I can be pretty sure what her conversational theme must have been — she felt old and rather useless. Frensham wasn't developing ... as she had hoped etc. — am I right? I've heard it all so often and can quite understand her view. After all, she borrowed one thousand pounds to begin the school then created Sturt from absolutely nothing. She really is quite a unique personality and apart from having the most creative mind of anyone I know, has a Cambridge Hons. M.A. in Maths, has a cricket and hockey "blue", played hockey for England, ... is an excellent musician (plays piano, harp and cello) paints very well and is an expert on birds, flowers and natives generally.[15]

Phyllis Bryant, Frensham's second Headmistress, was also a force in Joan's life. After visiting Australia with the English Hockey team in 1927, she joined the school in 1931 as a physical education teacher. From quite early days, West confided "several of us felt that she was the right person for the job — but the time was not right then." Bryant took over as Head in 1938 after working closely with West as her assistant. She is credited with caring "about all the things that had gone into making Frensham the kind of school it was."[16] Shy compared to West, she was a highly talented woman whom Joan "liked and respected ... enormously".

Joan began her Frensham years teaching Geography and the Year 11 English class, a late Friday afternoon class that included reading Shakespeare in the rose garden. At least one of her students, Patricia Conolly, did go on to have a stellar stage career.[17] Geography was taught under the guidance of Mrs Chipps, a staunch Presbyterian, a helpful point of connection for Joan. Joan also taught History with two German sisters who had fled Hitler's Germany: "Their father was a professor in Germany, and they pretty much kept to themselves."

An occasional treat was to take some of the girls by train to Sydney on a Saturday to visit the orthodontist, Dr Thornton Tayler. It was an easy task of simply escorting them to meet their parents at the journey's end and later accompanying them home. The dividend was a day of freedom in Sydney.

People who taught at Frensham were bound into a tight network. For Joan, many people associated with the school became life-long friends, including Cynthia Parker who had taught at Frensham in the 1960s and then followed Catherine Sandberg as Head. Sandberg had replaced Phyllis Bryant as Principal in 1965 but resigned due to ill health in mid-1967. Barbara Broughton was a secretary to Phyllis Bryant and would later share a flat in London with Joan. Dorothy Ross, a Frensham old girl, who had returned from P.E. training in England to join the staff, also became one of Joan's long-standing friends.

Joan left Frensham in January 1952, planning to travel soon after to England with a friend, Val Turnball. Joan and Val had met at university. Val, who had attended St Michaels, lived in Illawarra Road, Hawthorn, and the two women would often catch the tram to university together. After Val fell ill and required surgery, their travel plans had to be postponed for another three months. While she waited for Val to recover, Joan took a temporary position for first term teaching Year 10 girls at Methodist Ladies College in Elsternwick. Significantly, this meant that Joan was in Melbourne in April for Margaret's marriage to

Donald Knox. She had been away at Frensham when Margaret began dating Donald in 1950 and when they became engaged in 1951 on the day of Donald's graduation. They married in April 1952 and Elizabeth was bridesmaid. Margaret recalls Joan wearing "a little grey hat with a pink bird sitting up on it" and, not surprisingly perhaps, giving them Frensham coasters as a wedding gift.

The event brought Joan once more into contact with her later nemesis, Max Bradshaw. Bradshaw led the boys' groups at the Hawthorn Presbyterian Church where the Montgomery girls were members. Margaret met Donald through the Hawthorn branch of the Presbyterian Fellowship Association. She recalls the "tremendous respect" the boys had for Bradshaw and the "profound influence" he had upon them. "Strangely enough, out of that group of eight or so that Donald was a part of, two of them did theology and became ministers—Bruce Adams and Robyn Denholm." Yet, Margaret recalls, he didn't like women and "we found him profoundly odd." Another figure who was part of the group but not at the Montgomery-Knox wedding was Brian Bayston who also would emerge as a key adversary in the years ahead.

In the hiatus before leaving for England, Joan first met Jean Ford, who would become a significant lifelong friend. Miss Bryant, a friend of Jean's, had gathered several women recently returned from England to meet Joan.

"I don't feel the cold and it was a cold night and she had a lovely, raging fire and I was put beside it," Joan recalls. "I had just had my vaccination that day and though I wasn't ill with it, I did feel distinctly shivery and peculiar, and there was the oppressive heat of the fire. I have a recollection of various people through a sort of haze, and one of them was Jean Ford."

Jean also remembers the evening clearly: "At that stage Joan had short hair ... It was before the days of permanent waves and it was a very black shiny cap of hair, pink cheeks, those very alive eyes."

The next day, Joan wanted to thank Jean for her help but couldn't remember her surname. She did remember Jean taught at Tintern and contacted Miss Bryant to find out her name. She needn't have, as Jean had already contacted Miss Bryant to find out hers—to send her some material. A year later, Joan would write to her youngest sister Helen, by that time a student at Tintern:

"I must say that Miss Ford at least at first meeting, was most charming and amusing."

The feelings were mutual. Jean, who was 11 years older than Joan, would later say:

"Until I became friends with Joan, life was hardly a barrel of laughs and Joan brought a sense of fun to my life, and enjoyment for which I am forever grateful."

The bond between the two women would strengthen over many years, but first Joan had some travelling to do.

5

CORONATION

As bitterly cold winds swept the wharf at Port Melbourne on Saturday 31 May 1952, Joan embarked on her first trip to England, farewelled by Anne, Elizabeth and Helen and a group of 20 Year 10 girls from MLC. Her ship, the *SS Otranto*, left an hour after the scheduled departure, steaming across the bay to Port Phillip Heads and out into Bass Strait to begin the five-week voyage to Europe.

The 1950s were the twilight of the golden era of ocean travel as the aeroplane began to make its mark. And the 20,000 ton *Otranto* was an aging echo of that passing era. Built in 1925 for the Orient Stream Navigation Company, she had already had a long and hard life before Joan came aboard and would be scrapped five years later. During the war, the *Otranto* has served as a troop transport, taking part in the invasions of French North Africa, Sicily and Italy. And she was accident prone. In 1926 she was slightly damaged after striking a rock at Cape Grosso in Greece and two years later was heavily damaged after colliding with the Japanese steamer *Kitano Maru* in the North Sea. Then, in 1932, she collided with and sank a barge in the Thames Estuary.

Joan would describe her voyage with Val as "respectable". "That word really characterises our whole trip I'm afraid," she would write rather dolefully to her sisters, almost a month after leaving. Her letters would paint a dull picture of life on board: "Dress is informal—and how!—and one does little but eat, read, write letters and sunbathe—you could omit the latter. I've even taken to deliberately sleeping to kill time on some occasions. It's quite usual for people to sleep all afternoon, stirring only to partake of afternoon tea then retiring again."[1]

Meals gave a framework to the day: "Breakfast 8.45am, beef tea 11am, lunch 1.30pm, afternoon tea 4.30pm, dinner 7.30pm. I'm always ravenous so am afraid I'll put on weight but these breaks provide the only highlights to the day so far."[2] Adding to her disappointment was the abundance of women on the ship, appearing to scotch any prospect of meeting an interesting man: "There are just so few men and so many women. However, another 'Carnival Night' last night and I at least had a few dances — though I didn't enjoy one of them! ... I shall be in no fit state to apply for a job in England — my self-confidence will be at an all-time low!"[3]

The hundreds of letters written home to Anne, Elizabeth and Helen (with a request for them to be passed on to Margaret and Donald) would be a rich window into Joan's life over the next two years. But there would be cause for hesitation about their private nature, as she wrote to Helen: "It rather alarms me to think of outsiders reading it when it was written really only for home consumption!"[4] But there also were hints that she would not mind her letters finding a wider audience: "Though it sounds a strange request, could you keep my letters? Everyone else seems to be keeping most elaborate diaries or writing letters in duplicate so that I feel quite out of it. But in view of my skimpy diary I might like to look back on the letters I suppose."[5] Later still Joan would write to Elizabeth: "I don't keep a diary so if there seems anything worth remembering in my letters perhaps you'd keep them for me — perhaps for my memoirs later!"[6]

The younger Joan is brought to life in her letters home. Here we encounter her humour, her self-deprecation, her concern for family and finances, her thrill at being in the United Kingdom and her love of food. But most importantly, we see how important the time in the UK was to her growth as an individual. They are luminous threads in the larger story of what influenced Joan Montgomery to become a school principal, to be so committed to excellence in education for women, to command such respect from others and admiration from those who worked with her.

Joan began crafting her minutely handwritten letters home on Sunday 1 June 1952, the day after the departure from Melbourne. Within the first week she had written more than 20 letters and postcards. Yet it wasn't until two months later that she asked Anne, Elizabeth and Helen: "Please tell me ... if you object to my microscopic writing—others scorn it but if you can read it I can't see the point in making it large."[7]

A meeting one day with fellow travellers Joan and Marion Ormsby stirred memories of a young man Joan's sister Margaret had once spoken of: "Margaret had mentioned a 'Lionel' someone, I thought they might know him. They didn't but as soon as they left, a husky young six-footer came over from the adjoining table and introduced himself—the said 'Lionel.' He is quite nice, rather gauche and shy but I've seen him a few times since—very temperate and a great bushwalker!"[8]

Joan and Val shared their four-berth cabin with two other women—Mrs Endwhistle, in the bunk below Joan and, below Val, a young woman in her mid-20s who would return to the cabin regularly in the early hours of the morning—"having a lot more fun than we did!" She would be remembered for her laundry: her "smalls hanging everywhere", to Mrs Endwhistle's displeasure. Daily life aboard a ship passing through the tropics did have glimpses of romance: "Being on the promenade deck the early morning noises are probably accentuated because literally hundreds of people are sleeping on the deck. But it's really superb to wake at five and see the ever-changing horizon."[9]

The ship's first landfall was Ceylon, a country in its first few years of independence from Britain and yet to become the modern state of Sri Lanka. Her first encounter with the East would puncture Joan's boredom and stir a travel bug that bit with a fill of "outstanding impressions". She was struck by the "unbelievable vividness of the vegetation—every conceivable shade of bright green", the "wonderful physique of ... the Sinhalese men and boys and the beauty of the women and girls", the chaotic traffic and the "substantial buildings even in the most squalid outback villages".[10] She was appalled at the way the English residents addressed the locals: "No please or thank you but just a glance that implied out of my way dog—I was quite staggered."

After passing through the Suez Canal and crossing the Mediterranean, Joan awoke at 6am one morning to find the *Otranto* "steaming up the Thames". It was three days before her 27th birthday. Having berthed, breakfasted and lunched on board, Joan and Val straggled through Customs at 1.30pm not reaching St Pancras station until 4.30. From there, they took a taxi straight to the Trevose Hotel, 70 Queensborough Terrace, Bayswater, where they climbed four flights of stairs to their room. "It's a good many stairs, bed and breakfast only but our double room with bathroom and all bed-sitting room comforts is very clean, bright and airy. So, for one week only we'll be living in luxury!" Joan wrote "in haste" to her family telling them how "thrilling" everything was.[11]

When she next wrote it was to confirm that "London is everything everyone promised it would be—just wonderful!" And no wonder, as the Trevose Hotel was close to Kensington Gardens, Knightsbridge and Hyde Park's beautiful fountains. On her birthday, Joan recounted to her family just one night of her adventures: "On Thursday evening, after seeking out our snack at the nearby centre (very Bohemian) at Queensway, we couldn't resist a bus ride so though it was raining, we went all round Oxford Circus, Piccadilly, Trafalgar Square, and finally ended up wandering over Westminster Bridge through the grounds of Westminster Abbey, and gazing at the adjacent House of Commons. We even heard Big Ben strike. Wonderful!"[12]

Within two weeks of their arrival in London, Joan and Val set off on a Green Line Coach first setting down at Southborough, a town between Tonbridge and Tunbridge Wells. There they had their "one and only night at a hotel ... wallow(ing) in the hot bath, knowing it might be days before we had another." The next day, with packs they could barely lift, they set off for Bexhill via Rye, Winchelsea and Hastings, hitch-hiking the 20 miles to Rye and spending more time there than intended due to their driver's insistence that they see it fully. On their way again at 5pm, after two more lifts, they reached the outskirts of Hastings. They had little hope of reaching Bexhill and, as Hastings had no Youth Hostel, they happily slept by a haystack outside the town warmed by small tins of "canned heat": "The field was even equipped with the proverbial brook where we performed our ablutions."[13]

They reached Bexhill before midday the next day. There Joan sounded out an acquaintance teaching at an exclusive boarding school and leading an easy life on a handsome salary. The response was promising: "There's a cosy little niche there for me if only she can dispose of one person. She believes—anyway she thinks she'll try."

After Bexhill, it was on to a Youth Hostel at Patcham, Brighton and the chance to wash, cook and retire "to an adjacent green" to write a letter home: "Tomorrow we'll be moving towards Cornwall as the cars and the spirit move us. We plan to take nearly a fortnight over this trip then return to London only to pick up a few clothes then make our way by hitch-hiking stages to Edinburgh where we've booked in for a week at that cheap boarding house—that's from August 29-September 5th."

The thirst for travel and not ancestral connections drew Joan to Edinburgh. Nonetheless, church attendance was an integral part of her overseas experience: "This morning we went to the 11am service at St Giles Cathedral. This is a Presbyterian church or what's known as the Church of Scotland. Actually, this one is built and furnished on exactly the lines of a big Anglican

Vetting of Wisdom

Cathedral, complete with chapels etc. The board outside described it as High Church of Scotland. It was rather a mixture all through. There was no prayer book of course but we recited creeds and responses in what sounded a pretty Anglican way to my ears! How Robert Swanton would have been upset."[14]

After many weeks of travel, Joan still found the experience thrilling but her thoughts began to turn to work: "Frankly, I'll be quite pleased to have a settled job to return to — you can have too much of a good thing." But finding regular work was difficult and so she spent the remainder of 1952 doing odd jobs. While awaiting a suitable teaching position, she cleaned a Princess Milckoff's Mayfair flat for two hours a morning for 5/- plus fares. The British and Overseas Book Service (referred by The Labour Exchange) offered her several days putting calendars into envelopes for 98/6 per 1000. She worked at it like "one possessed" pleased to earn 32/- in a session. When she went back for another session they soon ran out of calendars and she was "pensioned off" at 2pm.

Joan continued to follow local and world news with an appetite developed since childhood. She wrote home: "I hate to think of the C.O.L (cost of living) increases at home — it looks as if the Government's not too popular at the moment. Over here, it's just the reverse — Mr. Churchill and the Conservatives seem to be doing pretty well — the new housing target has been passed and … Britain has a favourable trade balance for the first time since the war and rations are to be increased."[15]

Her cultural life was swirling and she was making the most of London, mindful that the high cost of living would limit the time she could stay there: "In a few minutes though we're off to the Round Pond in Kensington Gardens to feed the swans; then tonight we're going to the Royal Albert Hall to hear a concert by Eileen Joyce and the Royal Philharmonic Orchestra (all for 2/6!). Of course, I always patronize the cheapest seats."

After working over Christmas and New Year at a tedious and poorly paid job in a toy shop, a teaching job finally arrived in

January 1953. It was a relief teaching role at a school in Kilburn and far from a dream job, despite the money. Joan would write grimly of her "chamber of horrors" and striving to hold out until the end of term. "If not for every half hour being worth 6/- I certainly couldn't endure teaching everything from Arithmetic to Games, Scripture, First Aid, Hygiene and French—everything in fact except Geography and History, the only two about which I even pretend to know anything. Still, what one does for twelve pounds per week."[16]

In the hours when she was not teaching, London continued to delight. Late in February, she would write home describing the preceding fortnight: "*Giselle* at Covent Garden ... with Maria Sharen (Red Shoes star) as guest ballerina—it was superb ... A short, modern and most entertaining ballet *La Boune Nmouche* set in Kensington ... *Escapade*, a new play based on the adventures of several schoolboys which has taken the West End by storm ... Several good films too (including)—*Trent's Last Case* and *The Prisoner of Zenda* – all these outings of course from the height of the 'gods' or the proximity of the stalls." Cultural events were packed around other engagements—dinner with friends at the Cumberland Hotel, catch ups with others, games of squash with Val, an exhibition of Coronation Regalia at St James Palace.

In the midst of the tedium of relief teaching, a flattering offer from home arrived, but one that was not tempting enough. Winifred West wrote inviting Joan to return to Frensham to head their new junior school. A letter to Anne and Elizabeth soon after would hint at her internal struggle: "I've just written to Miss West, finally turning down the junior school offer—hope I don't live to regret it!"[17]

Regret was not a common characteristic of Joan. She seemed always to face forward, throwing herself into each stage of her life. Perhaps the only thing approaching regret came later with the dawning realisation that she might not be destined for a married life. In the meantime, as a twenty-something single woman in England during the 1950s, the idea of meeting and courting eligible young men was certainly on the agenda. Indeed, while meeting the challenge of keeping sane in a range of jobs, social events were often orchestrated to introduce her to prospective young men. The results, however, were often disappointing, as she would write to Anne in cold November 1952: "I spent this weekend with Rose at Newport ... Her brother Christopher, and his wife Ruth, had a friend Bill staying with them and I think our weekends were engineered to coincide. Alas, he was pleasant enough but I'm sure there'll be no further contact. Rose, who at the moment is desperately in love, seems to feel that everyone else should be too."[18]

In the same letter Joan would write of a coincidental meeting at a lecture on Australia by a visiting speaker. The whole school was sitting waiting and Joan was asked to fill the void: "That was bad enough ... but he arrived shortly afterwards. It was John Robertson the most eligible (though only relatively!) tutor I had at the 'Shop' [Melbourne University]. The headmistress was very tactful — left us together for tea, sent us off to the bus together etc. Result — several invitations in the next morning's mail. It's amazing how much closer the most casual friendships become, twelve thousand miles from home. Don't misunderstand me. Remember John Baker — this one has all the same faults only more strongly!"

Joan had high standards and the men she encountered often failed to meet them. There was an Earl's Court contingent of Australians during her time in England — "they had their beer and they were set" — and while it was fun occasionally, it wasn't Joan's thing.

By May 1953, Joan was living at 24 Scarsdale Villas in Kensington. She would write home about its prized but pricey location: "I'm sure that in London anything in the inner West End suburb, that runs to both a tree and a bed of tulips, that have been really glorious, is quite superior. Certainly, its semi-basement,

Coronation

and quite modest in size but at least it's a very respectable address—the Royal Borough of Kensington, where you're not even allowed to hang washing on an outside line."[19]

All of London was fixated with the impending coronation of Queen Elizabeth II. The crowning of a young queen in an era when old verities stood largely unchallenged was a significant world event. For Joan, being in London and alive to the history, pageantry and theatre of the occasion, it was a not-to-be-missed chance to savour the moment in all its rich detail. She would see a lot of her own experience in the young monarch. Both of them were first born, bereaved of a father, young, attractive, sporty, intelligent and capable women just beginning their journeys in life. "No! You must not compare me to the Queen," Joan insists on reading this, yet there is no doubting the usefulness of the comparison in drawing her character.

Ten weeks before the coronation, Queen Mary, the Queen's grandmother, died peacefully in her sleep. This would give Joan a first taste of what royal occasions involved as Queen Mary lay in state at Westminster Hall and was later buried at Windsor Castle—the hours of waiting, the crush of crowds, the queuing and the sheer intensity of the experience. She used the waiting time on Sunday 29 March to write airmail letters home composed on the back of her flatmate, Barbara Broughton, "as we stand in about the third row lining Parliament St along which Queen Mary's funeral cortege is due to pass in about 2 and 1/2 hours ... there's hardly room to move my hand". They are a few hundred yards from Big Ben which has just struck one: "We're midway between the Houses of Parliament and Downing St and Mr Churchill with a poodle in the back beside him has just passed by to No. 10. It's horribly windy, and the horses are very frisky—superb things—all blacks today—I don't know if intentionally. Several RAF caps blew off in the last gust and a young RAC has just fainted. Most of them are 18-19 years old National Service trainees and an officer has just walked by telling them to relax."

Vetting of Wisdom

At 2.10pm, with hundreds of thousands lining the route, "writing, in fact, breathing, is becoming increasingly difficult. Every window is just bulging with people but of course, in view of the occasion, the great crowd is very quiet." At 2.20pm — with only ten minutes until the procession begins — a small dog ran down the middle of the road and was apprehended by a policeman: "Little men with handcarts are now appearing — following up the horses! Something must be about to begin. Mr and Mrs Churchill have just driven past. The forty-one-gun salute has just begun, and at any minute it looks as though it may pour with rain."

With massed bands playing funeral marches, the gun carriage of the King's Troop, Royal Horse Artillery, moved forward carrying Queen Mary's coffin draped with her personal standard and the Queen's all-white wreath surmounting. This was followed by attachments from all the services in slow march with reversed arms: "Immediately behind the gun carriage were the four royal dukes; Phillip looking just too wonderful in the uniform of Admiral of the Fleet, the Duke of Windsor also in Admiral's uniform; but quite unimpressive beside Phillip — in fact he looked and marched like a really broken old man. Beside him was Gloucester and on the other side the young Duke of Kent, hardly looking his 17 years despite his topper and mourning dress. Completing the procession were army detachments of Queen Mary's regiments, and the Queen Alexandra Nursing Service. It wasn't vast, but it was wonderfully impressive."

Joan had then made her way to St James tube station across Birdcage Walk. Seeing the crowds, she realised the Royal cars would return that way to the Palace after the short Westminster Hall Service. Within a few minutes her prediction proved correct and she had a prize viewing position "right on the kerb" as the car carrying the Queen and the Duke of Edinburgh passed, following by cars carrying the Queen Mother and Princess Margaret, the Duke and Duchess of Gloucester and the Duke of

Windsor and the Princess Royal. "It was a wonderful spectacle though and all very solemn—even if every second person was sucking a meat pie or something similar."

Joan's letters home recounting her experiences revealed her personality and style—detached, observant, critical, amused, respectful but never over-awed. The approaching coronation would give her a further opportunity to observe the Queen in her new role. Later many PLC girls would compare Joan's style and bearing with that of the monarch, qualities perhaps infused in those heady weeks in London. She certainly was swept up in the "magnificent, quite unforgettable" events: "You felt you were right in the centre of everything." She carried a pad everywhere she went and wrote a 25-page letter hoping to give her family "ball-to-ball descriptions" of Coronation Week. Falling rain and gathering crowds kept pen from paper, but she left her readers in no doubt about the intensity of the experience: "I feel if I lived at this pressure much longer, I might burst!"[20]

A bird's-eye seat at the coronation itself came by chance. Flatmate Barbara Broughton won a coronation seat for herself and friend through the office where she worked. The seats were on the roof of Liberty's, the department store in the West End, "complete with TV and luncheon, and all free! I am delighted because (otherwise) I should have had to sleep out."

Wandering the streets of London in the days before the coronation on 6 June 1953 provided an exhilarating rush of sights and experiences: floral displays in Parliament Square with wattle brushes and waratahs flown in from Australia; thousands of troops camped out in Hyde Park; the exclusive clubs of Pall Mall decked with colourful crests and banners; the grand trees of Berkeley Square draped with pink bunting and lamps entwined with pink roses; worship at St Margaret's in the grounds of Westminster Abbey.

By Coronation Eve it was damp, cold and growing colder but no one seemed to care. Thousands camped out on the footpaths, some having been there for days to secure their vantage points: "We couldn't bear to miss anything so set off about 8pm merely to look at the crowds. We walked along Piccadilly, the Haymarket, the Mall, to the Palace and then to the Abbey ... Everywhere the scene was the same—you couldn't move on the pavement, the settled crowd was eight or ten deep, so everyone just walked on the road—the little traffic there was, was very good-natured, usually open cars or taxis with people standing up inside, and others clinging precariously." Whole families from grandmothers to small children waited out on newspapers, stools and rubber 'lie-lows,' cooking, reading, singing, listening to the radio, buskers or the nearest wag: "It was the most wonderful cross-section of the community, with well-dressed and down-and-outs, every possible English, Continental and Commonwealth accent."

In Piccadilly, Joan bumped into Kat Smith, a PLC old girl who had arrived that morning from Australia and headed straight to the West End from the ship. The evening with the waiting crowds "was so wonderful that I almost regretted having a comfortable bed to return to." But nearing midnight they headed homewards via tubes still crammed full of people.

Joan woke at 4am on Coronation Day, heading off at 7.30am for Regent Street and her vantage on the Liberty roof space, "much featured as London's highest". But it was "a foul day—bitterly cold and showery" with an Arctic wind: "I can't remember being so cold for ages." The rooftop position meant she could "at least see each shower approaching."

The appearance of the procession at 3.15pm changed everything: "The whole spectacle was quite unforgettable." It may have been the Queen of England's day but it was Queen Salote, the formidable Tongan monarch who would reign for 48 years, who "quite took the thunder" when she appeared in an open horse-drawn carriage with drivers in frock coats and top hats: "Six feet three's a bit hard to overlook at any time, but the only one who withstood the inclement weather, and clad in her national dress, bright red and short sleeved, she was thoroughly enjoying it all. All along the route she received a tremendous ovation and, in fact, has been mobbed everywhere ever since."

After the procession, it was home for a hot bath and to listen to the Queen's speech before setting off again, warm and dry. The aim was to reach the Palace by 10pm when the Queen was to switch on London's illuminations. Alas, they missed her but no sooner had they reached the Palace gates than the cheering of thousands greeted the reappearance of the Queen and the Duke at 10.30pm: "She looked glorious and everyone went quite mad with excitement." They then headed on to Westminster Bridge where a colossal crowd gathered on the bridge and Embankment to see the spectacular London City Council's £14,000 fireworks display. After being caught in a crush at midnight, they finally reached home about 1am: "What a day! I'll never forget it, I'm sure."

The day after the coronation was an anti-climax and bitterly cold – "an all-time low for June". But Thursday morning with the sun shining again brought the spectacle of the rehearsal of Trooping the Colour at Horse Guards Parade. The most thrilling moment came "when the Household Cavalry at the change of time in the music, without any apparent signal, suddenly broke into a brisk trot, and then a canter, in very close formation, eight abreast!" From Horse Guards it was on to Sloane Square to see the Queen and the Duke of Edinburgh in the second of their four London Coronation Drives. "We were allowed to line the middle of the road, leaving a lane of only 15 feet or so, along which the open car came. The Royal car was moving at about 12 mph and I was so busy taking a snap that I hardly saw her though I could have touched the car."

Derby Day on Saturday brought Joan another unexpected close encounter with the Queen, not from Royal enclosures but rather from Epsom Downs where there was free entry. Joan saw little of the races and had no money for "flutters" but there was plenty to see and do as the Downs was like a huge fun fair: "Merry-go-rounds, whirly gigs, scooter-cars ... and fairy floss, fish and chip stalls and every conceivable coconut shy." After touring the fairground, Joan prepared to cross the course at the only opening: "People had been lining the rails for hours in an effort to see the Queen and her Royal retinue driving down the course. Just as we were half-way across the 20-yard-wide track, mounted police galloped up in an effort to close up the temporary opening in the fence. As a result, I was forced back and found myself in the very front row when the gap was roped off. Hence, I had my second close-up of the Queen and the Duke in a week."

The tempo of coronation festivities continued apace: Sir John Barbirolli, conducting the London Symphony Orchestra at Festival Hall, "something noisy of Vaughan Williams", then Beethoven's No. 2 Concerto in B flat, with Clifford Curzon as solo pianist; a Sunday morning service at the Naval College, Greenwich, in almost below-zero temperatures; the last Coronation Concert at the Festival Hall with Barbirolli again as the conductor and, especially composed for the coronation, *Orb and Sceptre*—"rather noisy and scrappy, to my untutored taste"; back to Festival Hall in the evening for a Burl Ives program; and on Monday evening, 8 June, to Sadler's Wells for an opera and ballet program—"operetta really, *Die Fledermaus* and thoroughly enjoyable".

Tuesday evening brought a thrilling recap of it all with the viewing of "the just-released, and really superb" *A Queen is Crowned*. The Technicolour documentary ran for an hour and twenty minutes with Laurence Olivier as commentator. Joan gave a rave review to her cousin and sisters: "You must all see it—there is another long one too, but this is the better of the two according to critics and general impressions."

The spell cast by the coronation on Joan would endure long after the enthralling events faded into history. In 1977, on the day the Queen arrived in Australia on her Silver Jubilee visit, the then Principal of Presbyterian Ladies' College would relive the moment for girls at School Assembly.

> It was one of Britain's first celebrations after years of war, of hardship and rationing. Seats at windows overlooking the ... procession were balloted or sold at high prices. Thousands of people slept on the footpaths for one or even two nights before Coronation Day to make sure of their place to watch the passing procession — and then in some cases fainted as it appeared. The morning dawned to the shouts of the newsboys announcing that Mt Everest, which had so often claimed the lives of mountaineers, had been conquered — and by a team of British climbers, including the New Zealander, Edmund Hilary! Everywhere, there was excitement and optimism — the feeling that under a new young monarch, Britain was entering an era of peace, of prosperity and unlimited opportunity.

Joan would acknowledge that in the years since the coronation, Australians' views about the monarchy had changed: "This time the Queen arrives amidst increasing expressions of doubt and even opposition. But whatever one may think of the institution of the monarchy or the conduct of its representatives, no one could criticise the unfailing devotion with which the Queen has fulfilled her most demanding role in the past 25 years."

While the attitude of many Australians towards the monarchy might have changed, Joan's had not. In Queen Elizabeth she found a role model, kindred spirit and virtual mentor; a young woman who had embraced the great challenges of leadership with strength, dignity and humility; a woman after Joan Montgomery's heart.

Vetting of Wisdom

......

The time of the coronation would see Max Bradshaw make another unwelcome intervention into the lives of the Montgomery family, a year after he had been a guest at Margaret and Donald's wedding. Anne and Elizabeth had decided to move their weekly worship to the Toorak Presbyterian Church — and Helen had independently resolved to move to Kew — and the men who ruled the Hawthorn congregation were not amused.

The women had long been unhappy with the male-dominated conservatism of the Hawthorn congregation and it seems their displeasure at the Reverend Robert Swanton's handling of the prayers at the Coronation Day service may have been the last straw. While the exact nature of their grievance is unclear, their decision to quit the Hawthorn church while still living in Hawthorn stirred an indignant response from Max Bradshaw.

Writing back to Anne a month after the coronation, on Sunday 5 July 1953 — the day before her 28th birthday — Joan expressed her sympathy: "I can see that it was ticklish especially as our address hasn't changed. Did you state in your letter to Mr Bradshaw the Coronation Day Prayers incident? Did you get a reply to your letter or just the bare cards?" What came next might have driven Bradshaw from indignation to apoplexy, had he been aware of Joan's heretical sentiment: "It's unlikely that I'll stay there long once I get back. In fact, though I don't think I'm likely ever to change over permanently, I really prefer the Anglican Service and now equipped with a Prayer Book am 'learning' the various creeds."

While none of the surviving parties to the events can remember the nature of the "Coronation Day Prayers incident", Joan included, it may well have been the failure of the Scots clergyman to pay due homage to the newly affirmed young woman leader of the Church of England that stirred the

Montgomery women. And while they might have thought they were free to choose when and where they worshipped, the sticklers of the Presbyterian Church of Australia had other ideas.

Under the Presbyterian rules, a baptised member listed on the Communicant Roll of one parish could not be a member of more than one parish and needed the blessing of the parish where they were registered to move to another. And it appears Bradshaw's response to the impertinent request for a transfer from Anne and Elizabeth was to deny it. The Hawthorn Presbyterian Church has no archival record of Anne and Elizabeth's transfer to Toorak in 1953.

The Montgomerys had never been comfortable with Robert Swanton's ministry. He had been at Hawthorn since 1940 and had formally welcomed the family to the Glenferrie Road church when they moved to Kembla Street after William's death. Swanton was a bachelor and awkward with young women, perhaps particularly with a family of four recently bereaved sisters and their guardian cousin as the family presented in 1944. Both Max Bradshaw as Session Clerk and Swanton as minister were not easy for the Montgomery girls to relate to. The pair were of similar disposition and age—Swanton was born on 13 November 1910, 19 days before Bradshaw's birth, and both were 33 years old and unmarried when the Montgomerys arrived. Joan regarded Swanton as an intellectual who lacked "people skills"; an erudite man not well placed as a parish minister. In his history of Scotch College, James Mitchell would note Swanton's determination to follow literal interpretations of the Bible: "A tall and learned man, his virtues did not include an ability to engage boys."[21]

While the transcript of Swanton's Coronation Day sermon on 31 May 1953 gives no clue as to what might have displeased the Montgomerys, he did make clear the Bible's ascendancy over the humble affairs of men and monarchs. He told the congregation of Zadoc's anointing of Solomon with a horn of oil from the tabernacle: "And they blew the trumpet; and all the people said 'God save King Solomon'. These words are substantially reproduced twice in the Coronation. They remind us how the Coronation Service is founded on the Bible." (1 Kings 1:39)

......

While Joan had been captivated by the coronation celebrations, her view of England and the English was always that of an Australian patriot and she viewed all she saw with a restless, critical, wry, even patronising, eye. England was her base to travel, to work, to check off sporting, cultural and historic experiences and to write home to her family about it. And for the next 18 eventful months there was a lot to report on.

Hard upon Coronation Week came Australia's excruciating Ashes tour of England, four drawn tests followed by a thrashing in the fifth and final Test at The Oval in August. Joan had been at the Lords and the rain-affected Headingly Tests ("wasn't altogether scintillating cricket").

Until just before the fourth Test at Headingly, Joan had endured the gruelling experience of temporary teaching stints at Highgate, Kilburn and St Vincent's. "Supply teaching is soul destroying but worth over eleven pounds per week," she would remark. That practical philosophy kept her going but, for now, she was gloriously free until mid-September to enjoy the long summer vacation. And did she have plans, with cricket forming an enjoyable part of the interlude: "I'm off to Leeds with Joyce, to stay with a friend of hers who's anxious to show us Yorkshire — and incidentally, the 4th Test Match. Then I'm going straight on to Southport with Barbara for a long weekend (Bank Holiday) then setting off after a fortnight with Joyce and Barbara to Norway. We'll be there for almost a fortnight when Barbara must return, then Joyce and I are coming back through Sweden, Denmark, Belgium, Holland and perhaps having a few days in Paris."[22]

Coronation

Within days she added the acceptance of an invitation for ten days motoring in Scotland immediately after the Bank Holiday weekend. The return visit raised her interest in her Scottish roots. The previous July, soon after her arrival in England, she had travelled to Land's End, Cornwall, England's most westerly point. On her first visit to Scotland, she travelled across the north from Tongue through Thurso and out to John O'Groats: "I stood on the end of the J of G jetty, then looked up to the points all round me that appeared to be farther north. Still, I've now been to Land's End and John O'Groats for what that's worth!"[23]

Her second time in Scotland also brought the bonus of glorious weather and "one of the loveliest holidays I've ever spent". Having a car enabled her to sample "the most wonderful collection of bed and breakfast establishments you could imagine – average cost – 12/6." Ever mindful of her finances, on reaching Edinburgh there was a windfall: "Joyce's Uncle Albert's will was finally settled today, a grand meal tonight had to be on her!"[24]

On her return to London, Joan was in time to listen to the final Test debacle from her new accommodation at 80a Woodstock Avenue, Golders Green: "England with nine wickets in hand, need only forty odd runs to win, and two and a half days in which to get them! – They're batting so slowly you'd think they were intent on using all that time. Quite disgusting – you can imagine the English excitement when it was 1932 when they last won the Ashes – still suppose I shouldn't grudge them a little pleasure."[25] There were rich experiences ahead in her travels to Scandinavia – Oslo, Stockholm and Copenhagen – and then Paris.

Before her vacation, Joan had negotiated a permanent teaching position at Crouch End High School, an independent girls' school in north-west London. Having rejected an offer of £375 as too low, the school upped the offer to £445 which was still about £100 below scale: "I finally decided that small classes, a free half-day a week, and congenial surroundings, would more than compensate for the lack of cash. This supply teaching is really dreadful—I've now got to the stage (which everyone reaches eventually apparently) of just watching the chaos all round me, and thinking that at least every minute is worth about 11/2d."[26]

But it would be a depressing introduction when, at the end of the holidays, Joan attended a morning staff meeting the day before school resumed at Crouch End: "The staff were mostly middle-aged or elderly and the headmistress the 'bosomy' blousy style—oh dear, and it's for a year!"[27] Some days later she revealed the extent she had been spoiled by her Australian schools: "I'm afraid my 'Crouch End School for Girls' hardly provides what I'm used to. The children are quite pleasant, likewise the other staff (though a trifle elderly!) and the whole atmosphere is alright. But after PLC, Frensham, and MLC, all highly organised, whatever other faults they may have had, it does take some getting used to when the Headmistress, having finally found the hymn book she wants, announces the hymn, then disappears behind the piano on the tiniest of stools—her bust and hip measurement must be in the 60inch region—to play the hymn!"[28]

Compounding the gloom was the approach of winter and the fact that many of Joan's Australian friends were heading home. "How I wish the blossoms were out and spring was beginning here—the thought of the English winter is a bit depressing really, especially as most of my friends who waited just for the coronation and summer will have returned in a month or so ... I'll miss Joyce especially as being on nine months pure holiday, she's been more or less free to fit in whenever I've been free and our tastes are fairly similar."[29]

Joan's letters also tracked events at home, including the birth of her first nephew, David Knox, and youngest sister Helen's unhappiness that led her to switch schools. After receiving an eight-page letter from Helen with enthusiastic details of her move to Tintern Grammar, Joan confessed: "Right now, for perhaps the first time in my life, I feel homesick." She had occasional longings to be at home while at Frensham but nothing serious. "I'm beginning to wonder why anyone in their right mind voluntarily faces an English winter. Today, it's bitterly cold and wet so maybe I'm prejudiced this evening."[30]

Helen also raised the prospect of teaching jobs in Australia. This appealed to Joan: "The new Tintern sounds wonderful—yes! I think you're right I should like to teach there, so will have to see what can be done about it! That is—unless you've ruined my chances—though you may equally have enhanced them!"[31] Within days, Joan had written to Miss Constance Wood, the headmistress at Tintern, enquiring whether she might have a vacancy the following year.

In the meantime, post-war London life offered Joan a diet of rations, royalty and disappointing men. Clothing was becoming cheaper, eggs and sugar were free of restrictions and meat was plentiful. "Butter is still quite carefully rationed though I can't tell the difference between this and marg. Bacon too is rationed though not always hard to get as so many can't afford to take out their allowance."[32]

A post-coronation thrall enveloped the new monarch and Joan's fascination was undiminished. In November, she turned out to watch the Queen drive to the State Opening of Parliament but was thwarted when, just at the crucial moment, her view was blocked by a large man raising his hat in enthusiasm: "Result—Royal couple in the Irish State Coach were obliterated. However, I crossed the Mall and found a front row position for the return trip an hour later. The Queen was on the far side of the coach and I didn't see her properly—the Duke however was looking as handsome as ever, and the Duchess of Kent, together with Princess Margaret, in a closed car, both looked quite superb. It was Lady Churchill, however, whose car brought forth the most spontaneous waving and excitement—and she always looks as if she's thoroughly enjoying herself."[33]

Later in November, a Royal Concert at Festival Hall, given by

Australian and New Zealand artists in the presence of the Queen and Duke brought the new Queen into closer view. It was a full-dress evening and Joan had borrowed furs for the event: "We had seats where we could take in the Royal Box and the concert platform in one glance though I must confess that we could neither stare nor see too clearly when we did cast a surreptitious glance. But the most wonderful moment came later. We were close to our exit and so escaped in time to see the Royal party leave. In fact, we were on a foyer balcony and they passed just a few feet below. I'd seen the Queen by day at close range before but this was quite incomparable. I've never seen anyone look so beautiful—that radiant beauty together with tiara jewellery make-up frock and furs par excellence was overwhelming! What a wonderful looking couple."[34]

Less enchanting were four days Joan spent on a farm late in October at the behest of her sister Elizabeth who had implored her to meet a bachelor Liz had found particularly attractive: "Well, I must say, conditions weren't all I'd hoped and neither was my opinion of Andrew!" she later reported back to her family. Arriving at 8.30pm on a Friday, she was met by Andrew, his mother and aunt.

"The farmhouse is being thoroughly renovated, so Aunt and I had to share a room! Andrew went off to a party ... and as he was going shooting the next morning didn't reappear until 4pm on Saturday. Then he took a little nap, before leaving at 6pm for a cocktail party. From this he returned at 9pm on Sunday, having turned his mother's car over on the way home the night before and been forced to spend the night with friends. Apart from a few scratches and bruises he seemed none the worse for wear but suffering from a certain 'hang over' spent the afternoon asleep in front of the only available fire! Such trifles wouldn't have worried me, except that it rained very hard from midday on Saturday and sharing the kitchen with three dogs and two cats, not to mention Mother and Aunt (both darning industriously!) rather curtailed my activities. However, his lordship was awake on Sunday evening, and I agree, he's rather charming. But he certainly needs a change—a bachelor, living alone, can easily slip into very selfish habits!"[35]

The negative critique, continued in a later letter to Elizabeth: "By now you'll have received my reactions to the eagerly anticipated visit ... You'll realise too, that I constitute no rival in the field. He was really rather pleasant (I can feel you snorting at such lukewarmness!) but what hope has he against a mother that in the middle of a meal asked me to move as I was in Andrew's chair—and he let me go and get another!!! I ask you! Still, what it is really, I guess, is that I just hadn't got what it took!"[36]

Joan would spend another year in Europe and there was much still to do and see. On New Year's Day 1954 she confessed to mixed emotions at the prospect of returning home: "I have just 309 days until I sail—3rd deck down on the *Largs Bay* ... Of course, I've had a fair time and can't complain and am dying to see you all again. But I just feel that once home I'll spend ages repaying debts and may never get back again—must save for my old age you know!"[37]

With her departure from England now fixed for 5 November, Joan gave six months' notice of her intention to leave Crouch End High School—"pleasant enough" without being "wildly exciting."[38] At the end of the first term of 1954, she set off for Spain, after packing up her apartment in Golders Green ahead of a move to Chelsea with Barbara and Ruth, one of Barbara's office friends.

The trip to Spain would bring more male attention, not all of it welcome: "Spain is making me a changed woman—it's very good for the morale if every second man whistles appreciatively as you pass or whispers what you hope are compliments every time you're caught in a crowd. In Seville, I made the mistake of wearing a low-necked frock, and at least half a dozen times men just walked beside me nearly bending double trying to peer down—I suppose it's a spinster's paradise, though I'd prefer a little attention on a more personal line—in southern Spain, every senora receives it—irrespective of size or shape."[39] While "a social failure in Norway, even though a brunette ... in Cordova—never!"[40]

Joan spent Good Friday in Madrid. While processions were due to start at 3pm it was after 7pm before the first one left the cathedral. It could only invite comparison to the precision of the Guards and the orderliness of English crowds: "Even the military bands wander along, munching rolls, smoking and chatting, and playing tunelessly, but only when the spirit moves them! The crowds too always happy, wind their way between the hooded figures, while the children race about in their efforts to catch the wax."[41]

The move to 31 Tedworth Square, Chelsea, after Joan's return from Spain, would have a touch of drama. Their landlady, Lady Diana Mills, was linked to dark events through her sister, the Countess of Derby, who had been in the news recently. As Joan recounted to Anne: "One of the footmen at their family home went berserk, murdered the butler, wounded several others and finally took a pot shot at her ladyship, hitting her in the shoulder!"[42]

Several weeks after writing enquiring about teaching opportunities back in Australia, Joan had still not received a reply from Miss Wood at Tintern Grammar. Her mood turned from anxiety to irritation until she finally wrote home: "I've quite given up hearing from Miss Wood which I think rather rude of her."[43] While she waited, Joan visited the Society for the Settlement of British Women Overseas, a provider of English staff to Australian schools. She met with a Miss Ogden who told her that there were two outstanding schools in the view of most English visitors—Frensham in New South Wales and PLC in Victoria: "As this was before I'd told her anything about myself, I was pleased to think that I was educationally well-connected!" Miss Ogden also gave favourable mentions to Tintern, Fintona, Lauriston and Ruyton and left Joan hoping that something may come of her visit. But soon after, the long-awaited reply from Tintern arrived: "Don't faint but I had a letter from Miss Wood yesterday. Quite a nice one but necessarily non-committal because she isn't quite sure whether anyone is leaving. However, I've to send testimonials so that if there's any vacancy I can be considered."[44]

Joan turned 29 on 6 July with the return to Australia increasingly in her thoughts, teaching opportunities primarily but lesser concerns also—Davis Cup tickets, a bed in Sydney offered to her by Joyce Layton and her sleeping arrangements at 7 Kembla Street: "Perhaps it will depend on Helen's whereabouts. I know the mild shock I received on returning once from Frensham to find that 'my' room was now yours (Elizabeth). You doubtless had the same sentiments when you found that I'd temporarily taken possession again just before you returned from England."

The clearest marker of change came with the ending of school on 29 July and Joan's last day at Crouch End: "I was really quite sorry to leave. Many pleasant little parting gifts, including a very nice book from the Prefects, stockings and an ornament from the top form, and bookends from my own form. From the staff I had a book token. Somehow with everyone wishing me 'bon voyage' for the first time I felt that November 5th really was in sight!"[45]

Joan was now free to set off with Brenda Ladds, a teaching colleague from Frensham, on her "last Continental Grand Tour"—beginning with Brussels, followed by Cologne. The pull of change had perhaps featured in outbreaks of domestic tension in the lead up to her departure. A letter from Brussels to Barbara and Ruth alluded to discord before her departure: "How I wish you were here—I'm in such an obliging and eager to please mood, I'm really lovely to be with! And I fear that perhaps last week I wasn't always too lovely! Ah well, look out for a model of sweetness five weeks hence Ruth, and thank you both very much for your efforts to get me here—supplying the wardrobe grip, egg sandwiches etc. — I'm really very grateful."[46]

In a letter to Anne the next day she mentioned the testimonials she had forwarded to Miss Wood at Tintern: "I don't feel too hopeful." Her pessimism would soon be revealed as wholly misplaced. On her return to London, there would be letters back from two esteemed principals — Miss Wood at Tintern and Miss Elizabeth Kirkhope, a former dux, head prefect, teacher, owner and longstanding Principal of Lauriston — both offering her positions.

> The first offered senior Geography and senior History classes — if she really meant both to matric. I'd be preparing all night and having got used to a ... social life, prefer not to settle down for life just yet. However, to show I'm keen and I can't keep Miss Kirkhope waiting while I write to Miss Wood and see just how "senior" she means, tomorrow I'll indulge in a reply-paid cable. If my worst fears are confirmed (her wording was a little ambiguous) then I'll accept Lauriston — same salary, little travelling, senior Geog. And junior history — just what I'd like.[47]

She need not have worried. The reply from Tintern offered her a manageable workload and with that she felt comfortable declining the Lauriston position. Although she would write home after finally accepting Miss Wood's offer: "I only hope I don't rue it as I set off at crack of dawn during the winter months."[48]

Joan's final months in England were filled with more relief teaching, punctuated by weekend trips to the country, including Stratford, the Cotswolds, Leicester and the stately homes of Luton. Teaching in England broadened her general experience but added little to her skillset. One of her last and least satisfactory jobs was teaching art at a convent school near Victoria: "It's quite criminal really. I teach nothing really and can barely keep them within four walls, let alone quiet! This morning the hullabaloo reached such proportions that the Mother Superior felt bound to intervene—amazing what one puts up with for two pounds ten shillings per day."[49]

Britain became snarled in a dock strike that escalated from late September 1954. By 17 October, Joan wrote home: "All the dockworkers in London and Tilbury are on strike with the possibility of no work spreading to Southampton tonight. If that happens the Army is to be called in. As well, there's an unofficial London Transport strike with nine of ten buses off the road."[50] When she wrote again, four days later, the *Largs Bay* sailing date had been postponed, near 50,000 dock workers were on strike and troops were standing by, although "the Conservative Government which had had little industrial unrest so far, hesitates to take this drastic action."[51]

Joan's last few days in London were a blur of activity: "I worked on at my convent until Tuesday, then Wednesday, Thursday and Friday passed all too quickly in visiting bank, insurance company, taxation commissioners. Yesterday I almost ran all day—it was a filthy day too—out to lunch, tea … and 'final' farewell Soho dinner and theatre last night. Down to my last penny, and every second planned I was mildly alarmed when I discovered I'd collected ten pounds less than I'd expected at the bank. As it was practically my all, I was delighted when it turned out to be that rare thing—a banking error—fortunately I just discovered it in time."

The *Largs Bay* remained landlocked until 27 November 1954 when, almost two and a half years after leaving Melbourne, Joan prepared to embark on her return journey home "in dreary surroundings midst of sheds and wharves waiting to go on board. It's grey and raining and severe gales are blowing all around the coast. This morning's news was quite alarming—within sight of the coast, one ship blew up, one (20,000 tons) broke in half and two sank."[52]

Malta, Port Said, Colombo and Fremantle were the only scheduled ports of call with an arrival date in Melbourne of 3 January. Joan looked forward to arriving in time for the last two days of the Melbourne cricket Test. But the need to restore her finances with another summer job at the Fowlers factory loomed: "I never thought my cautious nature would let me get into the financial state to which I've sunk. However, with a job to go to, I hope I can work off all my debts promptly."

News that her friend Jean Craven was engaged to be married drew mixed feelings: "I'm looking forward to some tennis at home though — I'll miss Jean's court if she settles in the Western District — I'm certainly looking forward to meeting her fiancé. I felt quite dejected when you wrote of her engagement (delighted for her of course) — I'd always imagined that at least I'd have Jean as a confirmed fellow-spinster!"[53]

By 11 December, Joan was "dying to get home … it's hard to believe that we've only been aboard a fortnight today. It seems months."[54] Christmas provided a respite from the tedium with carols at breakfast, an outsize Christmas tree for the children, a morning church service, lunch, the Captain's Cocktail Party and a seven-course dinner with all the trimmings plus crackers and caps. After a further eight days of "plying our steady way across the Indian Ocean" the *Largs Bay* reached Fremantle on New Year's Eve with a revised arrival in Melbourne of 10 January. It would be too late for the cricket but just in time for a joyous reunion with family and friends.

6

EXCOMMUNICATED

Within days of her arrival back in Melbourne, Joan set about prioritising an early resumption of her teaching career. She arranged a meeting with the formidable Miss Constance Wood, Principal of Tintern Grammar, to follow up the job offer made while Joan was still in London. It would be an unusual job interview.

Tintern had moved in 1953 to new premises in Ringwood East but Miss Wood was still living in Glenferrie Road, Hawthorn. "I went to the front door and nobody answered," Joan recalls, wondering if she had mistaken the day or time. "As a first appointment, I didn't want that to happen. I thought maybe she was out in the garden—and there she was with a great washing basket."

Miss Wood had been doing school washing since the war years when the Americans took over the commercial laundry that had until then served Tintern. "They got all the girls' sheets and all their underclothes, they got everything," Miss Wood would later explain. "So, I just had to say, well, you send it back clean or dirty wet or dry, so it came back wet. And after that the School Council bought a special sort of washing machine and I did the washing with the boarders."[1]

Looking up from her great washing basket, Miss Wood caught Joan's eye and called to her. "Come on, you can put a few pegs on," Joan recalls. "That is how I had my first interview as we proceeded to put the blankets up together—a fairly informal start which was quite typical of her."

Vetting of Wisdom

Wood was born in England and a great believer in overseas teaching experience, so little wonder Joan appealed. As a young woman, Wood had landed jobs in India and Peru both of which her father had forbidden her to take. "It was no good going to either of those places as a poor white, and I wouldn't earn enough from the salaries and he couldn't offer to keep me," she would say. After teaching in England for three years, her father suggested she go to Australia where his brother lived. The uncle would be instrumental in landing her a teaching position at Clyde, the prestigious girls' school at Woodend, north west of Melbourne, starting in 1929. It was a pathway that Joan Montgomery would soon follow.

Miss Wood's academic staff in the senior school at Tintern were, without exception, university graduates and they were mostly, if not all, unmarried, so far as Jean Ford remembers. It was a small school of 300 students and fewer than 30 staff. Jean, a maths teacher whom Joan met shortly before leaving for London, had taught at Tintern for some years, returning in 1952 after four years in London. She had taught Joan's sister Helen.

Without a car, travel to Tintern was an ordeal with Joan taking a tram to Glenferrie Station and a train to Ringwood East. Joined by Jean Ford and Eileen Pike, the three teachers would then walk the remaining stretch, their journey to Tintern taking more than an hour. Jean, eleven years Joan's senior, had neither car nor licence. For her part, Joan had a licence but couldn't afford a car. A grand compact emerged, Joan would pay half if Jean bought the car. It took roughly a month for Jean to buy a Baby Austin car and gain her licence. At one stroke, travelling time to Tintern was cut by half, although Canterbury Road was not the highway of today and punctures were not uncommon. On one such occasion, they managed to pull the car into a garage and Jean Ford went inside to fetch a mechanic: "While he was coming out, Joan was out of the car, Eileen was out of the car, and the tyre was changed before the man got outside. How well trained the passengers were!"[2]

Jean and Joan had done a course in car maintenance at

Richmond Technical School. For Jean, it meant she knew enough to say to a mechanic: "I think there is something the matter … as if it sounded as if you knew what you were doing when you really didn't." For Joan, it meant she got a tyre change down to minutes. It was indicative of Joan's decisive character — whether dealing with a tyre, a teacher or a truant. "From a very early age she was making decisions," Jean would say. "She enjoys making decisions. And she never looks back. Once she's decided, that is it."

Joan was a great teacher, Jean recalls, and very well-liked by the girls and staff. Miss Wood remembers Joan as one of her best teachers: "I had a great admiration for her. She was one of the very best … her attitude, her general attitude to the other people." Jean attributes part of Joan's success to the fun she brought to the class and the staff rooms: "The school was small enough in those days where at the end of every term we wrote reports and the poor mistress had to, you know, produce a comment … There were over twenty of us sitting round, reading each other's reports and, of course Joan's were always a delight. You can imagine. She had to read them [aloud] and we were all very amused by them. But also, I think it improved the standard of report writing, because you had to keep up with her."

Joan's reputation in the classroom and staffroom was bolstered at an annual baseball match between the staff and students. Joan was the star of the staff team. Hilary McPhee, publisher and first female chair of the Australia Council, was one of Joan's students at Tintern. She has strong memories of her as an antidote to Miss Wood's traditional, disciplinarian approach. At times, Hilary felt victimised by Miss Wood's behaviour. In contrast, Joan was a great supporter of equality — a straight talker after "a genuine exchange, looking you straight in the eye." Her teaching was "like that too … [she] knew you had talents and could bring them out."

Hilary can still picture Joan, her Form Mistress and Geography and English teacher, as they walked together, Joan's dark hair and elegant black gown covering her tweed skirts. And standing at the blackboard in her shiny black heels, with her dark eyes and upright carriage, captivating the students with her freewheeling teaching style. For Hilary, Joan was a great source of "sensible comfort ... never sentimental yet always making you feel that she would stick up for what you were representing." She credits Joan with giving her the courage to leave Tintern in 1958 to join a group of four students doing matriculation in Colac. Joan inspired her "to do it off my own bat and made me feel confident in my own abilities." Joan seemed fearless to Hilary and made her feel that she, too, could be fearless. During what Hilary recalls were "a pretty tough few years" Joan remained a steadying role model. They would keep in contact down the years with irregular meetings at the Lyceum Club and other occasional encounters.

......

The return to Melbourne and the family home in Kembla Street, Hawthorn, meant Joan needed to decide where she would attend church. While she, Anne and her sisters had all been communicant members of the Hawthorn Presbyterian Church before she moved to London, Anne and Elizabeth had controversially transferred to the Toorak parish and Helen had moved to Kew. Joan's decision would provoke a confrontation with Max Bradshaw that steeled their enmity and presaged the later showdown over the fate of Presbyterian Ladies' College.

By the mid-1950s, Bradshaw was firmly entrenched as the power behind the pulpit at the Hawthorn church. He had held leadership positions for 20 years and had been Session Clerk, the most senior lay position in the congregation, for a decade. Joan's view of the man was already deeply unflattering: "Pudgy, flabby and unattractive; pasty and unhealthy." While she would never think to speak of such injustices of nature — and would caution students against such uncharitable views during her assemblies as a school principal — the instinctive reaction could not be denied. And her repulsion was about to move beyond the physical.

With Anne and Elizabeth now happily worshipping at Toorak and Helen at Kew, it seemed ridiculous to Joan that there should be three separate journeys from Kembla Street on Sunday mornings to attend church. She resolved to join Elizabeth and Anne at Toorak. And like them before her, Joan needed to apply to the Hawthorn Church's Session for a transfer. That required the support of the Clerk and Max Bradshaw refused. Their meeting would remain a vivid memory.

"You haven't been to three consecutive communions in a particular period," Bradshaw pronounced.

"But I have been in England for the last three years," Joan responded in disbelief.

"No, if you haven't ... you can't have one [a parish transfer]," Bradshaw replied.

"Oh, have I been excommunicated?!" Joan retorted.

With that, Joan went to see the Reverend Dr Alan Watson at Toorak, asking to join his church but explaining she was unable to get the transfer or "disjunction." Watson replied with a knowing smile: "Oh, you must be coming from Hawthorn." Church records show Joan's removal from the Hawthorn roll by resolution of Session on 31 August 1954 for "having left the district."

It is hard to imagine that Bradshaw's peremptory response to Joan's reasonable request to change her place of worship was not influenced by his previous clash with Anne and Elizabeth over their decision to quit the dwindling ranks of the Hawthorn congregation—and by his general disdain for assertive women in a church steeped in a culture of male dominance. His attitude must surely have been strengthened by her indignant refusal to accept his as the last word on the matter. Perhaps Bradshaw also saw the self-confidence of a 30-year-old woman claiming her right of choice as a further sign of the times that were threatening the foundations of his religious world.

When Joan resolved to attend a more congenial congregation, the Presbyterian Church of Australia was also on the move. As historian Ian Breward would write: "Pressures of rapid social change from the 1950s onwards underlined the inadequate resources possessed by any single church to respond to the changes in Australian society."[3] The formation of the Joint Commission on Church Union by Presbyterians, Congregationalists and Methodists in 1957 was a response to that pressure. Bradshaw himself acknowledged the pressures but never the solution. He opposed union from the outset and worked passionately against it from that time forward.

Life beyond teaching at Tintern and churchgoing on Sundays revolved around sport, with tennis on the weekends, and family life. Melbourne's hosting of the Olympic Games in 1956 provided a rich sporting and family experience. Joan attended the opening ceremony at the Melbourne Cricket Ground with Elizabeth, who was pregnant and craved apple skins that she happily munched throughout the event. Being back in Australia meant Joan could enjoy her new extending family and she had an easy relationship with small children. She relished the role of aunt and often read to Margaret's children.

Her life was full, but Joan still had an itch to travel again before settling down to more serious roles. One day in 1957, while driving to Tintern with Jean Ford in the Baby Austin, Joan mentioned an interest in going back to England. Jean was interested too, and the planning began. At the end of the year, when Joan said goodbye to Miss Wood the seeds were sown for her life beyond Tintern: "She said, 'Oh, you won't come back to Tintern. You'll come back as head of PLC'!" This was a prospect Joan had not entertained but Constance Wood clearly saw her as a principal in waiting, and not of just any school.

......

Excommunicated

In February 1958, Joan and Jean boarded the Norwegian-registered *MS Skaubryn* bound for England again. The ship was a mini-United Nations with a Norwegian captain, an Australian first officer and a Scandinavian, German and Italian crew. Their 660 fellow travellers were also a mixed lot, as Joan would write home: "The passenger list represents the normal cross section—a preponderance of attractive young women, a collection of oddments by any standards and a few you wish had never left Australia."[4]

As the voyage progressed, Joan would soften her snap judgment of her fellow passengers after many were revealed as highly talented and educated: "Every second person on board seems to be a university professor or lecturer going home on sabbatical leave. Appearances are no guide, and we had several shocks when I've seen people beside me on the rail who looked not only scruffy but a bit simple, producing volumes of Greek verse or modern poetry."[5] The nightly concert in particular was a revelation with "so much talent on board that would-be starters were auditioned first." A cello player, baritone, violinist, soprano, elocutionist and three ballet dancers among the more serious artists—"all bound for Vienna or London to further their studies." A professional comedian and three professional models also featured on one "conspicuously successful" night.

Soon Joan was relishing shipboard life: "It seems months since we left and I can hardly imagine any other existence but this one—eating, sleeping, getting tanned and being entertained!" She read nearly a book a day, watched films, swam, played deck tennis and shuffleboard and enjoyed the evenings—with community singing, bingo, quizzes, slide programs, treasure hunts, canasta and chess all on offer.

The journey was punctuated by stopovers in Singapore, Colombo, Egypt and Naples. In Egypt, Joan rode around the pyramids and the Sphinx on a camel, disappointed "they were practically in the streets of Cairo and the Sphinx was even covered

Vetting of Wisdom

with scaffolding."[6] In Naples, "the unrivalled majesty of Vesuvius was lost in the mist." The ship hit a severe storm after leaving Naples: "There was a tremendous crash and like a flash every table was cleared—sauces, sugar bowls and food in a hopeless muddle on the floor and everything in smithereens ... I felt quite ashamed that as everything shot through the air, I rescued my vanilla slice ... and in the following melee munched on happily."[7]

After their arrival in London, the *Skaubryn* would suffer much worse than a passing storm. On her next voyage, while crossing the Indian Ocean, a fire broke out which spread rapidly through the ship. All passengers were evacuated to lifeboats with no casualties apart from one person who suffered a heart attack and died. Luckily, the seas were calm and all passengers were eventually rescued by a passing cargo liner, the *SS City of Sydney*. While being towed to Aden, the heavily damaged *Skaubryn* sank.

Back in England the shocking news was slow to unfold. Joan wrote home anxious for more details: "If you could find any news of the *Skaubryn* disaster could you send it—sea mail. We missed all news because we were out of London and every letter's made passing reference to the 'fire' or 'explosion' or 'disaster.' It's all most tantalizing so we don't know what it's all about but we're very thankful we weren't on it."[8]

After their arrival in London on 13 March 1958, Joan and Jean took up residence at Crosby Hall, on Cheyne Walk, in Chelsea. They had arrived during a cold burst with the traffic snarled by snow. As it was mid-year, she and Jean could only hope for temporary jobs until September. Jean found work quickly at the Royal Masonic School for Girls, less than an hour by train from London, and by 23 March Joan also had accepted a job at a girls' grammar school in the East End.

Beyond September, Jean already had a position at a boarding school in Middlesex—The Welsh Girls' School—"highly spoken of at least in some quarters". Visiting the school to meet the staff, Jean mentioned that she was travelling with another teacher.

When pressed further, she said Joan taught Geography: "There was an electric silence and a few minutes later she was summoned by the Head ... The long and short of it was that ... I was invited to meet the staff and offered the job. At first, I think we were disappointed that 12,000 miles from home we'd be on the same doorstep. Against this however, it was quite the best job I'd been offered. Ashford is only 29 minutes by train from Waterloo, the school is very near the station, the duties light, and it will be very much easier for our shared car."[9]

The shared car was in fact a van they had purchased for travelling on weekends and holidays, a "Ford Thames — 5 cwt. model, lightest and cheapest on the road". Jean paid for it initially with Joan to contribute her half-share as soon as her income from teaching money allowed. Their van proved its worth almost immediately. On their third weekend in London, they took it on a test outing to Romsey Abbey and surrounds: "We're not really very highly organised yet, and to put down our Li-Lo's then sleeping bags, bedding etc. requires much transferring of boxes, bags etc. Still this is a minor irritation, and one we'll soon overcome I expect." Two months later, they were experts: "It's a really wonderful feeling just climbing into the van and taking to the road — no complications as to accommodation, routes etc. — we just set off often with a vague idea as to where we're going."[10]

Finding suitable places to park the van overnight could be challenging: "So many English roads have hedges to their edge or else concrete gutters which don't allow a run-off. Hence we've spent nights in main streets, in car parks, on grassy verges, in gravel pits or lay-bys — in fact almost anywhere."[11] In Devon, they found it especially difficult but managed to find a secluded green, or so they thought: "It turned out to be the old parish church entrance! We were awakened at eight by a great 'revving' of car engine nearby — the vicar then popped around the corner and apologised for disturbing us. Jean was sure there was no early Good Friday morning service so we had the Primus boiling merrily, the jaffles toasting and the cereals half eaten when the congregation appeared—cars, bikes and on foot, but we just had to munch on—very embarrassing."[12]

Joan's outings with men would be less satisfying than weekends roaming the countryside in the van. In June, Jean Craven's brother Douglas rang to invite her to visit Hampton Court: "As his route involved a 6-mile walk, I wasn't sorry to be committed elsewhere! I'm having dinner at the Cumberland with him tomorrow—he leaves for the Continent on Wednesday so I've little hope of frequent nights out I fear."[13] It would be "a very pleasant evening". A month later, Joan reported on another date: "Last Thursday I went to the Royal Tournament with Douglas. He's not exactly exciting but really quite fun and it's a pleasant change to receive chocolates and sit in the best seats."[14] There was another mention of dinner and theatre with Douglas "on the eve of his flying on to the States." Then nothing more.

Two days after her 33rd birthday, Joan had dinner with John de Witt, a friend of a girlfriend, before going on to *My Fair Lady* with Rex Harrison in the lead. The theatre was wonderful but the company was not: "Rather young—and he had a handshake like a dead fish … He made me feel like an elderly aunt—typical under-graduate humour and conceit perhaps, though it wasn't really nearly as bad as that sounds." But any regrets about her failure to find attractive men, were salved by Joan's busy lifestyle and exciting travel plans, expressed with her typical sardonic humour: "Ah well, spinsterhood needs its little compensations."[15]

Joan was saddened when news came of the death of Helen Hailes, the formidable PLC Vice Principal who had caught her escaping from the Latin class as a young student and had pronounced her position at the school to be in jeopardy: "I met her in Camberwell the day before I sailed and she said that before she came over here again, she and Miss Bryant hoped to see something of Australia. They'd been at school and university together and when Miss Bryant retired as head of PLC Goulburn recently she went to live with Miss Hailes in Burke Road ... Apparently, they were on a Murray cruise when Miss Hailes slipped, hitting her head and though she appeared alright a day or so later lost consciousness which she didn't regain before dying some days later — very sad, and a horrible shock for Miss Bryant."[16]

Female companionship was a natural consequence for women teachers in the late 1950s as Miss Hailes' and Miss Bryant's experience reflected. In a society that didn't yet see marriage and full professional lives as compatible, a successful and full teaching life, and certainly life as a principal, reduced the opportunities for marriage. But the spectre of "spinsterhood" didn't detract from Joan's appreciation of the life she was leading: "I sometimes feel so fortunate that I think it can't last and I'll never regret having chosen an occupation that allows, even encourages, travel. But I must come home to a good hard-working job to make the most of the experience I've had."[17]

Joan's East End job finished at the end of July "midst flowers, cheque from staff, chocolates" which she thought excessive: "Isn't it all so silly when I was there for under a term. However, as someone said, you just can't beat the East End children for their generosity and powers of forgiveness! By the time I finished I was getting quite attached to them anyway and I guess it was thirteen weeks of excellent, if sometimes, harrowing experience."[18]

With the summer stretching ahead of them, Joan and Jean loaded their van — now christened Issie — on a cross-channel plane and headed for Europe. They stopped first in Brussels for the international fair where almost every country was represented — but not Australia and New Zealand. Allowing a week or so to drive from Brussels to Greece, they headed into France and then Switzerland: "Issie took the Alps in her stride except for mild petrol vaporisation, which quickly recovered when we allowed her to cool down."[19]

The poverty they found in many villages caused the women

again to reflect on their own good fortune. In Greece they resolved to eat dinner always in a village restaurant: "As the waiter and proprietor rarely speak English or French we go into the kitchen and select our various dishes from great vats always on the stoves."[20] After filling all their containers at the village pump, they would drive off, find a suitable spot, wash, clean teeth, don pyjamas and set off again: "Then, when we reach the next settlement, we merely pull up, put up the *modesty veil*, a green and white check gingham curtain, and fall into our sleeping bags." In Italy, they slept in the protected, spacious and "quite luxurious" petrol station grounds where there was water, and toilets. Around 6.30am they would drive to collect fresh rolls and milk and while Jean prepared breakfast Joan made the beds.

So far so good until one day three young men on motor bikes offered Joan a bunch of grapes: "I accepted — I'd forgotten that while this would be the natural reaction in Greece, in Italy one has to be rude to every man, apparently."[21] Acceptance of the forbidden fruit was encouragement enough for the trio to materialise whenever the van stopped. The men waited two hours for them as they ate their lunch, disappearing and re-appearing close by whenever Jean and Joan left the towns. It was a lonely mountainous road and the van boiled frequently. At these moments, the unwanted companions suddenly reappeared: "We'd spoken no word to them and made it quite clear that they'd have no encouragement."

On reaching the last town at dusk before a 48-mile winding stretch of road, Joan and Jean visited the *polizia*! They had difficulty making the fatherly policeman — kindly enough, but with no word of English and seemingly simple — understand their predicament. It was only with the arrival of two of his colleagues, countless sketches, and, finally, Jean, mimicking the van galloping around the room closely pursued by Joan, the motor *bicicletas*, that the penny dropped: "They then became so protective that we were taken to the only garage and wedged in front of the four trucks … [then] taken to what seemed a private establishment for our spaghetti meal and finally barred and bolted into the garage. It was like a Turkish bath—by 3 or 4am I even wondered if it wasn't a high price to pay for safety but it certainly disposed of our escort. They stuck close for twelve hours but fifteen more in darkness we apparently didn't warrant!"

Their next adventure would be the Welsh Girls' School in Ashford, Kent, about 50 miles southeast of London. Their rooms, Joan reported back, weren't very exciting, "cream painted furniture, rather chipped—drawers that don't pull out smoothly, iron bedstead." But there were other compensations—pleasant staff, just two weekends on duty a term, no staff restrictions, only five minutes from the station and twenty-nine from Waterloo: "We breakfast at the Staff cottage, lunch with children and have dinner in another small dining room with the Head."[22] A few weeks later Joan wrote home of life settling into "a pleasant enough boarding school rut" with duties light enough during the week and with only two working weekends on a term.[23] But as someone who always made sure she was well-prepared, the routine of teaching had its pressures: "Every night there are corrections and preparation, and I've a tremendous admiration for those who seem to have time to watch TV in the staff sitting room all and every evening. On Tuesday, Jean and I both have a free half day and never return before 10pm or 11pm. That's necessary to keep one sane in a boarding school."[24]

While Joan was teaching in England, she still kept abreast of what was happening with schools at home. And late in 1958, Melbourne Girls' Grammar School was the centre of a divisive row that would have resonance for Joan's own experience some years later—not least for the way it was mishandled by church authorities. The dispute surrounded the dismantling of the legacy of Miss Dorothy Ross—the MGGS Principal from 1939 to 1955. The *Australian Dictionary of Biography* entry on Ross would encapsulate the crisis as the staff seeking to "maintain the structures in which

Vetting of Wisdom

Ross had embedded her ideas until 1957 when Edith Mountain, who had more conventional educational ideas, was appointed Principal. Nearly forty members of staff left and some sixty students followed." The controversy even produced a write up in *The Times* and that caught the attention of the Principal at the Ashford school, as Joan wrote home: "Our Head (very charming—if not over effective) claimed to be quite nervous, especially with three Australians on the staff."[25]

Joan urged her family to send more Press clippings to keep her up with developments: "I can imagine the furore that would have built up ... I'd be most interested to see how it all develops and ends up—who'd be a Head!" After receiving more news reports from home, Joan wrote back: "It is hard to know whether Miss Mountain is big enough for the job (after all, it took them two years to appoint anyone and no one knowing the school would take it on). Whatever Miss M's other qualifications, she can't, however, be lacking in courage and such is mass fickleness. She'll probably be being widely acclaimed in a year or so."[26]

The holidays arrived with the Christmas break on 18 December 1958 and again Joan and Jean headed off. This time, their travels included a trip to Brighton to visit "the Misses" Wood"—the sisters of Tintern Principal Constance Wood: "Only two of the three were there—one older than Constance, one younger. Imagine four spinsters out of four! As you'd expect, knowing Constance, they're not exactly bundles of charm, but they were both very pleasant and seemed very pleased to hear anything of Constance and Tintern."[27]

The following Easter, 1959, they took their van to Spain with a more than eight hundred-mile stretch through France to reach it: "We usually drive at 40-50mph on good roads, but as the Thames 5 cwt has the Prefect engine, without any of the interior padding, speeds above that cause strange vibrations! However, one can't have false pride in a delivery van, and we're quite happy to be passed by everything else on the road."[28] Earlier bad weather cleared by Easter Sunday when they reached the Costa Brava on a wonderful morning—perfect for cleaning their van and washing and drying all their damp bedding and coats: "Of course nearly every Spaniard who whizzed or peddled by nearly fell from their vehicles with curiosity, but we've long since failed to be moved by that. Like Greece, women here apparently don't drive, so we're an oddity before you go any further! As well, I don't think it would be usual for women to travel without a man, so you see, we're bound to be objects of curiosity."[29]

From the Costa Brava they travelled to Barcelona, Tarragona, Valencia and Alicante. With such exposure, little wonder Joan fell in love with Spanish food, the paella especially: "One evening I made a big decision and selected something that sounded fishy and most exotic. I should have been warned when the proprietor himself appeared and mentioned that said dish would be another forty minutes. Guess what arrived—a dish piled with thirty-one mussels floating in a sea of red luscious sauce! Scottish instincts prevailed. I dismembered and munched until only four remained—by then I was sauce to the wrists and had amassed a considerable pile of debris. Still, if there is anything you need to know about mussels, just apply to me!"[30]

In August, the travellers turned their sights on Germany and Austria followed by Italy and Switzerland before returning to Ashford by the end of September. After a long and mostly uneventful winter, a letter arrived in May 1959 that would give new focus to Joan's thinking about her career path beyond Ashford and her time abroad. The letter announced that Miss Olga Hay was retiring as Principal of Clyde and asked whether Joan might be interested in applying for the position. Jean received a similar letter.

Joan's initial response was equivocal. In a letter to her cousin Anne she said Jean had other plans and that she, Joan, was unsure of what she wanted to do in teaching: "I certainly would prefer the administrative side (I've a passion for lists, filling in forms etc!) but it needs an almost dedicated life I'm afraid, and I feel pretty sure that there's nothing too dedicated in my approach to children—not at the end of a weekend on duty anyway. Oh well, time will tell."[31]

Two months later, Joan resolved to chance her hand. Having come to the conclusion that you never get a principalship on your first attempt, she now thought interviewing for the position at Clyde would be good practice. She sent off an airmail reply suspecting it would be too late anyway. Soon after, a cable arrived inviting Joan to an interview with Mr Stephen Kimpton, a member of the Clyde School Council who was visiting London. After a pleasant interview, Joan was later invited to join Mrs Kimpton and several other Clyde mothers at Fortnums Piccadilly for what turned out to be a "luscious" tea "quite beyond my purse." She was left uncertain of what might eventuate: "I shall just add it to the list of pleasant experiences! Have no idea what the outcome of all this will be—am not even at all sure what I hope it will be. The job would be difficult. The salary quite good; the winter climate cold and the summer liable to bush fires. Against that, a Head's life I have always thought would be more interesting, and there are few schools which are Presbyterian in outlook."[32]

Despite Joan's reticence, events moved swiftly. The Council member was impressed. Dame Elisabeth Murdoch, also a member of the School Council and a former student at Clyde, would later confirm that Miss Hay favoured Joan to be her successor and encouraged her to come back to contribute to education in Australia.[33]

A month later it was all wrapped up. "An international search ... resulted in the appointment of Joan Montgomery late in 1959," Melanie Guile would write in her *Clyde School 1910-1975: an Uncommon History*. "It was a good appointment and everyone knew it." Confirmation of the job was cabled to Joan in England and she promptly informed Anne and her sisters so "they wouldn't just read it in the paper". There was a moment of panic when shortly afterwards a letter arrived from Clyde "stating that on no account could mention be made of said appointment before July 31st."[34] Even with the cat inadvertently out of the bag, the moment passed and by August Joan was being congratulated, including "a very nice — and quite unexpected — cable from PLC."[35]

With the appointment sealed, Joan turned her attention to booking a passage home on the *Orontes* ("more expensive and later than I'd like but beggars can't be choosers"), claiming an exemption from English taxes, paying Australian instead ("a favourable difference of fifty or sixty pounds") and spending up on clothes ("two suits and a fur!"). Her thoughts were increasingly about Clyde: "I'm not quite sure when I shall flee to Clyde but would like to see it as soon as possible … It's awfully hard to plan from this end when I'm so vague as to what I'm going to. At some early stage I'm to meet Miss Hay while I think my first visit is to be with Mr Alston, the school chairman. At present the *Orontes* is due in Melbourne on January 25th though the date is only for family consumption."[36]

Ahead of her departure, Joan visited schools in Suffolk and Caversham in preparation for her new role. Tying up loose ends meant saying a "very sad" farewell to Issie, Joan and Jean's beloved van: "It's served us wonderfully … it's cost us each twenty-five pounds for each touring holiday, so set against what we'd have paid for accommodation etc. it's been even more wonderful."

On the last stretch, Joan was farewelled at Ashford "as only the Welsh could farewell you" and drove to London for a very hectic last few days — a final tramp around favourite London haunts, last-minute shopping, dental and eye checks, a carol service at St Martin-in-the-Fields. The weather during this period was variously gusty, pouring with rain, and "a howling gale that swept all before it". It would soften the sadness of leaving

England as much as the excitement of anticipating the new era that lay ahead.

7

CLYDE

Clyde was founded as a private girls' school in 1910 by Isabel Henderson, a leading educationist of her day. Initially located in Alma Road, St Kilda, the school moved to Woodend in 1918 after Miss Henderson acquired Braemar House, originally a guest house and golf resort set in 172 acres of grounds in the foothills of the Macedon Ranges. A little to the north of the property lies the spectacular geological formation Hanging Rock. Clyde would gain celebrity with the publication in 1967 of Joan Lindsay's enigmatic novel, *Picnic at Hanging Rock*—the story of the disappearance of three schoolgirls and a teacher from a nearby school on Valentine's Day 1900—and the later acclaimed movie and television series. But while the fictional Appleyard College would never solve the mysterious disappearances, happily Clyde would not lose any of its boarders.

Presbyterian Ladies' College was always lauding its own and Joan's name was quickly noted as "the latest appointment of an Old Collegian as Headmistress" as Miss M.O. Reid put the finishing touches to *The Ladies Came to Stay*, her 1960 history of PLC.[1] Joan's public profile as an educator would begin when the *Orontes* docked in Melbourne and she was interviewed and photographed for two newspaper stories appearing the following day.

"She's home as the new head of Clyde" ran one headline with the subheading: "It's a good thing for a principal to have youth on her side, says Miss Joan Montgomery." The article continued:

"Attractive brunette Miss Joan Montgomery arrived home in Melbourne on the *Orontes* today to become the headmistress of a leading Victorian girl's school at the age of 34." PLC Principal Ruby Powell boasts of Joan being "the third of our younger generation of Old Girls ... to become a headmistress at an early age" (Miss Margaret McPherson, head of Clarendon Ballarat, and Miss Jeanette Buckham, head of PLC Goulburn, were the other two). Joan herself dismisses the fuss. She admits to being nervous but adds: "That has nothing to do with my age—after all, is 34 so young to be a headmistress?" She says sport is important but "must be kept in its right place". She thinks Australians, and not just the school children, don't work hard enough: "Most people get things too easily in Australia." And she believes Australian schools are slightly more liberal than English schools in their attitude to their pupils. Is she a progressive educationist? "I hope I'm reasonably progressive—but only reasonably."

The large photograph accompanying the story matches her candid outlook—a headshot with a glimpse of shoulder in which Joan flashes an open-mouthed, youthful smile. It contrasts with a more formal portrait published the following morning where she is still smiling but with her mouth closed. Her eyes are laughing; you can still see in them that Joan is up for a dare. But a string of pearls around her neck and a handbag tucked under her arm are revealing too.

Being principal of a country girls' school well suited Joan's style and temperament. Her love of the country nurtured through childhood would flourish in the rural environment of Clyde. Being only an hour from Melbourne enabled her to drive down to late-afternoon and night-time meetings, returning in the late evening or early morning in time for the next day's responsibilities at the school. But the travel carried hidden dangers, especially in winter when black ice made the local roads unpredictably treacherous.

At 7.45am on Saturday 2 July 1960, four days before her 35th birthday and less than six months after starting at Clyde, Joan set off from Woodend on the already familiar route down the Calder Highway to Melbourne. On this bitter winter's day, she was driving her new Hillman (HCV-098) and was accompanied by Clyde's bursar, Mary Allpress, 58, who had worked at the school for 15 years. They were heading to watch Clyde's sports teams competing against the PLC girls in Melbourne. Travelling by bus, the Clyde girls would pass them unknowingly as Joan's Hillman had come to grief on an icy bend near the Mt Macedon turnoff.

Joan recalls heading into a slight right-hand curve on the highway when suddenly she lost control, the car careening across to the opposite side of the road before coming to rest on the grass verge on the edge of the road with Miss Allpress, who had been thrown from her seat, lying on top of her. "I am sorry to get you into this plight," said Joan, to which Mary replied: "That is alright. How do we get out of it?" As they struggled to open the passenger-side door, a passing schoolboy, Brian Johnson, arrived and asked if they were alright.

Moments later, Walter Edwin Durbridge, driving his 1954 Morris Oxford sedan saw the Hillman up ahead and slowed to about 35 miles per hour as he approached. "I saw a lad standing by the car. Suddenly, the four wheels of my motor car broke away from the roadway ... I could not control the car in anyway whatsoever ... and I continued on and struck the other car in the rear boot portion with the off-side front of my motor car ... it canted up on its near-side. Both cars were still right way up after the collision ... There was a lady with quite a lot of blood on her face getting out of the other car ... I was told there was another lady lying on the ground, but I did not see her."[2]

The bleeding woman was Joan and the woman lying on the ground was Mary Allpress, who, according to Constable John Patterson, "received injuries from which she died almost immediately ... Dr Ormerod of Gisborne attended the scene and pronounced life extinct in my presence." A post-mortem examination by Dr Bryan Cohen, of Kyneton, found death was caused by the "rupture of the right auricle of the heart, rupture of the liver and multiple fractures of the thoracic cage." These injuries, he explained, "were the result of a sudden severe compressing force applied to the chest and are consistent with having been involved in a motor car accident."

Joan spent a week in Gisborne hospital where she was visited by her sisters, passengers from the other car, and a man from the local garage who came to show her photographs of the accident. She then spent a few more days in Melbourne recuperating. She missed Miss Allpress's funeral, although she remembers the school's tennis coach coming to tell her about it. Joan later visited Mary Allpress's sister.

Joan returned to Clyde within a fortnight with support coming from all quarters. One of the parents lent Joan a car. She would relive the terrible moment every time she had to pass the site of the collision on her drive to Melbourne during the next eight and a half years at Clyde. "You never get over it," she would reflect some 60 years later. "It was very sad, but life goes on."

Throughout her time as Principal at Clyde, Joan took a full teaching load in her specialist area—geography. In addition, she showed an abiding interest in the daily life of all Clyde students. When one girl made a twig and bracken cubby house named *Tamashanta* Joan went for an honorary visit, happily joining in. She continued a tradition going back to the 1920s of reading to the juniors in her study. In winter there would be a crackling fire and "her reading voice was lovely."[3]

Initially, her living quarters, shared with other staff, were too close for comfort with privacy impossible. Melanie Guile's history of the school notes it was common for girls to "come across the headmistress in her dressing gown and slippers in the corridors". And Joan found herself peered at in her private room by ten pairs of inquisitive eyes. Remedying this was one of the first changes she encouraged and separate living quarters for the Principal were made part of a new building program.

While a first-time principal, Joan was not shy of new initiatives and of changing existing practices. She certainly placed a greater stress on academic study than her predecessors, struck by how little schoolwork seemed to matter. It was such a contrast to her PLC experience where it was assumed that, if you had the intelligence, you went on to university.

She reintroduced debating: "Topics were pithy — euthanasia, disarmament, science education for girls."[4] Subject choices were widened — going from six matriculation offerings in 1959 to 10 in 1968. Leaving subjects increased from 12 to 19 over the same period. In 1963, Clyde ran October tests for the first time as useful practice for end-of-year external exams and to teach the importance of exam techniques as well as revision. At the end of her first year, Joan cancelled many of the prizes awarded at Speech Day. She told parents: "This does not reflect poorer work, but is a deliberate policy ... In a small school it seems a pity that so many prizes are given that mediocrity is sometimes rewarded."[5]

As part of the building program, classrooms were soundproofed, and special rooms were designated for Geography and French. In 1964, the old class names inherited from 1910 — IVA, VC and VB — and familiar to Joan as a school girl at PLC, were renamed Forms I, II and III, bringing Clyde into line with other schools. Guile reports that "for the first time since Miss Henderson's day, genuinely critical reviews by the girls appeared in *The Cluthan*, the school journal."

Exam results were mentioned each Speech Day and Joan was not afraid to say that they were "disappointing" in some subjects. However, she also catered for the needs of non-academic students: "Extra courses in first aid, hostessing and advanced domestic science had proved popular," she told an *Age* reporter in 1968. "I think the present system of extending (students) only in the academic field is wrong."[6] These were early expressions of Joan's approach to education — excellent academic standards did not mean abandoning a fully-rounded education.

Another of her strengths shone early: her ability to attract good staff, those with overseas experience among them. In 1962 she appointed Belgian-born Mrs Catherine (Annie) ten Brink, who had arrived from Europe two years earlier: "Strict, uncompromising, and with very high standards, 'Madame' quickly won the respect of the girls. One commented: 'If you made it to (year) 12 French, she was amazing and you always passed'!"[7] Under Mrs ten Brink's guidance, girls achieved outstanding results, as she recalls: "I had a certain freedom to develop my ideas on (the) teaching of French following the modern and more realistic approach of 'communication' and stressing the importance of the oral (listening and speaking) component." She pioneered the use of audiotapes in class and lectured her peers on their value in language teaching. At that time, cassette players were new and expensive, and other teachers were shocked to hear from Madame that her girls had their own. She also organised professional development weekends for fellow language teachers. Her interests extended beyond the classroom. In 1967, she organised camping weekends, establishing a program that gained great popularity in subsequent years.

Ten Brink also affirmed that Joan Montgomery wanted her teachers to keep up with the latest trends: "New programs and policies were being introduced ... teachers were given time off to go to in-service training ... they had to report back ... Staff had an extended morning tea and ... would talk about what they had done, distribute handouts for discussion. It was good for development."[8]

Weekend seminars were held at the school, staff attended conferences and curriculum workshops. Teaching staff came to feel that they were at the centre of educational development. And Joan was driving it. She joined the Victorian section of the Association of Heads of Independent Girls' Schools of Australia, later heading the Victorian branch. From the outset, Joan saw her role as contributing to the wider development of education in Australia. The Association also enabled her to stay connected to like-minded women principals of other girls' schools. Many became close friends.

Joan's love of sport enabled her to maintain a connection with her old Frensham friends. She initiated an annual weekend exchange visit to Mittagong, soon becoming the sporting highlight of each year, a tradition lasting right through to 1975. On their first visit in 1961, the girls were introduced to 'Holting' — a weekly bush working bee followed by a huge bonfire — one of Frensham's most hallowed traditions. On alternate years, the Frensham girls stayed at Clyde.

In addition to hockey, which was the premier game, basketball and tennis were played against other schools. Joan first met Ev Tindale on one of those visits. Ev remembers visiting Clyde with her girls as the Physical Education teacher at Firbank. Later, when Ev moved to PLC, there was a visit that Ruby Powell, the PLC headmistress, also attended. As would later be revealed, Miss Powell had more on her mind than sport, she may have had another purpose entirely.

Other sports were encouraged at Clyde. By 1966 judo was taught as a form of self-defence, perhaps with good reason. As Guile writes, Clyde's isolation generally made it a safe haven, but it also made the school vulnerable in unexpected ways. In Miss Hay's day as headmistress, Jean d'Helin had bravely outfaced a villain who had threatened Chef Platt with a knife.[9]

Playing on the fear of intruders, a group prank would lead to the arrival of a new dog. One of the pranksters, Sylvia McLachlan (Clarke) recalled the evening early in 1964: "I said to Tessa, 'Get out of the window and pretend you are a prowler' ... so she did. She was standing outside and leaning against the wall and the next thing we knew a girl came in from next door and said, 'Hey, kids, don't panic but there's a prowler outside your room!' ... we raced Tessa back in — she was about 5 feet tall and had long hair."

By the time Miss Brisbane, Joan's secretary, appeared to calm the girls, the story of the intruder had grown in the telling: "He's about 6 feet and smoking a cigarette! The police are on their way."[10]

When the police did arrive, a sceptical Joan asked: "Now is this likely to be genuine? And he named five men who lived within about ten or fifteen kilometres. He said ... 'when they've had a bit to drink (they can become) Peeping Toms. They won't go further but tell the girls never to attempt to bail them up ... You know, even if you call, we can't get here, even if we drop everything and run, it's a few minutes'."[11]

A police-trained Doberman arrived at Clyde the following Sunday afternoon: "The girls lined the balcony to view the arrival of this terrifying beast. A little VW pulled up and out of it staggered a very car-sick pup, and it lurched across the terrace (to) howls of derision from the balcony above ... Minerva, we called her, goddess of beauty, intelligence, and something else, she was a lovely dog ... she behaved beautifully."

But Minerva soon proved her worth, as Joan would recall: "One Easter I was there alone ... out on the terrace ... and suddenly this strange man, I just didn't like the look of him, ambled around the corner ... I said, 'Oh are you looking for someone?' and he said, 'Are you here alone?' I said, 'Oh, no, the school is never unattended. No, there are plenty about. Who do you want to see?' Just at that moment, the dog raced round and she went straight over and ... grabbed him by the wrist, just quite lightly. He was terrified, and ... went for his life ... but I didn't like it at all." The following week, Joan was out for a walk with the dog when the same man approached her: "He saw the dog, his face was as white as a sheet ... as he went for his life up the hill." The next weekend, a group of seniors reported that a strange man was loitering with one of the girls, who was crying, and Joan called the police. It turned out that the man was a rapist from New Zealand with a long criminal record.[12]

Clyde

Aside from Minerva, there were other dogs at Clyde. Binks was a shaggy mutt of indeterminate breed that Joan had brought with her. He was bought as a Scottie but grew into something quite different, as Joan recalled: "I met someone one day and I had Binks with me—'Oh', she said, 'how lovely, a Smithfield. I've not seen one in Australia'."

Binks overlapped with Sambi, a corgi, left with Joan when her sister Margaret and her family left for several years in New Zealand. Sambi was not a favourite with the Clyde girls due to her habit of retrieving cakes and other forbidden treasures from under their beds. One of the more obvious lapses occurred when the Bishop of Bendigo, the Right Reverend Ronald Richards, and Mrs Richards came to dinner one evening. While waiting in the hall to enter the dining-room, Sambi, with a box of talc in her mouth, raced down one side of the stairs and completed a figure eight in the hall trailing clouds of talc. She continued her lively ways for some months until one evening Joan had to ring New Zealand with the sad confession that she had run over and killed Sambi that day. Wondering how she might compensate the children, she was relieved when Margaret said: "Leave it to me." Margaret rang reassuringly a little later with David's reaction: "That dog didn't have a brain in her head."

One of the pleasures of Joan's return to Australia was getting to know her increasing number of nephews and nieces. David and Robin spent weekends at Clyde whenever there was a fancy dress or similar entertainment. On their last visit just before leaving for New Zealand, David, then six, was wearing new clothes, which from his suit, to his underwear, he offered for inspection! The Clyde girls looked after the children, taking them up into the tower of the main building, which was forbidden, entertaining, bathing and feeding them, and organising their fancy-dress costumes. David and Robin loved these weekends; their aunt had little control of the situation!

Religion in the school was represented by the Presbyterian

and Anglican ministers visiting on alternate Sunday mornings to conduct services. Dr Wilfred Paton was one of the Presbyterian ministers during Joan's time at Clyde. If a brilliant scholar, he was very absent-minded, as Joan recalls: "He'd come and suddenly you could see him feel in his pocket for his glasses and the nearest prefect would get up and go down to the study knowing that he'd probably put them down when he was talking to me." Once during a school service, Paton rummaged in his pocket and found a shifting spanner he had put there instead of his spectacles. But everyone liked and respected him: "He was very wise and very sincere ... a good man, and very human."[13] One of the Anglican ministers, Canon Fabian, was a less endearing character. He had been an army chaplain, and illustrated every point with military examples, earning the sobriquet, Cannon Fodder.[14]

......

While she had the option of staying overnight at the family home in Hawthorn when visiting Melbourne on school business, Joan would always return to Clyde so she could be on duty first thing each morning. But, eventually, the frequent travel to and from Melbourne meant Joan was more open to considering a move back to the city. An invitation to do so came early in 1968.

The PLC School Council advertised the position of Principal after Ruby Powell, the first Old Collegian to become the Head of her former school, advised her intention to retire. While the position was widely advertised, Joan had not applied. Perhaps Miss Powell's visit to Clyde on one of Ev Tindale's sports days visits was a step towards Joan being approached to be her successor. Ev certainly felt at the time that it was unusual for Ruby to come all the way to Clyde simply for a sports event.

The Selection Committee appointed by the Council approached Joan through her friend Dr Olive Mence (nee Wykes). Olive, while five years older than Joan, had known her from their

PLC school connections and had also met Joan in the UK on her travels in the late 1950s. She was a member of the Committee with the Chairman, Professor Johnson from Monash, and Dame Joan Roberts, a representative of the Old Collegians, and the Reverend Farquhar Gunn, Secretary of the Presbyterian Church. Joan was invited to lunch at Olive's house and later interviewed by the Committee which recommended her appointment to Council and ultimately to the Presbyterian Church Assembly. Joan was attractive to the Committee as another "old girl" with wide teaching experience in Australia and England. What is more, Council members were determined to appoint a woman.

It was in this context that Joan first met Ray Northrop. One month younger than her, Northrop had been invited to join the PLC Council in 1968, just as the search for a new Principal began. His two daughters were students at the school. Feeling very much the new boy on the block, he was struck on meeting Joan by her "very sensible, practical, down to earth" nature and "very good manner ... very good way of expressing herself" thinking carefully and giving good answers.[15]

By the time he joined the Council, Northrop had almost 16 years' experience as a barrister. In 1970, he would be made a Queen's Counsel and, in 1976, a founding judge of Federal Court of Australia. He would be elected PLC Council chair in 1972 and, with his great personal regard for Joan, become a vital figure when the bruising battle for control of PLC unfolded in the years ahead. Ironically, Northrop's election to the Council was proposed by the Reverend Bill Loftus, minister of the Camberwell Presbyterian Church, who would become a leading adversary in the move to church union: "We were members of the Trinity church ... and I was on the board of management. And when ... he retired from the PLC Council, Loftus said that I should get on."[16]

Born on the island of New Britain, in what was then the Australian Mandated Territory of New Guinea, Northrop returned to Melbourne with his parents at the age of two. He attended

Murrumbeena State School, Tooronga Road Central School and St Giles Presbyterian Church for Sunday School. He sat an entrance exam to become a telegraph delivery boy as a means of entry into the Commonwealth Public Service but continued his studies at Melbourne High School after being awarded a free place. After matriculating in December 1942, and having just turned 17, he joined the Navy, the only service that allowed enlistments under 18. In the final years of the war, he saw active service in the South West Pacific, New Guinea, the Philippines and Borneo. After being discharged from the Navy in 1946, Ray enrolled to study law at Melbourne University and, after graduating, went on to do a Masters of Law. A year after being admitted to the Bar in 1952, he met Joan Peacock. They married in December 1954. Joan Northrop would also become a key player in the struggle over PLC's future.

In 1968, the PLC Council had 22 members, including the Principal in her ex officio role, with Alex Ogilvy as Chairman. The Council's authority came from Regulation 36 (2) of the General Assembly of the Presbyterian Church of Victoria. Aside from Ray Northrop, Professor Maureen Brunt was a notable figure on the Council as a PLC graduate with a First Class Honours Commerce degree and a PhD from Harvard. Four clergymen gave the Church a strong presence and the eight women representatives exceeded the requirement of at least four women mandated in the regulations. This was an early form of affirmative action and while only a small percentage of women members was guaranteed, it was nonetheless an enlightened provision for its time. A more expansive affirmative action requirement was that "at least two thirds of the Council shall be communicant members of the Presbyterian Church."

The Council's duties included taking "all measures necessary for the welfare of the college, and in particular to provide for the more efficient teaching of the Holy Scripture, and the development of Christian ideals of citizenship and of personal character, and, in cooperation with the Principal, to promote a spirit of reverence in the entire life and work of the college." The Council was empowered to recommend the appointment of a Principal to the Presbyterian General Assembly and to fix the salaries, superannuation and retirement allowances paid to the staff, but the prerogative to appoint members of staff rested with the Principal (subject to confirmation by the Council) who had full powers of dismissal.[17]

Early in 1968, the Council recommended to the General Assembly that Joan Mitchell Montgomery be appointed Principal following Ruby Powell's retirement, declaring its admiration for her skills and personal qualities. A decade after she had left Tintern, Miss Constance Wood's prophecy that Joan was destined to become leader of her old school was to be fulfilled.

After the appointment was announced to the PLC community, Joan wrote to Vice Principal Helen Lade on 18 May thanking her for her "kind letter and good wishes". Joan had known Helen as leader of the Prefects' Student Christian Movement (SCM) group and admired her as "a wonderful woman – a true Christian." Describing how excited but humbled she felt about the appointment, Joan wrote: "I hope that you really do approve, because I know that I'll be very dependent on your help and advice." She said a meeting the previous Thursday with Ruby Powell had filled her with misgivings: "Why would anyone leave such a manageable little school as Clyde? However does one master the intricacies of PLC's timetables, or even learn the names of the Staff, let alone the girls! ... I drove back to the Mount in a state of mild panic, just hoping that my incompetence might take a little while to show."

Ev Tindale remembers Ruby Powell announcing to the staff one day during morning tea that Joan Montgomery was to be the next Head. The response was one of overwhelming delight — "which I think when we stopped and thought was probably a little disrespectful to Miss Powell, but it was quite spontaneous." Joan advised the Council that she would not be free to take up the position until the end of first term 1969, which was agreed. As she explained to Helen Lade: "The trouble with a small school is that it's far more a one-person affair ... I hope that it's not just that I cannot—or will not—delegate!" She applauded Helen's willingness to be Acting Principal in the interim: "Please don't retire for years—PLC will need you more than ever!"

Three days later, the *Age* published a feature by Anne Dalrymple headlined: "Aims for an all-round education."[18] It announced Joan's appointment as Principal of "one of Victoria's largest and best-known private schools." The article would open with an encapsulation of Joan's educational philosophy: "It seems to me that the aim of education today is to produce a well-rounded child, rather than simply a well-educated one". In comparing the challenges of Clyde and PLC, Joan would say: "The thought of PLC fills me with some apprehension. My role as headmistress will be very different. Clyde is unique in that it's run on such a personal basis—there one knows everyone. This will be one of the big differences for me."

Back at Clyde, Joan had given notice to the Council. Chairman Tim Moran wrote to parents expressing the Council's deep regret at being obliged to accept her resignation.[19] The girls were also saddened by the news, some bursting into tears.[20] By October 1968, Clyde had appointed Mrs Alice Pringle as the next headmistress with her husband, Grant Pringle, appointed as Science master. This meant that Mrs Lade didn't have to hold the fort at all, enabling Joan to start at PLC at the beginning of 1969, although Mrs Lade did stay on to assist Joan.

The girls at PLC would have been heartened to hear what their contemporaries at Clyde thought of their headmistress, had they read the tribute published in the school magazine in her final year: "Above all, Miss Montgomery has stressed the importance of character—of personal integrity, of magnanimity and of the realisation that each of us is involved in all mankind ... We would like to let her know that we have appreciated how fully she has given us of her time and attention. She has always been readily, indeed remarkably, accessible to each one of us ... and we would like her to know her qualities—her sense of humour, her dignity, her sense of fitness—have always made us pleased and proud to point her out as our headmistress."[21]

The PLC girls and parents had a chance to view Joan for themselves at the PLC Speech Night in 1968 to which she was invited as the incoming Principal. One of the new teachers at the time, who did not know much about Joan, was struck by her "young and glamorous" presence, remembering Joan adorning a black velvet gown.[22] Weeks later, Joan's homecoming to PLC would be complete when she took up residence at Hethersett, within the school grounds in Burwood, in advance of the 1969 school year.

8

PLC Principal

At 9.15am on Friday 14 February 1969 Joan Montgomery was formally installed as Principal of Presbyterian Ladies' College before the entire school community at a service in Wyselaskie Hall. The Moderator of the Maroondah Presbytery, the Reverend Neil Brown, and the Moderator of the General Assembly, the Very Reverend Reford Corr, presided. Sandra Barr, the School Captain, read St Matthew 5:1-16 and the Chairman of the College Council, Alex Ogilvy, delivered the Narrative. The Charge was delivered by the Reverend David Hodges—the same David Hodges Joan played squash with during their university days.

The magnitude for Joan of the transition from a small country boarding school to a big city college was graphically illustrated on the day before the service. Mrs Cohen, the receptionist, rang through to inform Joan that a Clyde student, Amy Wong, had arrived with thirteen suitcases. Amy had declared that she needed to start at PLC as she wanted to do science! Somehow Joan managed to sort things out for her: "PLC was so well organised and had such an excellent staff that for the first several weeks I wondered what the Principal did!"[1] In the first weeks, Helen Lade would meet Joan each day over lunch giving her the background of each PLC girl, their mothers, even their grandmothers: "I was very fortunate to have Mrs. Lade as my first mentor."[2]

It was not until late April, a few months after she had begun, that Joan signed the agreement between the Presbyterian Church of Victoria Trusts Corporation and Joan Mitchell Montgomery, prepared by Weigall & Crowther Solicitors. Crucially for events that lay ahead, her 'Period of Appointment' was set out:

> The appointment as Principal is in the first instance to be for a period of five years from the first day of June 1969 and thereafter by reappointment to the date of retirement namely the year in which the Principal attains the age of 60 years or if the parties mutually agree until the year in which she attains the age of 65 years.

Termination was possible at the end of any school term after the end of six months' notice. Joan could deliver that notice to the Chairman of the Council, but on the Council's side, notice of termination could only be given, "in pursuance of resolution passed at two special meetings of the Council held at an interval of not less than 14 days, such resolution being affirmed at each meeting by not less than two-thirds of the whole number of the Council for the time being." In addition: "Full notice of and opportunity for explanation at one or both of such meetings shall be given to the Principal who may if she so desires be accompanied by the President or Vice President for the time being of the Head Mistresses' Association of Victoria." Joan's signature was witnessed by Alice S. McLean, her secretary who continued in the role after being secretary to both Mary Neilson and Ruby Powell.

Joan would make many changes as Principal. One of the first, announced in August, was the introduction of a two-year fifth form course, which sought to accommodate those "girls who have shown they cannot maintain the pace or the standard expected of their class." Joan acknowledged this could be due to prolonged absence, poor teaching in the early stages of sequential subjects like mathematics, or "because their abilities do not lie in the mainly academic courses that PLC offers." From 1970 they were going to try something different and "if this scheme is to succeed, it must be planned by those who believe in it and accepted by those who undertake it." The outline of the proposed courses was set out in a memorandum to parents of girls who were being considered for the course and they were invited to an evening discussion to move things forward.

Dealing with PLC parents obviously was a key responsibility of the new Principal. Managing her staff was another. Some of Joan's staff were old friends. Their respective abilities to manage, and to an extent keep separate, their private connections was exemplified in her appointment of Joan Battersby as Head of Geography for 1970. Joan was the younger sister of Joan Montgomery's childhood friend Olive Battersby who had in turn become a good friend in her own right. Another protégé of the fabled geography teacher Miss Wilkinson, Joan Battersby, who had recently returned from Tanzania, had more than 13 years' teaching experience, including time overseas and at Melbourne University in the Department of Education. In a letter outlining the responsibilities of the role, Joan Montgomery offered some flexibility in how Joan Battersby would balance her own teaching with being head of department: "I understand that you would be interested in the possible re-organisation of the curriculum from Forms 1 to IV."

Nine days later, Joan Battersby wrote to "Miss Montgomery" thanking her for her letter: "I am sorry I have wavered over accepting this, but as you know I still have enthusiasm to be involved in education in a developing country and I honestly don't know whether teaching here will generate the same enthusiasm. If you are happy to appoint me, knowing there is doubt regarding long continuity of service, I am happy to accept." Joan Montgomery knew keenly from her own experience how challenging a choice it was. Her letter in reply was enthusiastic: "I was delighted to receive your acceptance of October 4th, and to know that for 1970 at least, our geography was in the best possible hands. You would have been flattered at the reception that your appointment received ... I further understand that you are considering this appointment for 1970 although I would hope that you might find satisfaction in the position and that if you accept, your stay here will be a long and rewarding one."

The friendship and the professional relationship would be tested within two months when Joan Battersby was compelled to write two letters to the Principal on 3 December 1969. The first was strictly professional, to "Dear Miss Montgomery", and began: "There seems to be some misunderstanding between us about the role I am intended to fill at PLC next year, so I am writing to clarify matters to enable me to plan accordingly. When we first discussed the possibility of my joining the staff at PLC, I was under the impression that my function [was] to be a dual one; to undertake a certain amount of basic teaching and to develop the geography department by introducing new courses in 1970. From our telephone conversation this morning, however, it appears that with the proposed timetable loading, the latter function cannot be an effective operation in 1970. I want to stress that my concern with the proposed timetable is not with the number of periods involved but with the number of students." The letter would continue with an explanation of numbers before declaring: "Sorry to have to abandon the development side of the work. It was this aspect of the work that swayed my decision in favour of accepting the position at PLC. If the proposed loading of 25 periods (involving 200 students and two matriculation classes), head of department and sixth-form mistress is inevitable, then I think we are being too ambitious in attempting to both formulate and introduce new courses for all four years in 1970."

The second letter, partly typewritten and completed by hand was personal: "Dear Mont, Forgive the formal approach in the attached letter. It is adopted to protect you from any attack of favouritism on the basis of friendship, should you need to lay my case on the table with other staff. This more informal and detailed letter is to spell out to you the puzzle I now find myself in." She continued with an intricate explanation with tables, showing the difficulties of student numbers and staff numbers, based on her experience teaching at St Leonard's full time in 1966 and a further telephone call that very day to St Leonard's "to see what their current student load is for staff taking matriculation classes."

The two letters did the job: Joan Montgomery can't remember having to lay out her case with other staff—and Joan Battersby can't remember exactly how it worked out save that it was done professionally but leavened with the trust and understanding that came from a long friendship.

At the end of 1970, Joan Battersby went back to Tanzania to marry Jack Kent, who had proposed to her some two-and-a-half years earlier. They married early in 1971 and then returned for a short time before moving to Iran from 1972 to 1977. Joan Montgomery would meet Jack Kent in Teheran late in 1977 and, on learning the couple were thinking of returning to Melbourne, wrote offering them both jobs, in Jack's case the position of head of Science at PLC. The Kents returned in 1978 and would stay at PLC throughout Joan Montgomery's principalship.

Joan's transition to Principal of PLC and her first year is beautifully captured in a letter she wrote in December 1969 after Helen Lade announced her decision to retire:

> Dear Mrs Lade, I still can't really believe that you won't be back but have no doubt that you'll be about when advice is needed. This year has flown, and so many of its happiest aspects have been shared with you. I've still so much to learn but you've been a wonderful help—I wish I had a little more of your greatness though. I know you'll enjoy your 'retirement' but will always be grateful that it has been delayed until now. With love and every good wish both for Christmas, and for all the exciting things that lie ahead. Joan.

Running a large school depends on tight schedules and precision timetables. Left to her own devices, running to time was not necessarily Joan's strong suit but there were others to buffer her whenever the need arose. Ray Northrop recalls one famous occasion when Joan was missing with the start of the annual Speech Night drawing dangerously close. There was mounting anxiety among Council members when Joan finally rang through—her car had broken down in Union Street, Hawthorn. To the horror of some of the other Council members, who feared a double calamity, Northrop raced off in his car to pick her up. Don Macrae was all for getting started without the pair of them, but they made it back in the nick of time. Most of the time during Joan's time as Principal at PLC, however, she wasn't late.

......

The moves towards church union that unfolded dramatically early in the 1970s had their roots in Australia's own Federation story when the colonies joined to form the Commonwealth of Australia in 1901. That same year, the Presbyterian churches of the six Australian States joined to form the Presbyterian Church of Australia. To enable this federal union, each State legislature enacted a Presbyterian Church of Australia Act 1900, which provided for all of the trust properties of the State churches to be held subject to the scheme of union and the decisions of the General Assembly—effectively the Presbyterian Supreme Court—which was authorised as a judicial committee of the Church.

The church unity cork had been popped. As Max Bradshaw would write: "Hardly had the inauguration of the Presbyterian Church of Australia occurred in July 1901 than there were suggestions of union with other churches. In the twenties, a basis of union with the Methodists and Congregationalists was prepared and a vote of communicants was taken. However, such was the opposition ... that the matter was dropped."[3] In fact, the Methodists and Congregationalists voted strongly in favour of union while the Presbyterians were split — the position that would be replicated half a century later.

A similar vote of the three denominations in Canada in 1925 succeeded, despite several hundred Presbyterian congregations, predominantly in Ontario, rejecting union. Moves towards church union were revived in Australia at the 1945 General Assembly but again stalled. A vote of communicant members of the three denominations in favour of reopening negotiations for union led to the formation of a Joint Commission on Church Union in 1957 to prepare the way. After a hiatus, the JCCU resumed work in 1968. A new "Basis of Union" to reconcile theological and administrative differences between the three churches was drafted, largely by the Reverend Dr Davis McCaughey who would become the first president of the Uniting Church in Australia.

But the marriage of the Presbyterian, Methodist and Congregational churches required parliamentary legislation and it was here that the opponents of union had the mechanism to fight the plans supported by the overwhelming majority of the faithful. As Max Bradshaw, the most prominent of the recalcitrants, would explain it:

> The ordinary position is that if parties desire a private bill to be enacted there must be general agreement in the body seeking the legislation. It was there that the opponents of union were in a strong position, enabling them to insist on constitutional provisions to safeguard a minority. It was felt better for those against the proposed union to participate in negotiations on these matters than to oppose enactment of enabling legislation. At that stage no one had any idea of the numerical strength

of the opposition to union, and among opponents, some thought there were very few, in which case there might be a great danger in opposing.[4]

In 1971, the Victorian Parliament passed the Presbyterian Church of Australia Act which enabled the Presbyterian Church in Victoria to be completely united with the Presbyterian Church of Australia, thereby enabling the national church to enter into union with other Churches. Similar legislation was passed in each state. Under the Act, any agreement on union could be implemented "only when approved by a majority of synods and at least three-fifths of the members present when the final vote of the General Assembly is taken."[5]

But as Bradshaw had noted, the legislation also ensured that if the General Assembly did resolve to enter into union then it should "provide just and equitable safeguards of the rights of minorities who do not concur with the decision to unite, including that the General Assembly set up a commission consisting of two groups of equal numbers, one representing those approving and one representing those disapproving, together with three independent persons acceptable to both groups, one of whom shall be Chairman."[6] This commission would be responsible for determining what Presbyterian property would be inherited by the new Uniting Church in Australia and what would remain with the Continuing Presbyterians.

Importantly for Presbyterian Ladies' College and many other church schools, the Act also provided for the commission to identify and grant to the Continuing Presbyterian church "at least one school for girls and one school for boys in each State where at the date of the said union there is more than one Presbyterian School for girls and more than one Presbyterian School for boys". There were further instructions for those States where there was only one boys' and girls' school.

The Continuing Presbyterians — with Max Bradshaw leading

the legal charge—were determined not only to fight to prevent union but also, in the likely event they failed, to secure the consolation prize of control of the two plum Presbyterian schools in Melbourne, PLC and Scotch College. And there are signs they began plotting well before the 1971 legislation was enacted. Ray Northrop, who would emerge as Bradshaw's principal legal adversary, had early grounds for suspicion: "I think Max Bradshaw had a good idea in advance of the Property Commission's work, of orchestrating things to ensure the continuing group got PLC and Scotch. There was a small girls' school in Hawthorn called Stratherne Presbyterian Girls' Grammar School. At one of the General Assemblies of the Victorian Assembly it was resolved that Stratherne be sold—well before the vote for Union occurred."[7]

Had Stratherne still existed, it could have been granted to the continuing group to satisfy the requirement that they receive one of the girls' schools. Northrop suspects that in Bradshaw's mind, the closing of Stratherne strengthened the Continuing Presbyterians' claim to PLC. However, Stratherne faced a financial crisis that had made its closure almost inevitable, regardless of the church politics. With fewer than 50 students enrolled for the 1969 year and a projected loss of $25,000 to $30,000, there had been little choice but to relocate the staff and students and close the school.

The Presbyterians opposed to union exemplified by Max Bradshaw were determined to preserve the sanctity of their church's forms of worship and doctrine, steeped in its Scottish ancestry. As Brian Bayston would write of his friend and mentor: "He was anxious to preserve it [the Presbyterian Church] from union with other churches on a basis which involved the loss of the doctrinal substance of historic Calvinism and of Presbyterian polity."[8] Many anti-unionists shared Bradshaw's abhorrence at the modernism creeping into the church and new definitions of evangelism: "Max considered that the appointed method of evangelism was to bring people under the sound of the Gospel in the context of a worshipping congregation and he repudiated appeals for decision, such as became commonplace after the Billy Graham Crusade of 1959."[9]

The lead up to the vote on union in 1974 would polarise Presbyterian congregations across Australia that were swept up in a campaign as fierce and acrimonious as the most heated secular elections. To advance the anti-union cause, the Presbyterian Church Association was formed under two driven stalwarts of the Hawthorn Church—the Reverend Robert Swanton and Max Bradshaw. Another vociferous layman, Charles Homer Fraser, was the public relations officer. "It was waged like a political campaign," Brian Bayston would write. "There were meetings and brochures and leaflets and how-to-vote cards. The theological arguments were substantially the work of Robert Swanton; the legal, the work of Max. My impression was that Max was prepared to work with anyone who would work to the same end. There were therefore supporters from a wide range of theological perspectives, and some whose support was merely traditional and Scottish ... The mixed character of the opposition to church union was used as an argument by the unionists: the continuing church would, they said, tear itself apart. They were wrong but not far wrong."[10]

The Presbyterians committed to union were equally fervent in their belief that change was essential. In the wake of the social upheaval of the 1960s many wanted "an Australian church called to bear witness to a radical vision of Christian unity that rose above cultural, economic, national and racial boundaries."[11] The Basis of Union envisaged a united church that was not merely a new denomination but a "movement for Christian unity". It would have a strong ecumenical commitment to build closer ties with Australia's nine other Christian denominations and other faiths. It would champion multiculturalism and indigenous reconciliation with self-determining congregations from Asian and Pacific migrants and Aboriginal communities. And it would strongly affirm the role of women in ministry, a simmering grievance of many of the Continuing Presbyterians.

Before the vote on union was taken and before the Property Commission began its work, there was a curious visit to PLC by a delegation of senior Presbyterian officials. Under the Presbyterian system of governance, congregations and other church organisations are grouped into regional 'presbyteries' of clergy and lay elders which, in turn, form the State general assemblies of the church. Presbyteries are required to conduct "visitations" to all of their congregations at least once every five years to "promote fruitful gospel ministry that glorifies God", encourage pastoral leaders and provide guidance to congregations in their work: "The Presbytery members who conduct these visitations are servants of the gospel who seek God's best for every congregation that they visit and for all the leaders of those congregations."[12] Despite the noble mission statement, there were suspicions that the purpose of the men who came calling at PLC was more political than pastoral, if not a real estate inspection in disguise. The school had never before, at least in the memory of Joan Montgomery, received a visitation.

The Visitation Committee from the Presbytery of Maroondah, the territory of which included the PLC campus in Burwood, comprised the Reverend Dr David Merritt, the Reverend Tom Howells and Mr John McArthur. The committee's convenor, Dr Merritt, whose wife Joy taught religious education at PLC and whose daughter Carolyn was a student, was wary of the visit and expressly questioned the reasons for it in his report:

> A Presbytery visitation to a church school involves different procedures and objectives to a Presbytery visitation to a congregation. Indeed, there is some uncertainty about the purpose and potential benefits of such a visit. The visit undoubtedly

serves to remind both school and Presbytery of the existence of the other, to raise some basic issues about the church's ministry in and through its schools, and to create an occasion for consideration of particular questions about the school's provision for the Christian education of its pupils. It should be clear, however, that the members of Presbytery undertaking the visit are in a relatively unfamiliar situation. On a short visit it would be presumptuous to assume that they came to know very much about the life of a large educational institution. It seems appropriate, therefore, that a report should be modest in its descriptions and very modest in its recommendations.[13]

The committee attended morning worship and met with Miss Montgomery and representatives of the School Council, staff and the minister of the local church attended by PLC boarders. They lauded what they had seen and commended the school for "creating and sustaining a community" concerned "with a high level of learning but also with the qualities of caring and respect for people that are at the heart of the Christian understanding of life lived according to God's purposes." They noted the existence of daily morning assemblies and the Principal's "careful thought and planning" of them. Joan's stressful weekends preparing for assemblies were clearly worth the effort!

Significantly for the impending deliberations about ownership of the school, Dr Merritt also said: "The links of PLC with the structures of the Presbyterian Church are relatively tenuous. The Council is appointed by the Assembly and the Assembly guarantees borrowing. The association of the school with the Presbyterian Church is more strongly in terms of its name and spirit, than in terms of its structures." But concerns that the Visitation Committee might have been a scouting party for the

PLC Principal

Continuing Presbyterians plotting to secure control of the school would prove misplaced. Tom Howells and David Merritt would emerge as passionate advocates for union and John McArthur, a partner in the law firm Wisewoulds, would become a key member of the legal team that fought to have PLC vested in the Uniting Church.

The path to the formation of the Uniting Church in Australia was secured on 1 May 1974 when the General Assembly of the Presbyterian Church of Australia voted 230 to 143 in favour of union—a majority of 64 per cent, just above the "three fifths" threshold required. The Congregational Union had already voted in favour with a majority of 98 per cent and the Methodist Church with a majority of 85 per cent. But the rift within the Presbyterian ranks became a full-blown schism the moment the die was cast.

The night before the crucial vote was taken, the Assembly convened to conduct a final debate on the Basis of Union. Anticipating an overflow audience, the leadership hired Dallas Brooks Hall in East Melbourne—site of the original home of Presbyterian Ladies' College. In the audience was a young minister named Bob Thomas, who would later become the Very Reverend Dr C.R. Thomas, Moderator of the Presbyterian Church of Australia. According to Thomas, it was a very poor debate. "By now, pretty well everything that could be said both for and against the union had been said, over and over again, and everyone was running out of steam," he would later write. "Basically, the uniting people just got up and said it was a good thing and the Presbyterians got up and said it was a bad thing. Call me biased, but I did think the better speeches were made by the continuers. Ken Gardner and Neil MacLeod in particular nailed the Basis of Union for its departure from Biblical standards and watering down of the subordinate standards of all three uniting churches."[14] But there were touches of levity amid the rising enmity.

"A moment of light relief was provided by the Reverend John

Perkins, minister of Lismore (NSW) and one of the 'characters' of the NSW Assembly. The Very Reverend Fred Mackay, successor of Flynn of the Inland and a former Moderator General, spoke in favour of the Basis, telling the Assembly that he had been out on patrol in the Outback one night when he rolled out his swag under the stars and just before going to sleep he took out the Basis of Union and read it, and it made him feel excited. Perkins interjected: 'Some people are easily excited.' Then it came Perkins's turn to speak. 'I suppose we'll all go down Bourke Street tonight,' he said, 'and there we'll find Fred boiling the billy and reading the Basis ... '. He went on to do a complete demolition job on Fred's speech. In the end they resolved to accept the Basis of Union."[15]

The following day, the Presbyterian leaders reconvened at Assembly Hall, beside Scots' Church, in Collins Street. After a protracted ballot, the meeting resolved that on 2 June 1976 or such earlier or later date as is determined, the Presbyterian Church of Australia would enter into union with the Methodist Church of Australasia and the Congregational Union of Australia, and further stated that "until the Presbyterian Church of Australia enters such Union it shall continue to function pursuant to its existing Constitution, its existing Basis of Union and existing Acts of Parliament."[16] Importantly, it was also resolved to protect those who did not agree with union, "providing just and equitable safeguards" and by "instructing officials of the Assembly to provide needed information to assist any continuing Presbyterian church and its congregations."[17]

No sooner had the historic decision been taken than "general mayhem broke out", according to Bob Thomas, who was not a delegate but was watching from the gallery. The Moderator of the NSW Assembly, the Right Reverend Neil MacLeod, immediately stood up and delivered a fiery speech said to have borrowed heavily from the words of Thomas Chalmers, who became the first Moderator of the Free Church of Scotland after the breakaway from the Church of Scotland in the Disruption of 1843.

> I crave to dissent and I protest that this resolution just passed is unacceptable to those of us who in conscience cannot enter this union; and I lay on this table this protest on behalf of those who elect to remain in the Presbyterian Church of Australia ... and we finally protest before the great God, Searcher of all our hearts, that we and all who adhere to us, are not responsible for this schism in the Church or for any consequence which may flow from this enforced separation ... I invite all of those who adhere to this protest, since there is not room in this place for two assemblies, to follow me to another place, namely 46 Russell Street, 'The Amethyst Hall', where we, the continuing General Assembly of Australia, shall resume the sittings of this house. In olden times that Bush flamed—*nec tamen consumebatur*. Let no one say that we here stamped on the ashes of that fire.[18]

The minutes of those who remained in the Assembly Hall would record that "after the reading of the Dissent and Protest, some 20 members followed the Rt Rev Neil MacLeod out of the Assembly to 46 Russell Street."[19] Bob Thomas would demur: "By my estimate the ... minute suffers from either poor proof-reading or dishonesty, as there were more like 120 who followed MacLeod."[20] Striding hot on the heels of MacLeod were the three other most prominent leaders of the Presbyterian revolt—Max Bradshaw, the Reverend Ted Pearsons and the Reverend Bill Loftus.

The minister of St Andrew's, Canberra, the Very Reverend Hector Harrison, was waiting for the protesters in the Amethyst Hall. He immediately inducted MacLeod as Moderator General, "claiming on good grounds (because they were Maxwell Bradshaw's grounds) that the moment the GAA voted to unite they altered the essential doctrine of the 1901 Basis of Union and were no longer legally entitled to be the Presbyterian Church of Australia. They then set themselves up as the shadow, or what we believe, was the real General Assembly of the Presbyterian Church of Australia."[21] The meeting then proceeded to rescind many decisions taken by the General Assembly over previous years, not least the decision to ordain women to the ministry. The Hawthorn Church, home of Max Bradshaw and Robert Swanton, would become the temporary home of the so-called "Camberwell Group."

Before the walkout, the General Assembly had also resolved that the distribution of Presbyterian property between the Uniting Church and the Continuing Presbyterians be the responsibility of a special seven-member Commission comprising a chair, two independent members, two supporters of union and two opponents of union. The chair would be Ken Handley, QC, Chancellor of the Anglican Diocese of Sydney and a later NSW Appeal Court judge. The independent members were I.M. Hunter, an Anglican, and Geoff Stevens, a prominent Baptist layman. Representing the pro-union group were the Reverend Jim Mathers, clerk of the NSW Presbyterian General Assembly, and a Mr Gough. The anti-unionists were Max Bradshaw and the Reverend Sam McCafferty, minister of the Ann Street Presbyterian Church in Brisbane.

Membership of the Commission carried a rider directed at those members and their alternates representing the anti-union camp: they may disapprove but they were nonetheless to allow that until such time as union formally occurred the Presbyterian Church of Australia would continue to be governed as before. The legal expression of this was ever likely to run the gauntlet of the courts. It took aim at a member who "refuses to acknowledge that until the Presbyterian Church of Australia enters into union

Fig. 1 The much-admired PLC Vice Principal, Miss Helen Hailes, who confronted Joan Montgomery as a schoolgirl: "Stand up and return to your classroom. Your position at PLC is in jeopardy!"

Fig. 2 Joan Montgomery (front right) in the 1940 School Sports Team and the year after Miss Hailes delivered her threat.

Fig. 3 The formidable F. Maxwell Bradshaw, who confronted Joan Montgomery and her two Vice Principals in May 1980 and offered her a 'golden handshake' to go early.

Fig. 4 Brian Bayston.

Fig. 5 Ted Pearsons.

Fig. 6 Joan Montgomery (left) and her two deputies, Jan Douglas (centre), Ev Tindale (right), present at the 7 May 1980 'golden handshake' meeting with Max Bradshaw and Ted Pearsons.

Fig. 7 Jan Douglas, PLC Vice Principal (1980-87).

Fig. 8 Ev Tindale, PLC Vice Principal (1980-85).

Fig. 9 Grandpa Hugh (Jnr) Montgomery arrived in Melbourne aboard the *Loch Long* on 3 January 1878 with his father Hugh Snr and his older brother Robert. He is nursing Joan.

Fig. 10 Joan's father, William Montgomery (far right), enlisted in the First AIF and was twice wounded.

Fig. 11 William Montgomery's and Beryl Rankin Harvey's marriage at the Free Presbyterian Church in East St Kilda on 10 June 1922.

Fig. 12 Joan with two of her younger sisters, Margaret (centre) and Elizabeth (right). Joan's youngest sister Helen was born in 1936, more than 10 years her junior.

Fig. 13 Joan had a flinty independence and strength of spirit which the arrival of her siblings merely affirmed.

Fig. 14 Joan (centre) with Loris McPherson and Loris' father Alec in Numurkah.

Fig. 15 William's salary included an allowance for a horse. But Joan remembered the car, a big "Dodge; later he had the first sedan in the district. Father was amused to be asked to drive a bride to her wedding."

Fig. 16 Bank of Australasia, Middle Brighton Branch, where William Montgomery became Manager in December 1936.

Fig. 17 Joan (right) during her year at Hampton High School.

Fig. 18 Joan (left) wearing PLC's new grey uniform.

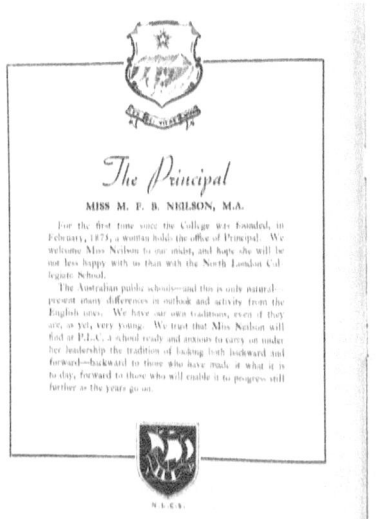 

Fig. 19 The December 1937 *Patchwork* announces Miss Mary F.B. Neilson's appointment as the first woman Principal since the school's founding in 1875. Joan would only know women Principals.

Fig. 20 Mary Neilson, Principal (1938-57), was the first woman to lead the school.

Fig. 21 Nora Wilkinson, PLC's inspiring geography teacher, taught there from 1928-66.

Fig. 22 Joan (left) in 1939 carrying the new sports uniform, folded and boxed, as Marjorie Cunningham stands beside her holding a baseball bat. The two were chosen to model the new sports uniform.

Fig. 23 Leaving House Captains, 1942. Joan sitting second from right.

Fig. 24 PLC Prefects, 1943. Joan sitting second from left.

Fig. 25 Val Turnball. First night "out", near Hastings, 13 July.

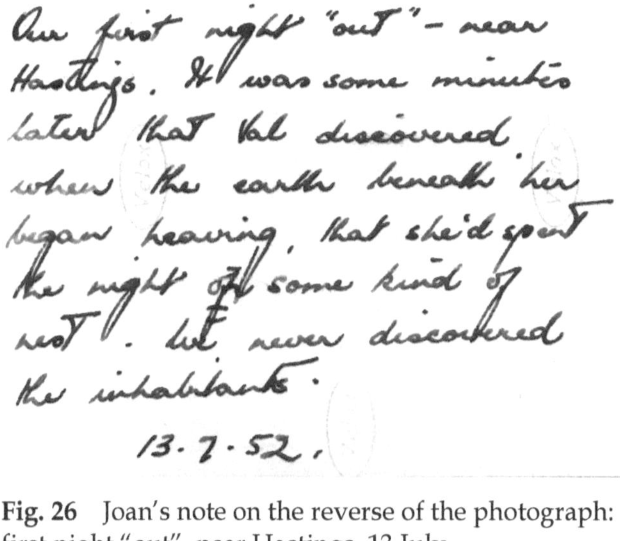

Our first night "out" – near Hastings. It was some minutes later that Val discovered, when the earth beneath her began heaving, that she'd spent the night on some kind of nest. But never discovered the inhabitants.

13.7.52.

Fig. 26 Joan's note on the reverse of the photograph: first night "out", near Hastings, 13 July.

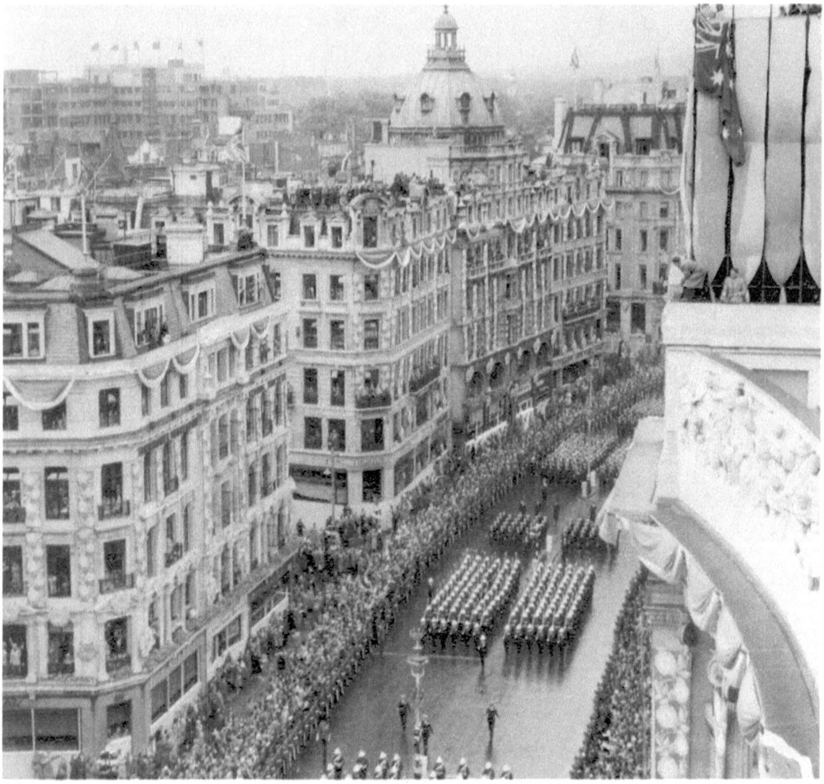

Fig. 27 Coronation Procession. Royal Marines, 2 June 1953.

Royal Marines in the
Coronation Procession,
marching down Regent St.
June 2nd. 1953.
(I was in back-row of
Stand in top R.H. corner !!)

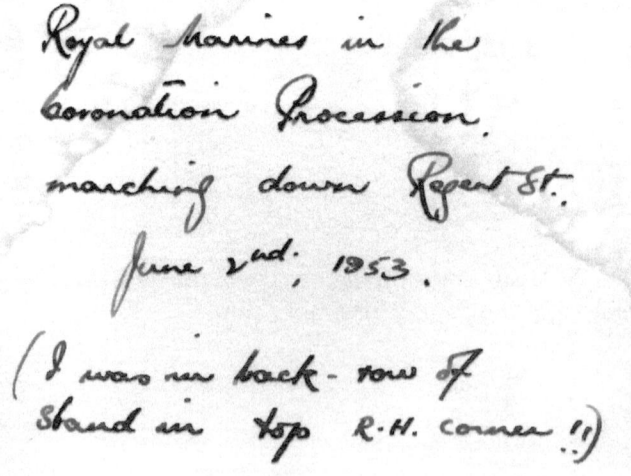

Fig. 28 Joan's description of the Coronation Procession on the reverse of the photograph.

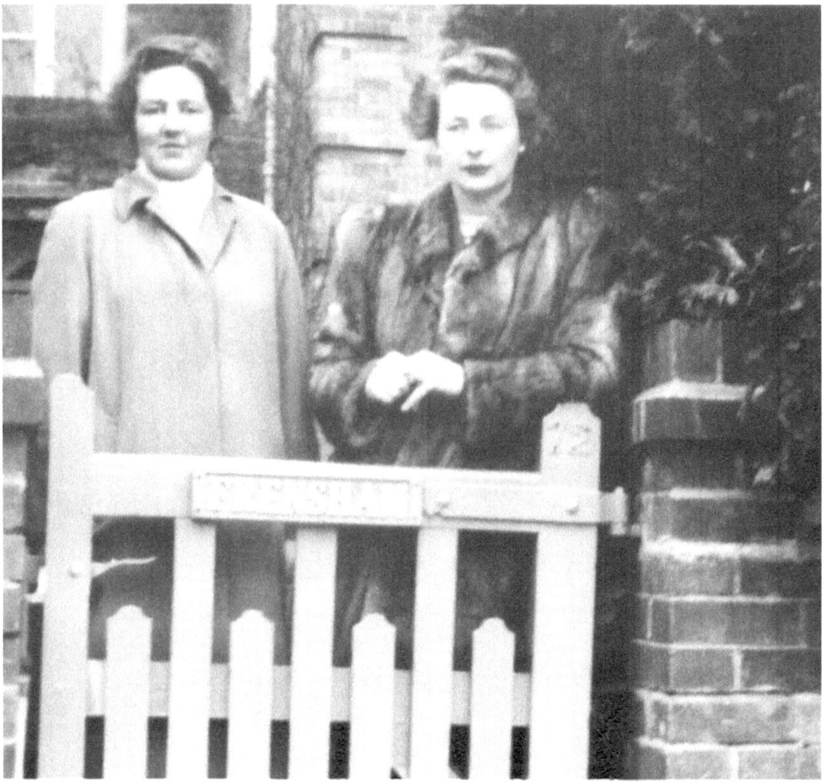

Fig. 29 Joan (left) with Barbara Broughton at Frensham, Surrey, UK.

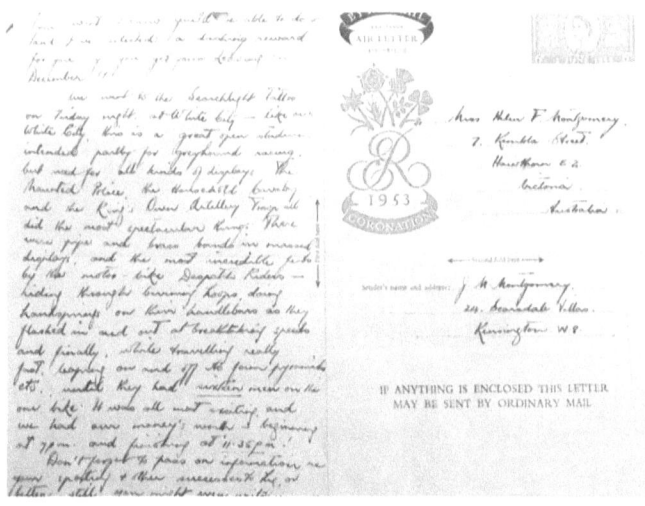

Fig. 30 One of hundreds of letters written home to Joan's sisters.

Fig. 31 The dark matted green "Ford Thames — 5 cwt. 12 model, lightest and cheapest on the road" purchased by Jean Ford (pictured) and Joan when they both taught at The Welsh Girls' School in Middlesex in 1958.

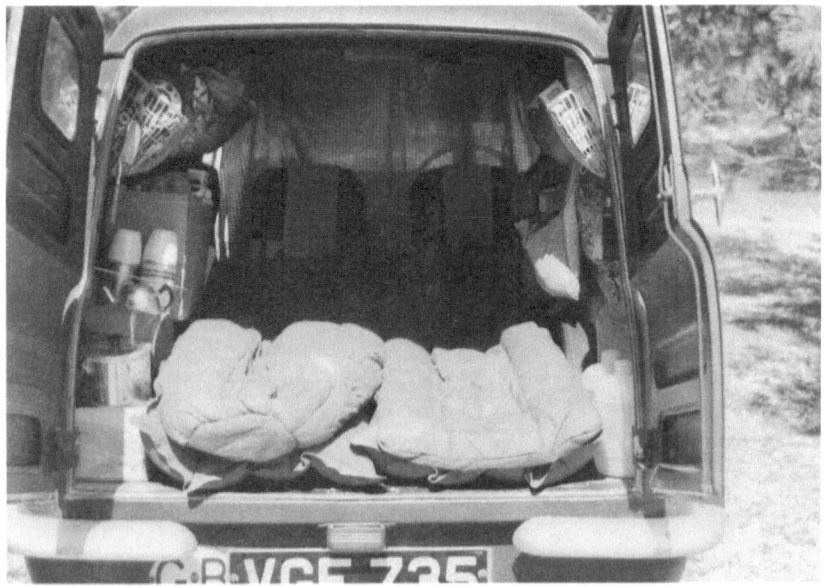

Fig. 32 "Li-Lo's, sleeping bags, bedding etc. require(d) much transferring of boxes, 19 bags etc."

on the 2nd day of June 1976 or such earlier or later date as is determined by the commission appointed it continues to function pursuant to its existing Constitution, its existing Basis of Union and existing Acts of Parliament." In that event, "then that person or persons shall cease to be members of this commission."

It was this last explosive nub that sparked the first of several court cases as the Presbyterian Church of Victoria Trust challenged the membership of Bradshaw and one of the anti-union alternate members, Charles Homer Fraser, citing their refusal to acknowledge the continuation of the Presbyterian Church as the General Assembly did.

The Trust case against Bradshaw and Fraser turned not only on their prominent role in the walkout from the Assembly meeting but also their leadership of the Presbyterian Church Association, which had declared that in the event the General Assembly voted in favour of union, the division of the Church "automatically took place and only those who disapproved of union would, from that time, constitute the Presbyterian Church of Australia." In essence, they asserted that from the moment a resolution in favour of union was passed, only those disapproving of union had the right and authority "to be, to manage and to control the Presbyterian Church of Australia."[22]

After a hearing in the Victorian Supreme Court, Justice Benjamin Dunn agreed with the arguments presented by the Trust and found that Bradshaw and Fraser ceased to be members of the Property Commission. In his ruling, Justice Dunn noted the intensity of emotion generated by the Presbyterian schism: "The feelings of its members were running high and displayed a somewhat intolerant and uncompromising outlook."[23] The judge also observed that not all of the people who were against the union were part of the Presbyterian Association, noting that while 82 members of the General Assembly had voted against union, only 20 to 30 joined the walkout from the General Assembly on 1 May 1974.

Two weeks after the decision was handed down, Bradshaw and Fraser lodged an appeal. At the Full Court hearing, Richard McGarvie QC, acting for the Trust, argued that the split had created three groups of Presbyterians. The first included those who approved union and who, if it eventuated, would join the Uniting Church. Then there were those who disapproved of union but saw themselves as part of the existing Presbyterian church which would remain until union, and then upon union would remain members of the "continuing" Presbyterian Church. The final group, including Bradshaw, were those who disapproved of union and represented themselves as the true Presbyterian Church of Australia that had separated from the others.

Justices Starke, McInerney and Newton determined that the proviso clause was invalid on technical ultra vires grounds and reinstated Bradshaw and Fraser to the Property Commission. Justice McInerney said the pair's argument "that the general assembly or those constituting the majority in the general assembly voting in favour of the resolution to enter into that union are by the very circumstances of the passing of that resolution to be deemed to have seceded from or separated out of the Presbyterian Church of Australia" was legally untenable. However, Justices Starke and Newton stated: "The question whether those views were legally or theologically right or wrong appears to be beside the point; we may however say that we regard it as a question of difficulty."[24]

So, from May 1974 through to the inauguration of the Uniting Church in June 1977, two rival Presbyterian Assemblies operated. When the Camberwell Group finally reclaimed control of Assembly Hall in Collins Street after union, they would have the last word — at least on the honour boards. Where the names of the moderators of the Presbyterian Church of Victoria are listed there are three obvious changes. In the last three years before union, the moderators elected by the Presbyterian majority were Donald

Macrae (1974 and 1975) and Farquhar Gunn (1976). Now, in an obviously different shade, the name claiming the authority in each of those years is W.A. Loftus—Bill Loftus, the minister of Camberwell Presbyterian Church and the man elected Moderator by the Camberwell Group. Bob Thomas would claim that steel wool was used to rewrite history.

What could not be so easily painted over were the personal rifts that flowed from the Presbyterian split. It had been Bill Loftus who invited Ray Northrop to succeed him on the PLC Council. Indeed, they remained good friends until union sealed their differences, with Northrop being appointed Procurator in place of Max Bradshaw after the walkout. Late in 1974, in a letter tinged with nostalgia and regret for times that could never be again, sent from Trinity Manse in Waterloo Street, Camberwell, Loftus wrote to Northrop as chairman of the PLC Council: "My wife and I were deeply touched by the gift of such beautiful flowers and your expression of goodwill and affection. Please convey to the members of the Council our appreciation. It has been an honour and a pleasure to have served on the PLC Council and to have been associated with so many who give their time and skill to the progress of the College."[25] As if looking back on a train wreck and tying to imagine a better future, he ends hopefully: "I trust that the difficulties which are now facing the Council will be happily resolved and that girls of many families in many circumstances will enjoy the privilege of a PLC education."

Loftus's views about union had obviously changed from the time when he first encouraged Ray Northrop to join the Council. Northrop believes Max Bradshaw was instrumental in turning Loftus from a supporter of union to one of the principal opponents. The two men knew each other well, both within the Presbyterian leadership and through the Victorian Bar where Northrop's practice, like Bradshaw's, involved a specialist knowledge of charitable trusts. Church union and PLC governance certainly put them at personal and professional odds when it came to PLC litigation involving the Presbyterian Trust of Victoria and a full-blooded skirmish about charitable trust principles that they both knew so well.

Northrop would be opposed to Max in another trust case. Still savouring the victory years later, he would recall: "Max sat in the court with his own notebook with every legal authority written up in it on charitable trusts, which he would cite from in argument in his case. But while he knew every detail of every case, he never understood the general principles themselves."[26] In Northrop's view, Bradshaw never truly understood the difference between charitable trusts and ordinary trusts and misunderstood the early church cases of Scotland, upon which he relied in arguing the Australian situation. He cites the High Court decision in *Attorney-General (NSW) v Grant ('Presbyterian Church case')*[27] as confirming his view that the General Assembly in Scotland had different rules to the Presbyterian Church in Australia. And he claims High Court judge and later chief justice Sir Harry Gibbs told him privately that Bradshaw was wrong. But whether right or wrong, when it came to their respective corners on PLC, Max Bradshaw always seemed to be one step ahead.

·······

The General Assembly vote in May 1974 came as Kathleen Fitzpatrick was finalising *PLC Melbourne: The First Century 1875-1975*, a book commissioned by the PLC Council. Fitzpatrick ended her narrative, as Ray Northrop would later remind the Property Commission, with the following forecast regarding the relationship between the school and the Presbyterian Church:

> Present in the background, today as ever, is the Presbyterian Church. As we have seen, PLC was one of the fruits of the happy union between

formerly separate branches of the church and when this book was planned, in 1972, it seemed probable that it would end, as it began, with the glad tidings of a wider union still. So, in a sense it does, for in 1976 a United Church will come into existence formed by Presbyterians, Methodists and Congregationalists. But the Basis of Union, which seemed so firm when it was laid in 1859 and for so long afterwards, has given way under the stress of changing times and some Presbyterians, fearing the loss of identity for their church, are not willing to form part of the Uniting Church and propose to remain as the Continuing Church. At the time of writing (1974) it is not possible to say just how PLC will be affected by these new arrangements. But all Presbyterians are united in pride in their great schools and we feel confident that as all desire to ensure their continuance and well-being, this will be effected, although no one can yet say precisely how.[28]

Precisely how was the work of the Property Commission, with the dispute over its make-up already the trigger for two cases in the Supreme Court of Victoria. With the challenges to Max Bradshaw and Charles Homer Fraser ultimately unsuccessful the Property Commission had now to determine the division of Presbyterian Church property between the major branch of the Church that had chosen union and the Continuing Presbyterians who opposed it. That division would start the chain of events that would end with Joan Montgomery's forced retirement as Principal of PLC.

The PLC School Council had been given an opportunity to state its position before the Property Commission set to work. In November 1974 the General Assembly of the uniting Presbyterian majority asked the Council to answer to the following question: "Does your Council desire your school to be vested in the Presbyterian Church of Victoria continuing to function after the inauguration of the Uniting Church in Australia?"[29] Meeting in February 1975, the Council resolved its answer was 'No' and responded accordingly. It would be an answer that carried little weight in the view of the Property Commission, as events unfolded.

After the school launched its centenary celebrations with a visit from the Governor of Victoria, Sir Henry Winneke, and Lady Winneke, Joan Montgomery received many letters of congratulation, including one from a parent, Mrs Jenny Pring: "My husband Jim and I wish to thank you, the chairman and members of Council for the memorable and enjoyable occasion of the Opening of the Centenary Celebrations. It was, as have been the subsequent celebrations, a great opportunity to travel back in memory to our own days in our great old school. We were, as are our daughters today, greatly privileged to have been members of this great school's community."[30]

The warmth of the letter to "Dear Miss Montgomery" would be fleeting. Jenny Pring would soon emerge as a determined adversary of the Principal and an implacable supporter of the Continuing Presbyterian Church. Like many of the critics, she was dismayed at the changes beginning to transform schools across Australia, including PLC. As the school's historian Kathleen Fitzpatrick would describe it, there was a broader societal "rebellion of modern youth against the mores of the past" and this called for some adjustment. While common to all schools of the period, it was of particular concern to girls' schools as, in the view of Fitzpatrick and many others, "perhaps the most important changes at present proceeding in affluent societies such as ours is a revolt of the women, on an absolutely unprecedented scale, against the position assigned them in society." Noting that PLC was founded partly in response to this movement in its "demand for the higher education of women in the wealthier classes of society," she continued: "Now, at the Centenary celebrations, one hundred years later the College was sharing with schools for girls of all classes, the logical outcome of the movement for the emancipation of women, which is no longer merely a demand for the right to work outside the home but also the right to earn as much as their brothers and to enjoy the same liberty in their personal lives."

PLC had arrived in the age when women believed that "no solution is acceptable which compels young women to choose between the role of mothers and that of free human beings."[31]

Jenny Pring was not amused. An Old Collegian, she had finished at East Melbourne in 1939 when Joan was in her second year at PLC. She was born Janet Mabel Patrick, the name she used on the paperwork when she later became a member of the School Council in 1982. Two PLC initiatives would stir her opposition to Joan Montgomery's "agenda" as she would describe it—the Human Relations program (dealing with sex education) and the Liberal Studies program. In Pring's view, Joan had a strategy to change the values of the school and convert the girls from Christian to Humanist, "not to mention Marxist!"[32]

For Pring, those two initiatives, "removed the girls' respect for their parents' values" and gave them the sense that they were "free to have their own views." This was "damaging to families" and the Liberal Studies course also led to a heavy workload for the girls, given its compulsory nature. Joan Montgomery had given those parents who had misgivings about its compulsory nature an opportunity to come and speak about them in advance. This may have satisfied some of the parents, but not Jenny Pring who felt it was not an authentic opportunity to take on board the parents' views.

Camberwell Grammar Principal David Dyer, whose daughter Sarah was also a student around that time, was also dubious about the Liberal Studies course, and sent his wife along to the information evening. Joan saw she had a prepared question in her hands. When it came time for questions, Mrs Dyer raised her hand and Joan could tell she didn't enjoy getting up to speak. Joan needed her to repeat the question because it was difficult to hear. When she asked whether it had to be compulsory, Joan told her it did and Mrs Dyer sat down: "To his credit, David Dyer later had the grace to write to me to say his daughter thought it was a wonderful course and one of the best learning experiences she had."

Parents with concerns were in the minority and the courses, while not designed by Joan, reflected one of her strengths. She encouraged teachers to be innovative and creative — and to take the initiative in their teaching and their own leadership. She gathered the best teachers and gave them the confidence to lead themselves. At least five of her staff would go on to become headmistresses themselves — Jan Douglas to Mentone Girls Grammar, Ruth Bunyan to Strathcona, Deborah Seifert to Fintona, Pam Chessell to Shelford and Barbara Fairy to Camberwell Girls Grammar.

The Liberal Studies course reflected what Kathleen Fitzpatrick described more broadly as a "quiet revolution" in pedagogic methods across the State and the academic curriculum in the 1970s at PLC. Joan's 1970 annual report had referred to an increase in self-instruction either in small groups or individually. This was seen as enhancing independence in learning and assisting the transition from school to higher education. It was coupled with other new initiatives such as self-government for the students, including meeting with senior students from other schools to discuss issues of common interest.

The Liberal Studies Course was launched in 1973 and was compulsory for all Fifth Form students who spent seven classes a week on it. While "an extremely interesting experiment," it was no flip offering but the product of two years' work by a Planning Committee convened by Sophie Borland, an experienced educator who had started teaching at PLC during Miss Neilson's term as Principal. Borland was a former Principal at St Catherine's School, and head of staff for many years at PLC. It was described as a course of study of the social, economic, political and technological changes in modern industrial society and the implications of these changes for the life of the individual in society. Its pedagogical innovation was its integration of subject matter and methods of approach—what would now be called an interdisciplinary course—covering English, History, Geography, Social Studies, Economics, Religious Education and Biology.

In the 1983 Senior School Speech Night booklet Joan reported on "a voluntary meeting of more than one hundred 1982 Year 12 students who had undertaken the course in 1981". The meeting had "recommended overwhelmingly that Liberal Studies be retained as a compulsory subject. This vote was expressed on the basis that the course raised serious questions about man, his purpose, his humanity, his basic nature, his social values and future, providing a context for discussion of important issues which are either not tackled, or not tackled with the same emphases in other subjects." Steeped in language that was unlikely to upset the patriarchy, it showed nonetheless that Joan was a cautious and respectful moderniser who inched things along without inflammatory discourse. To some, however, the whole notion of Liberal Studies was inflammatory. Liberal Studies was symbolic and concerns about it reflected an overall conservatism when responding to broader changes in society.

In her history, Kathleen Fitzpatrick noted the enthusiasm of Don Crofts, the then Vice Principal, for the course and the broader delight being taken by the teachers involved. It was also explained positively in the student publication *Quidnunc* where the learning process in the subject was described as "encouraging a lively involvement in a variety of educational activities—looking, listening, reading, assessing, meditating, talking and writing."

In 1975, with the Liberal Studies course well established, the

Schools Commission released *Girls, School and Society* produced by the Committee on Social Change and the Education of Women.[33] As Alison Mackinnon has commented, the committee membership reads today like a *Who's Who* of women's education and feminism.[34] Chaired by Ken McKinnon, Chair of the Schools Commission, it was led by Jean Blackburn and included other leading lights such as the sociologist Jean Martin, Elizabeth Reid (women's advisor to Prime Minister Gough Whitlam), Susan Ryan (later Minister for Education and the first Labor woman in Federal Cabinet) and Daniela Torsch—all of whom were or became prominent in women's educational policy and writing. In addition, an appendix lists consultants and research assistants employed on the report including Clare Burton, Teresa Brennan, Eva Cox, Wendy McCarthy and Anne Summers.

Deliberately using the language of the time, McKinnon would write that "clearly many leaders of the women's movement saw education as a key to women's liberation". Urging implementation of the report's recommendations, he added: "Australian schools will be better equipped to educate women and men so that they are both competent, high in self-esteem, self-reliant, independent and equally capable of cooperation, empathy and social interaction ... We believe that it is only if we educate men and women equally that we can achieve a democratic society where women and men regard and act towards each other as equals."[35]

PLC had been at the forefront of doing just this—as the first school set up in 1875 to provide equal education for women. But women like Jenny Pring, while proud of their school, were unhappy with its philosophy—a belief in women's equality in all aspects of life. Those discomforted by that concept were more likely to be aligned to the Continuing Presbyterian Church and would come to see Joan as part of a progressive movement that they abhorred.

Jenny Pring's "Marxist" slight against Joan presumably arose from Joan's two visits to China as part of Heads of School delegations—first in 1976 and again in 1982. She spoke to PLC staff about the experiences and acknowledged that two short visits to China did not make her an expert and her reflections were necessarily superficial. And while visiting China at two tumultuous times—during the Cultural Revolution and in the early stages of the country's reopening under Deng Xiaoping—made a vivid impression on the visiting Principal, there was no evidence of a political conversion.

In 1976, Chairman Mao still dominated the public sphere with the huge portraits in airports, railways stations and schools. But whatever the posters claimed, Mao was not immortal, and at the very moment the visitors were being entertained at a lunar festival party on their hotel roof in Guilin on 9 September 1976, Mao died. When his death was announced the next afternoon, the effect was remarkable. While the visitors spoke no Chinese, they witnessed genuine grieving as people huddled around transistor radios and listened to solemn music. Joan and her colleagues were due to fly out at 6.30pm but the hotel staff were so devastated that it felt almost indecent to think of eating and organising their departure. On finally reaching the airport, they waited several hours while messages of condolence were broadcast from each city and province. The symbolism was not lost on the group when a huge red moon rose into the night sky above the darkened Guilin airport.

Six years later, in 1982, the delegation toured educational institutions from crèches to universities. The changes since the previous visit were obvious. The long political introductions at every occasion had disappeared; the farm labourer with his worn hands and broken nails no longer was seen at universities and schools. And the older men and women who had been missing in 1976 were about again. Two of the Directors of Education they met were women. Some of the people who had been publicly humiliated during the Cultural Revolution were back, including the middle school principal who had been made to walk the streets in a dunce's hat and others who had been sent to the country for some years. One principal had been under virtual house arrest for ten years. And this didn't only apply to the world of education. A wonderful concert in Beijing included a fine baritone who had been confined for five years while his accompanist had been banished to work in the fields for ten years and forbidden to touch the piano.

While Joan's conclusion from her travels was that few Australians would want to live in China due to the lack of privacy and personal freedom, not to mention the communist ideology, she did observe: "If we were able to combine all the advantages we experience with the sense of purpose and dedication of the Chinese, then what a wonderful country Australia would be!" Was this "Red Joan" speaking, as Jenny Pring would have it, or Joan Montgomery OBE accidental tourist in the world's most populous country visiting as part of a Heads of School delegation?

Joan was appointed an Officer of the Most Excellent Order of the British Empire on 12 June 1976. The citation would declare: "In recognition of her valuable services as Headmistress of the Presbyterian Ladies' College and education." The OBE was also a badge of honour for the school and delighted members of the School Council, as it prepared to face the challenging fallout from church union.

After the unsuccessful challenge to the membership of the Property Commission, in October 1976 the Council resolved to make a written submission to the Property Commission explaining why the ownership of PLC should not be vested in the Continuing Presbyterian Church of Victoria. That submission began by acknowledging that the Commission had been empowered to allocate to the Continuing Presbyterians after union "at least one school for girls ... where at the date of the said union there is more than one Presbyterian school for girls." But while noting there were multiple girls' schools: "This power does not necessarily require that one existing school for girls in Victoria shall vest in the continuing Presbyterian Church, particularly where, as in the case of PLC, the Church provides no finance for either the providing or maintaining of the school. PLC is financed solely from fees charged to parents of pupils, government grants and gifts."

In support of the argument that a new school could be established in the name of the Continuing Presbyterian Church, the submission took the Commission through the regulations covering the duties of the School Council and the Principal's powers, emphasising that while the "Council of the College is a committee of the General Assembly of the Presbyterian Church of Victoria ... it exercises its powers with a large degree of independence." Moreover, the School was financially independent from the Presbyterian Church of Victoria.

In conclusion the submission said that given the history and nature of the school, the absence of any congregation of the Continuing Presbyterian Church in close proximity and the school's financial independence, the Property Commission "should not, in the exercise of its discretion, determine that the Presbyterian Ladies' College be retained by the Presbyterian Church." And—in a clear signal that it was keeping its legal options open—the Council added the words: "Even if it had the power to do so".

While the School Council was taking up the fight to prevent the school being handed over to Continuing Presbyterians, Joan was monitoring matters on the sidelines. On 16 March 1977, before the Uniting Church was inaugurated and before the Property Commission had made its determination, she sent a memo to Council Chair Ray Northrop and John McArthur, now a Council member and a pro-union alternate member of the Commission. She reported on a recent meeting of Heads of Presbyterian Schools in Victoria where it had been generally accepted that incorporation was the right move for schools. Further debate had centred on whether this should be under the Companies Act or by private Act of Parliament: "I contributed nothing to the meeting, since I felt this discussion seemed one for Councils rather than school Heads, but there was no doubt that most schools favoured very strongly a readiness for incorporation as soon as their fate was decided." Attached to the memo was a Private Act of Incorporation of Scotch College Adelaide, sent to Joan "since PLC's Council would appear to be the only one which has not had full debate on the matter."

By 11 May 1977, six months after submitting the Council's submission to the Property Commission, Northrop wrote as Council chair to the Right Reverend Farquhar Gunn, Secretary of the Property Commission, based at Assembly Hall in Collins St. This was an important letter—the Property Commission had deferred making its decision concerning PLC Burwood and the PLC Council felt it "desirable that a Supplementary Submission be presented on behalf of the College."

The four-page submission began by pointing out that the High Court had recently determined that the Continuing Presbyterian Church was not the Presbyterian Church of Australia.[36] In Northrop's view, the High Court had made it clear that Max Bradshaw's views were not correct regarding the impact of union on the Church.

The submission highlighted the 1869 decision of the General Assembly of the Presbyterian Church to consider establishing the school, noting that the Assembly at that time represented the "uniting churches" rather than those congregations that did not join in with the other Presbyterian congregations in Victoria "which in 1859 purported to reign true to the faith of their fathers."

The document went on to discuss the position of Bill Loftus, who had been elected Moderator by the Continuing Presbyterians after the General Assembly walkout in May 1974. It pointed out that he, Loftus, refused to attend meetings of the PLC Council from that time, although continuing to receive notices and minutes of meetings. When his term expired in October 1976, he was not re-nominated. The submission further noted that the Church made no financial provision for PLC. Rather, the school's future depended upon the community's demand for it and that if control were vested in "a minority of the existing membership of the Presbyterian Church of Victoria, there will no longer be available the wide range of persons with expert experience in education and business so necessary to serve on the Council of PLC." This, in Northrop's view, "would lead to a situation where PLC would cease to be a financial institution." The Council ended its plea with an emotive appeal: "It would be a travesty of justice if the control of the largest Presbyterian Church school for girls in Victoria was awarded to a minority of members of the existing Presbyterian Church of Victoria, particularly when, in the past, members of that minority group have not shown any particular interest in the management of the school."

It would soon be clear that these words had fallen on deaf ears.

9

RUINED

On 21 May 1977, the sword fell. Ten days after receiving Ray Northrop's letter and dumb to its wishes, the Property Commission determined that Scotch College and Presbyterian Ladies' College would be awarded to the Continuing Church and all the other schools in Victoria would be awarded to the Uniting Church.

Commission chairman Ken Handley QC called the chairmen of each of the school Councils. Ray Northrop, as PLC Council chair, listened as Handley informed him of the decision. Usually measured in what he said, Northrop's response was blistering: "You've just ruined the best girls' school in Australia, that's what I told him; just destroyed the best girls' school in Australia."[1]

The Commission had considered various submissions including a letter Max Bradshaw had sent to Handley after Northrop had written to Farquhar Gunn, the Commission's secretary, raising issues that the Presbyterians might like to address. Both letters were attached to a letter Northrop received from the Presbyterian Church of Victoria after the Commission's decision. Bradshaw's letter, dated 28 April, purrs with how reasonable the Presbyterian Church would be when it had control over PLC: "It must act with restraint and avoid any action that may be deemed to be at all provocative."

Actions would indeed speak louder than words. According to Brian Bayston, on a rainy day soon after the decision was confirmed, Bradshaw took a stroll around Ormond College at

Melbourne University, home of the Presbyterian Theological Hall. His appearance would alarm George Yule, Professor of Church History and an ardent advocate of union. "George didn't ask me why I was here, and I didn't tell him," Bradshaw would later tell Bayston, to their mutual amusement. The Ormond staff were effectively being put on notice that the Theological Hall was also vulnerable (Ultimately, the Ormond campus would be retained by the Uniting Church and the Continuing Presbyterians would create their own in Hawthorn).

The chairs of both the Scotch and PLC School Councils immediately sent a telegram to the Property Commission requesting reasons for its decision to award the schools to the Continuing Church—a first step towards mounting a legal challenge. By 17 June, Northrop had received a reply from the "Stated Clerk" informing him that the Commission had "unanimously resolved not to give reasons", with a PS at the end: "This also applies to Scotch College."

A few days before the Property Commission's decision, Joan was admitted as a Fellow of the Australian College of Education at the college's annual conference in Adelaide. The event was officially open by South Australian Lieutenant Governor Walter Crocker after a welcome from Justice Roma Mitchell, the state's first woman judge. Former PLC Principal Ruby Powell was also present. Of the 31 fellows admitted, seven were women and five of those were listed as Miss, one was a Mrs and one was a Dr. It was indicative of an era for women in which a professional life often precluded marriage. The citation for Joan's fellowship would recognise her "leadership as the principal of two schools and in the work and development of independent schools in Victoria and for valuable contributions to committees concerned with the development of education in Victoria in which understanding and cooperation between the Education Department and non-State schools are of importance."

Soon after her return from Adelaide, Joan attended a special meeting of the PLC Council on 2 June 1977 where it was resolved to obtain advice from Brian Shaw QC and Ross Sundberg on the legality of the Property Commission's decision. That advice was reviewed when Council next met on 16 June and concluded that it was necessary "for the welfare of the College that legal proceedings be instituted." To initiate the case, the Council needed a PLC parent to act as a plaintiff with the Council indemnifying them for any costs. The chairman and treasurer were authorised to instruct Mallesons solicitors and requested to keep the Council informed at subsequent meetings.

Proceedings were swiftly issued in the Supreme Court of Victoria on 21 June 1977 (No 3272 of 1997). Given the action involved a charitable trust, the Victorian Attorney-General was required to be involved as a form of "authorising" the action. The plaintiff would be John Thomson Macmillan, the husband of Helen Macmillan, an Old Collegian who graduated as Helen MacGibbon in 1949. Their daughters were students Sue (1980) and Wendy (1986). The defendants were the members and alternate members of the Property Commission.

The writ identified the Property Commission resolution No 287 of 21 May 1977 which resolved to: "Award the Presbyterian Ladies' College Melbourne to the Continuing Church on the condition that those members of the existing Council who desire to continue to serve after June 22nd 1977 are to continue in office until the close of the General Assembly of the Presbyterian Church of Victoria in 1979 and that the existing regulations of the General Assembly of Victoria, requiring a certain percentage of the membership of the Council to be communicant members of the Presbyterian Church of Victoria be amended as soon as possible to remove this requirement in relation to existing members of the Council."

Macmillan, by his statement of claim delivered with the writ, sought declarations that the Property Commission award was void, that the Presbyterian Church was not entitled to PLC pursuant to the award and that the award was ineffectual to vest in the Presbyterian Church of Victoria PLC or any of the items of property or assets held by the Presbyterian Church of Victoria Trusts Corporation for the purposes of PLC.

The following day—22 June 1977—the Uniting Church in Australia was born. In ceremonies broadcast live on ABC television, church leaders walked to the Lyceum Theatre in Sydney where the formal vote was taken to marry the vast majority of Australia's Methodist, Congregationalist and Presbyterian congregations. In a poignant moment, Farquhar Gunn, the Victorian Presbyterian Moderator and chair of the Joint Constitution Commission on Church Union, felt "aye" was an inadequate response to the historic vote and led an unaccompanied singing of the Doxology, "Praise God from whom all blessings flow ... ".

That evening, the Sydney Town Hall was packed for celebrations led by the Reverend Dr Philip Potter, general secretary of the World Council of Churches. Victorian Governor Sir Henry Winneke wished the newlyweds well: "The Church is the servant of God, certainly. But surely the church is no less the servant of all mankind. In your life together may you have the faith and courage to live out that dual concept." The secretary of the Joint Commission, the Reverend Dr D'Arcy Wood, would later write: "Despite the sadness of a sizeable minority of Presbyterians staying out of the union, there was great enthusiasm for the new church. It was a moment of renewal, a movement of the people, and, I believe, a movement of the Holy Spirit."[2]

But the celebrations would be short-lived for the community of PLC in Melbourne. Five days after the inauguration, Ray Northrop, as School Council chairman, sent the first letter to parents briefing them on the legal action: "On the 22nd June 1977 the Presbyterian Church of Australia entered into union with the Congregational and Methodist churches to establish the Uniting

Church in Australia. Thereafter, in the absence of any valid determination by the property commission previously constituted by the General Assembly of the Presbyterian Church of Australia, Presbyterian Ladies' College would have been under the control of the Uniting Church. The property commission, however, treating the College as property only, had purported to award the College to the Continuing Presbyterian Church of Victoria." Northrop pointed out that PLC's founders had sought to define the school's autonomy. When the Church finally moved forward with its report in 1869 on establishing PLC it intended "to assume only a limited financial responsibility for the Ladies' College. It would provide the site, build the school and a residence for the Principal, and give the advice and backing of the Church, but the school was to be self-supporting."[3] He said the Council was compelled to take legal action in an attempt to block the Property Commission's decision: "The College is an educational institution. It is not merely property to be awarded to any group without any consideration for those persons being pupils, staff, parents and friends, who together constitute the school community. The view that the College is no more than property of the Church is unsound since the Church does not, and never had, contributed to the capital costs or maintenance of the College nor does it receive any financial benefit from the College."

Soon after the decision was taken to launch legal proceedings, a confidential document was prepared to guide coordinated action to safeguard the independence of all of the former Presbyterian schools by seeking their incorporation. The "preliminary statement of case" was drafted by Davis McCaughey, the newly installed president of the new Uniting Church national assembly; the Reverend Professor Robert Anderson, Principal of the former Presbyterian and now Uniting Church Theological Hall; and the Reverend H.R. (Bert) Stevens, Principal of Penleigh and Essendon Grammar School. It would be distributed to the principals and school Council chairs of nine schools: Ballarat & Clarendon College, Penleigh and Essendon Grammar, The Geelong College, Haileybury, Hamilton College, Morongo Girls' College and St Leonard's, as well as PLC and Scotch College.

The document proposed: "Should the nine schools be able to agree on the form of government desired, an approach would be made by them jointly to both the Presbyterian Assembly and the Uniting Synod in October 1978, asking those two bodies to support an approach to the Attorney-General to put the proposal into effect." In the event that approach failed, it continued: "We should still put the proposal before the Attorney-General with as widespread support from the constituencies of all the schools as can be mustered." The authors were using the same Scotch College Adelaide model that Joan had earlier sent to Ray Northrop.

As an ex officio member of School Council, Joan was well aware of all details of the battle unfolding over PLC's ownership. Her focus, however, had to be on the day-to-day running of the school and her role as Principal. The letters in her files for the period are a time capsule of ordinary concerns: correcting information held by the Commission of Public Health about numbers of toilets, washing and drinking facilities at the College and reporting on the new hot drink machine in the foyer to the tuckshop. (In less than three days, it sold about 900 cups of coffee and hot chocolate prompting the comment: "The suppliers are such engaging and efficient young men that I hope their honesty is equally acceptable.") Joan authorised the use of Wyselaskie Hall by the First Church of Christ for a lecture and thanked the outgoing medical doctor for 20 years' service. She wrote to solicitors who had sent news of a bequest: "Legacies to girls' schools are rare, and therefore all the more appreciated."

But the legal battle was already casting a long shadow. On 16 June 1977, Joan received a personal note from School Council member Farquhar Gunn, who was conflicted as both a founding father of the Uniting Church and secretary of the Property Commission: "I rang your Secretary to tell her that I would be glad to conduct the service on the 17th July. I have just learned that PLC is joining Scotch in the action against the Property Commission. As I shall be one of the defendants in the action (though purely a nominal one) I feel I cannot conduct the service and suggest that you ask Donald Macrae to do so. I am very sorry indeed about this."

A month later, the Continuing Presbyterian Church began to make its presence felt. Joan received a letter from the Reverend Ted Pearsons, Clerk of the General Assembly of the Presbyterian Church of Victoria, advising her of the Assembly's forthcoming meeting, on 4 October: "Traditionally the schools have submitted a brief report of the activities of the school during the previous year for inclusion in the Assembly white book." Joan would duly submit a six-paragraph report — before Ray Northrop intervened.

After becoming aware of the exchange, Northrop wrote to Pearsons to correct his apparent "misapprehension" regarding school reports. He curtly explained that it was the School Council's responsibility to submit annual reports to the General Assembly and its report had been delivered on 14 June 1977 — a week before the Uniting Church inauguration — and a copy of that report was in the White Book of the State General Assembly of June 1977 at pages 23-24. Moreover, the brief report Joan had sent Pearsons, "is not and cannot be regarded as a formal report of the activities of the Presbyterian Ladies' College or as a report, annual or otherwise of the Council, PLC." After receiving a copy of the correspondence from Northrop, Joan wrote back to him apologising for her "thoughtless naivety." But Joan's self-described naivety on church matters would be short-lived, as the fight for control of PLC gathered momentum.

……

Vetting of Wisdom

In April 1977, Joan Montgomery had begun preparing to appoint a new headmistress in the Junior School. Mrs D.G.M. Flynn was about to reach the extended and mandatory retirement age for PLC staff. In June, parents were advised that Mrs Flynn would finish at the end of Term 1 the following year and that a replacement would be appointed. There was discontent expressed by some parents. Max Bradshaw was known to be a great fan of Mrs Flynn.

Late in November, Ray Northrop received a letter from Mrs Jowett, president of the Junior School Parents' Association, on behalf of "an increasing number" of parents "concerned" about Mrs Flynn's impending retirement. It referred to her "outstanding leadership" and included a signed petition requesting that the Council approach Mrs Flynn to stay on.

Northrop was happy to refer the material to the School Council but as it was not due to meet until the following February, he wrote to Mrs Jowett expressing his personal opinion and raising two issues of "vital importance to the welfare and education standards" of PLC: "Firstly, the Principal has the sole responsibility of appointing members of staff including the headmistress of the Junior School. Not only would it be wrong in principle for the College Council to interfere with this right of the Principal, but any interference could result in the College Council purporting to exercise powers over educational matters in which it has no qualifications to exercise judgment." He pointed out that all members of staff were appointed on terms with a specified retirement age. This avoided "any unpleasantness in deciding whether any particular teacher should be dismissed or requested to resign because of advancing age" and also allowed for staff renewal. He noted that Mrs Flynn's had already been extended by Miss Montgomery beyond the normal date of retirement "but she has now reached the second specified age where retirement is mandatory and cannot be extended."[4]

Mrs Flynn's position was advertised with a starting date of

Term 2 of 1978. Late in December 1977, after receiving applications, conducting interviews and making extensive enquiries, Joan offered the position to June Stratford, Headmistress of the Junior School at Melbourne Girls Grammar School (Morris Hall), who accepted in early January 1978. Through the summer, forces were readying in the Continuing Presbyterian world to scrutinise every move by Joan and PLC.

When the 1978 School Year began on Tuesday 7 February, June Stratford was still at Melbourne Girls Grammar. It is there that she received a letter from a stranger that would cast her at centre stage in the fight over the future of PLC. The typewritten, one-page letter dated 9 February was signed by Lilian Ganderton, of Murrumbeena. It was an epistolary hand grenade bent on blowing up Stratford's new position, if not that of the woman who had appointed her.

Describing herself as a person "completely unknown to you" and with "nothing to do with the running of the school or the Presbyterian Church," Ganderton referred to the legal challenge to the Property Commission's determination on the ownership of PLC and declared that "scarcely anyone thinks the litigation has any prospect of success." She then offered Stratford some gratuitous advice: "Before you resign your present position you may make some contact with the Presbyterian Church. That church is probably aware of a petition from Junior School parents that no change be made at the present time to the Headmistress of the Junior School and could well feel that an attempt is being made 'to beat the gun'." The letter concluded: "It would seem pretty clear that Miss Montgomery would leave the school when the Presbyterian Church's position is ratified, and I wonder what your position would be then?"[5]

Lilian Ganderton had voted to stay Presbyterian. She would claim that her minister at Murrumbeena had refused to allow one of the Continuing Presbyterians to come and speak to the congregation, so she switched to St Giles in Caulfield. While she had no connection with PLC, others at Caulfield, including the minister's wife, did and they encouraged her to write her provocative letter to June Stratford. "Maybe then I had my part to play in the school staying Presbyterian," she would later boast.

Lilian Ganderton may have acted as a freelance provocateur, but soon the professionals would join the fray. On 3 March, Ted Pearsons, the Presbyterian Assembly Clerk, wrote to June Stratford regarding her "purported appointment as Headmistress of the Junior School of the Presbyterian Ladies' College." It began in benevolent tone: "I write out of concern for your possible future employment by the Presbyterian Church of Victoria and School of the Presbyterian Ladies' College." Then came the sting in tail: "I would be failing in my duty as Clerk of the General Assembly if I did not draw these facts to your attention and caution you that the General Assembly will not be bound to honour your purported appointment by persons who had no authority to do so."

On 20 March, after learning that the PLC Council had confirmed Stratford's appointment, Pearsons again wrote to her, and dropped the kid gloves. His purpose was now, "to inform you that the General Assembly of the Presbyterian Church of Victoria will not tolerate an unauthorised appointment ... In the face of this intimation should you persist in attempting to take up the position you cannot look for payment of salary from the authorised funds of the Presbyterian Church of Victoria and must look for any payment from the individual members of the School Council."

Copies of the letter were also sent to Joan Montgomery and Ray Northrop. Unhappy about Pearsons' intervention, the School Council sought legal advice from barristers Shaw and Sundberg on whether to sue on the strength of the letters. Their strong advice was not to while concluding: "We have considered the circumstances of Mrs Stratford's appointment and we think that it is valid." Jean Stratford began work as the new head of the PLC Junior School as agreed at the start of second term, 30 May 1978.

She had received further letters from anonymous and named senders beforehand but was undeterred by the attempts to intimidate her. At the end of her first week, Acting Presbyterian Moderator Bill Loftus and two colleagues, "called on the Headmistress to inform her that if and when the College was finally controlled by the Presbyterian Church, the Assembly would not necessarily feel bound to ratify" Stratford's appointment. Twenty-four Junior School staff signed a letter to Ray Northrop as Council Chairman, declaring: "We fully support the right of the Principal of the School, Miss Montgomery, to employ all staff, and, of course to terminate that employment. The situation would be untenable for all parties concerned if this were not so … We, therefore, also fully support Mrs Stratford in her position here as Headmistress of the Junior School and of her right to employ staff and terminate their employment as she sees fit." When she spoke at her first speech night in December, Jean Stratford told the audience: "As you may imagine, arriving at a new school at the beginning of second term does have its difficulties … All I can say is that anonymous letters notwithstanding, I've felt welcomed."

Just before sending his first letter to Jean Stratford, Ted Pearsons had fired an opening salvo across the bows of the School Council. His letter, sent on 1 March, began gently enough, claiming the church had avoided exacerbating the legal dispute by not communicating with the Council over the previous months and had demonstrated goodwill by supporting retention of the present Council membership. While acknowledging neither the Council members nor the Principal were parties to the litigation, he said he was conscious it had "the backing of a majority of the Council" then warned: "[I] remind all concerned that both Council and Principal were appointed by the Presbyterian Church of Victoria. Their administration can only be on behalf of the General Assembly. It has no independent standing." And then an ultimatum that had the very familiar ring of Max Bradshaw, now Presbyterian Procurator and Pearsons' mentor:

> Since their [the Council's] authority is derived from the General Assembly, it follows that, like any other agent, they are not entitled to set up their own title or that of any third party, for to do so would constitute a repudiation of their agency. Yet that is what has been done. One may not blow hot and cold in these matters. If a person renounces the authority of the General Assembly, then obviously that authority ceases to be available for that person to exercise. If the Council and Principal have in this way denied themselves the authority of the General Assembly, where else is authority for their action to be derived? ... If what to us is the fantastic claim that the Presbyterian Ladies' College is really independent were to succeed, it would be for the Supreme Court, not the present Council, to set up the controlling body.

The letter went on to contest all the activity conducted or authorised by the Council since the Property Commission decision in May 1977, including the large expenditure on legal bills arising from challenging the Commission's determination and "most disturbing ... the purported appointment" of the new Junior School headmistress: "It is no answer to say that the present headmistress has reached the retiring age. When the best interests of the school are at stake such matters are surely of little weight and there is no adequate reason why Mrs Flynn could not have been asked to stay on until a proper field of choice should become available." Fuelling the rumours now abounding about Joan Montgomery's future, Pearsons then wrote: "The seriousness of the present situation is going to intensify rather than abate with the passing of time ... new problems may well arise, to give one example, should the Principal leave there is no means whereby a replacement could be made." And he would conclude with a threatening flourish: "If at a later stage we are compelled to take appropriate proceedings, we should not like it to be said that we permitted you to interfere in the affairs of the school in ignorance of the personal consequences to each member of the Council."

In response, Ray Northrop would give as good as he got. He said Pearsons' letter was, "the first communication I, either personally or as Chairman of the Council ... have received from any person claiming to be acting with the authority of the Presbyterian Church of Victoria or its General Assembly since the Presbyterian Church of Australia entered into union with the Congregational and Methodist Churches on June 22nd 1977." He then added: "There is a grave doubt whether the Presbyterian Church of Victoria, which you represent, is entitled to have authority over Presbyterian Ladies' College or me as a member of the Council of that College."

On the question of June Stratford's appointment, Northrop quoted from the Presbyterian Church of Victoria's regulations: "The Principal appoints members of the staff (subject to confirmation by the Council) and has full power of dismissal." Referring to Joan Montgomery's terms of appointment agreed by the Presbyterian Church of Victoria Trusts Corporation, he noted her power, "to appoint members of the staff of the College, subject to confirmation by the Chairman on behalf of the Council with full power of dismissal." Northrop would conclude on a defiant note:

> Is it suggested that the Principal should not exercise her powers to appoint persons as members of staff to fill vacancies caused by retirement or resignation? Is it suggested that the Principal has the power to extend the term of office of a member

of staff who has passed the retiring age, but has no power to fill a vacancy caused by retirement? Your letter is seen as an attempt to interfere with the authority and powers of the Principal. Respect for the authority and powers of the Principal in the conduct of the school is the basis upon which the greatness and success of the school has depended and still depends. This respect must be retained.

Northrop advised Pearsons that he was forwarding a copy of the correspondence to the chairman of the Trusts Corporation, the body registered as proprietor of the land on which PLC operated. This would become a central point in the legal challenges that lay ahead: a clear distinction between the school itself and the land on which it sat.

Dr Richard Chenoweth, a paediatric consultant who had been on the School Council since 1975, was also roused to send a three-page rejoinder to Pearsons. Chenoweth contested all aspects of the "ownership" of the school, drawing on Kathleen Fitzpatrick's history and examining the religious beliefs of the students (a matter he felt showed that family influence rather the school was the key determinant). He concluded with a passionate defence of Joan Montgomery. "The current Principal is, in my opinion, a woman who embodies an exceptional combination of intelligence, perception, energy, loyalty and common sense to whom the School, the Council and the General Assembly is in great debt. She inspires strong loyalty from the Staff. To attempt to replace her would be most unfortunate. She can look on society as it is and not be dismayed by what she sees yet encourage the best from staff and pupils by precept and example. Any veiled threats at security of her position are misguided, misjudged, mischievous and, hopefully, will miscarry."[6]

Chenoweth sent copies of his letter to Max Bradshaw and Brian Bayston, who replied the following week. Bradshaw was typically abrasive: "Circular letters to parents and statements at parents' gatherings repudiating the authority of the Presbyterian Church (and therefore of course repudiating all authority conferred on the Council by that Church), as well as apparently endeavouring to create hostility to the Presbyterian Church on the part of the parents ... It seems clear you were not aware of the significance of all of this, which provides a complete answer to the charge of hypocrisy you make."[7] Bayston responded on the issue of the religious beliefs of students: "What you say confirms my view that the Church schools generally have fallen behind in the task to which they are committed. That of course is no doubt due to a considerable extent to the fact that the families do not support the school in the inculcation of Christian knowledge."

The pressure being exerted on the PLC Council would have fallout in other directions. The heated exchanged between Pearsons and Northrop drove Farquhar Gunn to resign from the Council. Having been the Secretary of the Property Commission he wrote a letter of "great regret" to Northrop, saying he felt there was "no other course of action open" to him. He emphasised the serious consequences for other States as well as Victoria if there were a challenge to the procedures of the Property Commission: "I acquiesced in the proposed litigation believing, as I am sure other members of the Council did, that as we were told, the sole issue was the question whether the Victorian schools came within the jurisdiction of the Commission ... The litigation has gone far beyond this and has implications now that I cannot acquiesce in so therefore I must submit my resignation as a member of the Council." Gunn took strong exception to Pearsons' allegation of "a wilful misappropriation of funds" on the part of the Council. But the bullying—and the threat of personal liability—had the desired effect, as Gunn responded: "I have doubts as to whether members are covered in law and I have personally to face the fact that I would not be in a position to meet my share of costs were costs payable."

With letters going back and forth between the various interests, Joan wrote to Ray Northrop, thanking him for forwarding all the correspondence. "Life will be quite dull when there is no dossier to update so regularly," she wryly noted. Little did she realise that the dossier was in its infancy. As the conflict escalated, both parties turned to the State Government in an attempt to bolster their positions.

The idea of Presbyterian Church schools incorporating with both churches then being represented on school Councils of the new entities had been in development since union occurred. Northrop sent Victorian Attorney-General Haddon Storey copies of the correspondence detailing the dispute between the Continuing Presbyterian Church and the Council. By the end of March, Storey responded listing among the proposals he had received a document prepared in January — *Agreed Submission of the Uniting Church in Australia and the Presbyterian Church of Victoria to the A-G regarding the litigation over Scotch College and PLC* — with a letter from Pearsons about draft legislation prepared by Max Bradshaw. There were also proposals from the Presbyterian Church of Victoria's Trust Corporation and the Registrar of Titles and certificates prepared by the moderators of both the Presbyterian and Uniting Churches. Storey explained: "The Government is prepared to assist in any way it can in resolving the present difficulties. However, I would be unable to go to Cabinet with any legislative proposals in the absence of firm agreement of the interested parties." He sought Northrop's views on how this might be achieved and offered to "provide assistance in the drafting of any legislation required to implement the proposals."[8]

After meeting with Storey on 3 April, Northrop followed up on 10 April concerned about any lurking retrospective effect in Bradshaw's draft bill, given Pearsons' threats about June Stratford's appointment. He argued that it would be, "morally and legally wrong for Parliament to enact legislation of this kind at a time when the General Assembly [of the Presbyterian Church] is threatening personal liability against members of the PLC Council, and may well need to rely on that legislation to validate its own position."[9] What is more, PLC had not been consulted about the agreed submission of the two churches and as the agreement stood it was contrary to the Constitution of PLC and contrary to the terms of Deed entered between the Presbyterian Church of Victoria Trusts Corporation and the Principal.

The pace of the dispute was quickening. On 12 April 1978, another letter arrived from Attorney-General Storey alerting Northrop to a letter he had received from McCracken & McCracken, solicitors for the Continuing Presbyterians and the firm of which Brian Bayston was a partner. The letter alleged that the general funds of PLC had been used to meet the costs of the Relator (the plaintiff) in the litigation against the Property Commission and this represented a possible misappropriation of funds. Northrop hit back, using the opportunity to broaden his case with Storey. He argued not only had the Council been acting within its power, in the best interests of the College, based on advice of eminent legal counsel, but also: "Council would have been failing in its duty to protect property subject to charitable trusts if, in the circumstances, it had not taken that action."[10]

Correspondence ran back and forth through May, June, and July with further draft legislation and follow-up communication between Northrop and Storey. During that period, Pearsons sought a further report from Joan Montgomery for the General Assembly of the Presbyterian Church. This time, Joan forwarded the request to Ray Northrop who told Pearsons that the annual College report required by Constitution for the Assembly would, in view of the litigation, also be sent to the Attorney-General and the Synod of Victoria of the Uniting Church in Australia.

The August 1978 report was framed with the litigation hovering and with a "without prejudice" rider. Ordinary business noting student numbers, exam results, and activities within the school and beyond were reported in the usual way but an exposition of the underlying tension between the school and the Continuing Presbyterian Church was the real focus of the report. It charted the history of the litigation and detailed the proposal by PLC and the other Presbyterian and Methodist schools for their incorporation through an Act of Parliament, with representation from the two churches on the governing bodies of each of the schools. The controversy surrounding June Stratford's appointment was related in detail with the Council expressing "the gravest concern" at the attempts by the Continuing Presbyterian Church to thwart it.

Northrop's report was also critical of the purported agreement in January 1978 between representatives of the Uniting Church and the Presbyterian Church of Victoria — revealed to him by Haddon Storey — which had occurred without consultation with the School Council: "Not only is it undesirable that agreements of that kind be made without prior consultation with the College Council, but the failure to notify the College Council of the terms of the agreement can lead only to misunderstanding and feelings of resentment."

The report concluded with a spirited defence of Joan Montgomery's leadership of the school, calling out the moves against her as bizarre, regardless of whether the Property Commission had awarded PLC to the Uniting Church or the Presbyterians: "The Principal who, more than all others, has the essential experience and training, must have the authority and powers to direct the College ... The Council expresses its strong support for and appreciation of the work being done by the Principal, Miss J.M. Montgomery, and her staff in maintaining the high standing of the College."

Throughout this period, Joan sought to keep a low public profile, leaving legal and governance issues to the PLC Council. But she was stirred to react after receiving from Ray Northrop a copy of a memorandum prepared on 15 August by Allan Lobban, a partner at Blake & Riggall and a member of the Scotch Council (1971-80), which reported: "FMB (Max Bradshaw) said something to the effect that the principal of PLC had been speaking to the Senior and Junior Schools and to the Parent Association as though incorporation was a fait accompli."

Joan wrote to Northrop: "I know Mr Lobban as an ex-Clyde parent and felt that if only for his eye, I would like Mr Bradshaw's statement corrected or at least explained … I find it most irksome that anything said in the Junior School staff room is reported with such speed to Mr Bradshaw." A more detailed response followed in a letter she sent to Mr Lobban:

> Thank you for the Memorandum of 15th August 1978 concerning your telephone conversation with Mr. F.M. Bradshaw. As my alleged actions are mentioned in it, I enclose a statement of events as I saw them. Far from seeing incorporation as a 'fait accompli' I have had throughout the most pessimistic view of PLC's possible future … I desperately hope that incorporation will be possible, but inwardly feel anything but optimism. However, my statement to the Senior School Parents' Association and repeated to the Senior and Junior School staffs, was brief and factual, not a personal forecast! I am not entering into an exchange with Mr Bradshaw but felt that you should have a firsthand account of what was said.

By the end of August, Ray Northrop felt it was time for another letter to parents following up on his letter late in June informing them of the Council's decision to challenge the Property Commission decision. He gave details of the plan by the school Council chairs and principals of the nine former

Presbyterian schools to seek the support of the Victorian General Assembly of the Continuing Presbyterians and the Synod of the Uniting Church in Australia to approach to the Victorian Attorney-General for legislation to incorporate each of the schools, with representation from the two churches on the governing bodies of the schools. He said the key issue the schools wanted written into legislation, was that the chief object of each corporate body would be to, "provide for the students of the school vested in it by the Act a liberal, humane and scientific education within which the worship of the Christian Church, an understanding of the Holy Scriptures, and the development of Christian faith and practice may find appropriate expression." On the question of control, Northrop explained: "The proposal would ensure that each of the two Churches has a direct say in the management of each of the schools, but neither Church would be in a position to control any one of the schools." This would put an end to the current litigation and bring "about an amicable and reasonable solution to the existing problems." Given the Assembly and Synod would be meeting later in October, Northrop urged parents: "Any personal approach to ministers and representative elders of both the Presbyterian Church and the Uniting Church seeking their support of the proposal would be of great assistance."[11] A few weeks later, Archie Glenn, chairman of the Scotch College Council, and Ken Bethell, president of the Old Collegians' Association, wrote a similar letter to members of the Scotch community, also urging them to lobby in support of incorporation.

Northrop's letter provoked some unhappy letters from parents linked to the Continuing Presbyterian Church, including an indignant protest sent to the PLC Bursar by Brian Bayston: "That school funds and the school mailing system should be used to advance such a partisan view is, in my judgement, reprehensible. The reason that I choose to send my child to the Presbyterian Ladies' College is that it is primarily concerned for the advancement of Christian education, not 'liberal, humane and scientific education' ... kindly bring this objection to the attention of the Council."

Inevitably, Northrop's letter hit the press with the *Age* reporting on 18 September 1978, under the headline "Colleges Urge Ousting of Church": "Former students of two top Melbourne schools have been asked to lobby for a plan which would remove the colleges from the control of the Presbyterian Church." The story quoted Pearsons describing the move as "quite scandalous" and saying that "the Presbyterian Church was unanimously against it."

That "unanimous" view was made formal when the General Assembly of the Presbyterian Church of Victoria met on 3 October and rejected the proposal that it support legislation for the schools to incorporate. Pearsons wrote to Ray Northrop the following day to confirm the decision and advised that a "Special Commission" of the Assembly would follow up the matter with the PLC Council.

At Pearsons' request, a meeting was scheduled on 30 October. At 8pm members of the PLC Council—including Northrop, Joan Montgomery and Ewen McRae, the Bursar and Council Secretary—assembled at their usual venue in the school's social sciences wing. They were soon joined by the members of the Special Commission—the Victorian Moderator, the Reverend Hector Dunn, Ted Pearsons, Bill Loftus, Max Bradshaw, Brian Bayston and the Reverends Ray Russell and Don Carruthers. Joan Montgomery was seated next to Northrop.

Dunn, as the Moderator, immediately claimed the right to constitute the gathering as a meeting of the Special Commission of the General Assembly. Northrop, as the School Council Chair, then claimed the right to constitute the meeting as a Special Meeting of the Council. Ewen McRae suggested that in effect two separate meetings be constituted—Northrop agreed but Dunn refused. That was enough for Northrop. "If I can't open the meeting, then we can't start and I'm leaving," he declared and started packing up his material. Joan also rose to leave as did the other members of the PLC Council.

At this point in the procedural pantomime, the Presbyterians blinked. In line with McRae's suggestion, Dunn and his colleagues left the room. Northrop then asked Council member the Reverend Alan Crawford to constitute the Special Meeting for the Council members. When the Special Commission members returned to the room, Northrop informed them that the Special Meeting of Council had been constituted and Dunn confirmed that they too had constituted their own meeting outside. Now the business began.

Dunn explained the Presbyterians' purpose in proposing a meeting was to discuss the possibility of a committee of the Council and a committee of the Special Commission finding a solution to end the litigation over the ownership of PLC. Miraculously, there was agreement that any meeting between the committees would be on a "without prejudice" basis and, in the absence of any agreement being reached, the discussions would not be used against any person or party. On that basis, the visitors left the room to allow the Council to consider their proposition. The Council agreed and appointed Northrop, Crawford, Mary Murdoch and Bob O'Shea to be their committee. For their part, the Special Commission chose Dunn, Pearsons, Bradshaw and Bayston to be their committee. Both Council and the Special Commission then closed their respective meetings so that the two committees could meet that evening.

The two committees would outline starkly different positions. The Presbyterian view was that its General Assembly had authority over the School Council. Following the inauguration of the Uniting Church, the Council "had repudiated that authority, and the Principal, in accepting the Council's actions, had repudiated the authority of the Assembly." In their view, this meant the Council had no authority to conduct school business and the members of the Council would be "personally liable for the costs involved in running the school and, if need be, the Assembly would sue the individual members of the Council to recover the costs for running the school since June 1977." They further asserted that all actions taken by the Principal and members of the Council would need to be ratified by the Assembly before they became valid. In particular, every appointment of staff made by the Principal would need to be investigated before ratification, and there would be no certainty that the appointment of Mrs Stratford as Head of Junior School would be ratified or, indeed, any appointment of other members of staff.

The Council countered by rejecting the General Assembly's authority and pointed out that the litigation was being run to test that very point. They said in the absence of any final determination regarding the Property Commission and the vesting of property, it was difficult to say what authority the Assembly had over any general property of the former Presbyterian Church. In the meantime, the school must be kept running and all actions of the Principal and the Council must have full legal effect and, unless fraud could be established, no member of Council was personally liable.

The concept of "Christian education" was raised in a broad-ranging discussion. It was interpreted by the visitors as Presbyterian education leading to the "conversion" of students to that view. This was too much for the note-taker who added the gloss: "The visitors do not seem to understand how a large school operates and how the demand by parents to send their girls to such a school depends upon the standards set by the Principal and staff. The fact that a large number of staff would resign if Mrs Stratford was forced to leave is of no great concern to the visitors—they say there is an oversupply of teachers but do not understand that there may not be teachers of sufficient stature of those presently at the College."

Vetting of Wisdom

The idea of seeking the views of parents about who should control the school was rejected by the Presbyterians. The notes would conclude: "Each group says it is concerned for the welfare of the College. The difference between the groups arises in respect of what is best for the College and how the objectives are to be achieved." The two committees agreed to reconvene two weeks later — on 14 November 1978. In the interval, representatives of each of the nine Presbyterian schools and their principals, including Joan Montgomery, met with the Attorney-General Haddon Storey on 9 November to put their joint view opposing the legislation that had been drafted by the two churches without consulting representatives of the schools. The delegation was unanimous in pressing their proposal to incorporate all of the schools.

The dramatic intersection of Church and State in the school brawl would draw more newspaper headlines. In a feature headlined "Churchmen in Conflict", published in the *Age* on 14 November, Bruce Best — a former editor of the Church magazine *Presbyterian Life* before union — wrote that the Attorney-General's involvement was ruffling feathers. Best had contacted Joan but was rebuffed: "The sensitivity is such that the principal of PLC would not even provide the *Age* with details of her school's enrolment and staff numbers." But his last sentence had an ear to political realities — Haddon Storey was wedged: "To an Attorney-General whose Government will be facing an election inside six months, there seems little hope of any action which would win friends on both sides."

The *Age* feature stirred Camberwell Grammar School Head David Dyer to write to Ray Northrop worried about what Continuing Presbyterian management could mean for PLC. Dyer, who years earlier had questioned Joan Montgomery's approach to the new Liberal Studies course, had changed his view, as he confided to Northrop: "I have received an enquiry from a senior member of the PLC staff concerning a teaching position at this school. It was clear from the letter that she felt most insecure in her position, and that if there were a change in the management of the school then her own job would be at risk. To put it bluntly, I do not believe that a school with such a high academic reputation can afford to lose members of staff of that quality and I am also concerned as a parent that senior members of the staff, and in particular the Headmistress, should continue to be under such constant strain because of the apparent uncertainty."

The strain on all concerned was compounded with the sudden loss of a beloved member of the School Council. Two days after the *Age* feature appeared, the PLC Council held its November meeting. Soon after returning home from the meeting, Bob O'Shea died. The loss became a tragic metaphor for PLC's *annus horribilis*. It also forced the postponement of the proposed reconvening of the committees of Church and School Council delegates tasked with negotiating on the dispute, as O'Shea had been one of the Council representatives.

A glimpse of Joan Montgomery's own feelings during this intense time would come after Alan Crawford wrote to her advising that he would be unable to attend the annual Speech Night due to another commitment. In his letter, Crawford would write: "Could I take the opportunity to say how much I have appreciated the way in which you have handled the difficulties of this past year." Joan replied thanking him and, in her wry style, suggested an early invitation for the 1979 Speech Night: "Unfortunately, forward planning seems a little difficult at present! ... I have been very grateful for the help and support that I have had from Council members this year particularly. Although the situation that made it necessary is so sad, I am sure that in the days ahead most will look back gratefully to the present Council which stood firm in the interests of the school. May 1979 see a solution to the present difficulties." It was a vain hope.

By the end of November, Bert Stevens, the Principal of

Penleigh and Essendon Grammar who had taken the lead in advocating that the nine Presbyterian schools become incorporated entities, wrote a memorandum—*The Continuing Saga of 'The Schools.'* Attached to the memo would be a collection of documents charting the developments between the schools, the Attorney-General and the Continuing Presbyterians. It would record a key meeting convened on Friday 24 November.

At 11am that morning, Attorney-General Haddon Storey and John Finnemore, Assistant Secretary of the Law Department, met with representatives from the Victorian Synod of the Uniting Church (its Moderator, Ethel Mitchell, Secretary the Reverend Graham McAnally and solicitor Peter Webster), the pre-union Presbyterian Trust Corporation (John McArthur represented by Alex Gillespie and Ian MacKinnon), the Uniting Church in Australia Assembly (President Davis McCaughey and Secretary the Reverend Winston O'Reilly), the Continuing Presbyterian Church (Ted Pearsons, Max Bradshaw and Brian Bayston as their solicitor). Also attending were representatives of the nine schools, including Allan Lobban for Scotch College and Ray Northrop for PLC. Bert Stevens recorded that Storey stipulated that he would not act without the concurrence of all parties and, failing agreement, he would call another meeting to try to solve the problem.

Later that day, a smaller group met in Finnemore's office to see if an agreed Bill could be drafted but Max Bradshaw rejected the items referring to the validity of the schools' Councils from 22 June 1977, the day the Uniting Church was inaugurated. No agreement was reached and Stevens wrote to Storey: "It seems clear, Sir, that there is a complete impasse which is created by the failure of the continuing Presbyterian Church to accept the fact that the Schools had to operate with authority as set out prior to the 22nd June 1977. If litigation goes on for the suggested seven years (and Mr Finnemore and Mr Bradshaw agreed that it was a certain Privy Council case) then there is no doubt that the Schools and the members of the public who make up their communities will suffer greatly."

After the failure of the meetings, it was agreed that various representatives of the Uniting Church and the schools – including Stevens, Northrop, Allan Lobban and Davis McCaughey – would meet to discuss how best to proceed. But nothing had progressed by PLC Speech Night on Friday 8 December. Ray Northrop's address as Council Chairman acknowledged the media reports about PLC's future and reviewed developments in the legal battle. In her Principal's report, Joan characterised 1978 as a year of consolidation and uncertainty. She noted how newly-appointed staff and others had felt considerable anxiety about their future, with parents expressing concern about possible policy changes and how these might affect their daughters. But she reassured everyone, and for the schoolgirls present it rang true: "The day-to-day running of a school leaves little time for dwelling on problems that may not arise." That day-to-day business of the school was education and preparing pupils for life after school. An ever-present reality was rapid change. Joan addressed herself to what one writer had stated:

> Half the jobs of twenty years hence may not yet have been thought of, one of our aims must be to develop flexibility and the ability to respond to unprecedented situations. How does any curriculum prepare for this? Few teachers would answer identically here, but most, if not all, would agree that far more important than curriculum content is the long-term attitude that it develops. The responsibility to think, to respect facts and evidence, to assess conflicting points of view, and to examine the values of society as well as one's own – these are the qualities that all study should encourage.

Joan's report would finish with a warm public farewell to Jean Ford, her long-term friend and travelling partner in the UK in 1958-59: "After eighteen years on the Mathematics staff Miss Ford retires this evening ... If Miss Ford's approach could be described as velvet-gloved, the respect in which she is held has called for nothing stronger. As an excellent teacher and a delightful colleague, she will be greatly missed." For Joan, the farewell would resonate both personally and professionally. Jean Ford's departure was an echo of a happier and far less complicated time than the one she was now forced to endure.

10

MISS MONTGOMERY

As the struggle over the future of PLC intensified, Joan Montgomery increasingly became emblematic of the fight. For as much as it was a fight for ownership and control, it was also personal. In the eyes of many, Joan embodied the school and she and PLC seemed inseparably entwined. Pam Royle, a PLC "old girl" and Chair of the Parents' Association, was one: "If it hadn't been for Joan, none of us would have done this."

Pam More, as she then was, attended PLC in East Melbourne between 1948 and 1954. Like Joan, she had been influenced by their outstanding geography teacher Nora Wilkinson, whom she remembers having a long face, big teeth and a wonderful smile. Pam later studied pharmacy and ran her own business which gave her the flexibility to become involved in the school from the 1970s onwards. Her daughters Sue, Jenny and Julia were all PLC students.

Pam had been a member of the Parents' Association for a number of years before becoming Chair in 1979. During all those years and for many years after, she addressed Joan as Miss Montgomery and it wasn't until well after the struggle that Pam would start to call her Joan. She admits to having been "a bit intimated" because of her "enormous respect for her." But she admired Joan's "sparkle" and described her as "a real trick".

The objectives of the Parents' Association, as set out in its Constitution, were to "co-operate with the Council and the Principal generally in the promotion of the interests and welfare of the College; promote sympathetic co-operation between the home and the College; provide means for discussing problems affecting both parents and pupils and promote social intercourse between members." Joan was an ex officio member and attended most meetings.

In February 1979, Ray Northrop called Pam as the incoming Chair of the Association to inform her of a letter sent from McCracken & McCracken, the Presbyterian Church solicitors, to the School Council's lawyers, Mallesons, threatening legal action if the Parents' Association continued with a plan to carry out an independent survey of the parents' views on the future of the school. Northrop advised that the Parents' Association would need independent legal advice, but that he believed it would be quite in order for the Association to use its funds to carry out the survey. The survey wouldn't affect the litigation, he reasoned, but the parents' wishes would affect whether the Council continued to fight.

Pam and Joan had both been present at the previous Parents' Association meeting where a survey sub-committee had been formed comprising Eve Mahlab—parent of 1978 School Captain Karen and a prominent lawyer and businesswoman—John Jones and Alec Owen. The sub-committee discussed engaging Irving Saulwick—who for many years was the *Age* newspaper's pollster of choice—to conduct the survey. While aware of the threat from the Church's lawyers, the three members didn't think the survey would be in contempt. They were, nonetheless, conscious of the legal costs in just opposing any injunction and, through Northrop, asked the School Council if it was prepared to fund a legal opinion on whether the Parents' Association survey would be in contempt. The overture was unsuccessful. John Jones reported this to his fellow committee members along with the news that the Old Scotch Collegians had declined to participate in the survey and share its cost: "Whilst the sub-committee could recommend ... the Association get a legal opinion at its own expense, we believe that the threat of legal proceedings has placed the whole survey project well beyond the financial means of the Association."

Ray Northrop's call to Pam had, however, given the go ahead to the Parents' Association if they were prepared to cover the costs on their own. This was risky territory as the Parents' Association was made pointedly aware. Indeed, two days after Pam's first meeting as Chair, Brian Bayston, a partner at McCracken & McCracken, wrote directly to her home address repeating the threat: "It is our view that any such survey would constitute contempt of court so long as the present litigation is on foot (and) if we are right in our view, then each officer of the association becomes liable to penalties in the nature of attachment and committal."[1]

The Parents' Association had earlier sought its own advice. Ian Murray from Mallesons advised that the survey was relevant to showing support for a submission to the Attorney-General about the parents' wishes for the school and as backing the School Council in challenging the Property Commission's determination. Murray recommended sending a letter to interested parties — Pearsons from the Presbyterians, Davis McCaughey from the Uniting Church and an advocate for the independent body alternative — requesting a statement on how each saw itself as controlling the school. These statements could accompany the survey, which would virtually amount to one question: "Which of these alternatives do you prefer to have control the school? (a) an independent body, (b) the Uniting Church or (c) the Continuing Church." In the event of the Presbyterians issuing an injunction, the Parents' Association would have to oppose it, although Murray advised that the Association was definitely not in contempt of court. The costs of opposing the injunction could reach $3500 of which they would get back half if they won. He was confident any litigation on this issue would not be heard until well into 1980.

Meanwhile, the moves to have the nine Presbyterian schools change their legal status to incorporated associations, were proceeding. On 14 March, Bert Stevens, the Penleigh and Essendon Grammar Principal driving the initiative, wrote to Joan requesting further details from PLC. The letter was addressed, "Dear Headmaster". In her response, Joan would add: "Thank you very much for all the trouble you are continuing to take on our behalf. It really is appreciated even if you did spoil it by addressing me in your letter as the Headmaster!" In further correspondence, Stevens would add his own brand of handwritten cheek: "Note – I have had 'Dear Sir' changed to 'Dear Miss Montgomery' in deference to your previous complaint. HRS."

On 5 April, Pam Royle met with Joan to brief her on Parents' Association issues, including the survey, and urged her to take a leading role in the campaign in support of incorporation. She argued that parents wanted direction on the issue and "the person they will take most notice of is the headmistress." And she had a series of questions: "Would it be possible for the side of the Independent Corporate body to be written with Miss Montgomery's name on it? Is it possible to form an active, independent lobbying group to push for the independent body? Is it possible for the women's groups to invite guest speakers to inform groups of the independent corporate body idea?" But despite her strong commitment to the moves for incorporation, Joan wished to remain publicly neutral and said the information sent to parents should come from Pam, not her. By the end of April, Northrop confirmed to the Parents' Association that the School Council had resolved to allocate funds to conduct the survey and to cover the costs of contesting any litigation that might arise from it.

Not surprisingly, the row continued to draw media attention. In April, the *Bulletin* ran a cover story with the headline, "Uniters v Continuers: The Money Behind the Big Religious Split."[2] To promote the story, the magazine took out a full-page advertisement in the *Age*.³ It showed a photograph of three men with their heads down, eyes closed and hands firmly clasped in prayer. One man had the caption above his head: "Please God, give us the strength to continue independently as the Presbyterian Church and retain our beloved school properties worth millions of dollars." The next man's caption read: "Please God, give us the strength to become independent of both of them." And the third man's prayer was: "Please God, give us the strength to help unite the Methodist and Presbyterian Churches including their beloved school properties worth millions of dollars." Below the picture was the sub-heading: "Is God taking second place to the dollar in Melbourne's bitter religious split?" It continued: "David McNicoll unearths a bitter battle that has been engaged between the Uniting Church, comprising Methodists, Congregationalists and Presbyterians and the Continuing Presbyterian Church. The dispute involves some of Australia's top schools with real estate worth millions."

McNicoll's account was not on the money. While money, or at least very valuable property, was at the heart of the dispute, it was more about power and control, far more attractive commodities. Competition and gamesmanship also figured. There was a sense that some of the players, Max Bradshaw certainly, enthralled as he was with his strict and uncompromising brand of Presbyterianism, were enjoying themselves in the game of Church chess that inexplicably had given the Continuing Presbyterians the upper hand.

Pam Royle certainly was not focussed on real estate values. She, her fellow parents and many others joining the struggle for PLC were concerned about the educational values underpinning the school and the position of Joan Montgomery, who represented those values, guiding a school committed to equal education for women. Purer motives than money, property, power and control motivated many of the Continuing Presbyterians too. To be sure, they wanted to keep their beloved schools Presbyterian to 'provide a Presbyterian education for their children.

But what sort of education would that be? A year earlier, Pam Royle had noticed an article in the *Herald*, with the headline "It's Derek to the Letter."[4] It showed a photograph of the Bound family at their Werribee home — Derek and Joy with their children Faith, 8, Lydia, 6, Moira, 4, Jonathan, 3, and Daniel 19 months. The article began: "I allow no woman to teach or to have authority over men." Quoting the Apostle Paul, Derek Bound said this summed up why women could never become elders in the Presbyterian Church. The article went on to detail a row within the Presbyterian Church of Victoria that erupted when "six out of seven students at the Presbyterian Theological Hall signed a protest petition against women becoming elders". Derek Bound was their spokesman: "One reason why the Presbyterian Church survives is because the authority of scripture is paramount. And the Bible is quite clear that in the areas of marriage and the Church, man must have clear authority over woman." Joy Bound added: "My husband has authority in our marriage and I am subject to him, but I am not a door mat. I let him know when I don't agree."

The yawning ideological chasm between those in the Presbyterian Church with an unwavering belief in patriarchal Christianity and those in the Uniting Church committed to the equality of women, inflamed the struggle over control of PLC. The Parents' Association knew that Joan Montgomery shared the commitment of PLC's founders to provide equal opportunity for girls in education — and equal opportunity in life. At the beginning of second term in 1979, the staff met to discuss PLC's direction. As Joan would say in her end of year report, with more than 90 staff involved, complete consensus on priorities was unlikely, but what emerged clearly, "was the need to re-examine our aims, to advertise them widely, to implement them as fully and honestly as we can and to refer to them constantly in the day-to-day life of the School." The process was complete by the end of

1979, with the following statement issued, subtly pressing the importance of a liberal education, with integrity as the underlying quality:

AIMS

The aim of the school is to provide a liberal, humane and scientific education. Within this context, Christian worship, the study and understanding of Holy Scriptures, and the development of Christian faith and life will have their appropriate expression. In such a caring, responsible community, individuals of every point of view may find their place.

OBJECTIVES

The school seeks to carry out these aims by providing an environment where integrity is seen as underlying all other qualities, and by pursuing the following objectives:

To develop in each student her maximum potential in all aspects of school life, ‑ intellectual, physical, and creative.

To help each student: (a) To have a sense of her own personal worth and an understanding of her own strengths and weaknesses. (b) To become increasingly capable of organising her own studies. (c) To be a responsible, adaptable and constructive member of society.

To assist each student to be aware of, and sensitive to the needs of other people in the community, and to encourage her to participate in practical community service.

To foster in each student both self-discipline and initiative, so that freedom may be exercised in such a way that the good of all may be served.

Vetting of Wisdom

Adoption of the mission statement was complicated by the unfolding drama over control of the school, as Joan would also say in her end-of-year speech: "After a number of revisions, the final draft, supported overwhelmingly by the Staff, was submitted to the College Council. Unfortunately, this has been an inappropriate term for discussion of long-term aspirations at Council level." By late 1979, the Council was preoccupied with its own future and the future governance of the school.

Preparations for the long-awaited survey were confirmed when Pam Royle wrote to all parents on 22 May 1979 as Chair of the Parents' Association.

> Dear Parent
>
> This is an important letter. We urge you to read it carefully.
>
> Shortly before the date on which the Presbyterian Church entered into union, the Chairman of the P.L.C. Council was notified that the Property Commission had awarded P.L.C. to the Continuing Presbyterian Church. The P.L.C. School Council subsequently resolved to challenge this award and the court case will probably be heard in 1980 or 1981.
>
> In the meantime, the P.L.C. Council has supported a proposal by which each of the former Presbyterian Schools, including P.L.C., would become an independent corporate body having on its Council members nominated by each of the Uniting Church and of the Continuing Church.
>
> On the 13th February of this year, we the committee of the P.L.C. Parents' Association resolved to conduct a survey amongst P.L.C. parents for the purpose of ascertaining parents' preferences concerning the future control of the

Miss Montgomery

school between the following alternatives:
  i). The Uniting Church.
  ii). The Continuing Church.
  iii). An independent corporate body of the kind referred to above.

It was and is our intention to present the results of the survey to both the School Council and to the Attorney-General, so that parents' attitudes can be taken into consideration when any subsequent decisions are to be made concerning future control of P.L.C.

By letter of 21st March the Continuing Church through its Solicitors threatened our committee with legal proceedings if we proceeded with the survey. We have since received written legal advice that the survey we proposed would be quite lawful and we have therefore resolved to proceed.

This Meeting of Junior and Senior School parents is being called to inform all parents about the survey. The committee believes that this survey is of great importance and we would like to stress how essential it is that all parents reply to the survey when it is circulated.

PLEASE MAKE EVERY EFFORT TO ATTEND THIS MOST IMPORTANT MEETING.

The information evening was scheduled for Monday 11 June. The Parents' Association wrote to the Moderator of the Presbyterian Church, the Reverend Hector Dunn, who declined the Parents' Association's invitation to attend and to provide a 200-word statement summarising the Presbyterian position. He said this would be improper "as the matter is before the Supreme Court". Uniting Church Moderator Ethel Mitchell also declined: "The question as to which church the Presbyterian Ladies'

College would be related [to] after Union was a question for the undivided Presbyterian church and that church alone. The Uniting Church has never been a party to that discussion. It is still not a party to it or to the legal action which has ensued. It is therefore inappropriate for the Uniting Church to take part, at this stage, in any discussion as to the future of the College ... The Uniting Church in Australia (Synod of Victoria) will not be represented at your meeting."

Meeting notices were published in the *Age* and the *Herald* calling for parents, Old Collegians, Staff and friends of the College, to join the meeting in Wyselaskie Hall at 8pm on 11 June, "'to inform parents with respect to a survey to be conducted, concerning the future control of the college."

The turnout was overwhelming with more than 1300 people attending. Pam Royle opened the meeting stressing its informality and reminding those present that any questions about the litigation begun on 21 June 1977 would be ruled out of order. She explained and read out the letters that had been sent to each of the Presbyterian and Uniting Churches seeking a 200-word statement and their negative responses. Then she called on the Reverend Dr McCaughey, President of the Uniting Church in Australia, to address the question of an Independent body running the school.

Joan had first met Davis McCaughey when she was Head at Clyde and he had been Master of Ormond College at Melbourne University. McCaughey was born in Belfast and migrated to Australia in 1953 to take a professorship in the Presbyterian Theological Hall, at Ormond. Joan had come to see him more when Ormond, under his leadership, opened to women in 1973, enabling PLC girls to attend. McCaughey's daughters had been enrolled at PLC during Ruby Powell's term as Principal. It was in 1976 that Joan came to see him on a regular basis when she became a member of the Ormond College Council. She would be impressed by his urbane manner, amiable intelligence and

Miss Montgomery

approachability — qualities that all would see when he became Governor of Victoria in 1986 and dismissed the military *aide de camp*, traded the Rolls Royce for a Holden and opened the doors of Government House to the public.

On this evening, all the qualities that Joan saw in him were on display in his keynote speech, including a voice of reason: "While I am alone responsible for what I say, I know that I speak for many others, in the churches and in the community. I know that this proposal ... I put before you, has the support of all nine schools which were in any way associated with the Presbyterian Church of Victoria before the union of churches in 1977."

McCaughey shared Bert Stevens' proposal for all nine schools to be incorporated under an Act of Parliament with each school's governing body having representation from both the Uniting Church and the Continuing Presbyterian Church. Each school would therefore have more autonomy to control its own affairs: "In other words, let us cut under the unfortunate discussion about which school should be under the control of what Church. Let us say that none of the nine schools should be under any Church; but that all nine schools should be related to both Churches."

He then made three points. First, historically, the Presbyterian Church took over schools in the State, "as a service to the community" and these times had changed. Second, none of the schools wanted to break their historic connection to the Christian faith or to ignore its teaching in the curriculum. Finally, "the schools exist to fulfil an educational purpose. That is their primary objective: an educational purpose, not even in any narrow sense a religious purpose." He concluded with a strong message for PLC: "The School exists, always has existed, to provide young women, with an education, as full an education as is available in any day. It has been and is a liberal education, that is free to enquire into any subject of genuine interest, because it knows that God alone is the Lord of all Truth; it is humane, in that its scope is as wide as that of the human mind and imagination, its concern is the human lot, it is scientific because it believes that the ordering of human knowledge in rational sequence is an imperative which comes from the Creator—Lord of the Universe."

The speech enlivened the crowd, drawing enthusiastic applause. But not everyone was in agreement. During questions, with Ray Northrop responding on behalf of the School Council, there were many—questions and statements—from Continuing Presbyterians. Margaret Sandbach from the Old Collegians' Association was nettled by some of the behaviour and reported in the August newsletter on the "rudeness and heckling by a small group" calling it "regrettable, and ... foreign to PLC."

The future direction of the school was raised. One mother asked McCaughey about the Presbyterian Church's view of women as portrayed in the *Herald's* "It's Derek to the Letter" story the previous October. McCaughey responded: "First of all, I would hate any report in the *Herald* to be taken as representative of any group in this community ... but there are people [who] think that ... You have only got to have a look at the history of your own school over 100 years to know that that [women's rights to power] is well established. Now whatever any young man may say and get publicity in the *Herald* for saying it, that [is] not on and if anybody thinks it is on, they ought to be told what era they belong [to]—it isn't this one."

The controversy over June Stratford's appointment as Headmistress of the Junior School was raised. The Reverend Bill Loftus from the Presbyterian Church rose to take issue with Ray Northrop's account of the affair. Loftus recounted his experience of visiting Mrs Stratford in her first week at PLC and the courteous nature of the meeting. Later, Loftus reported in the July newsletter of his Trinity Presbyterian Church, Camberwell, and in the August 1979 Scots' Church *Leaflet*, that he was saddened by what he witnessed. It was not the move to incorporate the schools that upset him but that "this move was being made by blackening the good name of this church": "The risk of interference by the church was emphasised. There were accusations of narrow-mindedness. It was claimed that there would be interference with staff appointments ... Out of these bits and pieces of opinion, comment and action, it was evident that a campaign was under way to spread fear among parents and staff that the college would be 'at risk' if it came under the jurisdiction of the Presbyterian Church. Therefore, the solution was that the college should be made a corporate body to save it from the fate of being under the Presbyterian Church."

Soon after the public meeting, on 28 June, the survey was launched. Each PLC household received a package from the Parents' Association including a questionnaire accompanied by a statement briefly outlining the case for an Independent Corporate Body. It was explained why there were no accompanying statements from the Presbyterian Church or the Uniting Church. It assured the parents of anonymity, of the involvement of scrutineers and of pollster Irving Saulwick checking the rigour of the process. Parents had two weeks to return their papers and a reminder letter was sent a week later alerting them to the impending deadline.

The survey was conducted by post at a time when industrial disputes were adversely affecting the delivery of mail, but this didn't stop parents ensuring their voices were heard. Within a week of the deadline for completing the survey, Saulwick Weller and Associates reported back to Pam Royle on the results. They were a resounding vote in support of incorporation. From a total of 1086 questionnaires distributed, 81.2 per cent supported the creation of an Independent Body to control PLC, while 6.2 per cent supported the Continuing Presbyterian Church and 2.7 per cent favoured the Uniting Church. Informal votes totalled 9.9 per cent. A few months later, the Old Scotch Collegians distributed the same survey to old boys and parents. Their results were 70.5 per cent support for an Independent Body, 6.2 per cent support for the Continuing Presbyterian Church, 2.1% for the Uniting Church with 21.2 per cent being informal.

Buoyed by the outcome, the PLC Parents' Association authorised Pam Royle to forward the details to Victorian Attorney-General Haddon Storey. She wrote on 3 August: "In view of these results, which accord with the previously expressed wishes of all Councils and heads of all nine former Presbyterian Schools, our Association hereby urges you to take immediate steps to implement, by Act of Parliament, the wishes of the majority as clearly demonstrated by this survey. Your early response to this request would be greatly appreciated."

The uncertainty over the School Council's decision-making powers pervaded. In June 1979 Ray Northrop prepared a circular to parents about a new building appeal. Such an appeal had financed the Centenary School of Music in 1975 "but the need for capital funds specifically earmarked for building purposes continues." With the active support of the Parents' Association, the Council had authorised adding a suggested voluntary donation of $10 per family to all tuition accounts each term. In August, the Council newsletter to parents had included information about the redevelopment of the Junior School with plans for construction work to begin in October 1979.

The newsletter stirred Presbyterian Assembly Clerk Ted Pearsons, who promptly delivered a warning to Ray Northrop that, in light of the litigation: "It would be most inappropriate for the Council ... to authorise any building works, whether new buildings or alterations ... Should contracts for any such works be entered into, the Church will hold the members of the relevant Council personally responsible." It was enough to stay Northrop's hand. On 29 September, he explained to parents that the contract for the redevelopment of the Junior School would not begin in October. Instead, he offered the hope of "continuing to take steps to resolve this problem so as to allow the projects to proceed as soon as possible."

Miss Montgomery

Pam Royle's 3 August letter to the Attorney-General was still unanswered and so on 28 November she went higher and wider, writing to Premier Rupert Hamer and all members of the Legislative Assembly. There was an urgency to her communication: "The PLC Parents' Association is extremely concerned that introduction of the Presbyterian Trust Bill and the Presbyterian Schools Bill have been delayed. The Council of the School has been operating under uncertainty since 1977 and the Parents' Association Committee wishes this uncertainty to be alleviated as it is having a serious effect on the School."

Nine days later, Murray Hamilton, the member for Higginbotham Province, wrote back with good news. Legislation was "now under consideration by Parliament and I expect it will be passed through both Houses by the end of next week." But Hamilton's letter also delivered a rebuke: "I am quite distressed to find two branches of the Christian church squabbling over the division of property, and I have written to the authors of some of the intemperate letters I have received, suggesting that they should reflect on the matter and try to resolve their differences in prayer ... As a practising Anglican, I would suggest this is a much more appropriate way of resolving such deep divisions."

On the day their letters to the Premier and MPs had been sent, the Parents' Association and the Old Collegians' Association hosted a farewell evening for Vice Principal Donalda Crofts. Don's retirement marked a significant change for life at PLC and for Joan Montgomery. She also was an Old Collegian, finishing at PLC at the end of 1941 with Joan a couple of years behind her. She joined the History staff at PLC two years before Joan returned as Principal, had been elected Chief of Staff in the year of Joan's arrival and was appointed Vice Principal the following year. In her Speech Night report for 1979, Joan would say: "If PLC owes much to Mrs Crofts, no personal debt could be greater than mine. I have appreciated her abilities, respected her values and above all thoroughly enjoyed working closely with her for the last eleven years." Donalda Crofts left because in her view "the writing was on the wall." She likened the upheaval at PLC to the downfall of the Babylonian Empire, an interpretation Daniel ascribed to writing appearing on the wall during one of King Belshazzar's feasts.[5]

With Crofts' resignation, Joan had to think of a replacement as Vice Principal. In the end, she chose two, recognising the growth of the school and the increase in administrative demands. Her choices were already at PLC—Evelyn Tindale and Janice Douglas. Given the fracas over June Stratford's appointment at the Junior School, Joan resolved to record the appointments in a letter to Ray Northrop in his capacity as Chairman of the School Council, in September 1979.

Ev Tindale had been a year-level coordinator, Chief of Staff from 1973-75 and Director of Studies since 1977 and had known Joan since sports visits to Clyde when Joan was head and Ev was a physical education teacher at Firbank. Jan Douglas was such an outstanding history teacher in Ruby Powell's time that Joan had approached her annually in the hope of enticing her back to PLC as soon as family commitments allowed. Jan was teaching at Syndal High School, when Joan invited her to a meeting to discuss her possible return to PLC. "I'll never forget it," Jan would later recall. "In the 70s pant suits were very big, and I put on my only best outfit ... and I fronted up to PLC ... in a well-tailored jacket and pants. And when ushered into the study I knew immediately that I had misjudged the situation terribly, because here in front of me was somebody in a beautifully tailored dress. Her pearls; her hair, it was all perfect ... And I thought Janice, you have blown it." But she hadn't. Another interview was arranged as soon as Jan had resigned from her other job.

It was at that interview that Jan first met Ev Tindale who had been invited by Joan to attend. It was on a Saturday morning and Joan's dog was in the office. Jan made a fuss over the dog which promptly made a large puddle in the middle of the study. Joan had to set off to find some cloths and they became hysterical over the cleaning up while Jan tried to maintain some decorum. The incident came to represent the humour she always associated with the relationship between the three of them. It would not be until six months later, well after Jan had begun at the school, that Ev Tindale explained why, apart from the laughter over the dog, she had hardly said anything during the interview. Jan had looked like "the second coming" of one of Ev's sisters who had died. The striking resemblance had stunned her into uncharacteristic silence.

In thinking through Don Crofts' replacement, Joan knew that Jan and Ev had worked together in the History Department and in many other school spheres: "Their qualities are complementary; their mutual respect and trust obvious to all." They would be perfect as dual Vice-Principals. Indeed, Joan would later quote the respected Old Collegian Anne Fortune who was moved to remark: "I can't believe that they are not Old Collegians."[6] The pair would provide great support for Joan through the difficult years ahead. The three would meet daily before recess and, if there were no meetings or teaching pressing, they'd meet for half an hour at that time. Then often they would also meet for tea after school, reviewing the day's activities or discussing the evenings or forthcoming events. Jan Douglas would recall: "You could tell sometimes she'd had a terrible day and Ev and I would clown around and try and sort of lift that tension. Other times, she really wanted to talk and we'd cut the nonsense."

In October 1979, the Presbyterian Church moved to tighten its grip on the school—as the court challenge to the Property Council decisions on PLC and Scotch was set to begin and the Victorian parliament prepared to debate legislation safeguarding the interim school administrations. A delegation led by Ted Pearsons attended a meeting of the PLC School Council and promptly moved to sack it, as recorded in a letter Joan and the Bursar drafted to the Manager of the National Bank of Australia where the school banking was processed. A handwritten note across the top of the draft indicates it was 'Not sent on advice of Judge Northrop — 9.10.79' However, we learn from it:

> On Friday 5th October, we were visited by representatives of the Presbyterian Church of Victoria We were informed by those representatives as follows:
> 1. The General Assembly of the Presbyterian Church of Victoria had not re-appointed the existing members of the College Council.
> 2. The Assembly had appointed a Special Commission to conduct the affairs of PLC pending the outcome of litigation over the future of the College.
> 3. Any matters which would formerly have required a decision by the College Council should be submitted to the Special Commission through the Clerk of the Assembly (Reverend E.R Pearsons).
>
> No mention was made of any alterations to banking arrangements and we assume that the existing situation whereby cheques are signed by the Principal, Bursar, Assistant Bursar and Accountant (or his representative) will continue until further notice.

While the members of Council were notified that they had not been reappointed and that they were no longer members of the Council, the Church did not appoint a new Council. But it was an edict that the Council members chose to ignore.

It had taken more than two years, but the litigation initiated in 1977 by the Attorney-General on behalf of the Old Scotch Collegians' Association and John Thomson Macmillan for PLC to enable the two schools to incorporate was finally ready to proceed — now with the overwhelming support of the school communities demonstrated by the parent surveys. The case began on Thursday 1 November 1979 before Justice Robert Brooking in the Victorian Supreme Court.

The proceedings signalled the more pronounced entry of Joan Northrop into the PLC story, beyond her involvement as a former parent and the wife of Ray Northrop. A learned person in her own right, with masters' degrees in arts and education, she was a presence dedicated to the cause of women's education. Joan would attend each day the Supreme Court sat, taking notes as the case developed. During the lunch break, she would go across to see her husband (now Justice Ray Northrop) in his Federal Court Chambers at 451 Little Bourke Street and discuss the morning's events. Joan was "very alarmed" at the snail's pace of Richard Searby QC's opening of the case for the Attorney-General. She timed him at 12 words for half a minute! By Friday afternoon, Searby had finished his opening presentations, concluding with a technical discussion about the admissibility of the amended proceedings.

It was three weeks into the Court case when Allan Lobban, the solicitor from the Scotch Council, shared with Ray Northrop his diary note of a 23 November phone call with Max Bradshaw. Bradshaw had contacted Lobban with a proposal to reform the Scotch College Council with eight members appointed by the Presbyterian Church, two members appointed by the Old Scotch Collegians Association, two appointed by the School Council and one appointed by the Scotch Foundation. Lobban assumed a similar proposal would be put to PLC. He told Bradshaw that he would not comment on the proposal "and asked him had he heard of the Government's proposal regarding the interim position and, in particular, the proposal that the existing school Councils should be interim Councils."

The fruits of lobbying members of the State Parliament can

be seen in Hansard in the Presbyterian Schools Bill being introduced into the Legislative Council, in tandem with the Presbyterian Trusts Act Bill. The Attorney-General had decided to act upon the Schools advocacy to protect the Council members and had introduced both bills on 22 November 1979. The Schools Bill was about making "temporary Provision with respect to the Management and Control of certain Schools pending the Determination of certain Proceedings." The Trusts Bill was to "make further provision with respect to the division of certain Property in according with the Uniting Church in Australia Act 1977 and Part III of the Schedule to the Presbyterian Church of Australia Act 1971, to amend the Presbyterian Trusts Act 1890."

On 4 December, Brian Bayston, following Pam Royle's lead, wrote to every member of the Victorian Parliament on behalf of the Presbyterian Church of Victoria saying, "the passage of the Presbyterian Schools Bill would be unjust." Two days later, Bill Landeryou, the Labor Leader in the Legislative Council, confirmed the party's opposition to it: "The Bill asks Parliament to take an attitude on matters which should properly be determined outside the Parliament."[7]

The legal proceedings continued through December. At the Senior School speech night on 7 December 1979, in Dallas Brooks Hall, Ray Northrop advised the parents and girls that the legal challenge to the vesting of the schools in the Continuing Presbyterian Church was unlikely to be decided before February or March of the following year. He also briefed the audience on the Presbyterian challenge to the validity of the School Council, which explained the State Government's decision to enact legislation to protect the schools. In her speech, Joan Montgomery acknowledged the challenges, but with a determination to find a silver lining: "In some ways 1979 has been a difficult year. Any controversial issue, on which staff, parents or Old Collegians feel strongly, must be divisive. The frustration of deferred planning and building and the uncertainty that surrounds contradictory press statements is undermining. Yet from it all could come a stronger school."

In response to criticism that PLC was only interested in academic excellence, Joan said: "It is not a selective school except for those few girls who enter at Year 9 and above. Even here selection is based on a number of criteria, not just academic results. We do strive for excellence, but excellence in every field. Is it wrong to expect every girl to achieve the very best of which she is capable? The tragedy of unstretched faculties is a real one."

As much as Joan understood that students had varying abilities and aptitudes, she also understood that not all girls comfortably fitted the shoes of a model PLC pupil. Her pragmatism and humanity in managing such differences were part of what made her an exceptional teacher and Principal.

Ruth Stewart was a case in point. Ruth would later acknowledge[8] that she was a strong minded, determined adolescent with more energy than she knew what to do with and much more ability to ask why, than wisdom to reflect on the answers she might be given. In short, she was often getting into trouble in the boarding house, arguing about why things had to be done in a particular way. By sheer exuberance she found herself caught up the wrong ladder or behind the wrong bush. Perhaps Joan could see herself in Ruth from her own school days. Indeed, Joan would later reflect: "I was often at the discipline receiving end, but later was very grateful for the examples that I had had."[9]

Ruth remembers Joan eating dinner with the boarders in the dining room every Wednesday night. The rules in the dining room were very strict with a seating plan that changed weekly. It was hierarchical, with sixth formers and a mistress at the head of each table and seating rotating around the table during the week following the seat number you were allocated at the start of the week. There was a high table that had the Boarding House Mistress and Joan and a few girls each week. This meant each boarder would sit with Joan once or twice a year for a whole meal.

Vetting of Wisdom

After the regular formalities of prayer, carving, serving, clearing the table and folding of napkins, and after every diner had completed the meal, the girls would file out of the dining room past the Boarding House mistress or, on Wednesday nights, Miss Montgomery.

'Monty' would have a word here and there with one or other of the students. One Wednesday night she quietly indicated that she would like Ruth to wait at the end of the meal. Ruth had presumed it would be to make polite conversation, but Joan began: "Now, Ruth tell me exactly. Where did you go on Sunday?" Ruth's mouth dropped open, as she recalled the outing. She had been with several other boarders and they had gone further than their exit permission slips had indicated and in the company of several people who were not included in their parents' list of approved chaperones. What's more, they had imbibed several minor but not illegal stimulants that the school seriously disapproved of. How did she know? And what would become of Ruth now that Joan did know?

Ruth does not recall saying anything, but her body language spoke volumes. Joan continued: "You don't actually need to tell me where you went, as my friend who was on the tram with you gave a rather detailed account of your itinerary, and I have a good idea of who you were with. I merely suggest that you have a talk with each of the girls concerned and suggest that they come and see me. Anyone who does come to see me will be dealt with leniently. I can't say the same for any who do not come to see me."

Ruth knew what they had done would bring a serious disciplinary response, at the very least "gating" (not being allowed out of the school grounds for a specified time) but possibly worse. She wondered how many of the group Joan knew about? On reflection, had Joan asked who else was part of the adventure, she would have staunchly refused to reveal any names even under threat of torture! But the Principal had not asked Ruth to "dob" anyone in. More importantly, if Ruth didn't pass on the

Miss Montgomery

message they could be in even more trouble. "She had me absolutely check mated!" Ruth would recall.

Thirty years on, Ruth can't remember what exactly the punishment was. She has a vague memory that they were gated. But she vividly recalls the interview with Miss Montgomery and, as the mother of four children, still marvels at her astute handling of a rebellious and feisty adolescent.

Another time Ruth had an argument with her form teacher Miss Potter. It was the first week of the year. The class had four boarders in a class of 24. Miss Potter announced that each afternoon it would be the duty of the boarders to close and lock the windows as the day girls would all be heading off to catch buses. Ruth protested that this was unfair: "Four of us, twenty of them; do the numbers, it doesn't add up!" Miss Potter replied that she set the rules and Ruth must abide by them. Ruth re-joined: "This country has a strong tradition of democracy and I will not participate in such inequity." Declaring that the other boarders agreed with her, Ruth told Miss Potter she could do what she liked, but she would not be closing any windows. In response, Miss Potter chose not to take Ruth head on but merely concentrated her steely gaze on the insolent pupil and directed her to the Principal's office at morning recess to discuss the matter with Miss Montgomery.

Not intimidated and feeling like a freedom fighter, Ruth duly presented herself at the office, ready to wave the red flag high and wide, with many arguments forming on her tongue that were emboldened by her experience on the school debating team. Joan told Ruth to sit down, then gently began: "Ruth, let me give you some advice on how to deal with people." Ruth was totally disarmed. With one sentence she had acknowledged her grievance, treated her as a person who could be reasoned with and gave her the sense that she could help her through this predicament, which she did indeed do. Joan melded some compromise duty that the boarders shared with day girls, and that was the end of that. Ruth would later reflect that had Joan been a different kind of headmistress, Ruth would have made some kind of heroic, self-destructive stand and either been thrown out of the school or walked out. Indeed, she watched a good friend who was a boarder at Scotch College in the same year do just that. Instead, Ruth became one of the editors of the school magazine, *Patchwork*, and did well in her final year with marks aplenty to get into medicine at Melbourne University (where she admits she did struggle heroically and self destructively against the system). Ruth believes that in her handling of the students and staff, in her vision for her school and her students and in the mentoring and role modelling that she gave, Joan Montgomery was a brilliant headmistress and it was one of the great privileges of her life to have attended PLC when she was Principal.

Ten days after the Speech Night, on 17 December, Joan Northrop recorded her last entry detailing the court proceedings before the case was adjourned for the summer recess. On the first day back, 21 February 1980, she would note: "The intervening period has been one in which our counsel have attempted to force us to settle on terms which would give control to the Continuing church. I am not happy that Searby has been party to this." What Richard Searby QC, counsel for the schools, had been a party to, was a joint memorandum dated 18 February prepared by him, Brian Shaw and Gavan Griffith. In it they set out their position as to costs in the event that the Continuing Church succeeded in the court action. Given the Presbyterian Schools Bill 1979 had not yet been passed by Parliament, and even if had been, they raised doubts about whether the school Councils could indemnify the parties, who might be personally liable for costs.

The sitting was adjourned so that the PLC Council, of which Ray Northrop was still Chairman, could discuss the settlement proposal later that day. As Joan Northrop would record the next day, Friday 22 February: "PLC Council stood firm." She observed that while Max Bradshaw had arrived at the court in a cheerful mood, he had turned a "pale shade of livid" on hearing this news.

That afternoon, the Presbyterians decided to turn up the heat. They hastily fired off a writ in the Victorian Supreme Court with Clerk Ted Pearsons suing on behalf of the members of the Presbyterian Church of Victoria and Presbyterian Church of Victoria Trusts Corporation. Such was the rush that many of the defendants' names were misspelled as Brian Bayston, solicitor and protagonist, scrambled to file the writ. *Jean* (not Joan) Margaret Montgomery was the 16th named defendant. But there was no ambiguity in the charge: "Since the 3rd October 1979 (being the close of the General Assembly of the Presbyterian Church of Victoria for the year 1979) the first [to the] fifteenth defendants (the Council members) have (a) purported to act as lawfully appointed members of the Governing Body of PLC, although none of them was appointed, (b) have asserted authority over and dealt with and turned to account as they saw fit the finances and property of PLC, (c) have disbursed the funds of PLC in payment of legal expenses and outgoings in connection with the said actions or either of them and/or given an indemnity based on PLC funds to the said relators or relator, all without any authority of the Plaintiffs, or any lawful authority in that regard whatsoever."

The Presbyterians sought an injunction, restraining the defendants from further dealing with or authorising the expenditure of finances of PLC without the consent of the plaintiffs, and damages. The tactic, in law as in politics, was age-old, to squeeze "as a lemon is squeezed — until the pips squeak." But before applying the final squeeze, the Presbyterians hesitated.

As Brian Bayston would later recall, Bill Ormiston QC, the Presbyterians' barrister, "had prepared a further action against all the PLC Council ... He said, 'if you don't hear from me by quarter to three, issue the writ.' So, at quarter to three, I'd heard nothing and I headed off to issue the writ. It was a hot day and with my corpulence and the heat I was covered with sweat — I rushed off to get this writ in and got it in. In the meantime, Bill was ringing furiously to say, 'Don't, Don't.' He sent a person racing up after me to try to stop me—but it was too late. Bill tried to speak with the Registrar to keep it under wraps, as it might frustrate settlement."

But the heavy-handed tactics worked. On the following Sunday, the Scotch Executive and their Old Collegians' Association met and resolved that the costs involved were "not warranted in regard to possible benefits" and that they would "settle on any terms." The capitulation by Scotch triggered a downward spiral. That same Sunday afternoon, 24 February, the PLC Council met and resolved that it could not go it alone and would settle on the same terms as Scotch. As an exasperated Joan Northrop would write that night: "Are we Polish people when Hitler marched in, or small holders in the Ansett Takeover?"

The subsequent negotiations "were protracted, difficult and accompanied by some heat and rancour." The terms of settlement, which included the creation of a new body corporate to be called "Presbyterian Ladies' College" were drawn up and settled over many weeks by lawyers for the parties. The documents went through a series of drafts and were finally agreed on only after "much consideration, much anxious reflection and some give and take on both sides."[10]

The cave-in by the Scotch College had been the decisive factor that made any further resistance by PLC impossible. More than four decades later, Ray Northrop was still convinced the Presbyterian action would not have succeeded in the Supreme Court. There was absolutely no doubt in his mind that the Council had the authority and responsibility to keep the school running. The regulations of the General Assembly of the Presbyterian Church of Victoria itself clearly gave the Council the power to administer the finances of the college, and clearly gave the Principal the power to appoint members of staff, subject to confirmation by the Council.

It was a disastrous outcome for those advocating an independently incorporated PLC and, ultimately, for Joan Montgomery.

11

A 12 TO 5 CARVE UP

In December 1979, the Presbyterian Trusts Bill, which provided for the validation of the Presbyterian Church of Victoria and the transfer of certain property to the Uniting Church in Australia, was passed by the Victorian Parliament and became law. The nine former Presbyterian Schools, including PLC and Scotch College, and the property of those schools were excluded from the operation of that act. However, the Presbyterian Schools Bill, making provision for the nine schools awaited the March sittings of State Parliament. In the meantime, negotiations continued over a settlement of the legal proceedings commenced by the PLC Council in June 1977.

The proposed settlement looked good on paper, in principle enabling the PLC community to maintain some influence over the school, now to be characterised as a corporation owning the school property and being run by a board (the School Council but with a change of name). The Articles of Association would name the members of the *first* Council and would thereafter provide for the constitution of the ongoing Council. That new Council would consist of 17 members (to retire annually or biannually) who would be appointed by the General Assembly of the Presbyterian Church of Victoria and would comprise three groups. Group A was to be made up of five people nominated by the Presbyterian General Assembly (the Presbyterian contingent). Group B was to consist of five people nominated by a committee of three Parents' Association representatives, three Old Collegians representatives and the Chairman of the School Council (the PLC School community contingent). And Group C was to be nominated by the Council itself (the Council contingent), with the General Assembly having the power to veto one or more of the nominations and request new nominations.

To determine the first seven Group C members, the Presbyterians would nominate their first five, the PLC community through its representatives in the Court action would nominate their first five and then seven people would be drawn from a list that had been proposed in the settlement papers, comprising of two Baptists, two Anglicans, 11 Presbyterians, one Uniting Church person and one Jewish person. In Brian Bayston's view, the fact that the Presbyterians had come up with that first group of Group C members made clear it was never meant to have been 'independent' — whereas the school community saw it from the outset, according to Ray Northrop, as a third 'independent' group. From the Presbyterian side, as Bayston would later claim, "we saw it as a 12 to five carve up". While he would acknowledge the words of the settlement didn't reflect it, the terms of the negotiations were "clear that the Presbyterians had control over the appointments onto the Council".

The establishment of the Presbyterian Ladies' College, incorporated under the Companies Act 1961 as a company limited by guarantee (No C-164958L), ultimately provided for the College to become, as planned, an independent corporate body controlled by a Council of 17. The property of the school was transferred to the corporate body and its business affairs and property were to be managed by the Council, the members of which were the members and directors of the corporate body. It also provided, importantly for the Presbyterians, that the College would have a formal connection with the Presbyterian Church of Victoria but, as central to the concerns of the school community, would continue to provide a humane, scientific and general education for pupils of all faiths. Also, important for the school community was the condition that, as it always had been in the past, religious instruction on non-sectarian lines would remain a fundamental part of the education at the College.

More importantly for those who were concerned about Joan Montgomery's future, Joan would continue as Principal. The Parents' Association reported that, under the terms by which PLC would become a corporate body, the Principal would continue to have complete control of the organisation and management of the school and the employment and dismissal of staff. The Principal would also have the supervision and complete control of the courses of study, the enrolment, discipline and dismissal of students and the conduct of student activities generally. The Association also confirmed that the Presbyterian Church had withdrawn its opposition to the Presbyterian Schools Bill, and that all parties to the settlement agreed to support the passage through Parliament of a Bill containing appropriate provisions validating all proceedings of the present School Council up to the time when the corporate body was incorporated. Importantly, the costs of the plaintiffs were agreed to be paid out of the property of the school. The plaintiffs' financial positions were therefore no longer in jeopardy.

But the printer's ink had barely dried on the settlement when it became clear that while the powers and prerogatives of the PLC Principal had been confirmed, it was now Joan Montgomery's tenure that was in real jeopardy. Well in advance of the first meeting of the new School Council, Max Bradshaw and Ted Pearsons came calling at PLC for the "golden handshake" meeting at which it was made clear that the Presbyterians wanted Joan out.

Immediately after that meeting on 7 May 1980, Joan contacted solicitor Ian Murray at Mallesons. Six days later, Murray sent a draft letter to Bradshaw and Pearsons "seeking confirmation and clarification of certain matters arising out of the abovementioned conference." It had been drafted after careful consideration of the written statements made by Jan Douglas and Ev Tindale immediately following the meeting. Joan was told that she should sign the letters and arrange for them to be personally delivered to Bradshaw and Pearsons at their home addresses and that the person delivering them should keep a note of the time and place of delivery. On 14 May, the following letter was sent to Bradshaw and an identical one was sent to Pearsons:

> Dear Mr Bradshaw,
>
> I refer to the conference you attended with the Reverend Pearsons at my office on 7 May 1980. Two other members of the Staff of the College (Mrs Janice Douglas and Miss Evelyn Tindale) attended that conference.
>
> It was made apparent to all Staff present at the conference, including myself that—you and the Reverend Pearsons were consulting me on behalf of the Presbyterian Church of Victoria, and the Presbyterian Church no longer wants me to remain as Principal of the College and is willing to make me 'a not ungenerous settlement offer', if I am prepared to resign without delay, and the Presbyterian Church is not concerned at the possibility that my leaving the College in the circumstance may adversely affect the Staff and students of the College.
>
> I was amazed that such a proposal could be put with total disregard for the welfare of the College.
>
> My amazement was compounded by the fact that your proposal is entirely contrary to the terms on which the litigation was settled.
>
> I wish to make it perfectly plain that I have no desire to resign as Principal and therefore will continue to serve the best interests of the College in that role.

I do not believe I was mistaken in my assessment of what took place at the conference and will assume that this letter accurately reflects the attitude of the Presbyterian Church on this matter unless you advise me, in writing, to the contrary within forty-eight hours.

In the absence of any satisfactory response to this letter I will refer this matter to my legal advisors for appropriate action.

I am forwarding an identical letter to the Reverend Pearsons.

Yours sincerely,
Joan Montgomery
Principal

Ev Tindale and Jan Douglas also took action following the 7 May meeting. Ev prepared a letter to Pam Royle as President of the Parents' Association enclosing a copy of each of the contemporaneous notes they had made after the meeting and advising of their plan to send a joint letter to each new member of the School Council before its first meeting. They explained that they would present the letter to the whole Staff on Monday 26 May and suggest that a telegram be sent to the Council via the Moderator of the Presbyterian Church and the incoming Council Chair, Mary Murdoch, confirming staff support. The letter, sent on PLC letterhead, was explicit:

> Dear (each member of the new Council)
> On Wednesday 7 May we were present when Mr F. Maxwell Bradshaw and the Reverend E.R. Pearsons raised with Miss Montgomery the possibility that the new PLC Council might not wish her to continue as Principal, and sought to put to her a proposition as to terms upon which she might

relinquish her position. It was mutually acknowledged that Messrs Bradshaw and Pearsons raised these matters in a spirit of kindness. However, Miss Montgomery declined to hear Messrs Bradshaw and Pearsons' proposition on the ground that she did not contemplate resigning before her normal retirement date.

Knowing that the general feeling among the staff was that the settlement of the recent litigation promised a stable future for PLC we felt obliged to advise staff of this meeting. This we did at a staff meeting on Thursday 8 May. After praying on the matter, the staff discussed our news at length. It is no overstatement to say that the staff were astounded and dismayed at the suggestion that the new Council might not confirm Miss Montgomery in her office of Principal.

We are now writing to you, without Miss Montgomery's leave or consent, to state that in our view, if the new Council does not confirm Miss Montgomery's tenure of office as Principal, it will do her a grave disservice, and seriously erode the morale of the staff and student body, the support of the parents, and the reputation of PLC as one of the foremost schools and places of witness to Christian faith in action in Australia.

Miss Montgomery has performed remarkable service as a stabilizing influence in the difficult period from which we had all hoped PLC was about to emerge. Whatever may be Miss Montgomery's legal rights in this matter, we urge on you the opinion that it will be overwhelmingly to the advantage of PLC and to the credit of the new Council if she is confirmed in her office.

A 12 to 5 Carve Up

The new Council held its first meeting at 10am on Saturday 24 May in the hall of Trinity Presbyterian Church in Camberwell. It would be chaired by the Reverend R.C. Russell on behalf of the Presbyterian Moderator. Ray Russell was a former Moderator, former Air Commodore and Principal Chaplain of the RAAF and associate minister at Melbourne's Scots' Church. The proceedings would soon be etched in the mind of many who were present, not least Joan Montgomery.

The new Council members in attendance were Barry Murdoch Armitage (C—Presbyterian), Frederick Maxwell Bradshaw (A—Presbyterian), Keith Shaw Campbell (C—Presbyterian), the Reverend Donald Carruthers (A—Presbyterian), the Reverend Alan Stewart Crawford (B), the Reverend Gordon George Garner (C—Anglican), Valerie Jean Griffith (C—Presbyterian), Ian Leslie Hore-Lacey (C—Anglican), Thomas Lionel King (B—School community), the Reverend William Arnold Loftus (A—Presbyterian), John George Rennie McArthur (C—Uniting), George Edmund Morgan (A—Presbyterian), Mary Jean Murdoch (B—School community), the Reverend Edward Ross Pearsons (A—Presbyterian), Ian Ronald Waddell (B), and Dr Anne Jennifer Warr (C—Anglican). There was an apology from Henry Robert Holmes (B). Only one of the seven group C people, John McArthur, was aligned with the school community, having been on the previous PLC Council.

Russell began by welcoming those present and thanking them for agreeing to serve on the Council, then constituted the meeting with a prayer. The first item of business was the election of a Chairman. One of the terms of the settlement was that the first Chairman of the new Council would be elected from "those persons set forth in the schedule who were members of the Presbyterian Ladies' College Council on 21 June 1977 and before the College was incorporated". This is where the first heated battle of the Council occurred.

Ian Waddell moved and John McArthur seconded the nomination of Mary Murdoch as Chair. With no other nominations at that point a vote was taken—five in favour, nine against. Motion lost. Ted Pearsons then nominated John McArthur, who declined. McArthur then again nominated Mary Murdoch, noting that the Chair must come from among those who were members of the previous Council. Pearsons then nominated Waddell, who declined. The Reverend Don Carruthers nominated the Reverend Crawford, who declined.

John McArthur moved and Mary Murdoch seconded a motion that the election of the Chair be by ballot. The required number of five members duly requested a ballot. Carruthers then nominated Lionel King, who declined. As Murdoch remained the only nomination, the ballot was taken. The result was eight in favour, seven against. Motion carried. Just. But while that fight had been won by Group B—the school community—the struggle had only just begun.

Mary Murdoch would later recall the politics behind that first vote. The Group B members had agreed in advance that they would nominate her to be Chair. But on the way into the meeting, John McArthur—who had been selected onto the Council as part of Group C, and was the only Group C member who had been on the previous Council—showed Mary a letter he had received from Max Bradshaw "in his spidery little writing" asking him to agree to be Chairman.

Indeed, it would later come to light through a statement prepared by Val Griffith, one of the Group C appointees, that a meeting had been held in Ted Pearsons' office in Assembly Hall late in April: "It soon became apparent to me that we had been called together to plan strategic moves for the future of the Council and the School and that both Group A and Group C would be expected to vote as one body." Griffith said the Presbyterians' preferred candidate for Council Chair was John McArthur, who was not at the meeting and would decline the nomination. And she was struck by another matter: "We were told that Miss Montgomery would be approached in the near future regarding termination of her services and a 'golden handshake' would be offered regarding termination pay." Mrs Flynn—the former Head of the Junior School whose retirement had caused such a stir—was mentioned as a successor to Joan Montgomery. Val Griffith would reflect that she should not have been so surprised when, after being approached to accept a Group C position on the Council, she was advised that they were "expected to vote together on issues."

Immediately after her election, Mary Murdoch—shaken by the fierce politicking that resulted in her narrow win—took the Chair with a positive message, speaking about working for the good of the school and of the need to work together. As the Reverend Russell left, no longer being needed as convenor of the meeting, he paused at the door of the church hall with a concerned look on his face. Mary interpreted it as a feeling of concern that Group B hadn't rolled over: "I think we were seen, as we saw them, as villains ... I don't think there was any love lost at all."[1]

While the Presbyterians might have failed to get their preferred candidate as Chair, their domination of the new Council was confirmed as the meeting unfolded. Eleven days later, Lionel King, would deliver an explosive resignation letter to the secretary of the new Council—starkly summarising the extent of that domination:

> I herewith tender my resignation from the new Council and in doing so, I wish to register the strongest possible protest at the way in which, in spite of Mrs Mary Murdoch's most able and impartial chairmanship, the first Council Meeting, held on Saturday morning, 24 May was so completely and ruthlessly orchestrated by the Group A members to their own advantage. I was

Vetting of Wisdom

incredulous and appalled by the following:
1. The total opposition of both Group A and Group C members to Mrs Mary Murdoch's nomination for election as Chairman.
2. The utter domination of Group C members by Group A members, which was so transparently obvious by the way in which the former voted unanimously in support of all motions put by Group A
3. The voluminous position papers on all items in the agenda, copies of which only Group A and Group C had.
4. The relentless determination of Group A members to seek exemption of Section 121 (6B) of the Companies Act which, if granted, will allow any or all members of the Council to serve beyond the mandatory retiring age of 72.
5. The election of a Group A dominated Executive and Finance Committee which will henceforth control the Council. This Committee will meet 10 times during the year while the full Council is required to meet only 3 times a year.

Considering the above matters in the light of the recent and blatant attempt by two Group A members to force Miss Montgomery to resign as Principal and the unbelievably rude and ungracious manner in which the majority of Group A members either ignored or refused an invitation by the School Community to a 'get-to-know-each-other' evening.

I am now convinced that the College is headed for deep and serious trouble, under the domination of the Presbyterian Church through this Group.

Furthermore, I am convinced that, until the

Articles of Association of Incorporation are changed to enable ALL members of the Council to be elected or selected by the School Community, nothing will prevent this unhealthy domination and its certain extension into every aspect of College life.

I also have a strong feeling that my professional expertise as an Architect, and my experience of some 7 years as Convenor of the former Buildings and Property Committee, will not be called upon by this Council. Even if it were, I do not believe, in view of the foregoing, that I could bring myself to work with any of the members of Group A or Group C, particularly whilst the latter fail to recognise their duties and responsibilities as directors of the Company, Presbyterian Ladies' College.

I request that this letter be read in full at the next Council Meeting and I advise you that I have forwarded copies to the Parents' Association, the Old Collegians' Association, members of the Council, the Principal, the Bursar and the Moderator of the General Assembly of the Presbyterian Church of Victoria. For the moment I do not intend releasing copies to the newspapers for publication.

It is with the deepest regret that I take this course of action, but I do so with the utmost conviction that the School Community must be informed about these matters and events and the disastrous effects I believe they will surely have on the future of the College.

On the same day, 3 June 1980, Mary Murdoch prepared a

Circular Letter to Parents, as the new Council Chair. She reported on the first meeting—her election, with Bill Loftus as Vice-Chair and Ewen McRae, the school's bursar, as Secretary. More importantly, she further noted the confirmation of Miss Montgomery's appointment as Principal, with immediate effect and continuing until her retirement in five years' time or, if she and PLC agreed, after a further five-year term.

While many parents would have read the circular and rejoiced at the news that the position of their beloved Principal was now secure, Mary Murdoch had been somewhat economical with the truth. While the Presbyterians had indeed voted in favour of the resolution relating to Joan Montgomery's tenure, this had been no more than a tactical retreat, and a begrudging one.

While the meeting was underway, Joan had waited outside the hall from 10am until the Council had completed Item 8 — "Appointment of Principal". Luckily, it was a clear, mild day. Nonetheless, having planned to be on holiday in Queensland, there were better and more dignified ways to spend her time. Term 1 had finished on 8 May and Term 2 was not due to begin until the following Tuesday, 27 May. But Ray Northrop had earlier called Joan to say that given there was some tussling over her position it would be best if she were present for the meeting, and so she cancelled her holiday. Joan recalls Bill Loftus, whose church was host for the meeting, coming out to collect her after the discussion on Item 8 had concluded.

The minutes of the meeting note the tabling of a letter from Miss Joan Mitchell Montgomery dated 23 May 1980, in which she consented to act as Principal of the College. It was then noted that Pearsons had moved and Bradshaw seconded a motion that Joan be appointed Principal pursuant to and on the terms described in a resolution circulated to members. The motion was carried and then Joan joined the meeting.

In the lead up to the meeting, Bradshaw and Pearsons had

certainly attempted to engineer a far different outcome. So what happened between their "golden handshake" meeting with Joan Montgomery on 7 May and the meeting of the new School Council? Had they been influenced by Joan's letter to them or by the PLC staff protests? Brian Bayston would later reveal that it was a legal warning from their own camp that had been a significant factor in persuading Bradshaw and Pearsons to take a step back. Bill Ormiston QC, who had led the Presbyterian team during the court battle over control of the school, had given advice confirming that Joan's employment contract was secure. Moreover, all teaching staff and other employees of the School prior to PLC's incorporation were re-engaged on the same terms and conditions.

On paper then, nothing had changed in the way the school would continue to operate. But beyond that appearance of normality, nothing had changed in the attitude of the adversaries and the battle would continue. Joan, though Principal for the term of her contract, would now be subjected to a change of tactics, to make her life as uncomfortable as possible for the remainder of her tenure.

The first Council meeting had signalled the beginning of the fresh hostilities. Three days after Lionel King sent his letter, Max Bradshaw replied with a letter of his own. It was a mixture of good-cop-bad-cop, regretting that King was "so upset over the initial meeting" but then warning that "those who live in glass houses should not throw stones". Bradshaw disagreed with King's desire for the "school to be run as formerly." In Max's view: "It is abundantly clear that the Presbyterian Ladies' College is a charitable institution in law existing for educational purposes in connection with the Presbyterian Church of Victoria ... It is surely axiomatic that the Presbyterian Church should be so placed as to be able to ensure that the purposes for which the school exists should have effect given to them. What charitable institution is ever conducted on a different basis?"

Bradshaw went on to threaten King with a possible defamation suit, claiming "serious errors of fact" and "inferences erroneously drawn" were calculated to damage the reputation of Council members: "It is one thing to send such a letter to members of the Council ... whom may be covered by ... qualified privilege. But in sending copies of your letter to the Parents' Association and the Old Collegians' Association you have disseminated and published an actionable libel."

Having received his own legal advice, King would have none of it, writing back denying libel and contesting Bradshaw's view of the relationship between the Presbyterian Church and the school: "Following incorporation, the College is to be carried on, conducted and managed by the incorporated body in accordance with the Memorandum and Articles of Association, the Companies Act and the general law ... Contrary to your inference that it is for the Presbyterian Church of Victoria to ensure that the purposes for which the School exists are given effect to, it is clearly the responsibility of all members of the Council to perform their duties according to law rather than at the direction of the Presbyterian Church, or indeed any Church, association or group." King ended with a blunt full stop: "I now consider the correspondence closed. If you wish to take matters further, please address any communications to my Solicitors, Mallesons."

......

The contested relationship between churches and their schools had been an issue from the time of union. In May 1980, the education committee of the Uniting Church's Victorian Synod had reported on the church's involvement in primary and secondary education in both the independent and State school systems. Prior to the merger of the former Congregational, Methodist and Presbyterian churches, there were 14 schools of those denominations in Victoria and Albury. With union, the former Methodist schools were inherited by the Uniting Church along with all of the Presbyterian schools apart from PLC and Scotch College which were awarded to the Continuing Presbyterian Church. The report's recommendations therefore applied only to the former Methodist schools—Wesley College, Methodist Ladies' College, Cato College and Kingswood College—and the remainder of Presbyterian Schools.

The Uniting Church resolved to readjust its historical relationship to the former Methodist and Presbyterian schools by setting up the schools as incorporated companies, in much the same way as PLC and Scotch had been in the settlement that had resolved their future control. But in their new status, the Uniting Church schools would be legally free to run their own affairs through governing bodies only some of whose members would be elected by the Church. The education committee recommended that representation be a minority of between 15 and 20 per cent of its total and added: "Apart from the power to appoint nominees to the governing body and to receive reports, we envisage ... that the links would be creative and mutually beneficial ... we have deliberately avoided stipulating specific requirements in areas such as school worship or religious education."

This was a very different mindset to the Bradshaw model, without kicking over all traces of Church instruction. It remained a question of balance, eschewing extremism and dogma: "We would expect the School Council and Principal and Staff together to offer an educationally acceptable programme and to remain sensitive to the expressions of Christian concern on educational matters which arise in the Synod ... to which the school is related. A church which accepts for itself a process of self-criticism and renewal in a changing world will expect a similar discipline of the schools which would relate to it."[2] Religious teaching in schools was regarded not as an end in itself but rather a means to enable a person to enter into the worshipping life of their community.

Max Bradshaw envisaged something far more granulated and controlling for PLC and Scotch College under the paternal control of the Continuing Presbyterians. He had amplified his views in a draft resolution for a meeting of the PLC School Council in 1982: "To assist the Council to fulfil its responsibilities ... the Principal is requested on or before the next meeting of the Council to furnish information on the religious education given to pupils of the college grade by grade and form by form specifying in each case—a) the syllabus; b) the set texts; c) teachers, including their qualifications and church membership, and d) the Principal's assessment of the effectiveness of this program in—i) religious instruction; ii) teaching of holy scripture; iii) development of Christian ideals of citizenship and personal character; iv) promotion of a spirit of reverence in the entire life and work of the college."

So the fight for PLC between a Uniting Church-leaning school community and the Continuing Presbyterians was of no small difference. At stake for the school community was the style of education being offered to their children, whether instruction be "a process of self-criticism and renewal in a changing world" or the narrower dogma of minority opinion on the part of those who had opposed union. The high stakes would drive continuing animosity on the new School Council.

There had already been a delay in selecting a replacement for Lionel King when apologies came from 10 of the members, mainly from Groups A and C, at the Council's second meeting on 27 June. The meeting folded for want of a quorum with Mary Murdoch recording in the minutes: "It had been proposed that the meeting appoint a Chairman of the Selection Committee so that the vacancy caused by the resignation of Mr King be filled in accordance with the Articles. In the absence of a quorum it was not possible to make the appointment or to transact any other business."

This triggered a formal letter from Pam Royle, as President of

A 12 to 5 Carve Up

the PLC Parents' Association, to Murdoch the day before the third scheduled Council meeting on 17 July: "The Parents' Association Committee is extremely anxious that the Selection Committee meet as soon as practicable as is required by the Articles of Association of Presbyterian Ladies' College."

To shelter her from any procedural bullying arising from Groups A and C voting together on all matters, Mary Murdoch invited lawyer Phillip Aitken from the firm Aitken, Walker and Strachan to the meeting. Ian Hore-Lacey (Group C) was appointed Chairman of the Selection Committee and there was then an adjournment to allow the committee to meet and report back. When it did so, Hore-Lacey announced Alex Chernov as King's replacement to Council.

Alex Chernov was the Lithuanian-born son of Russian parents who had migrated to Australia with his family as a teenager in 1949. After attending Melbourne High School, he studied law at Melbourne University and was admitted to the Victorian Bar in 1968. Appointed a Queen's Counsel in 1980, he would become a Victorian Supreme Court judge in 1997, and move to the Court of Appeal the following year before being sworn in as the 28th Governor of Victoria in 2011. His intellect and courtly demeanour would prove a great asset for the school community group on the Council, but he was a late entrant to a long simmering feud and some wilier foxes had broken into the PLC Council coup well before his arrival.

When Chernov took his seat at the reconvened 17 July meeting, the Council moved immediately to address a matter that would flare into another divisive dispute directly affecting Joan Montgomery. Architects had been invited to display preliminary drawings for a new residence for the Principal in the grounds of the school. The living conditions for Joan were far from ideal; she was still living in Hethersett with the boarders.

Another controversial agenda item would be the mandatory retiring age of members of Council. As PLC was now an incorporated body, the Companies Act required directors to retire before they reached the age of 72. Some of the Presbyterian Church nominees on Council were close to that age. To mend their vulnerability, there was an application to the Commissioner for Corporate Affairs, Jan Wade (later Victoria's first woman Attorney-General) to be exempt from that section. Not surprisingly, Group B members opposed the move. Pam Royle, on behalf of the Parents' Association, gave the Association's backing, writing several times urging Wade not to grant the exemption. The skirmish would continue until June 1982 when, against the trend, Group A and C members retreated, asking Wade to take no further steps on their exemption request for the time being.[3]

Speech nights had increasingly become the focus for set piece presentations on PLC's direction and for Delphic hints to the broad school community at the roiling tensions in the school's governance. As 1980 wore on with no sign of goodwill between the parties, there was a prefiguring of dangers lurking in the annual event. At the 20 November Council meeting, Barry Armitage (Group A) launched a pre-emptive strike by the Presbyterians, moving: "That no address be delivered by a member of the Council at a Junior or Senior School Speech night unless the Chairman for the time being or such other member of the Council nominated to deliver such address has first submitted a draft of his/her address to the Council or, if there be no convenient meeting of the Council, to the Executive and Finance Committee, for discussion and ratification before the delivery thereof and such draft has been approved with or without modification."

The motion, moved by the Reverend Ted Pearsons was debated and carried by 9 votes to 7. At that point, John McArthur, Alex Chernov and the Reverend Alan Crawford all recorded their dissent. They declared that the resolution was "demeaning of the office of Chairman", contained "inferences which continue the divisive approach to matters before the Council" and said those inferences and that divisiveness were "hindering a proper approach to the development of students, staff and property". Furthermore, the rising barrister Chernov noted that the Council had "no power, legal or moral, to control the contents of the Chairman's address to be given at Speech Night or anywhere else."

Mary Murdoch suffered but a small dent to the contents of her speech when she read to Council a draft of her proposed report to be delivered at both the Junior and Senior speech nights and "after some amendment to the opening paragraph this was accepted by Council." But the dent to the authority of the chair was substantial as the dissenters had perceived.

There was more to come. Having flexed their muscles against Mary Murdoch, Group A was then emboldened to move against Joan Montgomery in their very next motion. Prior to the meeting, the Reverend Bill Loftus had circulated a draft motion: "That no position shall be established which will add to the permanent staff of the College without the prior approval of Council. This provision shall not apply to the replacement of any existing appointment and shall not derogate from the Principal's right to appoint and dismiss members of staff." Pearsons seconded the motion and again it was the subject of debate before being carried. This time, dissent was recorded from Henry Holmes (Group B) as well as McArthur, Chernov and Crawford, who raised the same issues about the treatment of Joan as they had made in relation to Mary.

Joan was unbowed when delivering the 106th Principal's Report at the 1980 Speech Night. She began on a positive note, saying that while 1979 had been a difficult year for the school, 1980 had seen the beginning of an improvement: "The unhappy dispute which undermined the College has been settled, building and planning projects are proceeding again and unwelcome publicity has ended."

While her farewell to unwelcome publicity was premature —

there was plenty more to come—her welcome to members of the new School Council was more perspicacious, expressing a hope rather than an expectation that "mutual trust will grow." And she would conclude with a direct reference to the struggle over her tenure as Principal: "My personal debt to those with whom I work most closely is enormous. Had it not been for the intervention of Mrs Douglas and Miss Tindale, supported by Miss Walker [Hilary Walker, then Chief of Staff] and the teaching staff, I might well not be presenting the Report this evening."

Jan Douglas and Ev Tindale had stood beside Joan when Max Bradshaw had sought her resignation in the infamous "golden handshake" meeting—and rallied the staff to forcefully oppose her removal as Principal. That battle might have been won, but the bitter contest was far from over.

12

CHURCH TIGHTENS PLC HOLD

The Parents' Association held its first meeting for 1981 on 3 February, soon after the school year had begun. Pam Royle reported that plans were well underway to produce a regular newsletter with topical content, including "items of interest covering the appointment of the school Councillors, the Council structure and its progress to date, general items of interest, restatement of important dates, personal glimpses etc."

Notes and News of PLC was to become the first combined community newsletter to parents with contributions from the Parents' Association of the Senior and Junior Schools, the Combined Women's Group, the Old Collegians' and the Boarders' Parents. It was an energetic exercise driven by esprit de corps, love of school and the sunny promise of a new year. Yet within days of the first edition being sent to parents and Old Collegians early in March, Pam Royle received a formal letter from McCracken & McCracken Solicitors, signed by Brian Bayston in his capacity as "Law Agent of the Presbyterian Church of Victoria." Writing on behalf of the Commission of the Presbyterian Church of Victoria, the body appointed to take charge of institutions awarded to the Church at the time of union and responsible for the settlement of the litigation concerning PLC, Bayston protested: "This circular contains much false and misleading information and we desire to know whether your Association accepts responsibility for its contents."

As intended, it was received with a jolt. While Bayston did

not go into detail about his grievances with the content of the newsletter, it would soon become clear that they encompassed a range of issues that would define the deepening conflict over the following months between the Continuing Presbyterians and the more liberal school community representatives on the PLC Council.

That polarisation was demonstrated in other feedback from readers of the newsletter. No sooner had Bayston's protest arrived than Mary Murdoch received a handwritten card from Russell Rechner, who would later become Chair of the Council, and his wife, praising *Notes and News*: "Congratulations on your part in the preparation of a fair, even-handed and interesting publication that lets the facts speak for themselves. There must be times for you and your colleagues when it all seems very trying and difficult. By your grit and determination to keep playing and fairly in difficult circumstances you are building up much goodwill in the minds of the silent majority, the parents. When and if the rules need to be changed, your perseverance will be rewarded."

The newsletter, printed in Collingwood by John D Harris & Co, contained fresh information about PLC and its Council. It was a volunteer effort representing many hours of work. Beyond the time spent preparing content, checking and proof-reading, the material had to be delivered to the printers, then the finished newsletters needed to be collected, folded into 1200 envelopes and delivered to the post office.

It was a labour of love and there was much to crow about: "For the first time in the history of PLC, the school community is now required by law to take an active and direct part in nominating persons who will become members of the School Council. In fact, the school community first exercised that right soon after the new Council took office." This was a reference to the replacement of Lionel King with Alex Chernov, which was reported in greater detail later in the newsletter. It was also a peg for the inclusion of Council material in the newsletter: "With this requirement comes the obligation on parents to be familiar with the affairs of the school, including its Council, and to be vigilant so as to ensure that the interests of PLC and its pupils are in the forefront of the minds of those who are charged with the responsibility of controlling its affairs. The following information will assist parents to understand the new and extended role of the school community in the affairs of the School." The newsletter went on to explain the make-up of the Council with Groups A, B and C and how they were nominated, then stated: "Despite the fact that persons who become members of Council have been nominated by different groups ... all members of Council are obliged by law to exercise the responsibility vested in each in the best interests of the school as each director sees them, and not pursuant to any direction of the body which has appointed or nominated them to office. The ultimate superintendence of the affairs of the school, of course, rests in the hands of the Attorney-General and the Courts of Law."

While this, at one level, was a simple statement of fact, the implied declaration that the secular courts rather than the courts of the Presbyterian Church had ultimate authority over the affairs of PLC would undoubtedly have raised the ire of Brian Bayston and his colleagues. Was this a veiled threat that the school community was prepared to go back to court to fight for its position? Heaven forbid.

It is also unlikely that the Presbyterians would have been impressed with the newsletter's explanation of the abrupt resignation from the Council of Lionel King: "On June 3rd, 1980, shortly after the first meeting of the new Council, Mr Lionel King, a member of Group B, resigned as a mark of protest at the way in which decisions of the new Council appeared to be pre-determined and uninfluenced by discussion and argument, no matter how well informed."

To those who saw the school fight as being principally about

Joan Montgomery's tenure and independence as Principal, another vexing issue, also dependent on the Council, was her accommodation. Around the time of the first newsletter's distribution, Pam Royle on behalf of the Parents' Association, wrote to Ewen McRae, secretary of the PLC Council, about the delay in providing Joan with permanent accommodation: "It is my Committee's understanding that Miss Montgomery agreed to give up her flat at Hethersett in favour of the boarders, in the expectation that the Principal's residence would be completed by about the middle of this year or very soon after." The lease of the house Joan was now living in, around the corner from the school in Barnes Avenue, Burwood, was due to expire that July and construction on her new dwelling had not yet begun.

The Parents' Association was also continuing to battle against a move by the majority of the Council members to seek exemption for its members from the compulsory retirement age of 72. At the end of February, the Association followed their three previous letters to the Commissioner for Corporate Affairs arguing against the granting of any age exemption and requesting an opportunity personally to put its case to Commissioner Jan Wade. This was driven by the Association's belief that a PLC Council Committee had been appointed to seek a personal interview with Wade to push the case for age rule exemptions. Pam Royle wrote to Wade that her Executive Committee was seriously concerned as, "the Council Committee is not truly representative of the Council of the Company because no representative of Group B has been included ... [and] not all members of the Council are in favour of the application for exemption." The letter, which was copied to the Attorney-General, argued that Wade should call a meeting of all the parties to discuss the issue.

The controversy over *Notes and News of PLC* continued. At a meeting of the Parents' Association on 6 April it was reported that Barry Armitage, one of the Group C Presbyterians on the School Council, had telephoned Pam Royle to raise issues about the newsletter. An informal meeting over coffee was arranged at her home and Nan Falloon, President of the Old Collegians' Association and Mrs Bean, President of the Combined Women's Group, were also invited. As the Parents' Association minutes would record, it was not clear "in what capacity" Armitage had sought the meeting but it was soon abundantly clear that he had a long list of grievances that echoed and expanded those of Brian Bayston.

Armitage declared that *Notes and News of PLC* was inaccurate and biased. He began by taking issue with the account of the application for exemption from the age limited provision of the Companies Act. He said it had been agreed by both parties involved in the litigation, prior to settlement, that such an application for exemption would be sought at the first meeting of the new Council (a claim checked for the Parents' Association by Mallesons and confirmed to be untrue). Armitage did not like the newsletter's section on the Executive and Finance Committee. He expressed concern at the statement that "the ultimate superintendence of the affairs of the school, of course, rests in the hands of the Attorney-General and the Courts of Law." He objected to the account of Lionel King's resignation. He did not like the section on the "Fun and Fitness Trail" as the Council had not been informed. He further claimed that a School Council circular sent to parents had misrepresented the handling of the matter of the Principal's new house. He said that as chairman of the Council sub-committee formed to investigate a residence for the Principal, he was investigating alternatives and the sub-committee had the power to recommend building, buying off campus or renting.

But most of all, Barry Armitage was upset about the Parents' Association opposing the Council's application for an exemption from the age limit provisions of the Companies Act. Returning to the matter, he threatened legal action unless the Association withdraw its opposition. This would involve going to the Supreme Court and obtaining a writ against the Association to prevent them seeing Corporate Affairs Commissioner Jan Wade.

Armitage might have saved his breath. Pam Royle reported to the April meeting of the Association: "A meeting will be held with the Commissioner for Corporate Affairs, Mrs J Wade, and the Deputy Commissioner Mr Mitcham, and Mrs Falloon representing the Old Collegians' Association, Mrs Royle and Mr Macmillan representing the Parents' Association, and Mr Murray of Mallesons, on Wednesday 15 April 1981, in support of the submission opposing the application by the PLC School Council to be exempted from the age limit provision of the Companies Act (1961)." The meeting also "resolved that the action taken by the executive in arranging a meeting with the Commissioner be ratified together with the actions engaging Mr Murray of Mallesons to prepare relevant material."

A month later, in the May minutes, Pam explained that she had omitted a section from her report at the last meeting: "Presbyterians were conservative people, and Mr Armitage believed they would like religion at the school to be more structured." This difference of approach about the place of religion in the school became increasingly significant as time went on.

......

Since the folding of the court case and her bitter reflection that PLC had been "scotched by Scotch"—when the Scotch College Council had been first to buckle under weight of further Presbyterian legal action and agreed to a settlement—Joan Northrop had maintained her rage and her readiness to help further.

Joan wrote to Nan Falloon of the Old Collegians' Association on 7 April after Falloon had sought suggestions during the Association's annual meeting for Group B representatives to join the PLC Council. Joan saw this as an opportunity to identify "the sorts of people my 'Council-watching' activities suggest are necessary for the future of the school." She envisaged a bleak two or three years ahead for the Council and made a prescient forecast: "First, the present situation. I see this as very serious. We must face as an almost inevitable fact that following October, the combined voting of Groups A and C will be sufficient for the removal of the headmistress—not necessarily immediately, she will be allowed to stew in a sea of uncertainty, harassed by accommodation deficiencies and any other irritant available ... although I am prepared to hope for, and believe in miracles, we must act as if they will not occur."

In Joan Northrop's view, the qualities desired in members of Group B were determined by "how one sees" the future of the Council: "Is it to be the scene of continual warfare? This is a rhetorical question—either we are prepared to accept the harassment of the principal, the erosion of the assets of the College, the limitations of its educational function, or we object—strongly ... The opposition (being the Presbyterians) regards all conciliation or, rather all concessions, as spoils of his [Max Bradshaw's] personal victory—not as acts of grace from our people. Conclusion: there is no alternative to continuing opposition to undesired actions and policies." She conceded that many "might oppose my suggestions on the ground that I am a hawk, but these are insufficient grounds unless you have reason to believe that a more dove-like approach will bring the desired results."

Alex Chernov for one would later wonder whether the hawk-like approach that Joan Northrop would take when she became a Group B member of the Council in 1982 was necessarily the best: "There are times when I've thought—well, maybe you're better off to give a little when it didn't matter (when) dealing with disputes during those meetings." But by 1981 it was all rear-guard action for the Group B members of the PLC Council who had little to give when so much had already been taken. And there were still years of scrapping ahead.

Vetting of Wisdom

Throughout April, Pam Royle received a stream of letters from parents who had attended the AGM and wanted to voice their support for the Parents' Association opposition to the School Council's application for exemption from the Companies Act retirement age. Many also voiced their concern for Joan Montgomery's position. One set of parents wrote: "We were sorry that at the meeting on 11 March we did not express our confidence in and support for Miss Montgomery as shown by the overwhelming vote at the referendum last year. We are deeply concerned at the strain being placed on such an outstanding principal by the attitude of the majority of the Council. Surely the function of the Council should be to aid her in every way possible in the tremendous task to which she is committed. In particular we trust she will soon have adequate accommodation on the premises of the school."

Mary Murdoch had responded to Pam's letter to the Council about the Principal's accommodation explaining that a decision had been made by Council about the plans and it was expected the new house would be finished by the end of the year. The good news was well received at the May meeting of the Parents' Association, but bad news soon followed. Just before the meeting concluded, Pam Royle reported that the Reverend Bill Loftus was stepping down as Vice Chairman of the School Council and Vice Chairman of the Executive and Finance Committee due to ill health. At its meeting on 9 April the Council had accepted the replacement of Loftus as a Group A member by Brian Bayston, Max Bradshaw's right-hand man. The vacancy on the Executive and Finance Committee was filled by Keith Campbell, another Group C Presbyterian. After an extensive and dismaying discussion, the Parents' Association resolved to write to the Council to "record its concern and disappointment that the Council had not taken the opportunity to appoint to the Executive and Finance Committee such members as are necessary to ensure that that Committee reflects the proportionate membership of

Church Tightens PLC Hold

Groups A, B and C on Council."

Brian Bayston's arrival would cement the Presbyterians' already firm grip on the PLC Council. As a parent, the Presbyterian Church's legal representative and now a Council member, Bayston would be a formidable player in the still unfolding drama. And the newly reconstituted Council, for starters, would be taking no cheek from the Parents' Association. Pam Royle's letter to Council was sent on 1 June, and the response by Council Secretary Ewen McRae, dated 25 June, was direct: "Dear Mrs Royle, I have to advise you that your letter of 1 June 1981, was read to the Council's Executive and Finance Committee at its meeting on 18 June 1981. The Committee resolved that the letter should not be received." The notion that a letter obviously received can "not be received" is a curious if not unique circumstance — but the Council's message was unambiguous.

Parent concern for Joan's position was now running high. Norman Gipton, father of Jill and Sara and husband of Old Collegian Peggy Trevorrow, was one who acted on his disquiet. On 17 June, he wrote to the Chairman of the Executive and Finance Committee, "as the Council is not meeting until August and I feel the matter is most urgent." Gipton raised the Council's decision not to go ahead with plans for an architect-designed residence for the Principal and instead commission a cheaper house from the firm Vindin Suarez: "This change of plan is of great concern to my family and me. My wife is an Old Collegian, both my daughters have attended the School from first grade Junior School; and we hope that our children's children will have the privilege of attending the School in later years." He believed Joan Montgomery should have "a residence befitting the eminence of the School and the status of the Principal." This was essential for PLC "to attract and retain school Principals of the highest calibre." Like most parents he had "voluntarily contributed each term to the Building Fund for many years ... to provide and upgrade school buildings to a standard worthy of the past history and future expectations of the school." If it could be shown there was a shortage of funds behind the decision to downgrade the standard of the Principal's residence, Gipton was prepared to immediately donate $1000 to ensure the original architect-designed house could be built.

The generous offer was spurned. Mary Murdoch, as Chair of the Executive and Finance Committee, told Gipton the Council believed "the proposed building fulfils all the requirements of a Principal's house and that the overall expenditure is appropriate to the project."

Describing her "nomadic existence", Joan would move from Barnes Avenue to another rented house in Windsor Crescent in Surrey Hills while waiting for the new house to be built. When the Council had made the decision to build the house, she was asked if her preference was to live on the school grounds or elsewhere. She made clear it was easier to live on the grounds given there were so many evening meetings. Her housekeeper continued to prepare her evening meals and look after domestic concerns, lessening the disruption of living off the school campus in the interim.

......

Joan's tenuous hold on her position as Principal again came into full view with the upheaval at Scotch College that came to a head in August 1981 with the forced resignation of Philip Roff, Scotch's seventh and first Australian-born Headmaster. The fortunes of PLC and Scotch, melded by a century of history as Melbourne's pre-eminent Presbyterian schools, had been entwined by the fallout from the schism. As James Mitchell would observe in his history of Scotch: "Throughout the crisis Scotch acted in concert with PLC. The link with PLC ran deep because many families with sons at Scotch had daughters at PLC, and this bred a habit of cooperation."[1]

Only 35 when appointed in 1975, and 15 years younger than Joan, Philip Roff's leadership of Scotch had become another battleground between the Continuing Presbyterians and a school community. But the context and circumstances of his demise were not identical to the troubles at PLC. Two differences would stand out. In the first instance, the Scotch school community was divided over Roff's style with several controversial incidents causing disquiet during his term, as James Mitchell would write: "The story of Roff's fall is how he lost the support of a majority of his key constituencies. He lost the support of the church, failed to secure the full or formal support of the staff, and eventually was abandoned by the Old Boys and dismissed by Council."[2] In contrast, Joan Montgomery had overwhelming support from parents, staff, the Old Collegians and Parents' Association and all Council members prior to union. The only antagonism towards Joan came from the new Presbyterians on the PLC Council driven by Max Bradshaw, who would also ply his scriptural intrigues as Vice Chairman of the Scotch Council.

Secondly, Roff's contract was different from Joan's. Hers specifically provided that she could continue until the age of 60, with the possibility of extending to 65 by mutual agreement. In contrast, Roff was first appointed in 1975 for an initial period of five years. Then in 1977, Council changed the Principal's employment agreement to unlimited tenure, with a specific period of notice required for either party to terminate. What was intended to secure Roff's position—the change coming with a substantial pay rise and a unanimous expression of appreciation for his work—would have the opposite effect. Curiously, at the same time, the Scotch Council praised Joan Montgomery in her role as Principal at PLC—acknowledging the common cause of the two schools to defend their principals "against the perceived threat to them from the Continuing Presbyterian Church."[3]

That perceived threat materialised on 27 May 1980. When the newly constituted Scotch Council met for the first time since the settlement, the Presbyterians moved immediately against Philip Roff. Max Bradshaw began by objecting to Roff's presence at the meeting but his objection was overruled by the Chairman, Sir Archibald Glenn. After an appeal from Glenn for the Council to set aside past divisions and work together for the good of the school, Bradshaw and Pearsons promptly resumed the fisticuffs. They moved a motion to immediately appoint as Principal "William Morton Mackay, MA, Dip Ed, of 87 Spotiswoode Street, Edinburgh" — and proposed a $50,000 golden handshake if Roff agreed to resign.[4]

Since the Presbyterians had been awarded Scotch in the asset carve up after the formation of the Uniting Church in 1977, rumours abounded, according to James Mitchell, that "Roff was going to be replaced by the General Patton of school headmasters ... who would be flying in from Scotland to completely overhaul the running of the school and, like Richard's Crusaders, give us religion whether we liked it or not."[5] William Morton Mackay was an unlikely casting in the combat fatigues of the great American general. The bookish, Spanish-speaking religious scholar and academic had most recently been headmaster of a boys' school in Peru. But the Dundee-born Mackay was certainly Max Bradshaw's secret weapon in his crusade to impose Presbyterian orthodoxy upon the wayward secularists running amok at Scotch. His impeccable Presbyterian credentials would be affirmed two decades later when Mackay was appointed Moderator of the General Assembly of the Free Church of Scotland.

Bradshaw had brought Mackay to Melbourne in 1978 in anticipation that the Principal's job at Scotch would fall vacant after union, according to James Mitchell: "Outside Presbyterian circles, his visit was known to the then [Scotch] Council, which refused to meet him, but most people were flabbergasted that he was now produced as a Principal, ready-made." Bradshaw's brazen gambit — which confirmed most people's fears about how

It's a good thing for a principal to have youth on her side, says Miss Joan Montgomery.

She's home as the new head of Clyde

MISS JOAN MONTGOMERY, new headmistress of Clyde, on board the Orontes today.

by SHIRLEY GOTT

ATTRACTIVE, brunette Miss Joan Montgomery arrived home in Melbourne in the Orontes today to become headmistress of a leading Victorian girls' school at the age of 34.

Miss Montgomery will take up her appointment as principal of Clyde School, Woodend, immediately. She succeeds Miss Olga Hay, who was head mistress of Clyde for 23 years, and retired at the end of last year.

"How do I feel about my new job? Very nervous at the moment," confessed Miss Montgomery. "But that has nothing to do with my age — after all it is so young to be a headmistress?

The singing Welsh girls

"It seems to be the trend today for heads to be appointed younger. It is probably a good thing."

For the past two years, she has been teaching geography at Welsh Girls' School, Ashford, Middlesex.

"It's more than 100 years old, and naturally, since the majority of the pupils are Welsh, music is a speciality," said Miss Montgomery.

She also taught in English schools from 1952 to 1955.

We're on easy street

"On the whole, I think they are not as advanced as we are here in allowing the girls social activities and freedom in dress and make-up.

"I cannot discuss my own views on educating girls until I have talks with the school council," added Miss Montgomery. "But I do think we don't work hard enough here — and I don't mean just our school children. Most people get things too easily in Australia.

"We're over - emphasising sport. I'm very fond of sport, especially baseball, but it must be kept in its right place."

In her student days she had Bachelor of Arts and Bachelor of Education degrees from Melbourne University. Miss Montgomery represented the University and Victoria in baseball, cricket and tennis.

Melbourne - born, she was educated at Presbyterian Ladies' College.

The principal of PLC, Miss B. E. Powell, said today: "Joan Montgomery is the third of our younger generation of Old Girls to become a headmistress at an early age. I taught her here. I'm sure she'll do very well at Clyde."

The other two youthful ex-PLC headmistresses are Miss Margaret MacPherson, head of Clyremont, Ballarat, and Miss Jeanette Burkhan, head of PLC, Goulburn.

Fig. 33   *Herald*, 25 January 1960.

new job

MISS JOAN MONTGOMERY pictured in Melbourne yesterday.

FROM London's East End "tough" schools to one of Australia's "top" schools that's the previous experience of the new, young head mistress of Clyde Girls' School, Woodend, Miss Joan Montgomery.

Miss Montgomery arrived home from England in the Orontes yesterday.

She was appointed head mistress of Clyde after being interviewed by school council members then in London.

At 34 she is young to be head mistress of such a school as Clyde.

She follows Miss Olga Hay, who retired after 23 years in the job.

An old girl of Presbyterian Ladies' College, Miss Montgomery graduated B.A. (in English and History) and Bachelor of Education at Melbourne University.

Later she studied geography at London University, and that is now the subject she teaches.

She has had two trips to England.

She was first there from 1952 to 1955. It was then that she acted as a relieving teacher at London Council schools in the poor areas.

Pupils at these schools — East End, Paddington and Euston schools were some she taught as — were very difficult to deal with, Miss Montgomery said.

"The breakdown rate among teachers is high in these schools and so the relieving teachers are kept busy," she said.

Before this trip she taught for three years at Frensham, Mittagong, one of New South Wales's leading girls' schools.

After her return from England in 1955 she taught at Melbourne's Tintern CEGGS for three years.

She has now just returned from two further years in England.

This visit she taught geography at a Welsh girls' school in Middlesex.

Miss Montgomery said she believed Australian schools were slightly more liberal in their attitude to their pupils than English schools — adding that she was judging only from the schools she had personal experience of.

Miss Montgomery is keen on sport, and is a former University baseballer, cricketer and tennis player. She also rides a little and plays golf.

And is she a progressive educationist?

"I hope I'm reasonably progressive — but only reasonably.

"I find you can only work by trial and error. You can't lay down hard and fast rules about girls."

Miss Montgomery said she hoped that girls at high-fee private schools got an "indefinable something" that they could not get at Government schools

Fig. 34   *Sun*, 26 January 1960.

Fig. 35 Joan as a young Principal of Clyde. "It was a good appointment and everyone knew it" — Clyde historian Melanie Guile.

Fig. 36 Clyde grounds.

Fig. 37 Joan (left) with Mrs Michael (sic) Hawker at a Clyde Old Scholars' luncheon.

Fig. 38 Ruby Powell, PLC Principal (1957-68).

Fig. 39 Helen Lade, PLC Vice Principal at the time of Joan's appointment in 1968.

Fig. 40 Joan (left) and Sir Henry Winneke — with the Centenary Medallion — with Lady Winneke, launching the school's centenary celebrations in 1975.

Fig. 41 Jenny Pring. Her early praise for Joan soon soured to implacable opposition.

Fig. 42 Joan Northrop's Ph.D conferral at the University of Melbourne, 28 July 1990.

Fig. 43 Mrs D.G.M. Flynn, PLC Junior School Principal (1962-77).

Fig. 44 Mrs June Stratford, PLC Junior School Principal (1978-88).

Fig. 45 Joan and Ray Northrop outside Wilson Hall at the University of Melbourne, at the conferring ceremony on 1 August 1981 where Joan received her M.A. degree. Ray was Deputy Chancellor of the University 1985-93.

Applause for Miss Montgomery (front row, nearest camera) at last night's meeting. Picture: ROB LEESON

Parents stand and cheer PLC head

By DAVID HUMPHRIES

A meeting of parents at the Presbyterian Ladies' College last night unanimously supported the school's principal, Miss Joan Montgomery, and overwhelmingly denounced a school council decision not to extend her employment beyond next year.

About 180 parents gave Miss Montgomery a standing ovation when she arrived at the meeting, but responded largely with derision when the school council's chairman, the Reverend Donald Carruthers, attempted to defend the council's decision.

Last night's motions of confidence in Miss Montgomery and no confidence in the dominant section of the school council follow receipt of 286 parents' letters by the school council in support of Miss Montgomery.

The issue has brought to a head differences at the school between parents and the controlling Presbyterian Church, which was awarded PLC and Scotch College in a division of church properties in 1977.

On 23 February, the school council decided by a vote of nine to five not to offer Miss Montgomery, a Presbyterian who joined the Uniting Church, a further five-year term from the end of next year, when she will turn 60. Her contract had allowed for the extension on a mutually agreed basis.

Mr Carruthers: "School has a right to be what it was intended to be."

Last night, Mr Carruthers reiterated the council's arguments put to parents in a circular last week. He said the council greatly admired Miss Montgomery's administrative ability, her progressive educational policies and her achievement of high academic standards. PLC, regarded as one of Victoria's best schools, has an HSC pass rate of about 96 per cent. Fees for day students are more than $3000 a year.

But Mr Carruthers said the majority of the council believed the school curriculum needed to be more "Bible-centred".

Asked what that meant in the teaching of the sciences, he said: "If you mean the Creation for example, I would hope that the teaching of science and biology at this school would give credit to God."

To an accusation that the right of parents to determine their children's education was being vetoed, Mr Carruthers responded: "I am not vetoing, sir. I am asserting that this is a Christian school and was awarded to the Presbyterian Church.

"I make no apologies for the theology that is expected to be promoted here. The school has a right to be what it was intended to be, what it has been for the past 100 years."

Mr Carruthers said the school council, the membership of which must be approved by the Presbyterian Church, did not select staff apart from the principal. The religious affiliations of staff members would not affect future employment. "As far as the council is concerned," he said.

But he said he could give no guarantee that the five parents and staff representatives on the council, who had voted to extend Miss Montgomery's term, would be able to vet any prospective replacements for the principal. "The appointment of the principal is in the hands of the council," Mr Carruthers said.

He said that "to my knowledge" the council would not re-open the matter if Miss Montgomery showed a desire to stay at the school.

The PLC badge.

"The prime concern of us all is the well-being of the education of your daughters," Mr Carruthers said. "I trust that working together, we will achieve maximum benefit."

The mood of last night's meeting indicated there is little prospect that the factions at PLC will soon be "working together".

A parent representative on the school council, Mr Alex Chernov, QC, said that on his reading of the school's charter, "there is no mention of any particular type of Biblical education".

Mr Chernov said the division within the council "lies at the very heart of what sort of education our girls should receive at this school" and that it was unfair "to lay the division at the feet of the Church as such".

"I do not think that the school in the short term can be served by anyone better than Miss Montgomery," Mr Chernov said. "It is difficult to imagine a more caring principal".

Miss Montgomery said last night that there had been "a misunderstanding" between herself and Mr Carruthers on whether it was her intention to retire at the end of next year.

She added: "It would be wrong to assume that it is my wish to continue at the school". She said the council should be asked why she had not been asked to stay on.

Fig. 46   *Age*, 6 March 1984, p. 1. The inset picture of Rev. Carruthers is captioned, "Mr Carruthers: School has a right to be what it was intended to be." Asked what "Bible-centred" meant in the teaching of the sciences, he was quoted: "If you mean Creation, for example, I would hope that the teaching of science and biology at this school would give credit to God."

Fig. 47 Alex Chernov, later 28th Governor of Victoria, was a PLC parent, one of five Group B Councillors and a staunch defender of Joan Montgomery's position as Principal. At a packed PLC community meeting on the evening of 9 April 1984 he outlined steps "aimed at preventing a handful of people ... dictat(ing) the future of the school with total disregard for the views of educationalists ... the school community and ... the paying parents."

Fig. 48 A gathering of Group B members of Council at the home of Alex and Libby Chernov in 1985.

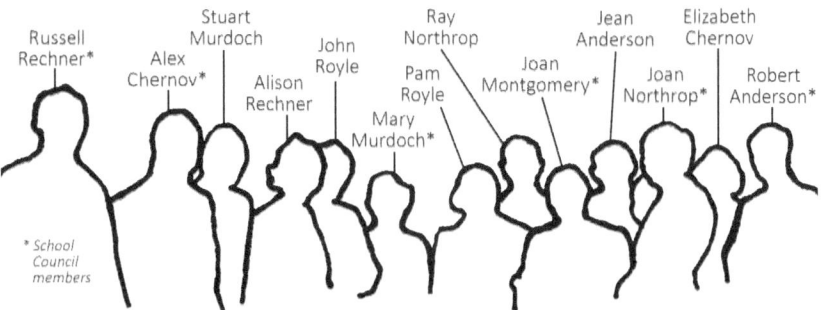

Russell Rechner*, Alex Chernov*, Stuart Murdoch, Alison Rechner, John Royle, Mary Murdoch*, Pam Royle, Ray Northrop, Joan Montgomery*, Jean Anderson, Joan Northrop*, Elizabeth Chernov, Robert Anderson*

* School Council members

Fig. 49 Farewell dinner for Joan (centre) in the Great Hall, National Gallery of Victoria, 8 November 1986, with Anne Dodds (left) and guest speaker Dame Phyllis Frost (right, seated). The author in black in background.

Fig. 50 William Mackay, PLC Principal (1986-97).

Fig. 51 Miss J.M. Montgomery, by Dudley Drew, 1979. The portrait as it now hangs in Wyselaskie Hall. (Photo courtesy PLC Development Office, reproduced with permission Presbyterian Ladies' College.)

Fig. 52 Joan (left), Ray Northrop (centre) and Brian Bayston at Northrop's home on 24 December 2013 — the first time the trio had met together since Joan's retirement 28 years earlier. The faces and body language say it all.

Fig. 53 Joan (left) with Ruth Bunyan in Argentina in 2016, off to learn the Tango.

Fig. 54 Kemi, Lapland, 2018.

Fig. 55 Joan (right) met up with Eve Mahlab in Japan, 2019.

Fig. 56 Japan, 2019.

Fig. 57 The getting of wisdom. Joan and the author, checking details in the manuscript, 2021.

Fig. 58 Joan at a film shoot for a documentary about *The Vetting of Wisdom*, May 2021. Excerpts can be seen on the biography and oral history website insidelives.org.

the Presbyterians would run Scotch—was thwarted when Glenn refused to accept the motion and, after a heated discussion, adjourned the meeting for a month.

In the interval, the Presbyterian General Assembly held a special meeting which produced a unanimous declaration that Mackay should become Principal. While the Presbyterians argued that Roff was no longer Principal because he was not appointed by the incoming School Council, Glenn's legal advice was that Roff remained Principal as the Terms of Settlement stipulated that the Presbyterian Church had acquired Scotch as a going concern that "included Mr Roff as Principal."[6] When the School Council reconvened on 25 June, it was clear that those opposed to forcing Roff's resignation did not have the numbers in the face of an anguished outcry from staff and the school community: "Bradshaw's motion, drafted in advance and sprung on the Council without notice, was intended to sweep all before it. He would have needed the votes of four of the seven men in Group C and it was possibly a shock to him to realise that he might not have obtained them. He had not fought the battles of the past years to end up in a minority."[7] In the end, a truce was called and the motion to replace Philip Roth lapsed.

Although Roff survived the Presbyterians' first attempt to topple him, his detractors were not reconciled, and from then on he was weakened as is any chief executive officer when a significant number of his company's board of directors has publicly declared against him. Fifteen months later, on 1 August 1981, the Scotch Council asked Roff to resign.

A souring in his relationship with Glenn and a series of controversial issues at the school—including a mishandled case of the alleged sexual abuse of a student that led to the sudden death of the accused teacher—sapped support for Roff. By July of 1981, matters had come to a head and Council members met at a private home to discuss Philip Roff's future. As Glenn would later recount: "Philip did not attend, didn't even know the Council meeting was taking place, which sounds rather an underhand way of doing it, but it had to be done in the circumstances. Then the whole thing was aired and when we discussed it I went around the individuals at the Council meeting and asked each one to honestly express his views on the situation, forgetting whether they represented the Church or anyone else. I said, 'We are discussing the headmastership'. Everyone was there, and it was absolutely unanimous. I was amazed at the strength of the attitude against him. You know, with a big group of people like that you would expect someone to speak up in favour of him, but not one."[8]

A deal was struck that would seal Roff's fate. The Old Scotch Collegians on the Council agreed to drop their support for Roff in return for the Presbyterians dropping their proposal to install William Morton Mackay as Principal and instead seeking an alternative replacement "by the usual world-wide advertising and rigorous selection procedures." Mackay could apply but would have to take his chances against the rest of the applicants. Max Bradshaw agreed. General Patton's understudy would be confined to barracks, at least for the time being.

In view of Roff's relatively young age—he was 48 at the time—Glenn "didn't want to ruin his career completely so the idea was that he would be given the opportunity to resign."[9] When Roff discovered the move against him a day or two later, he contemplated forcing the school to dismiss him but then decided not to fight. By the next Scotch Council meeting on 6 August 1981, Philip Roff had tendered his resignation and it was made public on 12 August.

The dramatic news was on the front page of the *Age* the next day under the headline, "Principal Quits Stormy Scotch" with Philip Roff's picture featured prominently. Essendon Grammar Principal Bert Stevens stirred further controversy by declaring the Presbyterian Church had achieved what it had wanted for a long time, "to get rid of Mr Roff". He then predicted that "next there would be moves to get rid of the principal of Presbyterian Ladies' College, Miss Joan Montgomery."[10] Always composed, Joan told *Age* reporter Sue Green it would be unwise to comment: "All I can say is that for the moment I am here."

On the small blue pad she used daily when writing to staff, Joan's notes the following day would illuminate the uncertainty of her situation—"for the moment I am here". Her elegant handwriting records: "Have been asked Q's concerning 'Age' article. As Council meeting proceedings already made public, I'll clarify." The Council meeting the night before, Thursday 13 August, had discussed new candidates to sit on the Council: "All moves to have individual names put forward defeated and it was actually stated that as the church would veto names they didn't want, why put them forward? It was never intended that they should be really independent!" She continued: "Three Ind(ependent)s off—Mr John McArthur, Mrs Val Griffith, Mr Ian Hore-Lacey—ON Dr Dorothy Moody, Old Collegian, allegedly fundamentalist, Mrs Harman and Reverend Lyman—No reason given for change; one can only assume that it was the three independents removed who often voted against Presbyterian representations. Significant change in Council membership in that it now has 12:5 support giving it 2/3 majority needed to remove the Principal."

In the formal Council meeting minutes, Item 3 would record "Selection of Council Members for the twelve-months period beginning 1 November 1981". Pearsons and Bayston had moved seven names, including Moody, Harman and Lyman. Ian Waddell and Alex Chernov then sought to add the three existing members in Group C—McArthur, Hore-Lacey and Griffith to the list of seven but this was defeated nine votes to eight. Then Russell Rechner, who was attending his first meeting after replacing Henry Holmes—who had resigned due to ill health—made another attempt at changing the list to include the existing Group C. His motion was also defeated nine to eight. The list of only seven names was then voted on and carried 10 votes to seven. Both Chernov and Rechner recorded their dissent because "in the circumstances the motion gave no effective opportunity to this Council to consider others for nomination to Group C at the next Council."

Waddell then put on record the extent of his unhappiness, saying he had voted against the motion not the individuals involved, "because: (a) this procedural method in selecting people for nomination for Group C Councillors is constricting the spirit of the Memorandum and Articles of Association; (b) the movers of the motion clearly indicated that no other names would be entertained 'by the Presbyterian Church'; (c) I do not believe the Presbyterian Church of Victoria's membership at large is aware of the 'raw political pressure' (quoting Mr Bayston) being wielded in the Council and I further believe that there would be a different course of approval by the Presbyterian Church if the Members were generally aware; (d) the determination of those Councillors voting in favour of this motion is to be deplored and is an indication of their unwillingness to entertain any other point of view besides their own and that this is not in the best interests of the School."

For Joan, the message seemed clear, as she wrote after the meeting: "Seems v. likely that I shall go—my concern now goes beyond the personal—I have been not only touched, but humbled by the letters and phone calls of support for the school, many from people who have no personal connection but who see the church's approach as an appallingly backward step." She had just returned from the national conference of Heads of Schools in Hobart where each morning began with an ecumenical service in which Jesuits joined not only with other Catholic orders but with all shades of Protestants. The comparison was obvious. It makes "the Presbyterian approach seem quite unbelievable to all present."

Two days after her front-page story about Scotch, Sue Green of the *Age* turned her attention to PLC under the headline,

"Principal May Go as Church Tightens PLC Hold". The story began: "Some parents of students at Presbyterian Ladies' College fear that the school's principal Joan Montgomery will lose her job." It reported that Val Griffith had found out on Wednesday night that she was not being renominated: "She knew of no reason apart from her desire to take an independent stand on Council issues."[11]

Green's article prompted two letters to the editor on Friday 21 August published under the headline "PLC is Not a Church Possession". Nan Falloon's letter commended Green's reporting and hoped "the Presbyterian Church will soon publish a strong denial of its intention to replace the principal ... who is the acknowledged leader in her field." Roberta Holmes, a parent and wife of former Council member Henry Holmes, wrote: "From whatever viewpoint, Miss Joan Montgomery must be one of the most outstanding heads any girls' school this country has ever had. She is acknowledged by her peers, respected and admired by her staff and students and valued by countless thousands of parents, past and present. Yet it appears from Sue Green's articles that her days are numbered; she is not only a woman but a woman of her time."

The following week the *Mercury* in Hobart featured Joan as President of the Association of Heads of Independent Girls' Schools of Australia in a way that made her troubles at PLC all the more perplexing. Her local patch was being threatened as her national standing as an educator continued to grow. The *Mercury*'s story—'Advantages in One Voice'—was about the proposed amalgamation of the "top policy making Councils of headmasters and headmistresses" following a joint national conference of the two associations in Tasmania. The conference, which Joan had co-chaired, was a key step toward that amalgamation. Tim Murray, the Head of Hamilton College, wrote to her on 5 September: "Thank you for all you did to make the Joint Conference such a success. Your work in the two years leading up to the Conference, was, I know, very considerable, and your handling of all your many official tasks during the Conference Week itself was done with ease, charm — and humour ... even at the penultimate moment when the time came to elect the next Executive! ... How you manage it all given ... your own Council/Church problems I don't quite know. It is probably that 'human' bit that sees you through."

Letters from other principals praised Joan's "courtesy and consideration", how she ran it "so gracefully", how she "inspired confidence" and how she took "personal care for every one of us." Perth College Principal Christopher Ellis wrote hoping "the finest aspects of Christian courage, tolerance and compassion will prevail" when it came to dealings with her own Council: "It has always impressed me that you have been able to find ways of supporting and caring for your colleagues — an expression of your Christianity in administration which is not always easy."

Joan's fellow principals then went a step further, taking their concerns to the public. On 7 September, Mary Waters, Chair of the Association of Heads of Independent Girls' Schools of Victoria wrote to the *Age* on behalf of the association and of the Headmasters' Conference of Independent Schools of Australia "to express the very considerable concern of our members at the uncertainty surrounding the future of the staff and girls of a great school, Presbyterian Ladies' College, and more especially of its principal ... a very distinguished headmistress and presently the Federal president of the Association of Heads of Independent Girls' Schools of Australia."

Her letter reflected the growing concern of principals around the country about Joan's position. Parents' Association President Pam Royle received letters expressing "shock and sadness" from Elizabeth Butt of Fintona Girls' School in Melbourne, Cynthia Parker, of Frensham in Mittagong, Joan Butler of St Margaret's School in Berwick, Nigel Creese of Melbourne Grammar and Kathleen McCredie of Abbotsleigh in New South Wales. Kathleen

McCredie said she and her colleagues stood ready to help Joan if there were anything they could do: "Her experience over many years, her untiring zeal to preserve standards, her principles, her ideals, her personal and professional integrity, her humility, her deep concern for staff and students make her one of the great Heads of one of the finest schools in Australia, a fact readily acknowledged by all her colleagues in the educational sphere. I realise I am not telling you or the members of your Parents' Association anything you do not already know, but we in the Association find it quite incredible to believe that the situation with the Presbyterian Church appears to be placing her position as Head in jeopardy, and this of course would be a tragedy for PLC and for the Independent Schools."[12]

The press reports also galvanised many parents to write to the Parents' Association, and some to the Presbyterian Church itself. Ted Pearsons, as Clerk of Assembly, wrote back to one set of parents declaring: "The Moderator, the Right Reverend F. A. Hoad, has asked me to assure you that the Church has, as always, the welfare of the great School at heart. The Presbyterian Church of Victoria founded the Presbyterian Ladies' College and, although the Church no longer owns the School, it still exists for her educational purposes. It would be unthinkable that we would do anything that would harm the School."

Brian Bayston's response to the media attention was less conciliatory. On 31 August, he wrote directly to Nan Falloon in her capacity as President of the Old Collegians' Association, about her letter to the *Age*. Bayston said he had determined not to respond publicly "as that may not be in the best interests of the School or of the resolution of the present tensions that exist between the Council and certain parties within the school community." But he couldn't "ignore the letter" which he claimed was internally inconsistent: "On the one hand you rightly say in effect that the School is now managed by a Council or Board ... and that therefore the Presbyterian Church has no direct control over its affairs. But, on the other hand, you call upon the Presbyterian Church to issue a strong denial of its intention to replace the Principal." Bayston claimed the public reaction had been provoked in part by Joan's comment "for the moment I am here" and that she should have said: "My position is different from that of Mr Roff. Mr Roff continued as Principal of Scotch College without ever receiving nine affirmative votes from the new Council as required by the Memorandum and Articles of Association of the incorporated body. My position is different. I was duly appointed as Principal of the newly appointed Council. I have a written contract with the new entity. The Council deserves my loyalty. It has my loyalty. I believe I have its. What is surprising is that she did not say this. Why didn't she? I forebear from speculation."

A firm letter in reply from Nan Falloon brought a sharper rebuke from Bayston: "I begin by saying that I take exception to your abrupt final sentence: 'I await your explanation'. It sounds like a headmaster addressing a recalcitrant schoolboy. Apart from the way it sounds there is of course a substantive objection to giving an explanation."

Bayston then delivered an extensive, and revealing, account of why the Presbyterians had found it necessary to "rely upon the exercise of power rather than ... simple persuasion" to achieve their objectives at PLC: "One is forced into the exercise of power when one is faced with the exercise of power." He said litigation involving Scotch and PLC had been initiated not by the church but by the former Councils of the schools: "It was a blatant exercise of power in which the funds for the pursuit of the litigation were provided not out of their own pockets but out of the school's purse. The litigation was not over ownership but over control." He went on to explain the tactics behind the Presbyterians' negotiations for the settlement.

"The terms of settlement were basically fought over two issues: incorporation and the structure of the Council. The church conceded incorporation: the property was to be transferred from one trustee (the Presbyterian Church of Victoria Trusts Corporation) to another trustee (the Presbyterian Ladies' College) ... When it came to the issue of the structure of the Council the issue was one of control. We were told: 'You can control the first Council so long as you do not have a majority of Presbyterians on the first Council. Alternatively, you can have a majority of Presbyterians on the first Council but no control' so the church elected for the first option and the first Council was contrived so that six places were filled by selection by the Plaintiffs from names supplied by the church. It was a somewhat cynical face-saving exercise for those who had expended hundreds of thousands of school funds on a fruitless expedition in the courts."

Bayston then confirmed the Church's strategy to ensure their ultimate dominance of the new School Council and to ensure that their brand of Presbyterian piety—the "ecclesiastical nexus"—would be an integral part of the PLC culture:[13]

> There was no doubt in the minds of those conducting the case on behalf of the church that if the people they chose for selection were chosen wisely, then the second Council and, if need be, subsequent Councils, could be so selected as to secure firm control of all but five places in the Council of seventeen. No doubt the plaintiffs, some of whom became Group B on the first Council, hoped that by using their skills over the period of office of the first Council, they would persuade sufficient members of the first Council to select its successors in such a way that progressively over the third and subsequent Councils, the control of the Councils by those who recognised the ecclesiastical nexus would be weakened. Once the control of the Council was lost by those who recognised the

ecclesiastical nexus, it could never, apart from action in the courts, be recovered. Control could pass to a Council such as that which was in control when the litigation was commenced, a Council which was made up of people who notwithstanding their appointment by the Presbyterian Church of Victoria asserted in their statement of claim that the school existed for secular educational purposes. Therefore, the selection of names for nomination for the second Council had to be made in the light of the history of the litigation and to ensure the preservation of the ecclesiastical nexus. I hasten to say that I have nothing personal against Mr McArthur, Mr Hore-Lacey or Mrs Griffith … but [none] of them were members of the Presbyterian Church of Victoria and the reappointment afforded an opportunity of replacing them with persons more closely associated with the church. Mrs Griffith by her published statement after the Council meeting has clearly indicated that she failed to understand correctly the function of Group C. It is distinguished, not to be 'independent,' but because of its method of appointment. As with Group A and with Group B it is to maintain the purposes of the school as set out in the Memorandum and Articles of Association. Whatever grounds may have existed before the votes for not reappointing her, that statement clearly showed that she misunderstood her responsibilities as a member of the Council.

……

Val Griffith well understood her role on the School Council just as those in Group B understood the role of Group C. She saw herself as independent. Val attended Scots' Church where the minister was the Reverend Norman Pritchard, who had been brought out from Scotland but had clearly different views to Max Bradshaw and his supporters. Pritchard counselled Val during the upheaval and would give a different perspective to Brian Bayston's account.

Pritchard recalls: "One of the early PLC spills involved one of my church members, Val Griffith, a PLC parent and wonderfully sensible person. She served one year, was re-nominated by the outgoing Council and then vetoed by the Special Commission, no reason given. Val and I knew the reason because we had discussed the issue when it arose. When the membership of the first Council at PLC was announced, either the Old Collegians or the school leadership (I forget which) invited everyone to an informal event to break the ice. The Special Commission let it be known that this was something they were not interested in. Val had surreptitiously gotten wind of this beforehand and discussed it with me. She was a very efficient person and I suggested she send her acceptance of the invitation immediately upon receipt and then when informed that the Special Commission were against the meeting, she could say that that information had come too late as she had already accepted. Something similar happened at Scotch. Council members were invited by the Principal to tour the school and I accepted, although I knew the Commission was telling people to ignore it. I was new to the country and hoped to be able to send our son to Scotch so it made all sorts of sense to take up the invitation. I learned several years after that I was the only one to do so."[14]

When the PLC School Council met on 10 September 1981 a motion was put: "That this Council re-affirms its confidence in Miss J.M. Montgomery as Principal of Presbyterian Ladies' College and her unanimous appointment at the initial meeting of this Council." It was carried by nine votes to five. Val Griffith called PLC Vice Principal Ev Tindale later that night but would be forced to write next day to correct her account of the event: "You may have thought (incorrectly) that I had rushed straight for my gin and tonic when I told you last night that the vote of confidence was 10-8, knowing there are only 17 members of Council – and only 14 were present at this particular meeting!!! The vote was actually 9-5. I would have been so happy had it been unanimous. Let us hope that this distasteful matter is now really over."[15] It was a sentiment shared by Mary Murdoch, who wrote to Pam Royle as President of the Parents' Association: "The Council sincerely hopes that this resolution will allay unfounded anxiety and rumour and that concerned members of the school community will now be reassured."[16]

But a vote that indicated at least five members of the PLC Council were not prepared to endorse Joan Montgomery's leadership and tenure did little to allay the fears of many in the PLC community. Signatures and addresses were gathered from more than 100 sets of parents for a letter of support sent to Pam Royle that declared: "Miss Montgomery is an outstanding headmistress with a deeply held Christian faith. In the years she has devoted to the school she has engendered a very genuine loyalty and respect in both staff and pupils. We are greatly disturbed by the implied threat in these recent changes [to the Council's voting patterns re Groups A, B and C] to her continuation as Principal. We do ask that you will use your own best efforts to see that she has a Council that will continue to give her the unqualified support she needs in her immense task."[17]

There was also unease within sections of the Presbyterian Church about threats to Joan Montgomery's position. In September, the Moderator-Designate, the Right Reverend Colin Harrison, received a strong letter from a member of 48 years of the congregation at Canterbury Presbyterian, who expressed his distress "at the unrest we are witnessing in the College due to the interference of a minority group of the Presbyterian Church led by Mr Maxwell Bradshaw. I disassociate myself with this group and urge all other clearer Presbyterians to do the same."[18] The tensions within the Church also continued to draw public attention. When the Reverend Norman Pritchard received the same treatment as Val Griffith, with his reappointment to the Scotch Council vetoed by his own Presbyterian Church, Sue Green reported in the *Age* that this was because he had taken an independent stand on PLC matters.[19] There appeared to have been a change of heart when Pritchard was eventually reappointed to the Council in November.

Joan Montgomery was acutely aware of how precarious her position was, although she could still make light of it. One evening she would pen a note to Ev Tindale on her ubiquitous blue notepad: "Please do not abscond with my picture! As a golden handshake is growing daily more possible, all resources may be needed! J.M." But the official position of the Council remained that there was nothing to see here. At its October meeting, the Council sought to douse the rumour and conjecture about PLC's future, with a motion: "That the Parents' Association, Old Collegians, Staff and any enquirers be reassured that no change is envisaged in the School's educational policy which will continue to accord with its objects expressed in the Memorandum of Articles and Association, especially Clauses 3 (1) (a) (b) and (c) and be mediated by the Principal."

Mary Murdoch wrote to Pam Royle on Friday 9 October informing her of the resolution and hoping the way was "now clear for all people with the welfare of the school at heart to work together in our common interest." But the Parents' Association was not persuaded. At its meeting on 21 October, the Parents' Association Committee (with Joan noted as an apology) recommended unanimously that the school community "explore avenues including litigation if necessary to ensure: 1. The interests of the school are at all times in the minds of all members of the

Council; 2. That Miss Montgomery, an outstanding Principal who is not only admired and respected by the PLC community but is held in the highest esteem in educational circles throughout Australia, is secure in her position as Principal of the College; 3. That the Council is made constantly aware of the mind of the school community."

The day after the Parents' Association meeting, Mary Murdoch signed off on her last letter to parents as Chairman of the College. The letter sought to reassure parents that things continued as before, even though it began by drawing attention to the recent upheaval—thanking the outgoing members of the Council and reporting on the new Church-approved members. The letter's failure to reassure was demonstrated by the barrage of mail from unhappy parents that landed in the office of the new Moderator. Late in November, Harrison was compelled to write a form letter to parents that began with an apology: "Please excuse me sending you a photostat copy of this letter in this way but the volume of mail has been large on the matters you have raised."[20] He promised to refer all the complaints to the special commission that had been established by the General Assembly of the Presbyterian Church of Victoria "to deal with matters relating to Institutions awarded to the Church" by the Property Commission. At its meeting in October the General Assembly had conducted a closed three-hour debate on the schools.

Mary Murdoch's term as PLC School Council Chair came to an end when she was not reappointed after her term expired on 31 October 1981. However, she sat in the chair during Council's November and December meetings with the Reverend Don Carruthers not taking over until the following February. This meant she represented the Council at Speech Night on 4 December—the last Speech Night to be held in the Dallas Brooks Hall, site of the original buildings of PLC in East Melbourne where Joan had been a schoolgirl. Why was Mary Murdoch still in the role, given she had not been re-elected as Chair at the

October meeting? Sue Green would write in the *Age*: "At its first meeting in November, the school's new Council which is strongly influenced by the church did not appoint a chairman because it said it wanted first to resolve differences with the committee of the Parents' Association at the senior school. But the parents believe the Council did not want to present a new chairman to the school community at speech night."[21]

Carruthers' formal election as Chair took place at the Council meeting on 1 December, just after speech night. The Church had been represented at Speech Night by Moderator Harrison and his wife, who would present the awards to School Captain Penelope Lowther and the Deputy School Captain Eve Darian-Smith. Joan Montgomery began her delivery of the School's 107th annual report with a note of gratitude and reassurance, acknowledging "the close liaison between the School's various supporting groups having strengthened further." She expressed sadness at the death of the Reverend Bill Loftus, the former Council Vice-Chairman, thanked the retiring Council members Henry Holmes and John McArthur and commended "two others whose stay was short, but whose contribution was generous" — Ian Hore-Lacey and Val Griffith.

There was now always a subliminal level to these large school community gatherings and even the most moderate calls to common sense picked up a rumble and then a roar. So it was with Joan's further words:

> The Council has every right to change its membership, but if morale and confidence among staff, parents and Old Collegians are to remain high, greater Council continuity and stability would be hoped for in future. The role of the Chairman of a Council in its formative years has not been easy and I should like to record the school community's gratitude to Mrs Murdoch for

her integrity, dignity, and constant attention to the needs of the school.

Joan's speech was raised briefly in "other business" when the Council met later that same week, although it was not formally recorded.[22] The next day, Brian Bayston was back on the attack. He wrote to Mary Murdoch, who was still acting chair, saying that he had not gone into detail at the meeting about his "other business" because of the "lateness of the hour." Now a fierce, four-page epistle would detail his "sense of disappointment" and, worse, "grievance which borders on anger."

Bayston declared that Joan's address showed "a failure to recognize the sphere of the Council's responsibility and authority." What is more, it disclosed "not that the Principal is the CEO and servant of the Council, but rather that she sees herself as the representative in some sense of 'the school' as conceived as over the Council." Adding to his grievance, he had not seen or heard much of what was in the report before speech night. Worst of all, he would intone, Joan had not addressed the perennial issue of utmost concern to the Presbyterian hardliners—the place of religion in the school: "The Report fails to direct itself to the way in which the Principal and her staff are seeking to attain the distinctive purposes of the College which mark it out as different from a High School in which excellence is both target and achievement ... the only reference that I can see to the Christian activity of the school is to a Christian Community Camp."

On Christmas Eve 1981, the *Age* reported Mary Murdoch's replacement by Don Carruthers under the headline: "Church Takes Firmer Control of Girls' School". That firmer control was now a vice-like grip.

13

I'LL HAVE TO ASK MR BRADSHAW

Pam Royle tried to start 1982 positively. She wrote to the new School Council chairman, the Reverend Don Carruthers, congratulating him on his appointment and inviting him to address a meeting of the Parents' Association Committee at a time of his convenience. He received her letter "with great pleasure" and was keen to oblige.

Don Carruthers was born in 1921 and had entered the Presbyterian Church as a mature age theological student. He was minister at Clarinda Presbyterian Church in Melbourne's south-eastern suburbs. Carruthers was fond of telling PLC parents that the only letters he had after his name were DAD. His lack of academic credentials and an anti-intellectual demeanour did not sit well with the school community. His speaking appearances at school events were not eagerly anticipated.

In the first week of term, Joan Montgomery — who had spent the summer break moving in to her new school residence — sent a 'Memorandum from the Principal' to parents. It would seek to reinforce the point that her focus was on the running of the school rather than the machinations over her position. After announcing the numbers of new girls and giving some background on new staff, she noted with delight PLC's "consistently good results" in the 1981 Higher School Certificate examinations, adding: "But while we remember the sound teaching through the school, the adequate resources, the parental encouragement — as well as the sheer hard work ... pride in our achievements must be tempered by gratitude for our good fortune."

The memorandum would chastise girls for "allegedly" opening their school reports without their parents' permission. Here was an echo of schoolgirl Joan Montgomery who had gone to Hillier's chocolate shop with her "unsealed report burning a hole in her pocket." She had resisted the temptation, however, as, "you did not look at something addressed to your parents." Now Joan urged parents of the class of 1982: "They are sealed, clearly addressed to you and should be delivered unopened ... we feel that it is discourteous; when they take comments out of context and quote them freely, it is insensitive and ill-mannered."

Brian Bayston's aggrieved letter about Joan's 1981 Speech Night address was tabled at the School Council's first meeting of the year on 11 February. Ted Pearsons and Mrs Harman moved that a committee comprising the Chairman, Max Bradshaw and Russell Rechner be formed to discuss the letter with the Principal and to report back to the next meeting of the Council. Joan Northrop was not impressed and recorded the first of what would be many dissents to motions as she pushed back against the domination of the new Council by the Presbyterians: "Since idiosyncratic interpretations of all written material are the rule rather than the exception, the time of members of Council can more profitably be employed in performing the tasks assigned to Council in the Articles than in the manner proposed by the motion."

By the next Council meeting, it was reported: "At the request of the Committee appointed to discuss her 1981 report, Miss Montgomery stated that she had confidence in the Council as the Council has faith in her. Naturally this did not necessarily cover the action of every individual Council member." This curious statement presumably meant there were some members who did not have faith in the Principal. It seemed that a formal truce had been reached but the threat remained.

Council meetings throughout 1982 blazed with tension with

Joan Northrop living up to the advice she had given the Old Collegians a year earlier: "Either we are prepared to accept the harassment of the Principal, the erosion of the assets of the college, the limitations of its educational function, or we object strongly." She came to her second meeting on 22 April armed with five motions dealing with the formation of the Executive and Finance Committee and the composition of the Council itself, which she had tendered in advance. She had sought advice from Garth Buckner QC on whether the resolution setting up the Executive and Finance Committee in its first meeting on 24 May 1980 was valid according to the power conferred by Article 50 of the Articles of Association of the school. Buckner provided four reasons why the Committee was acting beyond its power. The consequence of this opinion was so important to the continuation of the way the Council functioned — and in Group B's view to changing the power imbalance on the Council — that Joan Northrop sought to move it up on the agenda of items for discussion for the meeting, but the numbers were against her and her motion was lost.

Her sense that it needed to be dealt with earlier was prescient as it was a very full meeting, with the architects attending for discussion on the Senior School extensions and Brian Bayston armed with a motion to gather information on the religious education given to students. As three hours had passed by the time they got to Item 7, Joan Northrop's motion, Pearsons and Dr Moody moved for its deferral to the first item of business at the next meeting. Group B members recorded their dissent with Joan viewing the deferral as irresponsible and a dereliction of Council members' duty as directors. She did snatch a small victory by successfully moving to have Bayston's draft resolution on religious education also deferred.

In many ways, the Bayston motion represented the fundamental divide between Group A and Group B about PLC's purpose and this division of views drove the roiling tension enveloping the Council and flowing into the school community. It read: "To assist the Council to fulfil its responsibilities in co-operation with the Principal under Article 40 (1) (c) the Principal be requested on or before the next meeting of the Council to furnish information on the religious education given to pupils grade by grade and form by form in each case—(a) the syllabus; (b) the set texts; (c) teachers, including their qualifications and church membership, and (d) the Principal's assessment of the effectiveness of this program in—(i) religious instruction; (ii) teaching of holy scripture; (iii) development of Christian ideals of citizenship and personal character; (iv) promotion of a spirit of reverence in the entire life and work of the college."

Bayston and Northrop would have to wait until the next meeting on 10 June before grappling with their differences. In the meantime, the Executive and Finance Committee decided that a newsletter written by the Council be sent to parents. The 'Chairman's Report' drafted by Don Carruthers further reflected the tensions of the period. After setting out the school's achievements, he noted that "the success of these endeavours has only been achieved through sound co-ordination by the Principal, Miss J.M. Montgomery, whose expertise is revealed by the results." On her filed copy, Joan Northrop would write: "Report should end there!" But it did not, and Carruthers continued: "The Presbyterian Ladies' College is indeed blessed in having the prayerful support and interest of the Presbyterian Church of Victoria. The Church as a whole is deeply conscious of the need for a spiritual foundation if the school is to achieve a real and lasting success. This is apparent in that the Assembly has asked for a report on the spiritual activities of the school. God has richly blessed the Presbyterian Ladies' College throughout its long history, and it is the responsibility of each and every person however connected with the school to carry out the commission which our Lord has so graciously and lovingly bestowed for the glory of His Name, the upbuilding of His Kingdom, and the well-being of His Children."

To the school community and its representatives on the Council, the comments flagged a push towards a more fundamentalist Christian emphasis in the school rather than one that developed Christian principles more broadly under Joan Montgomery's leadership. Both Carruthers and Bayston, with their concerns about the development of "Christian ideals of citizenship and personal character", might have been better informed had they attended the first school morning assembly for second term on 25 May.

The morning assemblies invariably dealt with issues of citizenship and personal character and the implicit, if not explicit, Christian ideals involved. Students got a strong sense of Joan's religious convictions and values and her way of promoting a spirit of reverence in the entire life and work of PLC. The themes of her addresses during the period covered Boredom, Courage, Disaster, Encouragement, Faith in People, Gifts, Honesty, Indifference, Justice, Kindness, Love, Materialism, Nuclear War, Old Age, Perseverance, Quality of Life, Respectability, Success, Time, Unity, Values and Women.

For the 25 May assembly, Joan chose the hymn, "Now Thank We All our God" and the Old Testament reading of Ecclesiastes, Ch 3, V 1-13 — "There is a time for everything." In her address, she said: "In the words of the hymn, we thanked God for the ways most of us have been so fortunate most of our lives. In the words of the reading, we were reminded of the rhythm in our lives, that everything has its appointed hour. To the list of the potential opposites that are given we could add 'a time for play, a time for work' — not that the two are mutually exclusive. We have enjoyed our holidays — hopefully we've returned no less happily to begin a new term. A new term represents a fresh start. We all have things for which we are especially grateful, we also know that there are particular things in which we could do better. We could be more tolerant and less ready to condemn. We could be more aware of others' difficulties—more ready to share our time and talents. For a few moments, let us think quietly of those things for which we are especially thankful—the things in which we resolve to do better." And then she concluded with a prayer: "Give to each of us in the coming term, O Lord, the courage to do what we know to be right, the purpose that helps us to use opportunities to the full and the concern which helps us to respond to the needs of others. Beyond our own personal considerations, we pray for the peace of the world. That wisdom and good sense may prevail, and that wars and terror everywhere may cease. Through Jesus Christ we ask this. Amen."

When the School Council met again on 10 June 1982, the Presbyterians came prepared to crush Joan Northrop's postponed challenge. When the Notices of Motion were called onto the agenda and before their content was debated, Pearsons and George Morgan moved that the Garth Buckner legal opinion not be circulated to or received by Council, and they had the numbers. After Joan had spoken to her first motion that Council instruct solicitors to get an opinion from a QC who had not been involved with the school litigation regarding the validity of the Executive and Finance Committee, Bradshaw and Pearsons moved to amend her motion to nullify its effect and affirm the power of the Executive and Finance Committee. Having the numbers, they were successful, with Group B members recording their dissents. Beaten on her first motion, Joan withdrew two further motions dealing with the power of the Committee. She then moved her motion to establish a sub-committee to report to the June meeting on the expertise of the members of the Council. This motion was carried but, given the June meeting was already running, it was pointless. Her final motion requesting minutes to be distributed within five days of the meeting was also lost. The numbers were now completely against Group B.

Brian Bayston's motion on the religious content of the school was then tabled. Pearsons and Bradshaw moved that in view of the Principal's report to the Council—which contained an appendix with much of the information sought—the motion "should lay on the table until the next meeting." Joan Montgomery had acted on the notice she had on the matter and had tactfully included material on the subject in her report.

Joan Northrop's uncompromising approach to the conflict was beginning to create divisions within the ranks of the school community representatives in Group B. The June Council meeting was the last to be attended by Alan Crawford, who was now Moderator Elect of the Victorian Synod of the Uniting Church in Australia and the increased workload would preclude his continuation as a Group B member. Crawford fired a parting shot: "Our last Council meeting (my last Council meeting) was an unmitigated disaster and I feel compelled to make a few notes as I part."[1] In a two-page document, Crawford essentially challenged Joan Northrop's legalistic approach to dealing with the Council. In his view, this had alienated Groups A and C, and he felt a better approach would be to seek cooperation while maintaining a high level of vigilance: "In a situation of clear control by the Presbyterians (12 to 5 or less) the policy of confrontation is less than intelligent. If we want to batter our heads against a brick wall and ensure deep seated alienation which may cripple the School, then our path is well set at this point in time … If representatives of the School Community are prepared to adopt an approach that ensures more meetings like the last one then we, I regret to say, should accept responsibility for whatever effect this had on the Principal and the future of the School."

Three days later Joan Northrop prepared a rejoinder and, in direct response to Crawford's comments about the Principal, wrote: "Again, I express horror. If the Presbyterian Church's representatives use any criticism of their resolutions in Council … as excuse for unrelated actions such as 'blocking the building programme', 'sacking the Principal' then they are acting totally irrationally. There will be no limit to the constraints they seek to impose on their possible critics by this form of blackmail. There is no future in giving a bully this form of encouragement." The three-page response ended in capital letters:

EXPEDIENCY AND COMPROMISE IN MATTERS OF PRINCIPLE ARE PARTICULARLY INTOLERABLE IN ANY SCHOOL. THIS IS PARTICULARLY SO FOR PLC.

News of the internal disputes within Group B and the Council more broadly were communicated to Pam Royle through a letter prepared by the Chairman of the Boarders' Parents' Association, Tom Liley. In a letter to Council members, a copy of which he forwarded to Pam Royle, Liley hoped for some common ground in the conflict of opinions: "There seems to be an undercurrent of threats of damaging action to the school at large should objectors to one line of thinking not come 'to heel' ... I do not wish to appear the schoolboy teaching his grandmother to suck eggs, I am writing purely over my great concern the lack of harmony within Council is doing to the image of the School, Christianity in general and the Church in particular."[2]

In the end, Joan Northrop did not proceed with her formal objections to the lawfulness of the Executive and Finance Committee. She was influenced by the view of her Group B colleagues, in consultation with the Parents' Association, that it might jeopardise the building program. But this would be no more than a strategic retreat.

The Reverend Robert Anderson attended his first Council meeting in place of Alan Crawford on 15 July, a month shy of his 54th birthday. He had first met Joan Montgomery in 1973, when he was Presbyterian Moderator, and had developed immense admiration and respect for her. Anderson had been Principal of Presbyterian Theological Hall at Ormond College from 1966 to 1976 and then the Uniting Theological Hall from 1977 to 1980. He was, through those positions, a good friend of Davis McCaughey, and McCaughey's biographer notes that Anderson had, in the 1960s, presented the anti-Vietnam War case before the Presbyterian General Assembly narrowly voted against the war. An experienced Principal himself, albeit in a university environment, he had also been on the Haileybury School Council since 1975 and was later its Chairman. But while experienced in School Council matters, Anderson was not prepared for the confrontation he witnessed on the PLC Council.

At the July meeting the divisions were on display as Joan Montgomery was questioned after tabling her report. In an appendix, she had given details of a forthcoming Year 10 Human Relations Program to take place in the last week of term. The minutes would record: "Council discussed this in some detail and Mrs Murdoch asked that the Principal keep in mind the opinions which had been expressed and that she report to the next meeting of the Council on the results of the program." Minutes for the subsequent Council meeting would not formally record those reports, but the Human Relations program was a source of tension between the school community and the Presbyterian members. What, then, had transpired in those Council discussions?

Delys Sergeant, who was running the Social Biology Resources Centre at the University of Melbourne, had been in contact with Mrs Edmonson, one of the teachers involved in setting up the course. Delys had recommended Dr John Stanton to introduce the material to the girls. As a Jewish man, would his message be consistent with Christian views on human relations? The Group A Presbyterians determined they wanted two Council members, Mrs Harman and Dr Moody, to sit in on the Human Relations classes. Joan Montgomery was clear that if that happened, she would cancel the course. What was wrong, they responded, with them sitting in on the classes if there was nothing to hide? But Joan was adamant: these classes were designed carefully, and groups had been selected with a view to the dynamics surrounding the discussion of sensitive topics. There would be no way the course could be a success if two outsiders were sitting watching over it.

Robert Anderson defended Joan's choice of personnel for the course. Joan Northrop wrote to him after the July meeting: "While Thursday night's meeting may have appeared terrible to you, for the rest of us in Group B it must go down in history as one of our better nights. And while you might want to disagree, I believe a great deal of the improvement is associated with you being there." She gave two examples when the Chairman had listened and responded to suggestions made by Anderson. That had not happened at other meetings. She continued: "I was, and still am, concerned that Human Relations received so much attention. But we were relieved that you were present to defend the Principal's choice of personnel."

Joan Northrop also wrote to Joan Montgomery to thank her for hosting a dinner attended by all the Council members: "First, I should say how very pleasant I thought the dinner before the Council Meeting was last Thursday. Thank you. I did find it a little difficult, however, to get myself into a suitable frame of mind for the meeting—when you have shared a meal it is a little difficult to remember that we are not really friends, ideologically at any rate. Without my written notes the night might have passed for me in pleasant non-confrontationist acquiescence. Maybe in the hope that others are similarly affected, the meal together might be used as a secret weapon, which is not to say we achieved that much, but there were several incidents—enough to make me fear the next meeting may see the troops well-disciplined again."

Joan Northrop had done some strategic hosting of her own. In her letter to Joan Montgomery she described inviting all of the Group A and C women to her home: "When I invited all of them to a 'ladies' night here, I suggested its purpose included some discussion of how we saw our roles in regard to PLC. Any real discussion failed to take place, but in the course of the conversation it became apparent that ... they saw themselves as seeing that 'humanist' values were not taught in the Human Relations program."

Joan Montgomery would later recall that it had been a new experience to attend Council meetings where there was professional criticism and antagonistic questioning: "There were many grounds on which I could be criticised but several of their accusations were as ridiculous as they were untruthful." But these were feelings she would, at the time, keep to herself. She was scrupulous about keeping Council matters confidential, although all the Presbyterians suspected she was sharing and leaking. How did she cope with the pressures? "If the interesting and harmonious meetings of the past had gone, there were still Vivaldi and Beethoven to go home to."

But there was no place for reticence in Joan Northrop's armoury. She fought both within and without the Council meetings. A fresh line of attack was to try to determine whether Max Bradshaw was too old to sit on the Council. Section 121 of the Companies Act required that directors be no older than 72. She was unsure of Bradshaw's age so her husband, Ray, former Council Chair and a Federal Court judge, went during his lunch break on 20 July to submit Joan's application for a copy of the birth certificate. It would not be a successful outing. The following day, Ray Northrop recounted what happened in a letter written to the Government Statist on his Judges' Chambers' letterhead.

> On 20 July 1982 at about 12.10pm, on behalf of my wife I attended at your office seeking to obtain a document being an extract of the birth certificate of a named person in Melbourne. The appropriate application form had been completed by my wife. ... I presented the form to the officer at the counter. He read it, initialled it, and said he would have to

check it. ... Shortly afterwards he returned, handed the form to me and said that I could not get the extract unless I obtained approval of the person named on the form. I asked him under what Act and he said the Statistics Act. I said I would have a look at the Act and he replied that I could take it to the man at the top for all he cared.

Northrop duly went to the man at the top. He requested reasons for the officer refusing to accept the application form and "the relevant statutory provisions including regulations or rules." The Statist, Mr G.J. Kenney, wrote back the next day, referring to section 46 of the *Registration of Births, Deaths and Marriages Act*, and a proviso that a search may be refused by the Government Statist if, "in his opinion, the reason for which the search is required is insufficient" and added: "Many persons do not wish facts concerning their births to be disclosed and there is also public expectation that there should not be unlimited disclosure of information in government held records which affects the privacy of citizens."

The truth would not be revealed at the time, but Max Bradshaw was born on 2 December 1910. When the Northrops made their unsuccessful attempt to obtain a copy of the birth certificate, Bradshaw was less than five months away from the compulsory retirement age for directors, a fact the man himself would soon reluctantly acknowledge.

Rules and regulations governed life on the PLC campus, too. And in such matters the Principal was judge and jury. Late in 1982, Joan Montgomery was required to exercise that authority when she found girls with alcohol in the Boarding House. She would, as always, handle the administration of the School rules with compassion.

One of the girls, Marsha Watson, would later explain that she was in the library on a Saturday when she was informed that

"Monty" wanted to see her. When Joan explained she had been told Marsha had alcohol in her room, Marsha went hot and cold and initially denied it. But when Joan said she would have to search the room, Marsha showed her the bottle of marsala hidden inside her rolled up sleeping bag. Marsha was extremely upset and Joan sought to calm her down, but explained that it was a strict rule that she had to implement: once a student was found with alcohol on the premises they were expelled. Marsha would later recall her impression that "Miss Montgomery was more cross that we had it on the school premises than that we had it as such."

Joan told Marsha to come over to her office once she felt up to it. When she arrived, Joan called her parents. Her father came immediately and put his arms around Marsha and comforted her. Marsha would later reflect that her parents had always said never to do anything dangerous, and if she was to do anything silly, never to get caught: "They knew that as teenagers we would do silly things." Joan explained she would assist Marsha in finishing off the school year somewhere else. Marsha didn't want to go to another school and so she did the rest of the year by correspondence based primarily at home. During that time, she came to the school to meet with teachers from time to time. On each occasion, she felt sick: "I was so gutted I couldn't go back to the school without being sick—I literally had to have a bucket in between my legs in the car ... I was unwell for a long time after. I missed my friends, I missed school."

During that time, Joan called Marsha to ask her where she would like to sit the exams. She explained that Marsha could in fact sit them at the school. But Marsha didn't have anywhere in Melbourne to stay, so Joan suggested she stay with her. After each exam, Joan rang Marsha within half an hour to see how she had gone. Then when the results came out, she phoned: "Congratulations Marsha, you have done really well." She had achieved a score high enough to get into pharmacy and would go on to a successful career running two pharmacies in country Victoria.

Later Marsha would reflect: "I always speak in Miss Montgomery's defence. I broke a rule and I was to blame. I guess if she had made an exception because we were so close to our exams, anarchy could rule. She did all that she could do in the circumstances to minimise the effect on my results and do the best by me. I always admired her so much. She was so dignified—so wonderful—we all thought that she was like the Queen of PLC. I don't think anybody hated her—she always acted fairly and we always respected what she did. I was cross I got caught. I knew that what I had done was punishable by expulsion and it took me a while to get over it all."

On 23 September, the monthly Council meeting began with the Chairman welcoming Mrs Jenny Pring, who had been chosen by the Presbyterian Church to replace Max Bradshaw, who was indeed approaching the mandatory retirement age, as a Group A member. "What a tribute that was," she would recall many years later.[3] Max Bradshaw had known Jenny Pring through her membership of the Surrey Hills Presbyterian Church. She was already well known in PLC circles for her strident criticism of Joan Montgomery's "agenda", as she would put it, in the Human Relations and the Liberal Studies programs. Brian Bayston would credit her with a "villainous sense of humour" but not everyone was amused. Jenny Pring would often mimic Joan—who she declared to be "quite wicked"—with other group A members after Council meetings.

Inside the Council meetings, the acrimony was rising. After the September meeting, Joan Northrop would write to Don Carruthers, the Chairman: "I wish to object in the strongest possible terms to the displays of unrestrained temper provided at the last meeting by Mr Campbell and Mr Bayston, directed against Mr Chernov, the Principal and myself. I admit Mr Campbell apologised to me after the meeting, but an apology is no substitute for lack of self-restraint. On a previous occasion, he said in Council of me that I should think before speaking rather than apologise after — hindsight might suggest my earlier remarks were apposite. But Mr Bayston has not apologised, and I would request that no further intemperate outbursts against any member of the Council or the Principal should pass without rebuke. The position of the Principal is such that, lacking the right to object herself, she should be a particular object of your protection ... Those who lack self-control should not be given control."

Late in 1982 there was growing frustration among school parents and staff at delays in the building program. The matter had been hotly debated by the Council through the year. By October, proposed extensions to the Senior School were still awaiting the Council's approval. Pam Royle attended a meeting on 19 October with the Appeals Committee of the Council — comprising Bayston, Harman, Morgan, Murdoch, Chernov and Rechner — and the school community represented by a mixture of Parents' Association representatives. Joan Montgomery attended and spoke about the increase in demand for science subjects and the urgent need for these facilities. When the Parents' Association suggested that the success of an appeal would depend on the building having already started, Brian Bayston was unable to give any indication of a starting date. Rather, the Appeals Committee informed the meeting that they were considering holding a meeting at the school to explain to parents the plans for the south-eastern corner of the building and the financial support needed.

Another meeting was then held with the same group of parents and Appeals Committee members on 3 November, after the October Council meeting had examined amended plans for the building extensions. Joan Northrop had recorded her dissent at the October Council meeting to any further delays and Alex Chernov and Russell Rechner's motion that the architects be instructed to proceed to tender as soon as possible based on documents under discussion, was lost.

This delay was also a growing concern for PLC staff. On 4 November, Jill Sykes, the Chief of Staff, wrote to Don Carruthers: "The Presbyterian Church has a long tradition of excellence and fine leadership in the education field so the continuing delay to the South East Development and Staff Facilities project causes us considerable concern ... To alter the plans now would surely cause unnecessary delay and alarming additional expense. We are bewildered as we know the Council is aware of our pressing need for classrooms and laboratories. It is urgent that the project be completed if we are not to see a deterioration in the quality of the educational opportunity we are able to offer our students." By the end of November, the Parents' Association was notified that the mooted meeting for parents to inform them of the plans had been further postponed, so Pam Royle wrote to Carruthers, requesting that he include material about the building plans in the report for the coming Speech Night, the very first speech night to be held at the Arts Centre on Wednesday 8 December 1982.

In February 1983, Joan Montgomery received a confessional letter from a former student sure that Joan would have to "search her memory very hard" to remember her. It recalled Marsha Watson's experience, although this time the student wasn't caught. What the two students had in common was their esteem for Joan and the desire to thank her for the "great impression" the School had left on her: "While I was at PLC, I am afraid I was quite dishonest about where I went on weekends, I smuggled in alcohol and worst of all I had the fashionable attitude of cynicism and criticism ... For this I would like to apologise sincerely. I hope you accept this apology and realise how many of us are very grateful for the education you worked towards bringing us."

The measure of the school was the deep imprint it left on its students, sometimes only appreciated years after the event. It was also a measure of the stature of the Principal. But in early 1983, members of the Presbyterian Church continued to fret about the sort of education girls were receiving at PLC. Their chief concern was the Human Relations course and Council meetings were often consumed by the subject, with Mrs Harman and Dr Anne Warr particularly active. At the April and May meetings, Anne Warr reported on the Year 10 Human Relations program held at the School at the end of Term 2 of 1982. In July, the Chairman reported on discussions with Joan Montgomery and members of the teaching staff which had followed Anne Warr's report. Joan Northrop and Alex Chernov lost a motion to adjourn discussion of the matter and Brian Bayston and George Morgan moved successfully that "the Principal be requested to give serious consideration to inviting three members of Council who attended part of the program in 1982 to attend again this year." Joan Northrop and several others could only dissent: "This motion seeks to over-ride the powers given to the Principal by Article 58 which states she should also have the supervision and control of the courses of study provided by the College for students."

While the Presbyterians on the Council continued to carp, the Human Relations course remained very popular among the students and many of the parents. After the 1982 course, evaluation sheets were completed by the girls who had participated. Dr John Stanton, the Jewish doctor who had caused discussion in Council, was given excellent feedback: "Students found the two question time sessions with Doctor John Stanton very interesting and they very much appreciated his frank, authoritative answers. Time and again, the comments on their evaluation sheets included the words 'open' and 'honest' in connection with Dr Stanton. Of the 89 feedback sheets, 71 had favourable comments about his session, 11 without any specific comments and 6 that were not 'completely favourable'." Dr Barbara Thomson, a gynaecologist and parent of two daughters in the Senior School, would write to the School strongly supporting the course.

But while the Human Relations course would remain a continuing source of conflict and division on the Council, its November meeting would have a more far-reaching matter to discuss. The meeting began with the Chairman congratulating Joan Montgomery on her recent appointment to the Council of the University of Melbourne, and it then moved to Item 12 – "Matters related to Miss Montgomery's possible Retirement at the end of 1985". Joan left the meeting during the discussion. The Council resolved that the Executive and Finance Committee be instructed to draw up a timetable on all matters related to her retirement at the end of 1985. An amendment to refer the "Principal's contract'" to that committee for consideration before reporting to a special meeting of the Council was rejected.

With the resolution passed and the amendment rejected, the end of Joan Montgomery's illustrious career as Principal of PLC – the date her Presbyterian opponents had fought so long and hard to hasten and that her many admirers had equally struggled to postpone – was now at hand. Perched at this precipice, the Council had the option of extending her contract for a further five years. Exercising their own particular brand of human relations, the Presbyterian majority had decided not to extend but to push and, in so doing, the most admired educator of her generation fell. But it would not be before a further, final fight at an increasingly public, bitter and rising pitch.

The five Group B members of the Council – Anderson, Chernov, Murdoch, Northrop and Rechner – all recorded their passionate but futile dissent. Joan Northrop had her grounds minuted: "The motion as formulated at best ignores, at most overrides, the rights of Council and Miss Joan Montgomery as stipulated in the Principal's contract to agree to an extension of her appointment for five years after the end of the year in which she reaches the age of 60 years. Council has therefore not had the opportunity to consider how the best interests of the College can be safeguarded, in particular with respect to the advantage that accrues to it as a consequence of the presence of a Principal who enjoys such high standing in the community. Her high standing is evidenced by her recent election in a keenly contested ballot to Melbourne University Council. To fail to offer Miss Montgomery the extension — particularly when others have enjoyed such extension — can only reflect badly on this College." Alex Chernov also recorded his dissent: "This motion necessarily rejects offering the Principal an extended term without allowing the matter to be considered by the Council and this amounts to an abrogation of its duty to the School."

On the day after the November meeting, Don Carruthers called on Joan to inform her of what had taken place in her absence. What he said he would also claim in a letter distributed publicly the following March: "In our discussion, I became aware that there was a difference of opinion of what I believed she had told me concerning her intention to retire at the end of 1985." Joan would react with amazement and dismay at Carruthers' assertion that she had told him that she would retire at the age of 60. Knowing this was not true, she asked when the alleged conversation had taken place: "I'll have to ask Mr Bradshaw" was the extraordinary reply. Such an action would have surprised no-one, but its admission did! A year after stepping down from the School Council, Max Bradshaw was still the power behind the Presbyterian throne. Joan was certain she had not told Don Carruthers, Max Bradshaw or anyone else that she would retire at 60 — the false premise on which the Presbyterians would force her departure. Long after the event, Brian Bayston would admit being surprised to hear others say that she had intended to retire at 60.

On Wednesday 7 December 1983, the PLC school community gathered at the Victorian Arts Centre for the Senior School Speech Night. Not a word was mentioned by Don Carruthers in his Chairman's report about the Council decision, nor was there any allusion to it in Joan's delivery of the 109th Annual Report of the

Principal. The only sense of the impending change that astute parents may have picked up was the three full pages of staff resignations, with many long-term staff determining it was time to move on. The list would continue to grow in the 1984 and 1985 reports.

The following day, the Moderator of the Presbyterian Church of Victoria, the Very Reverend Alan Stubs, sent a letter of thanks to Joan Montgomery that revealed the disjunction between his view and the Council's decision. After praising the venue and the music, Stubs spoke of "the spirit of the School" beyond "the academic achievements, building plans, etc." He mused: "I fancy that the fine spirit that exists is due in no small measure to the fine work of yourself and your staff all of whom are so clearly dedicated to their work. We feel that you can be justifiably proud of PLC and that PLC should be equally justifiably proud."

Stubs was presumably taken aback to learn Joan Montgomery was not being invited to stay at the school beyond the age of 60, dramatic news that burst for PLC parents eight days after Speech Night. It came via a Parents' Association circular reporting the Council's resolution "the effect of which is that Miss Montgomery will not be offered any ... extended term". The circular acknowledged that the Association's Committee had taken the "unusual step of writing to the Chairman and all members of the school Council urging them to take all such steps as may be necessary to reverse the Council's earlier decision."[4]

The letter to the Chairman, written on the same day, mirrored the comments of Joan Northrop and Alex Chernov at the Council meeting and included a copy of the circular sent to all parents. After a five-day lapse, Carruthers replied to Pam Royle with a strident reprimand: "I hereby submit the following questions at your request so that your committee may consider them and give formal answers: 1. Who advised you or your committee of Miss Montgomery's retirement? 2. Who advised you of what took place at the Council meeting? 3. The final sentence in the second paragraph of your letter to me states, 'Any suggestion that such a course was forced upon it by the desire of Miss Montgomery to retire no later than the end of 1985, is unacceptable, and, we believe, contrary to the facts.' What facts? 4. Whose responsibility is it to advise parents of Council decisions? The Parents' Association or Council? I look forward to the receipt of your written formal answers to the above questions at your earliest convenience."

Pam Royle waited until the following February, and with the assistance of Ian Murray from Mallesons, responded with as good as she had got. After assuming that Carruthers letter was written in his "own right and not pursuant to any Council resolution," she said: "My committee was informed by members of the Selection Committee who had in turn been informed by Group B that the Council decided not to offer Miss Montgomery an extended term past the end of 1985. I assume that to be correct and if it is not, I would be grateful if you could advise me accordingly." Offering a rebuke of her own, she went on: "In the normal course of events it is the Council's responsibility to advise parents of its various decisions. The relevant events here, however, were anything but normal. Rumours about the Council's decision were widespread, the building appeal workers were constantly asked by parents and other potential donors about Miss Montgomery's position and parents generally, had the right to know as soon as possible about such a fundamental decision so that they could plan their daughters' future. Despite all this, no relevant information was forthcoming from you at Speech Night or otherwise. In those circumstances, the action taken by my committee was proper and any other course would have been an abdication of its responsibilities to the parents." She said she had received many verbal and written expressions of concern from parents and others dismayed by the Council's decision: "I have no doubt that parents and friends of PLC are most concerned about the failure by the Council to consider retaining Miss Montgomery's services beyond 1985. Once again, I would request that you take steps to ensure that the whole issue is reconsidered by Council at its next Meeting."[5]

Pam Royle's mailbox continued to fill with letters from parents and Old Collegians, mostly copies of what had been sent to the Chairman of the Council and the Presbyterian Moderator. They all expressed concern at the Council's move and all requested Council reconsider its decision. One had a radical proposal: "Cannot Miss Montgomery, her staff and students with the support of parents, Old Collegians et al, re-establish themselves in alternative premises by February 1986 and leave the Council out of it?" Another suggested that parents refuse to pay the term tuition fees as a last resort to get the Council to reconsider its decision if other methods failed: "If a sufficiently large number did this, it occurs to me that the Council would have to sit up and take notice." Yet another proposed "mass action" and went on: "One way of doing this would be to invite all parents who wish to do so to keep their daughters at home on a specific day ... to demonstrate very clearly the massive support which Miss Montgomery has from the school ... I realise such a strategy is drastic and one which would necessitate a great deal of co-ordinated activity, but I believe that if such an event transpired it would be merited."

Pam Royle alerted Don Carruthers to the many parents approached during the building appeal who were concerned about Joan Montgomery's position. As well as being head of the Parents' Association she had become President of the Building Appeal's Campaign Committee. The other committee members were Brian Bayston, Pam Buxton, Alex Chernov, Helen Macmillan, Ewen McRae, Allen Morris, Mary Murdoch, Jenny Pring, Mary Rayner, Russell Rechner, Heather Vickery and Joan. In an eight-page brochure presented to parents, a comprehensive case was developed for the need for funds to ensure the school buildings "adapt to the demands of the present ... despite the political and economic uncertainty that overshadows the future of the independent school."

Around this time, Pam Royle had a conversation with Russell Barton details of which she would note, undated, in a school exercise book. Barton is recorded as often seeing Max Bradshaw in Barristers' Chambers on a Sunday. The various comments include scheming so that the Council didn't get a quorum and references to it "being far too late to help the school now." The notes record a "plan to remove Joan Montgomery … and the Murdoch dame will be gone in October". They continue: "Parents may not like what Max has planned". But it "doesn't worry Max and what the parents want is of no interest to him at all, in fact Max wouldn't worry if he had an empty school". The record would end with Pam Royle commenting: "Don't think Miss Montgomery should be told about this. Keep her confidence up."

A month before the fateful Council meeting that would begin the process of finalising her retirement, Joan Montgomery sent out a circular to parents, notifying them of the death of Ruby Powell. Ruby, like Joan, had been a student at PLC in East Melbourne and returned as a teacher and member of the boarding house staff. She then had a period in Adelaide as head of the Presbyterian Girls' College, later Seymour College, before being appointed PLC Principal in 1957. She would be instrumental in securing Joan's appointment as her successor, when she voluntarily retired 12 years later. Her death late in 1983 seemed an ill omen, a sign that what she and Joan had helped build was being pulled down by those more concerned with their own power than in empowering future generations of strong-minded, independent and proud PLC women.

14

Outcry

Soon after the 1984 school year began, the February newsletter of the PLC Old Collegians' Association announced to those who had not received the December circular to parents that the Council had begun looking for a new Principal. This launched a fresh wave of concerned letters to the Council and the Presbyterian Church. Among many former students stirred into action was Marion Kainer, the 1983 Dux, who wrote to the Presbyterian Moderator, the Very Reverend Alan Stubs, saying she was shocked to find in her first newsletter as an Old Collegian that Joan Montgomery would not be offered a further term: "There cannot be a replacement for Miss Montgomery, for she is the very best principal one could ever dream of! The contribution she makes to the school is just marvellous and unsurpassable ... I therefore beseech and beg you, with all my heart, for the good of the whole school, to please reconsider your decision and extend Miss Montgomery's term."[1]

Ahead of its first meeting for the year on 23 February, the School Council received 269 letters protesting against the decision and calling for it to be overturned. In his report to the meeting, Council Chairman Don Carruthers sought to explain the "miscommunication" between himself and Joan Montgomery about her supposed intention to retire. Joan Northrop would later write to Carruthers complaining that it was insulting to Council to present such a report when it effectively was a response to a letter received more than three months earlier. She said the report would have been more credible had it been "circulated with the papers prior to the Council meeting." And she took particular issue with Carruthers' explanation that he had "discussed the retirement with Mr Bradshaw, a former member of the Council" as corroboration of his recollections: "I wish in addition to protest in the strongest possible terms at the fact that, on your own account, you informed Mr Bradshaw of your conversation with Miss Montgomery after the April meeting of the Council — as you recalled it — before you had informed Council that you expected Miss Montgomery to retire at the end of 1985. Mr Bradshaw is not a member of this Council and is not entitled for any reason to know Council business before Council itself knows." Carruthers' admission was proof of Max Bradshaw's continuing hand in the Presbyterian manoeuvring to replace the Principal.

Carruthers' claim that Joan Montgomery had told him months earlier of her intention to retire at 60 was demolished in a letter she wrote soon after he had visited her in the wake of the November 1983 Council meeting where he had referred to his understanding that she intended to retire:

> Thank you for visiting me on Friday morning. Reflecting on your visit, I am more certain than ever that the conversation which you felt that we had concerning my retirement at the end of 1985, did not occur. For the sake of the record I felt that I should set out my version of what took place. The only time that the question of my retirement was mentioned was a month or so ago when I raised with you the possibility of my taking study leave next year. You were kind enough to say that that would not be a problem and that, in any event, I had accrued leave to which I was entitled as of right. It was in that context, that I had mentioned my embarrassment in taking such leave since I had

Outcry

about two years until I retired. There was no other occasion on which this matter was discussed between us and I did not request or suggest that arrangements be made relating to my impending retirement at the end of 1985. In the circumstances, you may feel it desirable to bring the contents of this letter to the Council. I have no motive other than of ensuring accuracy in the matter.

In response to the outcry in the school community, a circular was sent to parents and others on 1 March in which Carruthers conceded: "The Council is very aware that the matter of the Principal of the Presbyterian Ladies' College is causing extreme concern to you the parents, former parents, future parents, Old Collegians, staff, students and the Principal herself." He then revealed details of the February Council meeting at which—despite the clear evidence that Joan had not wished to retire—the Presbyterian majority steamrolled a decision to force her out.

Still clinging to his discredited claim of a "misunderstanding" over Joan's intentions, but acknowledging the wave of protests from the school community, Carruthers said the Executive and Finance Committee had referred "the matter of the Principal's retirement" back to the full Council.

On Thursday 23 February the Council received all the letters,[2] noted their contents, and then proceeded to debate a motion that Miss Montgomery be invited to accept a further term of five years as from the end of 1985. Reporting in the March circular—on the Principal's letterhead, no less—Carruthers told parents of the three-hour Council debate "during which time every member of Council present participated, thereby giving their utmost consideration to the proposal":

> Summarising the debate, a number of opinions expressed in the letters were also generally held by

Council. For example: administrative ability; progressive educational policies and implementation resulting in a very high success rate in academic results; charm and dignity thereby encouraging students to develop similar qualities. However, it was the general opinion of the Council that, great as the academic and moral achievements have been, the Christian development of the students was of prime importance requiring a much greater emphasis on a Bible centred education as laid down in the Memorandum of Association. Further it was the opinion of the majority of members that the Council did not have the full confidence nor the complete co-operation of the Principal. The conclusion of the debate was that Council agreed not to offer Miss Montgomery a further five-year term from the end of 1985.

Joan Northrop's protest letter to Carruthers would indicate how heated that three-hour debate became: "I would have more confidence in you as chairman if you were to cease to tolerate such completely unprovoked, vicious and spiteful attacks as that launched by Mr Bayston against the Principal last Thursday night. His comment, for which he had no evidence whatsoever, should have been apologised for and withdrawn on your insistence. Too frequently such attributions to others are made by members in Council and you do not exert control of the meeting." The detail of Bayston's alleged attack is not explained. But the agenda of the Continuing Presbyterians was crystal clear. As Carruthers had put it in the circular, they were determined to get "greater emphasis on a Bible centred education as laid down in the Memorandum of Association".

The words would be read with dismay by many parents and others in the school community. On the back of her copy of the circular, Pam Royle would write: "Concern is enormous. Received many phone calls from worried parents since the letter arrived yesterday. Attitude of the PA Committee is that we are very concerned at Council's decisions. Miss Montgomery has our total support." In response to the many letters of protest he received, Presbyterian Moderator Alan Stubs sent out a form letter saying the General Assembly had no power to appoint or terminate the appointment of a Principal which was "entirely a School Council matter."

Joan Montgomery received many letters of support. One dated 4 March 1984 from Nigel Creese, Headmaster of Melbourne Grammar School, showed his admiration: "Our sympathy at this time, and on account of the whole rotten business, which I know has been dragging on for many years now; I only hope that your last two years won't be too much soured by it. I am assuming that there isn't much we can do. But please let me know if there is ... I think you know that all your colleagues, amalgamated or otherwise, are right behind you."

Camberwell Grammar Head David Dyer—who as a parent had earlier been sceptical about the Liberal Studies course before being won over—wrote to every member of the Council: "I have been privileged to work with Miss Montgomery and have seen at first-hand her outstanding ability and the generous way she has been prepared to give of her time and talents, not just to her own school but to the wider community as well. For this she has properly been regarded by those qualified to know as a most distinguished school principal of her generation and, in this way, she has done outstanding service for her own school and for the cause of Australia independent school education."[3] Dyer sent a copy to Joan with a covering note: "Words fail me, but both Betty and I want you to know how much we feel for you. For your information, you may be interested to have a copy of a letter I felt moved to send to each member of the PLC Council. I recognise that the letter will not, in any way, influence such a stubborn and unfeeling body but, as a parent who is most grateful for what you did for our daughter and as a professional colleague who had the greatest respect and admiration for your contribution, I felt bound to send it. You have countless friends and supporters, but if you ever felt it would help, do come and see us."

On Monday 5 March 1984 Joan spoke on the theme of 'Open Mindedness' at Morning Assembly. It ought to have given pause to her relentless Presbyterian detractors, who were convinced that she was driving a secular if not godless agenda at PLC.

> When speaking last year about the purpose of Assembly, I said that sitting in Assembly every morning there would be those of you from every Christian denomination—Presbyterian, Uniting Church, Anglican, Roman Catholic, Baptist, Church of Christ and many others. There would be others who are Jewish. There are others who are Buddhist, or other faiths. In those groups there would be those of strong conviction, those with genuine intellectual doubts, those who are just lazy and apathetic and don't think much at all. I see this mixture as a good thing. Assembly is one of the places where we try to make our Christian teaching more explicit—we do not assume ready-made answers to important questions. This religious teaching calls for honesty, even honest doubts. It concerns the need for truth, the readiness to think seriously about life's problems [and it] calls for great respect for views that differ from your own. I hope that one day you will all feel a full and honest commitment to your faith, which for most of us is the Christian faith. But I would feel very concerned if you felt that at PLC you couldn't ask questions, or express honest doubts about religious issues, as

you would in all other fields. It is good to ask questions—but when we do, let us make sure that we listen equally, honestly to the answers.

The address was followed by a prayer: "Uphold us, Lord, with your spirit. Save us from unreality, from praising what is lofty, while practising what is base, from thinking high thoughts, while living a poor life. Help us to be honest and not evasive with ourselves. And make us straight in anything that we do. Through Jesus Christ our Lord."

The hymn may have given momentary solace to the staff, conscious of Joan's predicament: "E'en the hour that darkest seemeth, Will His changeless goodness prove; From the mist His brightness streameth: God is wisdom, God is love."

Soon after the Assembly, notes from staff members flowed into Joan's office. Jan Douglas wrote: "Miss M, A magnificent Assembly—you're the best!" Another said: "Dear Miss Montgomery, I have sat in many Assemblies here. I have never found one as all-embracing or as impressive or helpful as this morning's—the prayer was beautiful, and the hymn said it all." Yet another: "Your assembly this morning was magnificent. I rejoiced inwardly to hear such a beautiful statement of the Christian faith within the school. 'Honesty' and 'Respect' have been key words between students and me in R.E. classes. Your support in these ideals has always meant a great deal to me. My (small) support for your position and ideals is unwavering." Joan's long-standing friend from Brighton days and long-time colleague Joan (Battersby) Kent wrote: "What you said in Assembly today was exactly what I would like to have put in a letter to Mr Carruthers if only I could have put it so well. I am full of respect and admiration for you."

That same day, Pam Royle wrote to Don Carruthers resigning as Chairman of the PLC Building Committee: "When I was asked if I was prepared to be Chairman of the Appeal, I was pleased to accept this position. I believed that this was an opportunity for the Council and the school community to work together for PLC. The school had Miss Montgomery as Principal and the expectation that she would have a further five-year term ... I visited many people and asked that they give financial support to the Appeal and they responded generously. As you know the target of $600,000 to be reached by the end of third term 1983 was exceeded. I have now received your Circular Letter to Parents dated 1 March 1984 and I am shocked and dismayed at the direction the school is likely to take in the future. I oppose the decision of the Council not to offer Miss Montgomery an extension of her term as Principal and believe that this decision is not in the best interests of PLC. Because of this I am not able to carry out my responsibilities as Chairman of the PLC Building Appeal."

At the next meeting of the Building Committee, Don Carruthers announced that Presbyterian stalwart and Joan Montgomery antagonist Jenny Pring would take over from Pam Royle. "Those meetings were very hard," Jenny Pring would later reflect. "Joan and her friend Mary Murdoch would place themselves in front of me at those meetings and Joan would fix her eye on me and give me a hard time." She claimed to have felt "ostracised by the entire Old Collegian community for about two to three years".

Carruthers was in the direct firing line of about 180 parents of Junior School students on the evening of 5 March. Having delivered her powerful school assembly address that morning, Joan Montgomery attended the Junior School Parents' Association Annual General Meeting that evening. A picture would appear on the front page of the *Age* the next morning under the headline, "Parents Stand and Cheer PLC Head."[4] There was also a picture of Carruthers with the caption, "Mr Carruthers: School has a right to be what it was intended to be." Asked what "Bible-centred" meant in the teaching of the sciences, he was quoted: "If you mean Creation for example, I would hope that the teaching of science and biology at this school would give credit to God." In response to an accusation that the right of parents to determine their children's education was being vetoed, he responded: "I am not vetoing, sir. I am asserting that this is a Christian school and was awarded to the Presbyterian church ... I make no apologies for the theology that is expected to be promoted here. The school has a right to be what it was intended to be, what is has been for the past 100 years." The report said, "the mood of last night's meeting indicated there is little prospect that the factions at PLC will soon be 'working together'."

The Junior School Parents' Association meeting carried two resolutions. The first, passed unanimously on a show of hands, declared: "That this Association has the fullest confidence in Miss Montgomery to achieve the objects as set out in the Memorandum of Association." The second, passed by "an overwhelming majority on a show of hands," was: "That this Association accept a vote of no-confidence in the members of Group A and Group C of the College Council of PLC."

The turmoil at PLC continued to create headlines. On 7 March, David Humphries wrote another piece, "Old PLC Girls Rally". He had spoken with Dame Leonie Kramer, Dame Phyllis Frost and Professor Maureen Brunt. Professor Brunt, cited as a member of the School Council sub-committee that in 1969 appointed Joan Montgomery, expressed her concern: "It is extraordinarily difficult—much more so than at boys' schools—to obtain a person of quality to become principal of such an outstanding girls' school ... It seems to me a very grave risk to try to replace someone of Miss Montgomery's outstanding qualities. The Council apparently wants an outstanding Christian educator. Well they have got that in Miss Montgomery."

Professor Kwong Lee Dow, Dean of Education at the University of Melbourne and former chair of the Victorian Institute of Secondary Education, wrote a letter to the editor "saddened to learn that Miss Joan Montgomery is to be removed from the educational leadership of the Presbyterian Ladies' College." Acknowledging that he had no affiliation with the school with his own daughters attending coeducational Government schools, he said "it would be hard to name another school which has offered greater opportunities and wider prospects for capable young women over a long period, but especially under the leadership of Joan Montgomery".[5]

Three more letters to the editor in support of Joan appeared three days later in the *Age*, and on 14 March another story reported that 60 former students from PLC met the previous day at Melbourne University with more than 100 former students from 12 faculties having signed letters of protest to be sent to the PLC School Council and the Presbyterian Moderator: "Students who had completed their education at PLC up to eight years ago told the meeting that Miss Montgomery was a remarkable woman who had been dedicated to the school and the girls' education. We are expressing our total support for her, an organiser of the meeting, Ms Carmel Crock, said."

A few days later, yet another article appeared in the *Age* — "Search for New Head by PLC" — then on Saturday 17 March a full-page feature appeared in the paper's Saturday Extra section written by Geoff Maslen.[6] It charted the history of the dispute and predicted it was "only the end of the beginning". Another full-page piece appeared in the *National Times* of 9-15 March entitled, "The Vetting of Wisdom", with the sub-title, "The liberal, humanist tradition of the Melbourne Presbyterian Ladies' College, and the school's popular principal under attack from the conservative Continuing Presbyterians." Susanna Rodell wrote: "PLC is not the kind of institution to air its dirty linen in public, however, and until last week's decision to get rid of Montgomery, the parents and old girls kept quiet, hoping for the best." Rodell had spoken to school community members, including Joan Northrop and Old Collegians' President Margaret Sandbach, who shared a conversation with one of the pro-Church members of the Council who had said to her: "I thought I'd booked my children into a Christian school; instead I find it's a left-wing humanist school. Why, they teach other religions!" Perhaps he was unaware that comparative religion was a Higher School Certificate subject.

The majority Presbyterian members of the Council refused to talk to the *National Times* but Moderator Alan Stubs—perhaps forgetting the glowing letter of praise he had sent to Joan Montgomery just a few months earlier, after attending the 1983 Speech Night—dismissed the problem as merely a few disgruntled people "not accepting the umpire's decisions." He said Miss Montgomery would have to retire "sooner or later". Joan herself is reported "with her customary discretion ... remaining silent". Rodell observed that "seven years of wrangling over the issue of control of the school [had included] enough dirty politics to make a Canberra journalist feel right at home."

While the decision not to renew the Principal's contract made sense to the Group A and C members of the School Council, the shock and sense of disbelief across the school community was pervasive. A further 175 letters were sent to the Council prior to its meeting on 22 March. The list of them attached to the minutes included many parents, teachers and high-profile names including former Monash University Vice Chancellor Professor Richard Larkins, whose daughter was at PLC. Ahead of that meeting, the five Group B school community members of the Council—Robert Anderson, Alex Chernov, Mary Murdoch, Joan Northrop and Russell Rechner—"felt compelled" to write to parents in response to Don Carruthers' Chairman's Circular of 1 March.

> 1. The Chairman referred to and adopted the Moderator's statement that 'what is desperately needed at the present time is willingness on the part of all concerned to sink their pride, get rid of their petty jealousies [and work together] ... This

characterization ... fails to recognise the fundamental differences that exist between the great majority of the School Community on the one hand and the majority of the Council on the other as to the type of education that should be provided at the School. To suggest that this difference can be explained on the basis of petty jealousies or pride is to misconceive the true basis of this division. It is our belief that the majority of the Council is of the genuine belief that PLC should provide an education which is more directly related to the literal interpretation of the Bible than is the case under Miss Montgomery. For our part, we disagree ... The teaching of secular subjects in the context of Christianity under her, is not only acceptable to us but, we believe, to the vast majority of parents.

2. In November last the Council was not prepared to debate whether Miss Montgomery's term should be extended and it was not until the receipt of almost 300 letters from parents and friends of the School that this issue was debated in Council and the motion to extend her term was defeated.

3. In relation to the Chairman's contention that 'it was the opinion of the majority of members [of the Council] that the Council did not have full confidence or the complete co-operation of the Principal', we say this:

(a) It may be that some members of the Council hold that view privately, but this has never been the expressed conclusion of the Council as such, (b) In so far as members may hold such a view privately, we believe it is without foundation. Miss Montgomery has more than co-operated with the Council and the individual members of it despite the fact that there were times when she had to endure remarks and queries which bordered on uninformed and unjustified criticism of her.

4. Miss Montgomery's position in the world of education need not be restated here. We only wish to emphasise that her value to PLC cannot be overestimated and to hold out to parents, as the Chairman does in his circular, the prospect of Miss Montgomery being replaced by someone better, is in our opinion unduly optimistic. In our opinion, a situation exists at PLC where a handful of people can act in total disregard of the School Community's views on matters as fundamental as the education of their daughters. The Committee just formed by the Council ... to draw up for Council the terms of appointment for the new Principal ... does not include any member of the Council nominated by the School Community. It is in the light of all the forgoing circumstances, that we felt morally obliged to put these matters to the parents.

The Group B note triggered a further avalanche of protest letters to Moderator Alan Stubs, who was already struggling to cope: "I have received so many that it has been quite a task replying to them all and I've almost forgotten those to whom I have already sent replies". Old Collegian Anne Fortune, a former student and member of the School Council, received replies from Stubs on 5 and 7 March each with different content in response to her 21 February letter. Stubs acknowledged the "high esteem in which the school is held" and that it was due "largely to the leadership given by the Principal, although it was undoubtedly great even before she became its head." Referring to the Property Commission's decision, he went on: "I am sure that had the Commission awarded the Church any other two schools, there would have been no fuss, but Scotch and PLC were the two most prestigious schools in Victoria and our Uniting Church brethren just could not stomach that. They would not accept the 'umpire's decision'."

Stubs then directly attacked Joan Montgomery, despite her attempts to remain publicly neutral: "With due respect to the Principal, she has allowed herself to become involved in this, and has made some public statements attacking the Presbyterian Church. This has not endeared her to her employers. It is not really 'for no reason at all' that the Council has refused to renew her contract." Exactly how she had "allowed herself to become involved in this" was not explained. But, the damage done, he went on to offer some token conciliation: "Despite this, she has nevertheless been an outstanding principal who has made a significant contribution not only to PLC but to education generally in this State. I hate to see anyone who has made such a contribution go out amid controversy, so it is my sincere hope and prayer that, before she retires upon the expiry of her present contract, as she surely will, Council, Staff, parents and Old Collegians will all get together and work together to the glory of God and the good of the School, so that Miss Montgomery may retire with dignity having pride in her achievement."

The staff room remained firmly with Joan. Ruth Bunyan, as Chief of Staff of the Senior School, and Susan Scott, Chief of Staff of the Junior School, wrote to Pam Royle as President of the Parents' Association and to the Council, Alan Stubs and Joan, expressing the staff's full confidence in the Principal: "Miss Montgomery has led and continues to lead the College in a manner which has ensured that the objects of the College as laid down in the Memorandum and the Articles of Association have been and continue to be fulfilled."

Former students were equally dismayed by the events. Lucinda McKnight, a Year 12 student in 1984, wrote to the Council expressing her love and respect for the school and concern for its reputation and future'. Lucinda said she had read the letters sent to her parents from the Parents' Association and members of Council "with shock, dismay and growing anger". If the Council's role was to work in the best interests of the school, then it was misguided "to discard one of the best principals the College has ever had" on the false assumption that the Christian development of students had been neglected.

> The Chairman considers that it is the responsibility of education at PLC to 'promote the development of Christian ideals' in each student. I support this view. I consider my Christian development, under Miss Montgomery, to have been more than satisfactory. I have studied the Old Testament in some detail, used a Christian youth development kit, which related teachings of Christ to my own life, highlighting religion's personal and social aspects, and combining it with interest and enjoyment, and studied different religions, in relation to Christianity. In Year 10, we covered a more general area of study, including the New Testament and discussion of issues with religious relevance. Again, this year, we are meeting in discussion groups, to consider our roles as Christians and the meaning of God in our lives. These discussions, and, in fact, our religious education at all levels, have presented a valuable opportunity for us to clarify and share our opinions ... I do not believe that a more Bible-centred education with greater emphasis on literal translation from the Bible, could be more important or beneficial to my Christian development. In my opinion, education under Miss Montgomery has fulfilled all the objects for which the College is incorporated, as set out in the

Chairman's letter ... Miss Montgomery has spoken to the school on many mornings, through the sermons, prayers, Bible readings and notices of Assembly, and I have conversed with her personally, several times. Her refinement and dignity are acknowledged and respected by every student, while a sharp sense of humour, combined with a caring, understanding nature, make her a person we can love, and with whom we share a bond. Miss Montgomery can discipline a crowded hall with a single glance, or put a smile on the faces of a thousand girls with a few words. The Council's recent treatment of her has sent waves of fear, frustration and confusion throughout the school, and has created turmoil in its community ... The only way to remedy this situation is for the Council to swallow its pride and 'petty jealousies' and vote again, in favour of Miss Montgomery remaining as Principal. In this way, the school could be free from anachronistic attitudes, and able to continue with a policy of education which is liberal, fair and most appropriate for girls in the 1980s.

Lucinda's letter was one of more than four hundred the Council received at the time, all alike in sentiment. The third meeting of Council for 1984 would record the receipt of correspondence from 'Past PLC School Captains, 30 March 1984' — a collective vote of support for Joan Montgomery from each School Captain since 1969. At the same time, Joan was receiving hundreds of letters of personal support from all quarters — principals of other schools in Australia and overseas, friends, parents and former students. One came from the then Chaplain at Scotch College, Archie Crow, who wrote on 13 March: "My warmest support to you at this time of crisis, and my sympathy in the most trying ordeal you have had to undergo. One very positive benefit, however, of this last week's reactions to the threat to your respected position and the aspersions cast against the good name of PLC has been to clarify and make public the questions at issue." Crow also offered some cryptic advice about "holding one's own ship together and riding out the storms" saying: "Such a noble cause as yours would be least well served if those well-wishers who felt most keenly and deeply about the school were to withdraw from the scene. Much base be lost by default and nameless fears can be gross deceivers."

But the publicity genie was already out of the bottle and bound to be rubbed further, as indeed it was when the Parents' Association decided to hold a public meeting on Monday 9 April — in conjunction with its AGM — to discuss the future of PLC. A notice went out as a circular to parents on 23 March and an advertisement was placed in the Public Notices section of the *Age* on 9 April: "Those interested in the affairs of the school are invited to attend the meeting which will start at 8pm sharp in the Wyselaskie Hall PLC — TONIGHT."

The Parents' Association had invited both Don Carruthers and Alan Stubs to attend and answer questions. Carruthers replied that it would not be in the school's "best interests" for him to attend. He had "already published a letter to all parents" and had nothing more to add. A further attempt by Pam Royle to persuade him to attend was also declined.

In the meantime, the Group B members of the School Council were taking steps to deal with their minority status, given Group A and C were voting as a block. Their proposed solution was to be announced at the public meeting. A draft resolution was prepared aimed at gathering support to change PLC's Articles of Association. The notice of motion sought to change the method of appointment of Group C members — effectively to exclude current Group C members from being involved in the nomination of new Group C members. It also proposed that the Attorney-General of

Victoria have a role in the appointments in certain circumstances. Moreover, it incorporated a request that the Attorney-General take steps to amend the Articles of Association if the Council did not agree to amend them.

While he had declined the invitation to attend the public meeting, on the same day Carruthers sent a letter to parents that included a report the Council had received on the process of finding a new Principal. In the covering note, he wrote: "When the Council forms a Selection Committee, it is my personal wish that such a Committee will contain members from Groups A, B and C of the Council." The report covered advertising and promotion of the position and the terms of appointment. It noted the "preference which the school community is seen to entertain for a lady Principal and our sensitivity to these preferences but without disclosing our preferences in such a way as to infringe anti-discrimination legislation."

And there was some genuine news that Carruthers might well have brought to a public meeting anxious to hear from him: "A special meeting of the Committee was held on Monday 12th March. Miss K.S. McCredie, the National President, and Mr Warren Stone, the State President, of the Association of Heads of Independent Girls' Schools of Australia met with the Committee. The meeting was at the request of Miss McCredie. The interest of the Association only formally arises in the event of the college dismissing a Principal. Nevertheless, a request having been made, the Chairman considered it appropriate to accede to the request. A frank discussion took place over matters of mutual concern upon an agreed basis of confidentiality."

While the conversation might have been frank, it was far from satisfactory in the view of Kath McCredie. She would later recall that Carruthers had failed to listen properly to her appeal for the Council to reconsider its decision not to extend Joan Montgomery's appointment. A week after their meeting, she sent a follow up letter: "The members of the Association of Heads of

Outcry

Girls' and Boys' Independent Schools find it incredible to believe that Miss Montgomery, one of our greatest educationalists and a most respected and admired Head, is suffering such hurt and humiliation. We would earnestly urge you and your Council to reconsider the whole situation most carefully and prayerfully and to take whatever measures are possible for reconciliation for the sake of the persons and principles involved."

Unmoved by the overwhelming appeals of the PLC community to save their beloved Principal, the Presbyterians were equally deaf to the chorus of dismay from leading educationalists across Australia.

15

FIGHT THE GOOD FIGHT

As parents and friends arrived in the foyer of Wyselaskie Hall on the evening of 9 April 1984 for the much-anticipated public meeting, a pamphlet was handed out. Typed on the back of it were just under 150 names who declared themselves to be "concerned Presbyterians, parents and old girls disturbed that misleading statements have been made about the Presbyterian Church."

The chief objection of the pamphleteers was to their being called "bigoted, fundamentalist and narrow-minded" and they wanted to "clarify some of the facts" about the nature of a Christian education. While they accepted the Bible as "the supreme standard of faith and conduct" they wished to make clear "this certainly does not imply that we interpret the Bible with crude literalism, a view that has been imputed to us." While not dealing directly with the School Council's refusal to renew Joan Montgomery's contract, the pamphlet declared: "We understand the difficulty in replacing a Principal of the calibre of Miss Montgomery. However, the problem is inevitable; sooner or later a replacement will have to be found. We would like to reassure you that the Presbyterian Church would like to see the high standards of the College maintained."

The meeting was thronged with estimates of more than 2500 students, Old Collegians and friends filling the hall to capacity with the overflow watching by video in the social science area and from outside the Principal's office. Pam Royle began by welcoming those attending, particularly special guests Dame Leonie Kramer and Joan Montgomery. She announced that for the sake of the record the proceedings would be tape recorded, before introducing the others on the stage, including Parents' Association solicitor Ian Murray and Council member Alex Chernov. She then explained the decision of both Council Chairman Don Carruthers and Presbyterian Moderator Alan Stubs to decline the invitations to attend.

Dame Leonie Kramer originally had been invited as the guest speaker at the 44th Annual General Meeting of the Parents' Association that was scheduled for later that evening but had since agreed to speak at the public meeting instead. Dame Leonie, one of Australia's most distinguished academics and educators, was the first woman professor of English in Australia and the first woman to chair the then Australian Broadcasting Commission. She would later become the first woman to be appointed Chancellor of the University of Sydney. After detailing her long and impressive CV, Pam Royle then added: "Most important to all of us at this meeting is that she is a PLC Old Collegian."

Dame Leonie began her speech by saying that the best thing about the night was being "back home" at her alma mater: "I am sure I am expressing the feeling of many parents when I say one of the things about this school that has been remarkable, is that it has been home to so many people. I don't know of many women who don't remember it with a special kind of affection and gratitude". In response to the rhetorical question of "what is a good education?" she declared: "The education you get and have always got at PLC and I would like to think will always be available at PLC."

She said the school had an outstanding reputation for its academic standard and the social and moral education that accompanied it: "PLC has sent out young women who have made a remarkable contribution to higher education, and to all walks of life. This school has never discriminated, as it never should. It has provided for children of all abilities. Everyone was encouraged to find out what she could do well—to prepare its students for whatever might come their way later in life—and I believe it has done." Socially, PLC encouraged its students to feel that the school was a community: "We were encouraged and expected to respect the needs of all people. We were not permitted to be snobbish or show favouritism, nor was it showed to us ... I met girls whose religion and race were different from mine—and I was not permitted to be censorious or snobbish—and that they had a point of view that was valid—and you made friends with those who were different."

As for providing students with a moral education and the "principles of honesty, integrity and courage—and that we are the fortunate inheritors of this world" these were taught by example—"I don't think one can teach principles"—and in this the head of the school provided the most important role model: "Ultimately it is the nature, character and ideals of the Principal and staff and the ability of the Principal to encourage the staff to infect the whole body of the school with those ideals too." That example had been instrumental in shaping her career: "I could not have done anything that I have done, if not for the education and training I received at this school. I was fortunate in having a family that chose this school at great personal sacrifice. I have absolutely no doubt that the education I received ... led to my inclination and desire to serve the community—a feeling that one had to give back. The other thing I acquired very early from PLC was freedom to learn, and to take risks in learning."

Dame Leonie was effusive in her praise of Joan Montgomery's leadership: "This school was 100 years ahead of its time in women's education from the beginning. It has had to live through a great period in Australia—no more so since Joan Montgomery's term as Principal. She has steered it with purpose and imagination, during one of the most difficult periods for leadership in our society—by preparing many fortunate young people for the modern world and for the future. It seems to me there is no scriptural authority for turning away from the present or the future. One of the things I learnt to love was the poetry of Milton—he defended the freedom of the press, because liberty was the test of character—and one could not shut people up to make them virtuous, 'I cannot praise a fugitive and cloistered virtue, unexercised and unbreathed, that never sallies out and sees her adversary, but slinks out of the race where that immortal garland is to be run for, not without dust and heat'."

Of Milton's injunction she was clear: "PLC does not teach people to slink out of the race." But over recent months, she had been asked what was happening at PLC: "One cannot replace that kind of reputation or set aside 100-plus years of liberal tradition without penalty, and one cannot survive by taking refuge in dogma." Again, she turned to Milton: "God uses not to captivate [a man] under a perpetual childhood of prescription, but trusts him with the gift of reason, to be his own chooser." It was a strong build-up to a rousing finish: "My favourite hymn was 'Fight the good fight' which I sang in the Old Wyselaskie hall in East Melbourne, and my father was the first chairman of the Building Committee that helped build this Burwood campus ... I never thought I'd be standing in the new Wyselaskie hall in these circumstances, having to fight for the PLC we know—it is worth the fight to preserve what it represents. So far as I am concerned, there is no fight more important to engage, and none more vital to win." After Dame Leonie sat down the applause rang for several minutes.

Alex Chernov, one of the five Group B members of the School Council, was then called on to outline the practical steps planned to fight the good fight for PLC's future. He explained that he and the other Group B members who were present—Robert Anderson, Mary Murdoch, Joan Northrop and Russell Rechner — were nominated by the school community via a Selection Committee and "although they do not act as agents of the school community when they sit in Council, there is an obvious affiliation between them and the school community."

In a calm and methodical way, as if he were opening arguments before a court, Chernov began to explain the actions initiated by Group B that were "aimed at preventing the perpetuation of the present situation where a handful of people that constitute the majority of the Council can dictate the future of the school with total disregard for the views of educationalists and the views and aspirations of the vast majority of the school community, and in particular the paying parents." He said Group B's reform proposals sought to achieve "a better-balanced Council in the future."

Before elaborating on the plans, there was a delicate point Chernov wanted to clear up. This was a public meeting and he was a member of the Council with a responsibility to maintain the confidentiality of Council meetings. The ordinary rule was to keep disagreements within the Council room. But this, he said, was no ordinary case: "In extreme cases [the Group B members] owe a duty to PLC to make available to the school community and to parents in particular, its views of what is wrong at Council level. Such an extreme case is now present because the course adopted by the majority of the Council in respect of the school has put PLC's future in some doubt. It is in the school's interests that parents know about that view so they can make decisions about their daughter's future education, taking into account that factor."

There were two further preliminaries. Chernov made clear that he was not blaming the Presbyterian Church as a whole, but rather, certain sections of it. And, on the subject of the Church, he wanted to dispel certain misconceptions about the relationship between the Church and PLC. He explained how the school had been established in 1875 as a result of the Scots respect for education, and that its object was "to provide for the daughters of our colonists as high an education as their sons are receiving at such institution as The Scotch College, The Grammar School and

The Wesley College." PLC's first Principal, Charles Henry Pearson, in speaking about religious education at the school, had said it should "be clearly understood that anything like denominationalism [at the school] is unknown and the authority of the parents in the matter is held to be sacred."

Chernov then sought to puncture the myth that PLC was owned or otherwise beholden to the Church because the Church funded it and was therefore "entitled to take the leading role" in the administration of the school: "Such a belief does not, however, accord with facts. Apart from the expense that was incurred in establishing the school at East Melbourne in 1875, the cost of procuring the funds necessary from time to time to provide the facilities at the school was borne by the school community. For example, when PLC moved from East Melbourne to Burwood in the 1950s, the cost of that move was borne not by the Presbyterian Church, but by parents and members of the school community. The same applies to the establishment of the Music School, the $1m spent on the renovations of the Junior School as well as the $1.5m now being spent on the South East extensions of the Senior School."

Referring to the decision of the Property Commission to award PLC to the Presbyterian Church, Chernov reminded the audience that the Supreme Court challenge to the decision, initiated by PLC's then Council, had raised squarely "the questions, to whom did PLC belong and who was to control its future." But the parties had settled before the court grappled with those issues. Nonetheless, the settlement was a new beginning for "whatever claims the Presbyterian Church may have had to PLC at the commencement of litigation, it gave them up in return for rights it obtained under the settlement." The settlement had led to the establishment of a company known as Presbyterian Ladies' College. Thus, PLC became a separate legal entity in its own right that was to be administered in accordance with its Memorandum and Articles of Association. Chernov then read out the relevant clauses and concluded by saying: "No mention is there made of 'Bible-centred education'." As ownership was vested in the new company and not the Church, it was "therefore no good saying, as some people do, that the Church was awarded the school at Union, and that gives it some sort of a proprietary interest in the College. The fact is that the Church accepted the establishment of the new company and the transfer to it of the school property, and no one can be properly heard to complain of that now."

Under the new structure, he continued, control of the school was vested in the 17 people who constituted the Council. Those 17 people were also members of the company, PLC, and were in a position similar to that of a board of directors of a company who also happened to be its sole shareholders. But, he argued, this was where the settlement took a wrong turn. Although the Articles had divided the 17 members into three groups — A and B each having five members and Group C with seven — what resulted was a Council controlled by those aligned with the Presbyterian Church.

Alex Chernov was in a rare and curious position. He was giving a legal seminar to the vast audience that spilled from the hall. In normal circumstances, it might be expected that some wander off or nod off. But the occasion and the cause, and Chernov's silky delivery, held the crowd captive. He proceeded to explain how the Council groups had formed. The Articles provided that the Council be appointed annually by the Presbyterian General Assembly with the school community nominating five Group B members, the Church selecting five Group A members and the retiring Council choosing seven Group C members. It had been envisaged that Groups A and B might, in the early days at least, be at odds and deadlocked. So, Group C was introduced to ensure the Council could work: "Group C was placed, so to speak, between group A and group B and was to be, in the relevant sense, independent of the Church and school community. It would, in this way, participate in the resolution of any deadlock that may exist between group A and group B on any issue." The independence of group C was, therefore, vital. But this did not happen: "Group A members did not accept that group C should be independent of the Church and looked upon it as and insisted that it be an adjunct of group A and at all relevant times both groups acted accordingly."

Thus, the new arrangement was doomed from the time of incorporation: "During the life of the first Council, three out of the seven Group C acted independently of the Church and the school community. The other four sided with Group A on every occasion when Group A and Group B adopted opposing positions."

The tenure of the three non-conformists would be brief, Chernov explained. When the time came to nominate seven Group C members for the second year's Council, Group A and the four conformist members of Group C voted as a block to rid the Council of the three independent-minded members and replace them with three members aligned to Group A and the Continuing Church. The four conformists kept their positions and so the four became seven members of Group C who thereafter routinely voted with Group A: "Whenever group A and group B took opposing views on any issues of substance, group C automatically sided with group A with the result that on each such occasion the vote was 12/5 against Group B ... Thus, twelve people on the 17 [person] Council will be selected directly or indirectly by the Presbyterian Church or those who are members or have an affiliation with it."

Chernov argued that this outcome clearly was at odds "with the understanding that the new company would have an independent group C to resolve deadlocks between groups A and B" and the School was entitled to demand that Group C members were chosen not on the basis of whether or not they would act in concert with group A, but on the basis of their proven ability. He said the unholy alliance between Groups A and C had led to the crisis over Joan Montgomery's position at PLC: "This in turn, raised the question of what type of education is going to be provided at PLC. The Council's decision on this point has highlighted again the fact that for practical purposes, groups A and C come out of one mould and that their philosophy and thinking is not reflective of community standards. They acknowledge that fact, but despite this recognition, are prepared to impose their wishes on the school community."

As Joan sat watching in the front row, Chernov turned directly to the issue uppermost in the minds of most of the audience—the future of their beloved Principal: "It would be preaching to the converted and embarrassing for Miss Montgomery for me to explain why Miss Montgomery is so well regarded." He referred to the hundreds of letters that had been sent to the Council and to the Presbyterian Moderator and the letters that had been published in the press from those associated with the school and others including renowned educationalists. This, he said, put paid to the question of whether or not Joan should have been offered the opportunity of staying on at PLC.

Then he turned his guns on the Presbyterian majority on the Council: "Any group which can say that education at PLC under Miss Montgomery is not good enough because it is not sufficiently 'Bible-centred' and that therefore she should not be afforded the opportunity of staying on at the school, is clearly out of step, not only with the vast majority of the school community but also expert educational opinion and common sense. It may lead one to question seriously the competence of that group to look after the best interests of the school."

At this point, the audience, who had been listening in silence, broke into energetic applause. After waiting for the clapping to abate, Chernov acknowledged that since the letter of Chairman Don Carruthers had been distributed, attempts had been made by some affiliated with groups A and C to downplay any suggestions that they wanted a more rigid and fundamental type of religious education at PLC, or that there would be any significant change in the educational emphasis at the school after Joan Montgomery retired. But he was not encouraged: "Group B is of the view that any such placatory statements should be treated with caution ... [it seems] what is desired is a more definitive nexus between the Scriptures and secular education. Moreover, the Chairman's letter states, in effect, that there is a deficiency in education at PLC under Miss Montgomery and what is required to remedy that is 'a much greater emphasis on Bible-centred education as laid down in the Memorandum of Association'." In Group B's view, the change envisaged would be at odds with the educational standards Joan Montgomery epitomised: "Can one feel comfortable in the knowledge that they'll select a principal under whom the education at PLC will be what the vast majority of the school community and the educationalists regard as first class and of the calibre and type that PLC has been renowned for the past century or so? In our views, these questions can only be answered in the negative."

Chernov then outlined Group B's plan to ensure that Group C was independent and selected on ability: "We have concluded that the only practical and enduring solution is to alter the Articles so as to provide that at the end of each year, Group C for the forthcoming year should be selected not by the retiring Council, but by groups A and B and if they do not fill all the vacancies by agreement then that should be done by the Attorney-General from the lists of names supplied to him by group A and group B. Each list will set out no more than two names per vacancy." He said the Attorney-General was an appropriate umpire as his office had an historic responsibility on behalf of the Crown "to keep an eye on charities, such as educational institutions", he was a party to the litigation that resulted in PLC becoming an independent incorporated entity and he was also responsible for administering the Companies Code under which PLC operated as a registered company.

Group B had already given notice to groups A and C of its

proposed motion to amend the Articles and to move it at the next annual general meeting of the PLC company scheduled for 31 May. Anticipating a combined vote against the amendment, Chernov said: "The Attorney-General has been requested to take such steps as may be necessary to procure that amendment." This was no radical move to twist the Articles into a wildly different shape. Group B was seeking "to restore the position to what was intended to be in the first place" and thus to produce a better-balanced Council. This was "the commonsense intention of the Articles," nothing more.

Chernov now moved to what he sought from the overflowing gathering of parents, friends and Old Collegians: "Group B believes that the school community will support the action that it has taken and, if that is so, it would be of great assistance if this meeting were to express that support. A strong and united expression of support will be of great assistance and may have a strong bearing on whether the Attorney-General will agree to assist in the resolution of the present problem facing PLC." The response was spontaneous and overwhelming. As Chernov resumed his seat, the applause thundered.

Pam Royle then opened the floor to questions. There would be many. One of the first was from Ruth Bunyan, a member of staff, who asked whether a change in the composition of the Council would mean Joan Montgomery's position as Principal was open for reconsideration? "The answer to that is yes, it would be open for it to do that," Chernov replied, drawing more rapturous applause.

One Old Collegian asked about the current state of religious education at PLC. Mrs Merritt, the head of Religious Education, explained that this involved more than what went on in RE classes. She said her department had the support and respect from all the staff and the Principal, and over the years the time spent on RE classes had been increased. Importantly, she noted, "part of the religious and spiritual life is in Assembly." The curriculum was largely biblically based but was related to everyday life and the style of teaching was about encouraging students to question and think rigorously about their values and beliefs: "We desire to make them freer to make inquiry—in the spirit of Christ, who did not enforce a particular view. We also see this as more educationally valid, by encouraging questions, not simply providing answers. And it is an approach that is more likely to work. We value and respect differences in the school community, not because we don't care, but because we do." This drew strong applause.

It was then the turn of Jenny Pring's husband Jim—the couple had signed the letter distributed at the beginning of the evening as concerned Presbyterians—who asked Alex Chernov: "Why does Group B assume that the Presbyterian Church which has successfully administered Church schools has suddenly lost that capacity?" Chernov responded: "I didn't state anything about the capacity of the Church because I hoped to make it clear that the Presbyterian Church has no legal right to administer the school and agreed to that situation at the settlement of the litigation." More strong applause.

From the balcony of the hall, Tom Ramsay, a past parent, raised concerns about the proposed involvement of the Attorney-General. Wouldn't it be problematic if the Attorney-General was casting the vote because of the divisions? "How do we move towards unity and the welfare of the future of the school? Can we move to influence the whole body of Continuing Presbyterian Church?" Chernov said the proposal was preferable to the present situation: "If it turns out to be the casting vote of one, that would be a relief to the casting vote of 12 to 5."

Yvonne Rentoul then rose in the main hall. An Old Collegian who had attended the school from 1916 to 1926, she explained that those were the days of the last male Principal. "Mr Chernov, in light of what we have been given this evening, is there a very real danger, with the presently constituted Council, of there being appointed a Presbyterian Minister and not an educationalist?" How prescient she would prove to be. Chernov couldn't say but agreed that Group B was genuinely apprehensive about the type of person to follow and sensed that change would not be change for the better.

Parent Fred McGuinis cut to the chase: "Can we win?" Chernov replied: "Yes, PLC can win. If we do not win, there will be a PLC that Dame Leonie Kramer doesn't know, that Miss Montgomery doesn't know and that the vast majority here do not want to know."

The last question would go to Brian Bayston. There were a few sighs when he identified himself. "Can Mr Chernov justify his belief on rational grounds?" With his lawyerly style, Alex Chernov calmly answered: "I hoped that what I said on behalf of Group B stated rational grounds on where the future of the school lies — I have set them out in summary form and would not want to repeat that again."

The motions were then put to the meeting by parent Mark Rayner, who read out:

1. That this meeting:
    (a) supports the action of group B members of the Council aimed at procuring independence of Group C and to that end, seeking to amend the Articles of Association of PLC so that group C will be selected by groups A and B and in default of agreement, by the Attorney-General, from a list of names supplied by groups A and B;
    (b) requests the Commissioner for Corporate Affairs to grant the necessary approval to such proposed amendments;
    (c) requests the Attorney-General to agree to participate in the selection of group C in the

manner proposed by said amendments;
- (d) requests the Attorney-General that in the event of members of PLC not resolving so to amend the Articles, he take such steps as may be necessary to procure such amendments.
2. That the Parents' Association obtain the names and addresses of those of the school community and of its friends who support the above resolution and forward those names and addresses to the Attorney-General and upon this being done, inform the Commissioner for Corporate Affairs of that fact.

After the motions were seconded by another parent, Caroline Larkins, Mark Rayner spoke briefly, expressing concern that the traditions and standards of PLC be maintained over the decades ahead. The motion was then opened for discussion and there was some debate about the wording. One parent said it was hard to make a decision without hearing the views of the other side. Bruce Teale, another parent, recommended a negative vote because he was not satisfied there had been an exhaustive effort to bridge the gap: "I am not a Presbyterian, and perhaps there are other Anglicans like me who are concerned by the thought of going to the Government, which absolutely appalls me — you cannot be sure that you'll get what you want, and this action runs the risk of polarising the feelings further ... Is it not possible for us as a meeting to recommend that this matter go before the Assembly of the Presbyterian Church so that every possible avenue has been explored? The letter from the Presbyterian Church tonight [the letter parents handed out] indicates that there are Presbyterians concerned too and perhaps they could be encouraged to do more?" Margaret Sandbach, an Old Collegian and past parent, had a response: "I have tried to rouse the Presbyterian Church to action—the Commission of Assembly has just met and the Education Committee and nothing was done. We can't wait until October."

David Wilson, another parent, was also concerned about engaging the Government. Alex Chernov explained that the motion did not involve going to the Government as such, but to the Attorney-General in his role overseeing charities. He gave a recent example of Camberwell Grammar relying on the Attorney in a similar manner to positive effect, then asked: "Where have the Presbyterians been for the last four years?"

Allan Harman, a parent and Presbyterian minister, questioned the ability of the Church to control the appointment of Group C members of the School Council and said there must be an opportunity of sitting down to talk—before going to the Attorney-General in whatever capacity. Chernov said it was important to sit down and talk, but that should be after the changes were made. In response to Harman's challenge about the way Group C operated, he referred to evidence in his possession from one of the Group C members who had written a statement about being directed how to vote by Group A. Chernov said he didn't want to read it out publicly, but Harman was welcome to see it.

After Caroline Larkins spoke as seconder, and Mark Rayner responded further to various issues raised, Pam Royle called for a show of hands. There was an overwhelming majority in favour in the hall itself and unanimous support in all the overflow areas. A smaller group of hands went up against the motion in the Hall. In order to record the passing of the motions properly, those attending were asked to sign their names supporting the motion before leaving, and Parents' Association volunteers went to the petition tables outside the Principal's office to get all the paperwork in readiness before people left after the AGM.

As the public meeting prepared to break up, Jenny Walker, a parent, rose and proposed a further motion: "That this meeting expresses its support for and confidence in Miss Montgomery as Principal of PLC." Almost the entire hall stood, including those on the stage, with a standing round of applause that went for several minutes. Helen Macmillan then seconded the motion. A sea of hands rose across the audience. Only one hand was raised in opposition.

At the brief Parents' Association AGM that followed the public meeting, Pam Royle opened by summarising the sentiment expressed by the standing ovation Joan Montgomery had just received: "The feeling that exists in the school at the present time is due not only to the fact that we care for this school and its future, but because we care a great deal for our Principal. I know that I speak on behalf of the vast majority of parents when I say to Miss Montgomery, we not only admire you for your educational ability and all that means for our daughters, for your standards and values that you impart to them, but you also have our confidence, respect and you have our affection."

At the conclusion of the AGM, as the audience was ushered out of the hall by staff, 10 rows at a time, Joan Montgomery, who had sat quietly in the front row through the evening, turned to face those behind her. She appeared pensive and self-conscious as she stood talking with her deputies, Jan Douglas and Ev Tindale. Did she feel uncomfortable? "Wouldn't you?" she would later say. Ev Tindale had suggested she stand up to respond to the applause during the meeting, but she found she could hardly move her legs. The evening had been an outstanding moment in bringing all the issues into the open and she was very grateful for the support, but deep down, Joan was pessimistic: "I had little hope of anything happening."

Pam Royle was more upbeat. Her letter of thanks to Dame Leonie Kramer was effusive: "Your address, with Alex's explanation of the problem that exists, and how we can help, has had a wonderful effect on the morale of the school community. For the first time in many months there is a feeling of hope for the future of the school. The first bundle of signatures was taken to the Attorney-General last Thursday and since the meeting hundreds of parents, old collegians and friends have collected petition books and are busy collecting more signatures. If we don't succeed with this petition it will not be due to a lack of support from the school community."

There were those in the Presbyterian Church who also were galvanised by the spirit of the public meeting. Members of the Canterbury Presbyterian Church organised a "Motion Concerning the Crisis at PLC" that was sent to their Presbytery on 17 April: "This Congregation expresses its deepest concern at the crisis at PLC caused by the division between Church and School community representatives on the Council ... It is our conviction that if the Church does not, as a matter of urgency, take appropriate action to resolve the crisis, it will have dire consequences for the Church. At the public meeting of approximately 2500 people at PLC on the 9th April, the Church failed to offer any explanation or counter view to that put forward by the school community. Presbyterians at the meeting were dismayed and disturbed by the Church being so thoroughly discredited. As the Church has direct and indirect oversight of the appointments to the Council, it has the responsibility to initiate reforms which will result in reconciliation between Church and School. We believe these reforms must include changes to the special commission of the Assembly which has responsibility for appointments to institutions, replacement of some members of Council and conciliation with School Community representatives. Such moves are necessary to preclude the legislative action which seeks to change the Articles of Association of the School."

Despite the mounting concern in the PLC community and sections of the Presbyterian Church, Brian Bayston and Max Bradshaw were unwavering in their approach to the way Groups A and C would continue to behave on the Council. Soon after the public meeting, Bayston briefed John Phillips and Hartley

Hansen, two barristers who had worked for the Presbyterian Church in the 1979-80 litigation, to provide an opinion on the way Alex Chernov had characterised the nature of Group C at the public meeting. In particular, they sought advice on Chernov's assertion that Group C's role was to resolve any deadlocks between Groups A and B.

Unsurprisingly, Phillips and Hansen's memorandum took a different view: "Although the appointment of members to Group C is dealt with exhaustively by Article 33 [of the Articles of Association], members of that group are not classified or otherwise designated as 'independent'; nor are they in any way indicated as being the holders of some sort of balance of power; nor are they required to be in any way 'independent' of the influence of the Presbyterian Church ... To say now that members of Group C should be 'independent of Church and the School Community' or to argue that 'the independence of Group C is vital to the proper and efficient working of the Council' is to speak of something which was never agreed, nor was it ever part of the settlement. So far as the agreement went, the only qualification of membership of Group C was that ... they should be nominated by the current Council and approved and appointed by the General Assembly of the Presbyterian Church, which to that end was given the right of veto as set out in Article 33. It was only on those terms that the Church agreed to forego its claim to the direct benefit of the award of the Property Commission; it was only on these terms that the Church agreed not to continue to press for a determination in the litigation that the Property Commission award was valid and effective according to its terms."

Phillips and Hartley dismissed the arguments for amendments to enable Group C to be independent. This, they asserted, was, "no more than a bold attempt to re-negotiate the settlement. It could be done only if the Church were to be given the opportunity of resurrecting the litigation and maintaining thereby its claim to the direct benefit of the award of the Property

Commission. That cannot be done and therefore any attempt to re-negotiate the settlements is on a false basis." They also dismissed the amendments proposed at the public meeting and endorsed by the overwhelming majority of those who attended. They argued the amendments were not "properly characterised as aimed at procuring the independence of Group C," and the meeting's support had been "induced by, and is based upon, some fundamental misconceptions, involving both the compromise reached in the 1980 litigation concerning PLC and the terms of the Articles of Association."

The lawyers also challenged the proposal to enlist the support of the Attorney-General: "The Attorney-General was a necessary party to the litigation concerning PLC ... and was in fact the plaintiff. As a plaintiff, he was a necessary party to the compromise achieved and he was, of course, party to the terms of settlement." They argued that the Attorney could not depart from what was agreed to in 1980, "simply on the ground that one group of persons, who now see themselves affected by the agreement then reached and claim loudly that the terms of that agreement should be altered ... The clamour for change that has been raised at the instance of members of Group B on the Council, is based upon an assertion of what was always intended when the settlement was reached. It is on that basis that the members of Group B now seek to have the Attorney-General assist in changing the Articles of Association." There was no basis for this as the "intention was plainly misconceived".

It was now obvious that Groups A and C on the School Council were not going to bend and would fight hard to resist an approach to the Attorney-General. The school community realised they would need to employ other strategies if there was to be any hope of achieving their ends.

Soon after the April public meeting, a public relations committee was formed. It included Council Group B members Mary Murdoch and Joan Northrop, and Lois Bell, Pam Royle and

Pam Buxton representing the Parents' Association. The committee prepared a document dated 2 May 1984 that was titled "Campaign to Unify the PLC School Community". It was marked "Strictly Confidential", as they were aware that "a quality public affairs advisor is acting for the other side". The document argued that a campaign was necessary because of the belief "that Council at its 31 May meeting will not refer the matter to the Attorney-General, so that he will subsequently have to be asked to intervene."

The committee mapped out a strategy that had six elements in the lead up to the 31 May meeting and 10 elements after it. They resolved to hire their own public relations adviser. Another "Strictly Confidential" letter confirmed the appointment of Alan Chipp, Managing Director of Professional Public Relations—the husband of a former student and father of a daughter in Year 12.

Alan Chipp's first piece of advice was not encouraging. In a letter to Russell Rechner, as Chairman of the Public Relations Committee, on 3 May, Chipp commended the committee's draft document as comprehensive and worthwhile, but then added: "Addressing the realities of your situation we must voice our grave doubts about any campaign, no matter how well structured or presented, overcoming and persuading the incumbent Labor government to intervene in an internal dispute in view of the overwhelming political dangers inherent in such action."

Chipp advised that he had taken the prerogative of arranging an urgent discussion with the Reverend Bert Stevens, the Head of Essendon and Penleigh Grammar and a leading member of the Uniting Church group that had fought the issues initially, two of his colleagues "who handle the bulk of our political manipulative work" and Pam Buxton, representing the Parents' Association, to get a full briefing on the background to the dispute and the current situation. On the basis of his firm's extensive experience dealing with the Victorian Labor Government, Chipp was not convinced they would obtain the support of the Attorney-

General, Jim Kennan, but even if they did, they would still have to win approval for any action at both Caucus and Cabinet level. This, he said, would be a tough task: "The Caucus education committee ... has a heavy socialist bias and could be expected to be totally unsympathetic with problems of the private schools."

Chipp was also concerned by a flippant comment Kennan had made in reply to a question from Joan Kirner in the Legislative Council on 17 April. Kennan had said, "the best thing he could do was to appoint the former Liberal Attorney-General Mr Storey to deal with the matter." On checking the Hansard record of that day, Chipp thought Kennan's detailed response, while jocular, still left the door open.

> The Hon. J. E. KIRNER — (Melbourne West Province): Has the Attorney-General received approaches from the school community of the Presbyterian Ladies' College on difficulties being experienced in relation to school Council matters? Given the Government's commitment to community participation in school decision-making, will the Minister advise the House whether he has made any response, or intends to make any response, to the Presbyterian Ladies' College community?
>
> The Hon. J. H. KENNAN — (Attorney-General): It seems that there are some factional difficulties on that school Council. I asked some of my colleagues for advice as a long-standing member of the phone-box faction may have been able to bring some expertise to bear on it. Those matters have been brought to my attention. I am awaiting a resolution from a meeting at the end of May. I have received a letter and some personal representations from

representatives of the school community. It would be best if that community could solve its own problems. I am tempted to appoint Mr Storey to deal with the matter but I feel it would be unfair. I shall await the outcome of the meeting of the community before I decide whether action should be taken.[1]

Alan Chipp identified the obvious political dangers that might pre-empt government intervention, including "charges of interfering in church affairs, trying to take over control of independent schools, trying to stamp out religious education and kowtowing to a privileged minority interest group (who are not Labor supporters anyway)." In essence, he felt the better course was to try to win the support of the broad Presbyterian Church community and motivate them to bring about a change in attitudes and/or personnel on the current Council, "either by confrontation or persuasion". By confrontation he meant: "Precipitating a public furore which would alarm Presbyterian Church members to such a degree that they exert their influence to insist that the matter be resolved to save the Church from further public ridicule and humiliation." One way to do this, he explained, would be for "parents to remove their children en masse, refuse to pay their school fees, picket the school, or some similar dramatic action (aimed) at generating media coverage." An alternative approach would involve, "working quietly behind the scenes on individual church members, identifying ministers and senior church people with more moderate views and approaching and demonstrating to them the injustices of the present situation and elicit their support to bring about change."

The Committee may have been less persuaded by the second plan when Pam Buxton received a sharply-worded letter on 6 May from Marion Mason, an Old Collegian (1933-45) and member of the Wangaratta Presbyterian Church: "Having been a pupil at Presbyterian Ladies' College for over 12 years and also being a member of the Old Collegians' Association, I have been concerned at the bias of the newsletters since PLC and Scotch College were awarded to the Presbyterian Church by the Property Commission after the formation of the Uniting Church … When I was at school, we were carefully taught to examine both sides of every question and the rights of the Presbyterian Church in all of this have never been mentioned by the Old Collegians' Association." She was concerned that the Presbyterian Church was spoken of as if it contained "a few bigoted geriatrics", adding: "The Presbyterian Church is one of the fastest growing denominations in Australia today and for very good reason. Its Theological College graduates are preaching the truth as contained in the Scriptures and whole families, weary of the sleazy humanism so widespread in State Schools etc., are flocking to hear it." She concluded by saying she would send copies of her letter to other Old Collegians, "in the hope that they will start to think of both sides of the question instead of following the instructions of this ruthless, faceless pressure group like a mob of silly sheep."

But Mrs Mason herself may have been influenced by mob behaviour. Pam Royle would obtain a record of the Wangaratta Presbyterian Church's "Order of Service and Intimations for The Lord's Day, Sunday 27 May 1985", in which the Reverend Peter Hastie would say: "Forming the minds of a future generation is the task of education, and you will surely be concerned, if you are a parent, whether the school teachers who guide your children's thinking are men and women with values and standards which are distinctly Christian. There is no such thing as educational neutrality. If you are not studying and teaching on the assumption that there is a life beyond this one, you are studying and teaching on the assumption that there is not. … Christian muddle-headedness on this matter has led us to send tiny Johnny to Sunday-School to learn about his desperate need for grace, but on Monday to send him to a school where in social studies/personal development he is taught that all man needs for personal well-being is to attend to hygiene and 'do his own thing'. This is a recipe for disaster, and the sooner the Christian community realises it the better. If education is finally a matter of ultimate issue and human destiny, the Church must become involved and take care of its own constituents. For too long the Church has sat on the sidelines and abdicated its responsibility. The time is fast approaching for decisive action."

Brian Bayston and Max Bradshaw were of the same mind. Control of PLC was a matter of vital importance to them. And the place of religion in the life of the school was central to why they had fought to ensure that Groups A and C became a single voting block on the School Council. No public meeting, however spirited, would shake their conviction.

The Parents' Association remained equally determined. On 28 May, three days before the crucial Council meeting, the Association sent a letter to all parents briefing them on developments since the public meeting. Community backing for the plan was looking formidable. More than 7000 parents, Old Collegians, and friends of PLC had given written indication to the Attorney-General of their support for the moves. A notice had been forwarded to Corporate Affairs Commissioner Jan Wade seeking her consent to changing the procedure for selecting Group C Council members. Approaches had also been made to the Attorney-General to become involved in the selection of Group C members in the event that Church and school representatives couldn't agree. The circular stressed: "The action is not an attack on the Church or its entitlement to a voice on Council. However, it must be understood that the Church does not own PLC which is an independent incorporated body controlled by its Council ... The objective is to ensure the Council has an appropriate cross section of expertise and is made up of people who are proven leaders in their respective fields who will work together for the best interests of PLC. Representation from the Church and school communities is to be safeguarded."

The next day, Mary Murdoch received a first draft of the submission to the Attorney-General prepared by Alan Chipp's colleague Harry Smith at Professional Public Relations. In drafting it, Smith's purpose was to "spell out the problem in human rather than legal terms" in a simplified form that might become a briefing document for the media "if we have to go public on the whole issue." The approach was to "push the concerned parents' angle because it is something that the vast majority of people can identify with and understand." This was in contrast to talking about how the Council members were in breach of the Companies Code which he felt would enable the opposing forces to say that the "Church only got two out of the nine schools and now they are trying to take that away." Smith spelled out the key argument: "The underlying fear of parents is that the basic foundation upon which the school was established, i.e. to provide an education for daughters equal to that available to sons, will be eroded."

The draft submission also addressed how to respond in the expected event that the 31 May Council meeting rejected the will of the public meeting. Smith suggested putting out "an aggressive statement" to emphasise the parents' motivation being concern for their children. It was not anti-Church. However, the statement should leave no doubt "that we intend to escalate rather than capitulate".

To the surprise of no one, the PLC Council meeting on 31 May followed the same pattern as all previous meetings: the vote was 12-5 against the motions put by the Group B representatives. On Saturday 2 June, a report by Graham Reilly appeared in the *Age* with the headline, "PLC Council Five Fail in Push for Intervention". He wrote that the "community representatives on the Presbyterian Ladies' College Council have failed to win support for their move to have the State Government intervene to resolve a dispute between the warring Council factions." Having lost the Council vote on the previous Thursday evening it meant that no further steps could be taken as "the Attorney-General, Mr Kennan, said earlier this week he would intervene only if asked by the Council, or if it could be proved that the Articles of Association had been contravened."

Holt Public Relations was engaged to carry the Council's message to the school community. At the conclusion of the Council meeting, a media statement had been prepared on the Principal's letterhead: "The Council of the Presbyterian Ladies' College tonight rejected a move by five dissident Councillors to amend the Articles of Association." The statement also confirmed "that the present Principal, Miss Montgomery, will retire at the end of 1985, having reached normal retiring age." The victors then proceeded to rub salt into the wounds of the school community. The statement went to attack the "dissenting group". Chairman Don Carruthers declared that, "Council had a number of areas of concern, including the fact that the dissenting group of Councillors favoured high fees and appeared unconcerned that the school could — if they had their way — become accessible only to the very wealthy. Council was determined that PLC would remain accessible to as wide a cross-section of the community as possible and that it would continue to be a 'caring' school."

The media statement was followed soon after by a Council news bulletin, sixteen pages long, again on the Principal's letterhead, with what Group B would later condemn as groundless attacks on Joan Montgomery, the PLC staff, the Parents' Association, and the Group B members. The bulletin catalogued a list of what were claimed to be serious allegations raised by parents that had not been thoroughly investigated by the school: "Allegations that staff time and equipment, particularly at the higher levels in the Senior School, is lavished on gifted girls at the expense of those who are less gifted; that the Principal has accepted into PLC children of parents who have community standing at the expense of others who are earlier on the waiting lists; that members of the Presbyterian Church who wished to have their children admitted to the school have been discouraged from putting their child's name on the waiting list; that certain members of staff have used offensive language in the course of teaching and other activities in order to humiliate some children, and the parents were fearful to raise the matters with the Principal or staff member because of possible repercussions."

The bulletin concluded: "Whether or not the allegations are true, the members of the Council have certainly reached the conclusion that the reputation of PLC as a caring institution has been put in jeopardy." This final statement particularly outraged the five members of Group B who were driven to respond with another circular to parents on 12 June—in light of the "recent material that has been sent to parents which contains some inaccuracies." It made the obvious point that serious allegations had been broadcast when it was not known—as the bulletin conceded—"whether or not these allegations are true". The Group B members said they did not wish to "dignify this misconceived public relations exercise by responding in detail" but felt "compelled to make some observations." Over three pages, the circular set out a blow-by-blow attack on the substance of the Council's bulletin. It concluded with the five group B members affirming that they would continue to "press through the Attorney-General and other means to produce a situation where the Council of PLC is better balanced and more responsive than is presently the case".

The Council bulletin also stirred the PLC staff to send a letter to all Council members on 15 June which declared: "The Staff affirms its belief in the fine tradition of the Presbyterian Ladies' College and accordingly are appalled and distressed at the unsigned document from our Council received by those Staff members who are parents of girls at PLC." The letter objected "in the strongest possible terms" to the circulation of allegations directed against the Principal and staff which the Council had admitted were unsubstantiated. As to the claim by the Council majority that PLC's reputation as a caring institution was in jeopardy, the staff wrote: "This method of attacking the Principal and staff is contrary to the Christian ethics upheld in the School." The staff "felt entitled to an apology".

While the school community continued to fight passionately in support of Joan Montgomery, her profile grew stronger in the wider world of education. In the minutes of the Parents' Association meeting of 3 July it was recorded: "The sincere congratulations of the Committee were extended to Miss Montgomery on her recent appointment to the Council of the Melbourne Grammar School." Indeed, Joan was the first woman to be invited to join the MGS Council. On 19 June, Ross Clayton had written welcoming her and letting her know how delighted he and his fellow members of staff were that she had accepted the position. Clayton said that when the news of her appointment was mentioned in the MGS common room, there had been a moment of "consensus, as we recognised how lucky we were. The ironies are unavoidable, but we are grateful that your recent experiences haven't caused you to lose faith in Councils or their role in education." It was beyond ironic that as the PLC School Council was determined to end its association with Joan Montgomery, the Council of another of Australia's prestigious schools embraced her. When she retired from the role 11 years later, Melbourne Grammar praised her contribution to their Council as having "brought an extra dimension to consideration of important issues and subsequently led to the appointment of further women Councillors which has added breadth and expertise to its activities". They also noted that "her grace, wisdom, expertise and warm personality will be greatly missed by her fellow members of Council."

Joan's 59th birthday, on 6 July 1984, was celebrated with a "white and gold arrangement" of flowers from the PLC Old

Collegians and a set of glasses—"an attractive shape, discreetly crested"—from the Parents' Association. As life at the school progressed in its usual routines and rhythms, largely unaffected by the continuing divisions over PLC's future, Joan was now moving into her 60th year and the final year of her contract, without an agreement to extend her term.

Most of the recent media attention on Joan had been about her precarious position at PLC. Yet an article appearing in the *Age* on 18 July 1984 had a familiar photo of Joan smiling beside the caption, "Resignation of PLC head from committee regrettable, says Fordham." This resignation did not involve PLC, but rather Templestowe High School. The Victorian Government had encouraged an initiative where selection committees at public schools could recruit people with appropriate expertise from the community to assist them, and Templestowe High had selected Joan. She would remember clearly her one and only meeting, which discussed the appointment of a new Principal: "It was a wet night and I set out for an abandoned school at Preston; the overhead projector didn't work and it was a little disorganised, but everyone was keen to do it properly. The fellow who was chairing the meeting said he felt a little embarrassed at his own inexperience compared to mine, but I was happy to be of assistance if I could. During the course of our discussion I asked whether they had asked for medical records of the short-listed applicants. Some of the Committee looked aghast—'we couldn't ask for those' they proclaimed indignantly."

Joan thought such a check was entirely appropriate, and necessary. During her time as president of the Association of Heads of Independent Girls' Schools of Australia she had to travel interstate one Melbourne Cup Day to deal with a situation where the head of a school had to be confined due to mental health. Later the head's referees for the job had all acknowledged that the person had a history of mental illness, but that it hadn't been asked about in the process of appointment.

Vetting of Wisdom

Joan's comment about health checks, together with her Independent School vantage point, led to some of the Templestowe High teachers writing to her with objections to her appointment on the selection committee. A parent at PLC was also on the staff at Templestowe High School and gave Joan feedback about what was being said in the staff room. Joan invited the teachers' union representative at Templestowe to lunch to clarify the union's concern about her membership — serving her usual sandwiches. The staff member and PLC parent later overheard criticism on the lunch offering in the Templestowe staff room and reported back. This was more than enough for Joan to tender her resignation: "I wasn't forced to resign ... but I thought it was the best thing to do. After all, I was also dealing with my own issues at PLC."

Ahead of the next PLC Council meeting on 26 July 1984, Don Carruthers met with Joan, her deputies Ev Tindale and Jan Douglas and Chief of Staff Ruth Bunyan to discuss the controversial criticisms contained in the recent Council bulletin to parents. The Council was briefed that the staff "were offended, hurt and very angry about some of the statements in the Bulletin and, in particular, at being accused of being uncaring." In his Chairman's report, Carruthers noted a motion that had been passed by the meeting: "That Mrs Bunyan be advised that the Council did not, in the Council Bulletin or otherwise, intend to damage the reputation of the staff of PLC and in so far as the language of the Bulletin was interpreted as damaging the reputation of members of staff, the Council, having confidence in their professional expertise and integrity, apologises to them for the concern and distress occasioned." After the Chairman's report, Joan left the meeting which then focused on the appointment of a new Principal.

The Council was briefed that advertising material had been prepared and a schedule fixed for an advertising campaign to run during November and December in Australia, Britain and New

Zealand. Important dates were also set. Applications would close on 29 March 1985, and a selection committee, yet to be formed, would meet on 30 May and 6 June 1985 in order that an announcement could be made by the end of June for the new head to take up the position at the beginning of 1986. At a special Council meeting on 11 October, with Joan attending, a revised draft of information about the position was approved and a budget of $20,000 agreed for advertising, printing, consulting fees, interviews with applicants and secretarial assistance to the Chairman and Selection Committee.

The inexorable steps towards the appointment of a new Principal did not deter those still desperately strategising to keep Joan Montgomery in the job. Further letters were sent to members of the Presbyterian Church in an attempt to arrange a meeting with those responsible for selecting the members of the PLC Council. On 28 September, Ruth Bunyan wrote to the Presbyterian leadership detailing the staff's concern "at the public controversy arising from the failure of the present Council to offer Miss J M Montgomery an extension of her term as Principal and the publication of unsubstantiated allegations which were distributed to parents and the media ... after years of unease, the events of 1984 have resulted in an unhappy polarisation between the vast majority of the school community and a small number, including some Council members." She urged the Church to endorse only those Council members mindful of the fine traditions of excellence in education at PLC and committed to their continuation.

The effort to persuade the Church to influence the membership of the Council was too late. The process of selecting new Group C members was already well advanced. At the July meeting of the Council, two of the seven Group C members had indicated they did not wish to be renominated—Barry Armitage and Dr Anne Warr. Although Group B members were unaware of this situation prior to the meeting, they had asked two members of the school community for consent to include their names in the selection process. One had considerable experience in company administration, was married to an Old Collegian and had a daughter at the school. The other was a parent who signed the letter distributed at the April meeting seeking to allay fears about the present Presbyterian Church. However, members of Group A and Group C had proposed two other candidates—an elder of the Hawthorn Presbyterian Church (Max Bradshaw's church) and an elder from South Yarra. One had a daughter at MLC and a son at Scotch, the other did not yet have school age children and neither had any connection with PLC. Inevitably, the majority ruled and the two candidates of Group A and Group C were duly chosen.

The view of the Presbyterian General Assembly was made clear in an open letter Moderator Alan Stubs wrote to church members after the PLC Annual General Meeting. Addressing "My Dear People", Stubs said he had been asked a number of questions about what was happening at PLC. After reprising the background to the Property Commission decision to award PLC and Scotch to the Presbyterians, he said there had been "an extremely well-orchestrated campaign" bombarding Don Carruthers and himself with hundreds of letters of protest. He urged Church members to rally in support:

> 1. Pray most earnestly for the Council, especially its Chairman, Reverend Don Carruthers, who has been under tremendous pressure as a result of all this unrest;
> 2. If you are talking with parents of PLC girls, acquaint them with the true facts, and attempt to allay their fears regarding the future of the school. Also disabuse their minds of the idea (if they hold it) that the Presbyterian Church is a narrow bigoted 'conservative rump' (as it was described in one

recent newspaper article), and

3. Be prepared, if called upon so to do, to write a letter to the Attorney-General asking him not to interfere in any way with the present articles of association.

Stubs reflected on the many days he had been forced to devote to answering correspondence, attending meetings and receiving deputations. He said he had been "tempted to take the phone off the hook as it rang incessantly". But he felt "if we can retain control of the school which is a great institution founded by and run very successfully for more than 100 years by the Presbyterian Church, it will have been worth it". He said the Church's sole aim in maintaining control of the school was to see that the girls who passed through it "were equipped academically, socially and spiritually to make an effective Christian witness and contribution to society in whatever sphere they choose for themselves".

The die was now cast for Joan Montgomery's departure from PLC. On 22 November 1984 during its eighth meeting for the year, the School Council appointed a five-member committee to oversee the selection of a new Principal. Two days later, an advertisement in the Classified Extra section of the *Age* announced to the world the official reality: "Applications are invited for the position of PRINCIPAL of the Presbyterian Ladies' College, Burwood, Victoria, for the school year beginning January 1986."

In her Speech Night address on 12 December 1984, her job now out to tender, Joan focused on defending her staff from the attacks in the Council bulletin several months earlier.

> Any school which has consistently good results is likely to be labelled 'academic' and PLC is no exception. Since the Higher School Certificate was

introduced 14 years ago, the annual pass rate has averaged 96%. This is a record of which any school would be proud. It has NOT been maintained by severe pruning, whereby girls of less than average ability 'are encouraged to leave,' as an unsubstantiated allegation in the unsigned mid-year Council bulletin suggested — no girl has been asked to leave the senior school for reasons of academic ability. Nor has it been maintained by discouraging Year 11 girls from proceeding to HSC. The only criterion for this is clearly stated — a pass in English and any other three subjects. Of the 869 girls who have passed through Year 11 in the last five years, only five have had to repeat the year before entering Year 12.

Joan then turned to reflect on a statement by the Vice President of the Victorian Secondary Teachers' Association that one third of Victorian classroom teachers suffered physical illness due to work stress. She light-heartedly reassured the audience "most of our staff appear very healthy — not nearly as fit as they will look seven weeks hence — but comparatively unruffled." She then cited the approach of Emeritus Professor Bill Walker:

> Without stress there is no conflict
> Without conflict there is no challenge
> Without challenge there would be little change

With conflict unabated, change now loomed large for Joan Montgomery and Presbyterian Ladies' College.

16

THE FINAL YEAR

Joan Montgomery's final year as Principal of PLC began with letters of support continuing to stream in. On 19 January, before the first term had begun, one family wrote "from the heart" with gratitude and affection for the way in which Joan led PLC and for her Christian example: "Your modesty is a lesson to us all and your firm graciousness makes us realise how much better this world would be if more were like you." The family felt privileged to be part of PLC during her time: "In your retirement you deserve to feel that you carried out your responsibilities at school very, very well ... Thank you Joan. May God continue to bless you."

There were three responses by staff to Joan's forced retirement. The first group were those who said "OK, we are leaving", and that was a large group. The second group, who for economic reasons had to have a job, stayed on. The third group said, "Why are we here? It is because of the kids, and if we walk out who is suffering? The kids!" Joan Kent was one of those who stayed on. Her daughter Nicola was at the school and Joan fell into the last camp. All staff respected each other's position and it had no impact on their respective relationships with Joan Montgomery, who treated all her staff in the same way. She had the job, however, of replacing all those who were leaving — and there were many of them.

The first School Council meeting for the year, on 28 February, granted Joan eight days' leave to join a group of school principals visiting the Soviet Union in April. Her previous trips to China with other principals had stirred controversy and the Russian trip would lead to more. Later in the year, in his final article in the *Age* about Joan's departure, Geoff Maslen observed: "At PLC, Miss Montgomery sometimes has been accused of appointing radical teachers, although she denies this. Students claimed that on the occasion of the death of Chinese leader Mao Zedong the socialist song 'The Internationale' was played in the school hall. Her visits to China and Russia, although with a team of other independent school heads, fuelled concern among her critics in the Presbyterian Church about the direction in which PLC was going."[1] Joan would later chuckle about Maslen's reference to 'The Internationale' being played: "I can't say if that is true because I was in China at the time, but I don't believe it is." Joan was not the only member of the PLC staff travelling in 1985. Study leave was also granted to Vice Principals Jan Douglas and Ev Tindale and for the Junior School Principal June Stratford.

A day after her 60th birthday, Joan wrote to Ray and Joan Northrop thanking them for the "exquisite" flowers and referred to the growing challenge of replacing departing staff: "I was cheered too by your good wishes—midst weekly searching by staff around me for alternative 1986 positions—the search accelerated by Scotch's RE [religious education] vacancy advertised on June 29th—it's all a little depressing!" She went on, alluding to Joan Northrop's role in the appointment of the new Principal: "Happy hunting next Saturday, Joan! Do beg your fellow Councillors to speak up—the arrangements seem well-known, and rumours abound. To hope for confidentiality these days seems sadly naïve!"

The abounding rumours were about William Morton Mackay, the Scottish headmaster whom Ted Pearsons and Max Bradshaw had unsuccessfully tried to install as Principal of Scotch College five years earlier. And they were true. Thwarted at Scotch, the paternalistic Presbyterians would complete their

The Final Year

ascendancy over the vast majority of the PLC community that had fought so hard to keep Joan Montgomery by imposing the school's first male Principal since the 1930s. It was a blast back to the past.

The saga had begun in 1978 when Pearsons travelled to Edinburgh on behalf of the Presbyterian Church of Victoria to sound out Mackay about the Scotch College job. Mackay was then brought out to Melbourne where he first met Max Bradshaw that September. At the time, Mackay, who had previously been head of a school in Peru, had also been offered a position as principal of a coeducational school of 2000 students in Argentina. It was a pressing offer, but he turned it down because of the expectation that the Scotch job would be confirmed. After missing out on two prestigious jobs, Mackay stayed working in Edinburgh where his children were able to complete their secondary education. He would later say: "It was a very rough time for those years—but I would say that the years at PLC made up for it."[2]

While Mackay had been offered an inside track to the top job at Scotch before his patrons were blocked, he would deny any preferential treatment during the PLC recruitment process. He claimed to have known nothing about the PLC position until he saw the advertisement in *The Times Educational Supplement* in 1984. Concerned he would be tainted by what had happened at Scotch, he talked it over with his wife and they decided it couldn't do any harm to apply. The application was lodged in the last 10 days of the advertised period.

On Saturday 13 July 1985, an all-day meeting of the PLC Council was convened with all members present except Alex Chernov, who was overseas. Each member was invited to speak, without time restraint, on the suitability of three candidates who had been short-listed by the selection committee and the desirable next steps. After an extensive discussion, it was resolved unanimously that the Chairman arrange for Mr and Mrs Mackay to be flown to Melbourne business class at the earliest opportunity, and accommodated at a first-class hotel for approximately two weeks, to enable the Council to interview him on his suitability for appointment as Principal in 1986.

Less than two weeks later, the Mackays were in Melbourne. On Monday 22 July, he was interviewed from 5.30 to 7.00pm, followed by dinner hosted by the Council for him and his wife. Immediately after the dinner, at 8.30pm, the Council resolved to offer him the Principal's job. Only Joan Northrop and Alex Chernov dissented from the resolution.

Chernov set out the reasons for his reluctant opposition: "All members of Council are aware of the fact that I was firmly in favour of the re-appointment of Miss Joan Montgomery, one of the outstanding educationalists in this country. Seeing that the Council has decided to proceed with a new appointment then it should appoint an outstanding woman as Principal of PLC. If no suitable applicant is currently available, an Australia-wide search for such a woman should be initiated. If no suitable person can be found (and this I do not believe) then the search should be extended overseas. If it is considered necessary, an Acting Principal should be appointed whilst the search proceeds, even if one year is involved." But Chernov and Joan Northrop were well and truly outnumbered. The text of a letter of offer was approved by the Council, and the Chairman was authorised to convey it to Mackay with a view to seeking his acceptance at the earliest opportunity.

The response was instantaneous, to no one's surprise. The following day, 23 July, Don Carruthers announced to the school community the appointment of Mr W.M. Mackay to take up the position of Principal of PLC in January 1986. They were told that he was 51 with 12 years' experience as Principal of a boys' school in Lima, Peru, and that for the previous seven years he had been involved in curriculum and assessment development work in Scotland, similar to changes presently being considered in Victoria. The letter ended: "It is the Council's belief and sincere

The Final Year

wish that the school community will welcome the new Principal and his wife into the life of the College in 1986."

In many ways the announcement confirmed the fears of all those who had fought to keep Joan Montgomery as Principal. For a girls' school to install a man as Principal was not the feminist message that had been subtly present since Joan was a schoolgirl herself. This was at the heart of Alex Chernov's dissent. Thirty years later, Brian Bayston would say that the Council had little choice as all the women principals at the time had effectively boycotted PLC because of the treatment of Joan. Or perhaps those who might have applied were dissuaded after seeing the way in which Joan had been treated.

Two days after the announcement, Joan attended the fourth Council meeting for the year, after hosting a buffet meal at her home. She was present for the Chairman's report which recorded thanks to "every member of the Council for their assistance in the selection of the Principal-elect, Mr W.M. Mackay." The report noted that Joan had been informed of the selection two days earlier and that arrangements had been made for her to meet the Mackays the following Monday and that she had undertaken to introduce them to the staff and show them around the school.

On 26 July, the *Herald* reported the news. "A Firm Scots Hand will Guide PLC," declared the headline. Mackay was quoted as believing that "over the past 200 years there has been an eroding of Christian teachings and the injection of 'threatening' philosophies, including nihilism and Marxism." But he expected to continue the academic tradition already established at PLC: "A girl has every right to have an education that maximises her aptitude and capacity as any boy has, it is a philosophy that I am in complete sympathy with."[3]

Joan's deputy Ev Tindale was absent on study leave but they would exchange letters. Ev was one of many senior staff members already looking to leave PLC. Joan would write "with my love and desperate hope that you really land a very influential plum!"

Ev would ultimately move to Ivanhoe Girls' Grammar School as Curriculum Coordinator the following year. On Thursday 15 August, Joan would write to her again: "Term ended today. I should be on top of the world but feel somewhat flat! Guess an early night is all that I need, but I was so pleased to receive your letter from Hamburg."

Joan then shared her thoughts about what lay ahead: "I have a feeling that the end is drawing close very quickly and when I see the obvious smugness of Mrs Harman, Pring and Dr Moody perhaps I can't wait. Mrs Harman's Acting Chairman at present – wrote to Ruth [Bunyan, Chief of Staff] suggesting that Council-staff relations might be helped if three Council members could visit the staff room and explain how the Council works!!! It was too much for Ruth—she resigned!" Ruth Bunyan would become the Co-Vice Principal and Head of Mathematics at St Margaret's School the following year and from 1990 until her retirement in 2001 she was Principal of Strathcona Baptist Girls' Grammar School in Melbourne.

On returning after the September break for her final term at PLC, Joan wrote her last *Memorandum from the Principal* to parents: "I would like to thank you all very sincerely for the support that you have given during the years of your association with PLC as parents. With few exceptions you have attended our functions, supported our policies and co-operated even when we have felt it necessary to suspend your daughters!" She noted that for the first time that year, the Senior School staff was complete, with teachers on long service and study leave having returned, including Ev Tindale. And Joan acknowledged her own final conference in Canberra of the Headmasters' Conference of Australia and the Association of Heads of Girls' Schools in Australia: "After 14 years of discussion, amalgamation took place and the Association of Heads of Independent Schools of Australia was born." In November, the Victorian Branch of the Association would propose Joan for honorary life membership. Joan's circular would end magnanimously: "At this time Mr Mackay will be looking forward to his new appointment. I know that he will have your full support and hope that his years here will be as happy as mine have been."

The Presbyterian hardliners on the School Council might have got their man—or at least got rid of the woman who was not theirs—but Joan Montgomery was not the only one being shown the door. On Saturday 12 October, Geoff Maslen reported in the *Age*: "The Presbyterian Church has carried out a purge of its representatives on the Councils of Scotch College and the Presbyterian Ladies' College ... The outcome means that the moderates in the church have taken control from a group of highly conservative Presbyterians." The report noted that the purge had come "too late to save Miss Montgomery's job". The Reverend Norman Pritchard was quoted as saying "the changes signalled a new era in the relationship between the church and the schools."[4]

Lexie Luly, the head of the PLC Art Department wrote to Joan the same day after reading the article: "Did someone pull the plug of the hotline to God? A Pyrrhic victory alas too late to salvage the PLC as we knew it. I only hope your last two months will be less of a strain in your relations with the Council though I guess it all depends on whether the 'independents' will now have the guts to think for themselves. The O.C. [Old Collegians] Ex staff phones have been running hot today and all are thankful to be rid of the Calvinist clique though wary of being too jubilant. The 'devil's advocate' could still be the power pulling the strings of a very inexperienced principal. I look forward to joining in all the celebrations in November though in some respects they will be sad occasions—the end of an era at PLC."

At the School Council meeting on 24 October, Russell Rechner was elected as the new chairman. In a circular to parents five days later, Rechner—after flagging a seven per cent hike in school fees for the following year—announced the dramatic news: "As from the conclusion of the Assembly of the Presbyterian Church of Victoria on 17 October, the Reverend D. Carruthers, Mr B.D. Bayston and Mr G Morgan ceased to be members of Council. The Assembly appointed Mrs Mairi Harman, Mr Ken McNie and Mrs Anne Neil as members of Group A. This left a vacancy in Group C in respect of which Council has made a nomination for appointment to the Assembly." Two nominations had been received to fill the Group C vacancy — Mrs J. Pritchard, Norman Pritchard's wife, and Brian Bayston, who had not been renewed as a Group A representative of the Church. After a vote, Bayston was declared to be the Council nominee, pending approval by the Presbyterian Assembly.

Amidst this upheaval, Joan's broader community contributions were being recognised. On 30 October, she was invited to deliver the Third Collins Memorial Oration at Melbourne's Royal Children's Hospital. In 1949, Vernon Collins had been appointed as the first medical director of the Children's Hospital and then, in 1959, became the first occupant of the Stevenson Chair of Child Health (later Paediatrics) at the University of Melbourne. Joan began her address rhetorically: "When asked the title of this evening's lecture, I unwisely suggested — Education, the greatest gift? It took little time to answer that question negatively, for there could be no argument that life itself is the greatest gift. Next, I would put good health — I suspect that few here would disagree with that. But education would come next." Her 17-page speech then ranged broadly about the state of education before concluding with words that would resonate with many of the thousands of girls who had studied at PLC under Joan Montgomery's leadership: "When any community can provide schools with environments of care, cohesion and direction, with teachers of vision and integrity, where students are challenged vigorously and excitingly, then that community has offered the greatest gift to its most important resource."

With only weeks remaining of her leadership, an intensive

The Final Year

round of farewell events began. On Friday 8 November, the Old Collegians' Association hosted a dinner to honour Joan in the Great Hall of the National Gallery of Victoria. It was a huge turnout, with almost 500 in attendance. The guest speaker was Dame Phyllis Frost, the celebrated criminologist and philanthropist who had attended PLC in the 1930s. The Association's February 1986 newsletter was a 'souvenir' issue with a front-page photograph of Joan at the dinner. Diana Cherry, teacher, wrote that it was a "night to remember", with local, interstate and country visitors dining in a beautifully set room decked in the school colours. The celebratory atmosphere inevitably was overshadowed by the rapidly approaching end to Joan's brilliant career. Anne Dodds, President of the Old Collegians' Association, concluded her toast to Joan by saying: "To say we are sorry you are leaving PLC would be, I think, the understatement of the year." There were many who still couldn't believe that it was happening. Cherry's report confirmed the evening's lingering wish that the time for leaving would never come: "The most obvious measure of the success of the evening was that the last guests left only after Gallery staff had repeatedly dimmed the lights."

Two weeks later, on 15 November, a large gathering of teachers from Joan's 17 years as Principal gathered for another grand farewell dinner in the Long Room at the Melbourne Cricket Ground, a fitting venue for a keen cricket fan. Kath McCredie, Principal of Abbotsleigh Anglican Girls' School in Sydney, and a good friend of Joan's, was guest speaker. Ev Tindale also gave a speech and reflected on how the PLC staff room was professional and happy thanks to Joan's leadership. Ev recalled Joan saying that failures were one's own as Principal and successes belonged to them all. She acknowledged how the staff all felt that Joan led from the front during the hard times and took the brunt of trouble, and in the good times encouraged them all from behind. The staff that Joan had brought together and who were sitting in the room — a balance of men and women and youth and experience — were all made to feel that they had something to give and something worth giving. She had encouraged democratic participation, consensus decision-making and a very broad base of involvement. As Principal, Joan had placed her own individual, indelible stamp on the life of PLC: "We do applaud you Miss Montgomery, for your 17 years of leadership and concern for us, for your dignity, courage and calmness. Thank you."

Earlier on the day of the staff farewell dinner, the Special Commission of the Presbyterian General Assembly responsible for approving members of the PLC Council, wrote to Ewen McRae, the Council Secretary. McRae was advised that at their meeting on 12 November the Commission had considered nominations for Groups B and C and agreed that Joan Northrop, Alex Chernov, Russell Rechner and Professor Anderson "be appointed and that these members be congratulated and thanked for their willingness to serve on the Council." Then came the bombshell. The Commission rejected "the nomination of Mr B. Bayston to the PLC Council" and added: "This resolution upholds the intent of the motion passed at the General Assembly in October." This was the resolution that had removed Bayston and others from Group A.

Norman Pritchard, the Senior Minister at Scots' Church, had successfully pushed to remove all the members of the Special Commission who were in Max Bradshaw's league. Then Donald Carruthers and Brian Bayston had been evicted from the PLC Council and Bayston's attempt to rejoin the Council had been rejected. A coup had occurred within the General Assembly against Bayston and Bradshaw. Wrangling over Bayston's position and the legality of the process would go on for months, but the change would not be overturned. Had it come a year earlier, it might have saved Joan Montgomery's job but that was not to be.

The Final Year

Joan attended her last Council meeting on 28 November. She spoke to her written report, including requests for additional capital expenditure on Junior School chairs and foyer curtains that were approved. But there would be no formal record of this being her final meeting, and no record of thanks in the minutes. These thanks would come in an overwhelming show of support on the afternoon of Saturday 30 November when more than 2500 people gathered in the school's outdoor quadrangle area. The official party was heralded to the dais by a trumpet fanfare. Speeches and presentations followed, including gifts for Joan of a Georg Jensen silver bowl and cheque. The event was also featured in the souvenir Old Collegians' Association newsletter in February.

The last School Assembly was on Monday 9 December. Joan began with a reading she had often chosen, 1st Corinthians Ch 13, describing it as the great hymn of love: "Though I speak with the tongues of men and of angels, but have not love, I have become sounding brass or a clanging cymbal ... When I was a child, I spoke as a child, I understood as a child, I thought as a child; but when I became a man, I put away childish things. For now we see in a mirror, dimly, but then face to face. Now I know in part, but then I shall know just as I also am known. And now abide faith, hope, love, these three; but the greatest of these is love." Joan continued with a prayer:

> Lord, as another year ends we thank you for the vision and wisdom of the founders of this College, for their insistence on high standards and ideals. We thank you for those who have served the school in the past, and for those who are serving generously today as teachers and house staff, as students, as administrators, as groundsmen or cleaners. We thank you for the good things we have enjoyed here—the friendship and opportunities, the

examples and traditions which have influenced us throughout. Lord, we have been given so much, may we in our turn show courage and integrity, sensitivity and compassion, and that understanding which will help us to live peacefully together in the spirit of your son, our Saviour Jesus Christ.

It was an emotionally charged moment in Wyselaskie Hall as Joan delivered her last sermon to the school. The next year William Mackay would take the helm as the Scottish male Principal of Australia's leading girls' school and it would herald a difference not seen at PLC for 45 years. It was an extraordinary turn of events and, for some, brought to mind other assemblies Joan had conducted that spoke of "a time to every purpose under the heaven" and that "all is vanity and vexation of spirit". In such an assembly, she might have been wry enough to include something else from Ecclesiastes: "That which is crooked cannot be made straight: and that which is wanting cannot be numbered."

The students would have had gained some solace leafing through their *Patchwork* school magazine, distributed before the school year finished. The first page carried a half-page photograph of a smiling Joan Montgomery. She is dressed in a full-sleeved soft grey chiffon-like dress and perched on the arm of a Victorian-style chair. Succeeding pages have shots of Janice Douglas and Evelyn Tindale, arms folded, open smiles, perched over the back of the same chair.

In "An insight into our Principal", *Patchwork* editors Louise Bowen and Helen Rodwell ask Joan a series of questions, including changes in the school from East Melbourne to Burwood, changes in the opportunities for students in the previous 15 years, changes in the relationships between teachers and students and changes in teaching methods. And then there were more personal questions about Joan's memories of PLC as a student—and the inevitable question many girls speaking about Miss Montgomery would mention—her dogs. What have been the different dogs you have kept and how do you remember them best? Joan could not resist an expansive reply: "Cindy, a Miniature Schnauzer, was frail but very affectionate. I was always sorry for her when people said: 'How can you get used to such a *little* dog?' She died at two! Minerva II, the third Doberman I'd owned, was very reliable and loved people. But she did tease by taking lunches and Junior School toys ... Soda was a very handsome Doberman but not quite so friendly, so she rarely appeared at school. At present it is Prudence, a German Short Haired Pointer. She loves everyone but is so curious and so disconcertingly fast that she might be a disturbance in the school."

Inevitably, the final question was what Joan planned for the future: "I have few definite plans! With more time I hope to improve on those things that I'd done badly and to enjoy to the full those things that have been increasingly put aside—gardening, reading, music, fishing and many others. I don't think that endless self-indulgence would be very satisfying, but at this moment it has a certain appeal! I cannot imagine ever losing interest in education but am uncertain about involvement. With so many changes and developments pending, there are exciting challenges ahead; but it may be easy to lose touch ... I should hate to cling on when of no use anywhere."

A tribute by Ev Tindale would once again counter the long-running claim of some Presbyterians that Joan had failed to give priority to Christian values in the PLC curriculum: "If it is possible to single out one influence that Miss Montgomery has made to the life of PLC, I would argue that it is the respect for religion in the school. In an age when some schools have had to cut down, or remove completely daily religious assemblies, PLC has continued to value and share in morning religious observance. Equally, Religious Education is not seen as a soft option subject, but rather as a challenging, thought-provoking part of the overall curriculum with real meaning for the students."

On Thursday 19 December, the *Age* reported Joan Montgomery's departure under the headline, "Contract Not Renewed, but Content with Her Time." The story noted that PLC was losing more than its Principal, with 18 members of staff having resigned. The paper's education editor, Geoff Maslen, referred to a "quietly content Miss Montgomery who reflected on her 17 years as head of PLC." Maslen ended his piece with Joan saying: "I've had a marvellous innings ... I think 60 is a good retiring age."

Joan would have the summer and beyond to review all the letters of tribute she received from parents, teachers and students. One teacher wrote: "Words are totally inadequate to express to you my thanks and appreciation for all that you do and are—for your unfailing high standards vigilantly maintained, for your graciousness and composure in all situations, for your delightful (sometimes wicked) sense of humour, for your courage and fortitude in the face of difficulties, for your inspiring leadership, but more than anything else for your kindness and concern for everyone with whom you come into contact. The last 13 years have been a source of immense joy to me; it has been a great privilege to work under you. My most sincere thanks and warmest wishes that your life will be richly blessed in the future."

In the same Old Collegians' newsletter reporting on the various farewells for Joan, there was also a farewell to another Old Collegian and teacher, Nora Wilkinson, who had died on 19 January 1986. Joan would be one of 46 individuals who, together with the Old Collegians' associations of Melbourne, Geelong and Sydney and the Combined Women's Group, contributed to funding a Nora Wilkinson Memorial Garden. The proposed garden would include an outdoor classroom, a weather station, named plants and areas where girls could mingle at lunchtime. A short tribute would record that Wilkinson's connection with PLC

The Final Year

stretched from 1928 to 1966 and she had been an inspirational geography teacher whose "interest in each individual endeared her to all; her rigorous standards and high values commanded respect while her extra-curricular activities and innovations made her a person far ahead of her times."

This was a timely connection to Joan. Nora Wilkinson had taught Joan geography and had been the teacher who had taken her aside in Year 11, transforming her from a mischievous and spirited schoolgirl into a purposeful school prefect. Like Helen Hailes earlier on, she was perceptive enough to warn Joan that her position at PLC was in jeopardy but not prescient enough to know the form that jeopardy would take. Who could have predicted that the PLC Council would, in its wisdom, decide that a male headmaster was better able to educate young women and bring them closer to God. It was indeed the end of an era at Presbyterian Ladies' College.

AFTERWORD

I was 14 on the fateful afternoon of Wednesday 7 May 1980 when Max Bradshaw and the Reverend Ted Pearsons called on Joan Montgomery hoping to induce her early retirement. I was sitting as a Year 10 student in a nearby classroom, one of more than a thousand other girls at the school that day. But we had absolutely no idea of the meeting or of any of the machinations of the Camberwell Assembly and their wish to see our revered school head removed. Indeed, not only did we miss the opening skirmish in what was to become a five-year battle over control of PLC but, due to Joan Montgomery's extraordinary composure, the unfolding conflict was kept well away from us. Remarkably, even though I had met with Miss Montgomery on a daily basis as School Captain in 1982, I learned nothing directly of the unfolding school drama that had been set in motion on that day in May 1980.

My personal history at the school had obscured from me the possibility that PLC's creed of female empowerment and religious ecumenism could be thwarted by narrow dogma with a sting of patriarchy and even, as I later learnt, a shot of long-remembered personal animus. For Max Bradshaw and Joan Montgomery had scrapped in much earlier days and Bradshaw had long nursed the perceived slight of Joan's spirited independence.

My own journey at PLC began in Year 4 as a nine year old transferring from Mt Scopus Memorial College, a four-minute drive up Burwood Highway. It was my mother, Sue, who sensed the opportunity PLC offered, recognising it as *the* school for girls. She was an MLC girl. My father, Leigh, went to Melbourne High. Both mixed easily with people from all backgrounds, cultures and religions and they were keen for their daughters, me and my younger sister Elana, to do the same. It was part of PLC and Joan Montgomery's Old Testament welcoming of strangers that no-one batted an eyelid at the Jewish girl from Scopus. The PLC that I attended was a roomy place encouraging of faith and religious diversity. Judaism and Presbyterianism have a shared history and not by accident did Joan the student choose an Old Testament prophet as the subject of her prize-winning Bible essay in 1942. The two traditions have the same genesis, were aboard the same ark and afloat on the fundamental cultural raft of education, so highly prized in Jewish and Presbyterian communities.

PLC's ecumenical ethos was embodied and shaped by Joan Montgomery. Each year, the Parents' Association gave every Year-12 girl a Bible on leaving PLC — a valedictory Testament. They were presented at a school assembly before speech night. I noticed, however, that my copy was different, a Sinai Publishing House version, printed in Israel in 1977. Yet, importantly, it shared the same bookplate as all the others — the PLC crest 'Lex Dei Vitae Lampus' (the law of God is the lamp of life) on the inside cover and underneath the inscribed emblem: "Presented by Senior School Parents' Association, Combined Women's Groups." How did this come about? Well, Joan had driven to a Jewish bookstore in Acland St, St Kilda, and bought a Tanach, the Hebrew Bible, rather than give me the Christian version. It was a moving gesture and, during my years practising law, I would lift this Bible to swear affidavits, knowing that it was unique — a burning light that would not go out.

The Tanach is central to orthodox Jewish practice; the Bible to understanding the Presbyterian Church. The Church's approach to it distinguishes Presbyterianism from other Christian denominations and this was part of the reason for the

Afterword

Presbyterian schism during the formation of the Uniting Church in Australia.

As a Jewish student and an elected School Captain, my own position may have been emblematic of what the Continuing Presbyterians thought was wrong with PLC. In their view, it had veered too far from a strict orthodoxy and narrow scriptural reading of the Bible and was overly concerned with producing well-rounded girls ready for university and for taking their place alongside men in the professions and leadership positions ahead. There is no doubt that the complex history of Presbyterianism and the beliefs and practices of the Continuing Presbyterians and the Camberwell Assembly were critical to the story of Joan Montgomery and the fight for PLC. Yet broadly the saga is reducible to an alliterative formula — power, patriarchy, property and, perhaps critically, personality. Indeed, force of personality, in particular the personality, character and zealous convictions of Max Bradshaw may be the key, the one factor making the critical difference and without which and whom the story would have ended differently.

For me, as for so many, Joan Montgomery was an inspiration and it was unfathomable why anyone would seek to curtail her tenure as PLC's head. Max Bradshaw saw things differently. A granite-like figure of deep commitment and steely, unremitting purpose, he was the leader of a cause bent on blocking Joan's way and ending her principalship. It was my first experience of a world where power seemed to trump reason. Making sense of what to my view was a counter-intuitive, highly-disruptive, unjust, unfair and destructive objective took some absorbing. It also hatched for me the riddle of why? What was it that drove Bradshaw and his followers in such antagonistic pursuit of their cause? And, indeed, what precisely was their cause and what was its urgency? If she exercised its option, Joan's contract had five more years to run. Why not wait it out?

While Max Bradshaw was the principal antagonist, Joan

Vetting of Wisdom

Montgomery was the regal Principal at the centre of a school and a community that saw her continuing presence as indispensable. What was it about her that inspired such loyalty and admiration? Alex Chernov, the School Council member from 1981 to 1990 who went on to become an Appeals Court judge and then Victorian Governor, says: "Those ten years live with me to this very day." For Chernov, "the whole thing ... revolved around one thing, there was only one thing that was of any importance and that was Joan ... Everybody was firing bullets around about her and it was a terrible predicament. But we could all go home, she couldn't."

It would have been a great bonus for the writing of this book to have met the redoubtable Max Bradshaw. But Bradshaw died in 1992, prior to the book project beginning, and his wife and daughter led intensely private lives not wishing to be disturbed. Ted Pearsons and Brian Bayston, both of whom regarded Bradshaw as a mentor, would help illuminate his role.

......

On 22 March 2005, almost 25 years after that ominous meeting in Joan Montgomery's office, I walked down the same long corridor as had her adversaries to meet with the then PLC Principal, Elizabeth Ward. There were different curtains, but the room otherwise looked the same as it had when Joan was Principal—a large desk by the window and a coffee table and chairs just inside the door. I explained my commitment to writing "a comprehensive biography canvassing the Joan Montgomery and PLC story from many viewpoints, including those not necessarily supportive of her at the time the school was in transition." I asked to interview members of the School Council during Joan's time and for my details to be passed onto them. As I was fishing in turbulent waters, I expected little of it, so I was taken aback when Brian Bayston called.

Bayston had attended the Hawthorn Presbyterian Church

Afterword

where Max Bradshaw had been an elder and session clerk. He had also been on the School Council after the settlement of the court case and, at that stage, was still a member. "Yes" he said in a strong and friendly voice, "I would be happy to meet with you." He then added, a little warily: "I don't know how much I can contribute." We rearranged to meet on 12 May 2005, almost 25 years to the day after the golden handshake meeting. Bayston also suggested I meet with Ted Pearsons, which I did the day before I met him.

Assembly Hall is a grand Gothic revival building at 156 Collins Street, next door to Scots' Church. As well as the meeting place for the ministers and elders of the Presbyterian Church, it houses the Church's State administrative headquarters. After ascending the fine wooden staircase to the mezzanine floor, Pearsons, a tall, broad-shouldered man with white hair, walked out of his office to greet me. I had no recollection of having met him before. However, sometime later, looking through Bronowski's *The Ascent of Man*, the book I chose to be given in 1982 as the Jean and J. Keay Troup Memorial prize for School Captain, I saw the book plate inscription, "Presented by the Moderator Right Reverend E.R. Pearsons."

The office of the Clerk of the Assembly is a modest room with a window overlooking elegant, green-leafed Collins Street. Pearsons had been Clerk since May 1974 and, by his retirement at the age of 70 in 2006, he would have held the position for 32 years, in addition to his term in the rotating role of Moderator. I am struck immediately by his warm and friendly manner. I explain that I have been looking at the archival records of the Presbyterian parishes in Bright and Numurkah, the country town where Joan had spent her first 12 years. Pearsons interrupts: "I think at one stage, was she not going to the Church at Hawthorn ... I remember Max Bradshaw saying that she had been a member there." Pearsons can't remember attending the 'golden handshake' meeting with Joan but he is quick to recall the issue of Joan's attendance at the Hawthorn Church when the Montgomery daughters moved back to the family home in Kembla Street, Hawthorn.

The next day, Brian Bayston says he only really knew of Joan Montgomery (before he became a member of the PLC Council in April 1981) through Max Bradshaw. He says Max had known Joan before she became Principal of PLC in 1969 because of the Hawthorn Church. There had been "some animus between Joan and Max dating back to those Hawthorn days. I don't know what it was, but I did know that Max was distrustful of her."

The meetings with Pearsons and Bayston impressed on me the significance of Max Bradshaw to their lives, to the whole Presbyterian Church saga and to this book. Both men said Bradshaw was a mentor or father-like figure to them. Both had been connected to him over the entire period of the Presbyterian Church split and the subsequent battle over the ownership of PLC. Both agreed Bradshaw had influenced their view of Joan Montgomery.

Yet Bradshaw's relationships with each of the two men were different. Six years older than Pearsons, Bayston had known Bradshaw since he was 20, when he had begun attending the Young Men's Bible Class at the Hawthorn Presbyterian Church in 1951. Bradshaw, then aged 40, was the leader. In his memoir on Bradshaw, Bayston would write: "As I look back, I think I should have sought to influence Max more. He liked to get his own way ... In the earlier years of our relationship, I found that he enlisted me on his side with remarks in Session such as 'You'd think that, wouldn't you, Brian?' The result was that I had the sense of being manipulated, and from time to time was forced to moderate an extreme position in the course of my concurrence. He often made the bullets that others were to fire, while he remained in the background. He would say: 'The Congregation wouldn't stand for that', which being interpreted was, 'I don't like it'. In 1974 I became Law Agent and from then on we were together as the

Afterword

Law Officers of the Victorian Assembly. I found that there were areas in which he relied on me, and I should have built on that."

In contrast, Pearsons first met Bradshaw when a committee had been set up to promote the Continuing Presbyterian position during the discussions about union. Pearsons was the minister at Cheltenham and Clerk of Flinders Presbytery at the time, and Charles Fraser, a prominent elder, asked him to join the committee that was comprised mainly of senior ministers. Pearsons, still only in his 30s, formed a close bond with Bradshaw from the outset. He describes Bradshaw as a "shy, retiring and very private gentleman" who was often misunderstood: "Few would have known … that for the last 10 years of his life he was legally blind. I remember taking him to Sydney one time and his wife Jillian was terribly worried. Jillian reported to me later that Max said I looked after him better than she did." After Bradshaw's death from a sudden heart attack, Pearsons wrote a tribute that described him as "one of the greatest servants of the Presbyterian Church of Australia".

......

While reflecting on my life at the time the PLC saga was unfolding, I recall the bit part I played at the packed public meeting addressed by Dame Leonie Kramer. It is a memory rekindled by a video of the occasion where I watch my 18-year-old self, a few months into my first year as a law student. I am quite emotional while thanking Dame Leonie and Alex Chernov for their speeches on that electric April night. Seeing it again brings back all the layers of feeling that surrounded the event—the school that I loved, the Principal I deeply respected, the values my education nurtured, the feeling of empowerment as a young woman that had been instilled in me by my schooling and, then, the spectre of all that I valued being trashed by what I increasingly regarded as a cynical expression of power. The move against the

Principal and the school community seemed to me then, and still, to be a pitting of forces—reason versus unreason, freedom of religion and expression versus dogma, education versus ignorance. No wonder I described that public meeting, called to inform the school community of ways to take back their school, as an "historic" event. It was historic, it was valiant, it was stirring but, not for the last time, I learnt that logic, reason, justice and fairness are not always enough. Power, and the intense drive of those with a competing vision can rise to trump those values.

In the final stages of writing this book, Ray Northrop mentioned to me that Brian Bayston and he had seen each other at recent PLC speech nights and the contacts had been civil. Joan Montgomery and Northrop had both been invited to the 2011 PLC Speech night where they had been directly and publicly acknowledged by name and as former Principal and School Council Chairman. And so began a process that would result in a remarkable reunion of the once bitter adversaries in the contest over the future of PLC.

Eight years after our first meeting, I emailed Brian Bayston, at first to see if he could help me further in my research. He wrote back: "At 83, I have had recently some ill-health, hospital confinement, and have stopped going to work each day. I am no longer fee-earning but have lots of trusts for which I am responsible in whole or in part, so I have a room and the use of a secretary, when I choose to use it. I have only recently been fit enough to do that." In a subsequent phone call, he agreed to what might have been unthinkable three decades earlier—a meeting with Joan Montgomery and Ray Northrop.

We met on the morning of Christmas Eve, Tuesday 24 December 2013, in Northrop's home. The four of us sat around the breakfast room table, while I took them back more than 30 years to the time when the battle was at its most intense. Jim Mitchell, author of the Scotch College sesquicentenary history covering the same period, later wrote to me: "What—Joan,

Afterword

Northrop and Bayston all in the same room together ???!!"

It was an emotional meeting. Ray Northrop was very clear about his feelings at the time. He acknowledged that in all his professional life, as a barrister and then a judge, he had been able to stand back from the issues and view them objectively in a 'professional' way, somewhat neutral, even indifferent. However, the PLC battle had been quite different: he had been emotionally involved. Now he acknowledged he was no longer so emotional about the events, but it had taken a long time for the intensity of those feelings to subside.

Brian Bayston revealed his own emotional side, although not at first related to the PLC conflict. He had recently retired and it had been a difficult transition for him: "I actually had a little cry when I stopped." Ill health had forced him to stop full-time work at the age of 83 and he was unhappy about his vocation of so many years ending abruptly. He seemed unaware of the irony of saying this in front of Joan Montgomery who had been forced to retire at the age of 60 — and deal with those emotions much earlier than he had — due to the efforts of him and his associates.

Joan then spoke directly to Bayston: "For 28 years I have wanted to ask you … I can give many criticisms I'd hold against me, but I don't know what it was that Max held against me. I only spoke to Max Bradshaw once in my life, and that was to ask for a transfer to Toorak. He told me I had been removed from the roll." She then explained how after she chose to move from Hawthorn Presbyterian Church to the Toorak parish, Bradshaw, the Session Clerk at Hawthorn, had refused to sign the transfer required by the Church authorities. Bayston was unable to explain Bradshaw's decision, but confirmed that there was clearly something Bradshaw had disliked about Joan. He agreed that Bradshaw disliked people leaving the Hawthorn church and said that when he himself left Hawthorn, some years later, his and Max's relationship was never the same again. There was agreement all round when I suggested that Bradshaw may have even taken more umbrage at being confronted by a self-confident, assured former PLC girl who challenged him, in her confident way, about the transfer decision, asking if she had been "excommunicated".

......

How might PLC have changed since Joan's time? I raise Joan's replacement by the Reverend William Mackay and what a strong statement it made—the first male Principal of PLC since the early days of the school. Bayston responded: "The Council was predisposed to appointing a woman, but it was blackballed by women teachers who were not prepared to apply for Joan's position."

Bayston argued that despite the claims of his adversaries, PLC was in very good shape a generation after the Continuing Presbyterians had asserted their control over the school: "I remember Alex Chernov saying that he had no confidence in the Council to make a good appointment of Principal and to maintain the standards of the school. And I think the standards have been maintained and improved." And he stood by the claims of him and his allies at the time of the struggle that had been necessary to defend the quality of religious education at PLC:

> It is my conviction that the so-called secular subjects can't be taught in a Christian school without seeing them as part of God's created order including the fall of man into sin and redemption and the providential care of the world through a long-term purpose ... The respect for the Christian faith is greater now than it was. I think there have been more teachers with Christian conviction appointed.

Afterword

This was too much for Joan. "I wouldn't agree with that," she responded, while acknowledging her view was informed by hearsay. She reflected on the teaching of religious education during her time as Principal — Sheila Griffith and Frances Boyd were both excellent and admired by the girls and staff alike. She said it would have been hard to find anyone better than Frances to teach religion. They were both good teachers who won the respect of the girls: "It is important that the religious education is respected in the way that other teaching is." I add that the school's outward public message is more overtly Christian in its culture and image. All agree, although Joan wonders if this is more on paper than in practice.

Bayston conceded the personal toll that the conflict had had on many of those involved. "I often felt when I was fighting those who were representing the PLC school community, that I was fighting with people who should have been my friends."

......

What might Max Bradshaw have said had he been able to join the strange reunion on Christmas Eve 2013? What drove him all those years ago and how would he have viewed the events that followed — and those against whom he fought so hard, not least Joan Montgomery?

A document submitted to the Presbyterian Church of Victoria's Commission of Assembly in 1986 discusses the Special Schools' Commission responsible for appointments to the School Councils of PLC and Scotch. Each paragraph begins with 'Whereas' in the quasi-legal format prescribed by the church rule book and which suited Max Bradshaw to a tee. In some ways, the document represents what I would have heard from Bradshaw if I'd had the opportunity of interviewing him.

Bradshaw explains that for most of their history PLC and Scotch were closely supervised by the Presbyterian General

Assembly through a School Council composed predominantly of members of the Assembly, but in more recent years those nominated by the Councils for appointment by the Assembly increasingly lacked commitment "to the place of Christianity" in the schools. As a result, a strong Christian witness was replaced by an "elitist secular education clothed in the trappings of Christianity". When it came to the division of property ahead of church union, those looking after the interests of the Continuing Presbyterian Church secured the right to be awarded one school for boys and one for girls. This was not a matter "of setting up an ideal educational system for the Church, but of making the best use of what was within our reach". Scotch and PLC were the most suitable of the existing Presbyterian schools to "enhance the efficient functioning of the Continuing Church" as they were centrally situated to Presbyterian families in Melbourne and had large boarding establishments that enabled country Presbyterians to "have their children educated in a Christian atmosphere and have the advantage of teaching consistent with the Reformed faith". Additionally, the schools provided "a field for missionary endeavour, and an opportunity to influence the rising generation of leaders of the community".

Bradshaw then recounted the awarding of the two schools by the Property Commission to the Continuing Presbyterian Church and the subsequent litigation initiated by the Scotch and PLC communities. His explanation of the settlement is illuminating: "After a court hearing over three months and an immense expenditure of money, the position was reached when the prospects of the relators [the school plaintiffs] had become distinctly precarious which proved an opportune time to compromise the proceedings on a basis that in essence preserved the position of the Presbyterian Church, required the relators to pay much the greater part of the Church's legal costs as well as their own legal costs, provided for the incorporation of the schools as corporations holding their property, in trust for the

Afterword

educational purposes of the Presbyterian Church, and with virtually the only significant concession to the relators being the grant of minority representation on the two school Councils."

Bradshaw goes on to confirm that the supposed diversity of the School Councils—giving representation to representatives of the Church, the school community and so-called independent members—was a mirage: "The highest legal tribunal in the British Commonwealth laid down [he does not cite the case] that where a school exists for the educational purposes of a church, a 'considerable majority' of the members of the governing body should be persons who are committed to that church, and in conformity with that principle it was insisted, in framing a compromise, that when giving representation to the interests of the relators, each school Council should consist of twelve members representing the Presbyterian Church as against five for the relator's interests [i.e. the schools] but to save face for the relators the church representation was to be in two sections, with five members appointed by the Church directly and seven appointed by the Church on the nomination of the retiring Council with wide powers of rejection by the Church." Bradshaw was absolutely correct when he continued: "Moreover, for the first Council the group of seven (Group C) was chosen exclusively from persons nominated by the Church, *thus giving the Church power to preserve its position in perpetuity.*"

And that is what happened—by having control from the start, the Church maintained and still has control over the schools' governance and operations. In some ways it is a miracle that Joan Montgomery remained Principal until 1985, given that from 1980 the Continuing Presbyterians had control. The Church's legal advice was powerful enough for Max Bradshaw to restrain himself and enable Joan's contract to continue, as it set out securely, until she reached the age of 60.

The document makes clear that Bradshaw was driven by his religious convictions, indeed his zealotry, to ensure that his brand of Presbyterianism was imposed on the students and staff of PLC: "It is of crucial importance, if what was achieved for the Church by the compromise of litigation is to be preserved for succeeding generations, that it has persons on the Councils who are zealous at all times to preserve the Church's rights with respect to Scotch College and the Presbyterian Ladies' College, and are prepared to uphold those rights, if necessary, in the face of opposition."

The document was prepared in response to the successful move by the Senior Minister of Scots' Church, the Reverend Norman Pritchard, at the General Assembly in October 1985 where, according to Bradshaw, Pritchard "pushed through" the removal from office of all the members of the Special Schools' Commission who were in Bradshaw's league. The decision removed the Reverend Don Carruthers and Brian Bayston from the PLC Council and Bayston's subsequent re-nomination was refused.

Bradshaw's pleading — later referred to by others as the "1986 Overture" — led to an undertaking by the General Assembly to reconstitute the Special Commission and instruct it that in making appointments to the School Councils it should only appoint persons committed to upholding the trusts on which the schools are held and "who have a vital church connection." The vote on it was split 50 in favour and 45 against. Norman Pritchard was one of those against.

......

Norman Pritchard moved to the United States in 1996 to become Senior Pastor of the Presbyterian Church in Bloomfield Hills, Michigan. He had been installed as Senior Minister of Scots' Church in 1979 and served as Moderator of the General Assembly in the mid 1980s. It was then that he began to have some influence over people like Max Bradshaw and Brian Bayston, and he was on the Council of Scotch College, including ten years as Deputy

Afterword

Chairman. After I contacted him several years ago, he replied by email: "I'm very pleased that Joan M is to be commemorated in your book, she deserves better acknowledgement than anything she received at the time she was forced to retire. I'm sure you're wanting to do everything her stature and achievements deserve."

Is this book that? Is it the acknowledgment that Joan Montgomery never adequately received? Can a book do justice to her stature and achievements? At the very least, this account highlights that no matter what Joan's stature and achievements, the Continuing Presbyterians were swayed by Max Bradshaw in their distrust of her. While the broader community was entirely supportive of Joan, those who wanted to keep her as Principal were ultimately unsuccessful due to the numbers against them on the body that had the power. It all revolved around who had the power — and, in the end, the school community did not.

Life, however, moves on and Joan is not the sort of person to look back and fret. After leaving PLC, she remained busy and engaged, serving on many education boards and continuing to indulge her passion for travel. She lives independently and was still driving at 95 and only in April 2021 did she part with her sporty Volkswagen car gratefully received by one of her grand-nieces. It was but one mark of her closeness to her sisters' children and their children and to the thinning ranks of those who worked with her and under her at Clyde and PLC. After finishing at PLC, Joan moved to live mainly in Shoreham while retaining accommodation in Melbourne and then in more recent years moved permanently to retirement accommodation in Melbourne. She continued in retirement to play a significant role in the community. She was on the Council of the University of Melbourne and many of its committees. She chaired the Council of Medley Hall and was on the Council of Ormond College. Membership of school Councils included The Geelong College, Melbourne Grammar, Woodleigh and St Margaret's.

She was on the board of the Alfred Hospital, the National

Health and Medical Research Council and the Baker Institute's Animal Ethics committees. The Human Ethics Committee of the Walter and Eliza Hall Institute and membership of the Lyceum Club and M.C.C. were other interests. But her 17 years as the beloved and universally respected Principal of Presbyterian Ladies' College remains the crowning achievement of Joan Montgomery's brilliant career, a legacy that the brutal politics of her departure can never erode or erase.

Notes to Chapters

Front cover

Portrait of "Miss J.M. Montgomery", by Dudley Drew, 1979. Photo courtesy PLC Development Office, reproduced by permission Presbyterian Ladies' College. The tearaway is taken from the front page of the *Age*, 6 March 1984.

Foreword

1. See https://www.si.edu/exhibitions/first-ladies-political-role-and-public-image-4091 viewed on 3 August 2018. The page indicates that that physical section of the exhibition may no longer be there — as it is dated *March 29, 1992–July 16, 2006*. I must have seen it, then, in its very early days.
2. Eleanor and Franklin were fifth cousins, once removed. They descended from Claes Martenszen van Rosenvelt who emigrated to the USA in the 1640s. His grandsons were Johannes and Jacobus. Eleanor descended from the Johannes branch and Franklin descended from the Jacobus branch. See further, Barry Jones, *Dictionary of World Biography* (ANU Press, 2017) and http://en.wikipedia.org/wiki/Eleanor_Roosevelt.
3. Blanche Wiesen Cook, *Eleanor Roosevelt,* vol 1: *1884-1933* (Viking, 1992).
4. Ibid., p. 4.
5. Ibid., p. 103.
6. Kathleen Fitzpatrick, *PLC Melbourne: the First Century 1875-1975* (PLC, 1975), p. 23.
7. Cook, *Eleanor Roosevelt*, op.cit., p. 11.
8. Jill Kerr Conway (ed.), *Written by Herself: Autobiographies of American Women: An Anthology* (Vintage, 1992).
9. Ibid., p. xii.

Chapter 1 – Jeopardy

1. Brian Bayston, "Frederick Maxwell Bradshaw: a Memoir", in *Proceedings of the Uniting Church Historical Society, Synod of Victoria and Tasmania*, vol. 22, no. 2, December 2015, p. 60.
2. Author interview 12 May 2005.
3. Joan Montgomery, Ev Tindale and Jan Douglas did not speak to each other before they wrote their own accounts and their records are with the Author.
4. F. Maxwell Bradshaw, "The early history of the Presbyterian Church in Victoria", Address to the Church of England Historical Society, Diocese of Melbourne, 20 August 1965, typescript in the Mollison Library at St. Paul's Cathedral, Melbourne.
5. Alan Rodger, *The Courts, the Church and the Constitution: Aspects of the Disruption of 1843* (Edinburgh University Press, 2008).
6. Fitzpatrick, *PLC Melbourne*, op. cit, p. 136.
7. Ibid., pp. 136-137, which Kathleen Fitzpatrick explains "she tended to frequent, partly perhaps as an escape from the harsher realities of her life."
8. Ibid.

Chapter 2 – *Loch Long*

1. F. Maxwell Bradshaw, *Scottish Seceders in Victoria* (Robertson & Mullens, 1947), p. 1.
2. Wilfred Owen, "Spring Offensive [1917]" in *Wilfred Owen: War Poems and Others* (Chatto & Windus, 1973).
3. Frank Huelin, *Keep Moving*, forward by Alan Marshall and an afterword by the author (Penguin Books, 1983).
4. Alan Marshall, *How Beautiful Are Thy feet* (Allen & Unwin, 1949).
5. William Henry Bossence, *Numurkah* (Hawthorn Press, 1979), pp. 213-214.

Chapter 3 – PLC Girls

1. Professor Joan McMeeken, "Remembering Australia's Polio Scourge", University of Melbourne, available at https://pursuit.unimelb.edu.au/articles/remembering-australia-s-polio-scourge, viewed 13 May 2021.
2. Letter from Joan Ritchie, 23 October 2005.
3. Fitzpatrick, *PLC Melbourne*, op.cit., p. 214.
4. Author interview with David Hodges, 19 May 2005.
5. This was debated in the House of Commons and recorded in debate

of 26 June 1868 and was published in 1869 (H.M.S.O., London).
6   Ibid., pp. 548-549.
7   Fitzpatrick, *PLC Melbourne*, op. cit., p. 32.
8   *Encyclopedia Britannica*, "Frances Buss | English Educator."
9   Ibid.
10 John Stuart Mill & Stanton Coit, *The Subjection of Women* (Longmans, Green and Co, 1906).
11 Fitzpatrick, *PLC Melbourne*, op. cit., p. 32.
12 Mill, *Subjection*, op. cit.
13 Josephine Butler (ed.), *Woman's Work and Woman's Culture: A Series of Essays* (MacMillan and Co, 1869).
14 Ibid., p. viii.
15 Ibid., pp. vii-viii.
16 Ibid., p. vii.
17 Ibid., p. 290.
18 Ibid., p. 294.
19 Charles H Pearson. "On some historical aspects of family life" in Josephine Butler, *Woman's Work*, op. cit., p. 154.
20 Ibid.
21 Fitzpatrick, *PLC Melbourne*, op. cit., p. 39.
22 Tregenza, John, *Professor of Democracy: The Life of Charles Henry Pearson, 1830-1894, Oxford Don and Australian Radical* (Melbourne University Press, 1968), p. 77.
23 Ibid., p. 79.
24 Fitzpatrick, *PLC Melbourne*, op. cit., p. 46.
25 This is noted by Tregenza, *Professor of Democracy*, op.cit. p. 75. There were other girls' schools and colleges but they did not provide equal education.
26 Ibid., p. 82.
27 Ibid., p. 85.
28 Ibid.
29 Ibid., p. 94.
30 Ibid., p. 97.
31 Ibid., p. 99.
32 Ibid.
33 Ibid., at p. 102, citing the *Age*.
34 Melbourne *Punch*, 22 February 1877.
35 Tragenza, *Professor of Democracy*, op.cit., p. 106.
36 Ibid., p. 108.
37 Ibid., p. 111.
38 Ibid.

39 Fitzpatrick, *PLC Melbourne*, op. cit., pp. 74-75.
40 Christopher Symons, *The Melbourne Symphony Orchestra: An Introduction and Appreciation* (The Orchestra, 1987).
41 Ibid., p. 10.
42 Ibid., p. 37.
43 "Speech Night, 1938" in *Patchwork*, No. 71, May 1939, p. 4. Speech night was on Monday 12 December 1938.
44 Author interview with Joan Kent (Battersby), 27 October 2005.
45 *Patchwork*, No. 74, May 1940, p. 34.
46 Leila Shaw, *The Way We Were: Adventures, Feats and Experiences of Pioneering Families of the Mornington Peninsula* (Somerville, Tyabb and District Heritage Society, 1998), "The War Years at PLC", pp. 214-215.
47 Joan Montgomery's eulogy at the funeral of Olive Battersby. Olive died 14 July 1996.
48 *Patchwork*, No. 76, May 1941, p. 28.
49 Lexie Luly, "Memories of PLC 1934-1940", PLC Archives, K4 76, ACC PLC 2059967 BRN 102991.
50 Marilyn Yallom with Theresa Donovan Brown, *The Social Sex: A History of Female Friendship* (HarperCollins, 2015), pp. 145-146.
51 *Patchwork*, No. 78, July 1942, p. 5.
52 Ibid., p. 6.
53 Fitzpatrick, *PLC Melbourne*, op. cit., p. 157.
54 Ibid., p. 192.
55 Ibid., p. 199.
56 *Patchwork*, No. 79 (New series), December 1942, pp. 17-18.
57 Luly, op.cit. 40-41
58 *Patchwork*, No. 81, July 1944, 6.

Chapter 4 – A Church in Hawthorn

1 Bayston, "Bradshaw: a memoir", op. cit., p. 60.
2 Ibid.
3 F. Maxwell Bradshaw, *Rural Village to Urban Surge: A History of the Presbyterian Congregation at Hawthorn, Victoria* (Hawthorn Session and Board of Management, 1964), p. vii.
4 Ibid.
5 Bayston, "Bradshaw: a memoir", op. cit.
6 Bradshaw, *Rural Village*, op.cit., p. 105.
7 Ibid.
8 Author interview with David Hodges, 19 May 2005.

Notes to Chapters

9. Victoria Peel, Deborah Zion and Jane Yule, *A History of Hawthorn* (Melbourne University Press, 1993), p. 185.
10. Priscilla Kennedy, *Portrait of Winifred West* (Fine Arts Press, 1976), p. 41.
11. Ibid., pp. 28-31.
12. Ibid., p. 27.
13. Ibid., p. 121.
14. Ibid., p. 90.
15. Joan Montgomery letter to Elizabeth Montgomery, 28 September 1952.
16. Priscilla Kennedy, *Portrait of Winifred West,* op. cit., p. 120.
17. Patricia Conolly was a star of the Melbourne Theatre Company, beginning her stage career in Australia but later performing in the West End with the Royal Shakespeare Company (https://en.wikipedia.org/wiki/Royal_Shakespeare_Company) and Chichester Festival Theatre (Laurence Olivier's company); and theatres in Canada and the United States. A spirited student, Joan remembers Conolly leading an attack on her teaching.

Chapter 5 – Coronation

1. Joan Montgomery letter to Anne, Elizabeth and Helen, 28 June 1952 (with Margaret and Donald recently married and living now in Beaver St, Malvern).
2. 5 June 1952.
3. 15 June 1952, to Elizabeth.
4. August 1952, to Helen.
5. 15 June 1952.
6. 9 March 1958.
7. 13 August 1952.
8. 21 June 1952.
9. 21 June 1952.
10. 15 June 1952.
11. 3 July 1952, to Elizabeth.
12. 6 July 1952.
13. 18 July 1952.
14. 1 September 1952, to Anne.
15. 15 November 1952.
16. 22 February 1953.
17. 22 March 1953.
18. 24 November 1952.
19. 23 May 1953.

20 6 June 1953.
21 James Mitchell, *A Deepening Roar: Scotch College, Melbourne, 1851-2001* (Allen & Unwin, 2001), p. 210.
22 19 July 1953, to Helen.
23 27 August 1952.
24 12 August 1953.
25 18 August 1953.
26 23 May 1953.
27 18 September 1953, to Helen.
28 22 September 1953.
29 3 September 1953, to Anne.
30 22 September 1953.
31 18 September 1953.
32 2 October 1953.
33 3 November 1953.
34 21 November 1953.
35 3 November 1953.
36 13 November 1953.
37 1 January 1954.
38 2 December 1954.
39 21 April 1954.
40 17 April 1954.
41 17 April 1954.
42 22 May 1954, to Anne.
43 28 June 1954.
44 11 July 1954, to Elizabeth.
45 31 July 1954, to Elizabeth.
46 31 July 1954, to Barbara and Ruth.
47 4 September 1954.
48 25 September, to Anne and Elizabeth.
49 5 October 1954.
50 17 October 1954.
51 21 October 1954, to Anne.
52 27 October 1954.
53 December 1954.
54 11 December 1954.

Chapter 6 – Excommunicated

1 Author interview with Constance Wood, 18 June 1993.
2 Author interview with Jean Ford, 17 February 1995.
3 Ian Breward, "Union and division" in James Jupp (ed.), *The*

Notes to Chapters

Australian People; An Encyclopedia of the Nation, Its People and Its Origins (Cambridge University Press, 2001), p. 658.
4   5 February 1958, to Elizabeth and David.
5   21 February 1958, to Anne.
6   9 March 1958, to Elizabeth.
7   2 March 1958, to Anne.
8   15 April 1958.
9   30 March 1958.
10 19 May 1958.
11 15 April 1958.
12 3 April 1958, to Liz and David.
13 4 May 1958.
14 13 June 1958, to Anne.
15 8 July 1958.
16 30 May 1958, to Anne, Elizabeth and David and Margaret, and Helen.
17 30 June 1958, to Anne.
18 31 July 1958.
19 3 August 1958, to Elizabeth and David.
20 13 August 1958, to Helen.
21 1 September 1958, to Anne.
22 21 September 1958.
23 3 October 1958.
24 19 October 1958.
25 25 October 1958, to Elizabeth and David.
26 7 November 1958, to Anne.
27 3 January 1959.
28 29 March 1959.
29 29 March 1959, to Elizabeth and David.
30 3 April 1959, to Anne.
31 3 May 1959.
32 30 June 1959.
33 Author interview with Dame Elisabeth Murdoch, 15 July 1993.
34 30 June 1959, to Elizabeth.
35 10 August 1959, to Anne.
36 25 November 1959, to Elizabeth.

Chapter 7 – Clyde

1   M.O. Reid, *The Ladies Came to Stay: A Study of the Education of Girls at the Presbyterian Ladies College, Melbourne, 1875-1960*, authorised by the Council of the College (Presbyterian Ladies College, [196-]).

2   Proceedings of Inquest held upon the body of Mary Everett Allpress at Gisborne dated 1 August 1960 and conducted by A.E. Scott Esq—SM Coroner.
3   Melanie Guile, *Clyde School 1910-1975: an Uncommon History* (Clyde Old Girls' Association [South Yarra], 2006), p. 279; from interview with Margie Gillett (Cordner), 3 March 2006.
4   Ibid., p. 253.
5   Ibid., p. 253.
6   *Age*, 21 May 1968, as reported in Guile, *Clyde School*, op. cit., p. 254.
7   Anonymous, Clyde Questionnaire 2005, for Guile, *Clyde School*, op. cit.
8   Notes of interview, Melanie Guile with Madame ten Brink, 4 November 1987.
9   Guile, *Clyde School*, op. cit., p. 276.
10 Sylvia McLachlan (Clarke), Clyde Questionnaire 1992 for Guile, *Clyde School*, op. cit.
11 Melanie Guile interview with Joan Montgomery, 24 November 2005.
12 Guile interview with Joan Montgomery, 24 November 2005.
13 Guile, *Clyde School*, op. cit., p. 276.
14 Ibid., p. 276.
15 Author interview with Ray Northrop, 30 December 1994.
16 Author interview with Ray Northrop, 30 December 1994.
17 Regulation 36 (2) of the General Assembly of the Presbyterian Church of Victoria.
18 Anne Dalrymple, 'Aims for an all-round education', *Age*, 21 May 1968.
19 Guile, *Clyde School*, op. cit., p. 284.
20 Ibid., p. 285.
21 Ibid., p. 285; *Cluthan*, 1968, p. 11.
22 Author interview with Judy Gregory, 10 April 2005.

Chapter 8 – PLC Principal

1   Speech to Old Collegians' Annual Luncheon, November 1994.
2   Ibid.
3   *Basic Documents on Presbyterian Polity*, With Introductions and Notes, F. Maxwell Bradshaw, MA LLM, Procurators, General Assembly of Australia, Christian Education Committee, Presbyterian Church of Australia 1984, pp. 102-103.
4   Ibid., p. 103.
5   *Presbyterian Church of Australia Act* 1971.

Notes to Chapters

6 Bradshaw, *Basic Documents*, op.cit., pp. 102-103.
7 Author interview with Ray Northrop, 29 April 2005.
8 Bayston, "Bradshaw: a memoir", op. cit, p. 60.
9 Ibid.
10 Ibid.
11 Ben Rogers, "When three became one in Christ", *Journey*, Uniting Church in Queensland, 31 January 2017.
12 Presbyterian Church of NSW, mmpcnsw.org.au/presbytery-visitations.
13 The report was tabled in the PLC Council minutes of 21 March 1974.
14 "The crisis of '77", paper by Bob Thomas at Ministers' Conference, Presbyterian Theological College, Melbourne, 23 March 2004, p. 20.
15 Ibid., p. 20.
16 Citing the resolutions in *The Presbyterian Church of Victoria Trusts Corporation and Frederick Maxwell Bradshaw and Charles Homer Fraser* at p. 5 of the unreported judgement handed down on 30 April 1975.
17 Ibid., p. 6.
18 Thomas, "The crisis of '77", op. cit., pp. 22-23.
19 GAA Blue Book 1974, Minute 45.
20 Thomas, "The crisis of '77", op. cit., p. 23.
21 Ibid., p. 24.
22 *The Presbyterian Church of Victoria Trusts Corporation and Frederick Maxwell Bradshaw and Charles Homer Fraser*, op. cit., p. 9.
23 Ibid.
24 Ibid.
25 Letter, 10 October 1974.
26 Author interview with Ray Northrop, 29 April 2005.
27 *[1976] HCA 38; (1976) 135 CLR 587 (3 August 1976).*
28 Fitzpatrick, *PLC Melbourne*, op. cit., p. 267.
29 This history is set out in a letter from Justice Ray Northrop to the Attorney-General on 24 April 1978.
30 Letter to Joan Montgomery, 11 April 1975.
31 Extracts in Fitzpatrick, *PLC Melbourne*, op. cit., pp. 221-222.
32 Author interview with Jenny Pring, 20 August 2005.
33 Australian Schools Commission, Committee on Social Change and the Education of Women, *Girls, Schools and Society: Report by a Study Group to the Schools Commission*, Study Group chair K.R. McKinnon (Australian Schools Commission, 1975).
34 Alison Mackinnon, "Girls, society and school: a generation of change?", *Australian Feminist Studies*, 21:50, July 2006, pp. 275-288.
35 Ibid., citing Schools Commission 1975, p. vii.

36 *AG (NSW) v Grant* (1976) 135 CLR 587.

Chapter 9 – Ruined

1. Author interview with Ray Northrop, 30 December 1994.
2. *Crosslight* magazine, Uniting Church, 21 May 2017.
3. Fitzpatrick, *PLC Melbourne*, op. cit.
4. Letter 12 December 1978, Ray Northrop to Mrs H.A. Jowett.
5. Letter 9 Feb 1978, Lilian Ganderton to Mrs J Stratford.
6. Reported in August 1978 *Annual Report*, R.M Northrop, Chairman, PLC College Council, pp. 3-4.
7. Letter 8 March 1978, Richard Chenoweth to Mr Pearsons.
8. Letter 31 March 1978, Haddon Storey to Ray Northrop.
9. Letter 10 April 1978, Ray Northrop to Haddon Storey.
10. Letter 24 April 1978, Ray Northrop to Haddon Storey.
11. Letter 29 August 1978, Ray Northrop to Parents.

Chapter 10 – Miss Montgomery

1. Letter 21 March 1979, Brian Bayston to Pam Royle.
2. *Bulletin*, 3 April 1979, "Uniters v Continuers: The Money Behind the Big Religious Split."
3. *Age*, Wednesday 28 March 1979, p. 4.
4. *Herald*, Saturday 7 October 1978, p. 3.
5. From the Book of Daniel.
6. Joan Montgomery's speech to PLC Old Collegians' Annual Luncheon, November 1994.
7. Victorian Hansard, 6 December 1979, p. 5785.
8. Ruth Stewart, email to Author.
9. Joan Montgomery, PLC Old Collegians' Luncheon, November 1994.
10. Memorandum, John D. Phillips and Hartley Hansen, prepared for Group A members.

Chapter 11 – A 12 to 5 Carve Up

1. Author interview with Mary Murdoch, 4 May 2005.
2. Uniting Church in Australia Education Committee – Synod of Victoria, *Report and Recommendations for Synod and Presbyteries*, May 1980.
3. Reported at the Parents' Association AGM on 19 April 1983.

Notes to Chapters

Chapter 12 – Church Tightens PLC Hold

1. Mitchell, *A Deepening Roar,* op. cit, Chapter 17, "Schism 1977-1980", p. 395.
2. Ibid, Chapter 18, "Roff's Fall", p. 417.
3. Ibid., p. 397.
4. Ibid., pp. 408-409. Mackay's address was Spottiswoode Street and was misspelt in the Council Minutes.
5. Ibid., p. 398 quoting J.R. Cormack, *Collegian,* 1978, p. 146.
6. Ibid., p. 411 quoting S.E.K. Hulme QC's advice.
7. Ibid., p. 412.
8. Ibid., p. 418, Archibald Glenn, interviewed by Tolson, 8 May 1990.
9. Ibid., p. 427, Glenn with Tolson, 8 May 1990.
10. *Age,* 13 August 1981, p. 1.
11. Sue Green, "Principal may go as church tightens PLC hold", *Age,* 15 August 1981.
12. Letters from Elizabeth Butt, 5 September 1981, Cynthia Parker, 3 September 1981, Kathleen McCredie, 7 September 1981 and Joan Butler, 21 September 1981. Pam Royle Correspondence and Notes file.
13. Letter Brian Bayston, 9 September 1981 in reply to Nan Falloon.
14. Email Reverend Pritchard to Author, 2014.
15. Letter Val Griffith 11 September 1981, to Ev Tindale.
16. Letter Mary Murdoch 23 September 1981, to Mrs P. Royle.
17. Letter prepared by Mr and Mrs Ramsay, 28 September 1981.
18. Letter H.A. Potter to Reverend Harrison, 28 September 1981.
19. Sue Green, "Church veto on Scotch College appointment", *Age,* 15 September 1981.
20. Letter The Manse, 17 November 1981 in Pam Royle Correspondence and Notes file–this one with the insert in the salutation space to "Mr and Mrs Potter."
21. Sue Green, "Church takes firmer control of girls' school", *Age,* 24 December 1981, p. 3.
22. Council Meeting, 10 December 1981.

Chapter 13 – I'll Have To Ask Mr Bradshaw

1. Notes for Members of Group B, 22 June 1982 in the Correspondence and Notes file of Pam Royle.
2. Letter 9 July 1982 from "Moonbool" Foster in the Correspondence and Notes file of Pam Royle.
3. Author interview with Jenny Pring, 30 August 2005.

Vetting of Wisdom

4   15 December 1983.
5   Letter 17 February 1984, in the Correspondence and Notes file of Pam Royle.

Chapter 14 – Outcry

1. Letter 15 February 1984, Marion Kainer (Dux of School 1983) to Presbyterian Moderator, the Very Reverend Alan Stubs.
2. There were 296 letters expressing concern and asking Council to reconsider extending Joan Montgomery's contract. Tabled in Item 7.1 in the Council minutes and accompanied in the Appendix with the names and addresses of all senders.
3. Letter David Dyer 5 March 1984, to members of Council.
4. David Humphries, "Parents stand and cheer PLC head", *Age*, Tuesday 6 March 1984, p. 1.
5. Kwong Lee Dow, "School at risk", Letter to the Editor, *Age*, Wednesday 7 March 1984, p. 12.
6. Geoff Maslen, "Religion in the classroom", *Age*, Saturday Extra, 17 March 1984, p. 6.

Chapter 15 – Fight the Good Fight

1. Hansard as scanned and online at http://www.parliament.vic. gov.au/images/stories/volume-hansard/Hansard%2049 %20LC%20V374%20Apr-May1984.pdf.

Chapter 16 – The Final Year

1. Geoff Maslen, "Contract not renewed, but content with her time", *Age*, Thursday 19 December 1985, p. 10.
2. Author interview with William Mackay, Edinburgh, 2005.
3. Michael Pirrie, "A firm Scots hand will guide PLC", *Herald*, Friday 26 July 1985, p. 2.
4. Geoff Maslen, "Conservatives purged at Scotch", *Age*, Saturday 12 November 1985, p. 5.

Index

The two tranches of illustrations appear
after p. 142 (Figs 1-32) and after p. 246 (Figs 33-58).

Age (newspaper), and PLC
  disputes   179, 182, *Fig. 46*,
  248-9, 250-1, 252-3, 259, 261,
  262, 294-6, 331-2, 335
  and Montgomery's
    appointment to Clyde
    112-13
  and Montgomery's
    appointment to PLC
    124
  on Montgomery's
    retirement   354
  on Montgomery's travel to
    China and Russia   342
  on purge of Scotch and
    PLC Councils   347
  and Scotch College
    resignation   248
Aitken, Miss   46
Aitken, Phillip   231
Alfred Hospital Board   371
Allen, Merle   22
Allenswood School, London
  xviii, 27
Allpress, Mary, death   113-14
Anderson, Jean   *Fig. 48*

Anderson, Robert   163, *Fig. 48*,
  270-1, 280, 297, 310, 350
Araluen, Hawthorn   51-2
Armitage, Barry   232, 238-40,
  337
Assembly Hall, Melbourne   3,
  140, 144, 156, 361
Association of Headmistresses
  (UK)   28
Association of Heads of
  Independent Girls' Schools of
  Australia   2, 116-17, 251-2,
  304-5, 335
Association of Heads of
  Independent Schools of
  Australia   346
Australian College of
  Education, Fellowship   160
Baker Institute Animal Ethics
  committees   372
Bank of Australasia, Hugh
  Montgomery's career   12, 13
  William Montgomery's
  career   13-14, 16, 18, 20,
  25, *Fig. 16*
Barr, Sandra   127

Barton, Russell 285
Battersby, Joan 40, 46, 129-31
  see also Kent, Joan
Battersby, Olive 39, 40, 49, 129
Battersby family 39-41
Bayston, Brian 63, *Fig. 4*, 175, 184, 211, 227, *Fig. 52*, 281, 360-2, 364-5
  on anti-union campaign 136
  on Bradshaw 53-4, 56, 135, 159-60, 360, 362, 365
  on Mackay's appointment to PLC 345
  and Parents' Association meeting 319
  on PLC Council 216
  as PLC Council member 242-3, 249, 253-6, 262, 264, 265-6, 276-7, 279, 290, 323-4
  on PLC dispute 366
  and Presbyterian Special Commission 179, 180
  as Presbyterians' legal agent 235-6
  on Presbyterian Schools Bill 206
  on religious education in schools 173, 178-9, 265, 268, 330, 366
  removed from PLC Council 348, 350, 370
  on survey of PLC parents 189
Beale, Dorothea 27-8
Bean, Mrs 239
Begg, Margaret 48
Bell, Lois 325
Best, Bruce 182

Blackburn, Jean 152
Boarders' Parents' Association 270
Borland, Sophie 150-1
Bound, Derek 192, 198
Bound, Joy 192
Bowen, Louise 352
Boyd, Frances 367
Bradshaw, Max 53-5, *Fig. 3*, 159-60, 172-3, 184, 259, 281, 323, 330, 359, 361, 363
  as Continuing Presbyterian 3, 134-6, 141, 191, 210-11
  draft legislation on PLC and Scotch College 174
  and Hawthorn Presbyterian Church 56, 63, 80-1, 96-7, 361, 362, 365
  and Montgomery dismissal attempt 1-2, 5-8, 217-20, 226-7, 285, 288
  opposed to church union 3-4, 55, 98, 132-3, 142, 145-6
  as PLC Council member 241, 242, 257, 264, 268, 273, 276
  and Presbyterian Property Commission 143-4, 147, 368
  and Presbyterian Special Commission 179, 180, 367-70
  Rural Village to Urban Surge 55
  and Scotch College Council 205, 245-7, 342-3
  Scottish Seceders in Victoria 12
  threatens Lionel King

Index

227–8
Brennan, Teresa 152
Bright, Victoria 16–18
Brighton, Victoria 25–50, *Fig. 16*
Brisbane, Miss 118
Brooking, Justice Robert 205
Broughton, Barbara 62, 73, 75, *Fig. 29*
Brown, Mrs 48
Brown, Neil 127
Bruce, Mary Grant 23
Brunt, Maureen 122, 295
Bryant, Christina 102–3
Bryant, Phyllis 58, 59, 60–1, 62, 63, 64
Buckham, Jeanette 112
Buckner, Garth 265
Bulletin, and PLC dispute 190–1
Bunyan, Ruth 150, *Fig. 53*, 300, 317, 336, 337, 346
Burrage, Miss 48
Burton, Clare 152
Buss, Frances Mary 27–8
Butler, Joan 252
Butler, Josephine, *Woman's Work and Woman's Culture* 29–30, 31
Butt, Elizabeth 252
Buxton, Pam 326, 328
Camberwell Assembly 4, 142, 144, 145, 357, 359
Camberwell Grammar 321
Camberwell Group *see* Camberwell Assembly
Campbell, Keith 242, 276–7
Canterbury Presbyterian Church 258, 323
Carruthers, Don 179, 222, 260, 263, 332, 336

letter to parents 304, 315–16
as PLC Council chair *Fig. 46*, 261–2, 263, 266, 278, 281, 282–5, 287–90, 294–5, 303, 338
removal from PLC Council 348, 350, 370
Ceylon, Montgomery's impressions 67–8
Charlesworth, Max 19, 20, 21, 25
Chelsea, residence in 87, 88
Cheltenham Ladies College 28
Chenoweth, Elaine 42
Chenoweth, Richard 172–3
Chernov, Alex 231–3, 236, 241, *Figs 47–8*, 249–50, 279, 280–1, 297, 344, 350, 360, 363
and Parents' Association meeting 308, 310–17, 321
Chernov, Elizabeth *Fig. 48*
Cherry, Diana 349
Chessell, Pam 150
China, Montgomery's impressions 153–4
Chipp, Alan 326–8
Chipps, Mrs 62
Church of Scotland, disruption of 1843 3, 140–1
church union 1, 2–3, 98, 132–7, 154 *see also* Joint Commission on Church Union
Clayton, Ross 334
Clubbe, Phyllis 58, 59
Clyde School 111–24, *Fig. 36*
approach to Montgomery 107–8

Montgomery's appointment to 112–13, *Figs 33–5*
Cohen, Miss 127
Combined Women's Group 239
Committee on Social Change and the Education of Women 152
Congregational Union, church union vote 139
Conolly, Patricia 62
Continental Europe, travels in 89, 103–5, 107, *Figs 31–2*
Continuing Presbyterians 3, 4, 134–6 *see also* Presbyterians
Cook, Blanche Wiesen, *Eleanor Roosevelt* xvii, xx
coronation festivities 77–8, *Figs 27–8*
Corporate Affairs Commissioner *see* Victorian Corporate Affairs Commissioner
Corr, Reford 127
Cowling, Judy 42
Cox, Eva 152
Craven, Douglas 102
Craven, Jean 42, 57, 92
Crawford, Alan 180, 183, 222, 232, 233, 269
Creese, Nigel 252, 291
cricket, Montgomery's love of 25, 34–5, 82, 92, 349
Cridge, Mrs 58
Crock, Carmel 296
Crocker, Walter 160
Crofts, Donalda 151, 201–2
Crouch End High School, London 83–4, 87, 89
Crow, Archie 302–3
Cunningham, Marjorie 42, *Fig. 22*
cycling, Montgomery's love of 22–3, 25–6
Dalrymple, Anne (*Age* journalist) 124
de Witt, John 102
Deakin, Catherine, as PLC foundation pupil 4, 31
Dodds, Anne *Fig. 49*, 349
dogs, at Clyde School 118
Douglas, Jan 2, 7, *Figs 6–7*, 150, 202–3, 218–20, 234, 293, 322, 336, 342
Dow, Kwong Lee 295–6
Dr Mac (radio program) 23–4
Drew, Dudley, portrait of Montgomery *Fig. 51*
Duffy, John Gavan 32
Dunn, Benjamin 143
Dunn, Hector 179–80, 195
Dyer, David 149–50, 182–3, 291–2
Dyer, Mrs 149–50
Edmonson, Mrs 271
education of girls, 19th-century England 27–30
Ellis, Christopher 252
Ellis, Constance 5
Endwhistle, Mrs 67
equal opportunity, PLC's commitment to 192
Fabian, Canon 120
Falloon, Nan 239, 240, 251, 253–4
Finnemore, John 184
First Ladies exhibition, Washington DC xvii
Fitzpatrick, Kathleen xviii, 31, 46, 146, 148–9, 150
Flynn, Mrs D.G.M. 166, 223,

Index

Fig. 43
Ford, Jean   63–4, 94–5, 98, 100–7, *Fig. 31*, 186
former PLC staff, farewell to Montgomery   349–50
former PLC students, support for Montgomery   287, 296, 300–2 *see also* Old Collegians
Fortune, Anne   299
Fowlers Vacola, Hawthorn   57–8, 92
Fraser, Charles Homer   136, 143–4, 147, 363
Free Church of Scotland   3
Free Presbyterian Church of Victoria   1
Frensham school, Mittagong   58–62, 117
Frost, Phyllis   *Fig. 49*, 295, 349
Galloway, Misses   51, 52
Ganderton, Lilian   167–8
Gardner, Ken   139
Gedge, Miss   37
The Geelong College Council   371
Gib Gate school, Mittagong   60
Gillespie, Alex   184
Gipton, Norman   243–4
Girls, Schools and Society   152
Glenn, Sir Archibald   246, 247, 248
Godfrey, Ethel   5
Golders Green, residence in   83
Goldstein, Vida   5
Gough, Mr   142
Great Depression, 1929–33   20
Green, Sue (*Age* journalist)   249, 250–1, 259, 262
Greig, Flos   5

Griffith, Gavan   210
Griffith, Sheila   367
Griffith, Val   222–3, 249, 251, 256, 257–8, 261
Guile, Melanie, *Clyde School, 1910–1975*   108, 114
Gunn, Farquhar   121, 145, 156, 159, 162, 164–5, 173
Hailes, Helen   9, 102–3, *Fig. 1*, 355
Hamer, Rupert   201
Hamilton, Murray   201
Hampton High School   25, 26, *Fig. 17*
Handley, G.W.   59
Handley, Ken   142, 159
Hanging Rock, Victoria   111
Hansen, Hartley   323–5
Harman, Allan   321
Harman, Mairi   249, 264, 271, 279, 346, 348
Harrison, Colin   258, 261
  letter to PLC parents   260
Harrison, Hector   141
Harvey, Beryl *see* Montgomery, Beryl
Harvey, Eleanor *see* Meyer, Eleanor
Harvey, William   15–16
Hastie, Peter   329–30
Hawker, Mrs Michael   *Fig. 37*
Hawthorn Presbyterian Church   53, 54–6, 63, 80–1, 96–7, 142, 361-2, 365
Hay, Olga   107, 117
Herald (newspaper), and Mackay's appointment to PLC   345
  and Montgomery's appointment to Clyde   *Fig. 33*

389

and Presbyterian view of women 192, 198
Hethersett, PLC residence 125, 231, 238
Hodges, David 57, 127
Holmes, Henry 233, 261
Holmes, Roberta 251
Holt Public Relations 332
Hore-Lacey, Ian 231, 249, 256, 261
Howells, Tom 137, 139
Human Relations, PLC program 149, 271-2, 273, 279
Humphries, David (*Age* journalist) 295
Hunter, I.M. 142
Hutchinson, Alison 47
immigration, Australian policy 20
Irving, Martin Howy 34
Ivanhoe, Victoria 16-17
Jewish refugees in Australia 37
Johnson, Professor 121
Joint Commission on Church Union 98, 133, 162
Jones, John 188
Jowett, Mrs 166
Junior School, Parents' Association 166, *Fig. 46*, 294-5
    redevelopment plans 200
    staff support for Stratford appointment 169
Kainer, Marion 287
Kennan, Jim 327, 332
Kennedy, Priscilla 59
Kensington, residence in 72-3
Kent, Jack 131
Kent, Joan 293, 341 *see also* Battersby, Joan
Kerr Conway, Jill, *Written by Herself* xxi
Kimpton, Eleanor *see* Meyer, Eleanor
Kimpton, Stephen 108
King, Lionel 222, 223-5, 227-8, 236, 237, 239
Kirkhope, Elizabeth 90
Kirner, Joan 327
Knox, David 84, 119
Knox, Donald 62-3
Kramer, Dame Leonie 295, 308-10, 363
Kurrle, Stan 57
Ladds, Brenda 89
Lade, Helen 123, 124, 127, 131, *Fig. 39*
land tax proposal 32-3
Landeryou, Bill 206
Largs Bay (ship) 87, 91-2
Larkins, Caroline 320, 321
Larkins, Richard 297
Lauriston School 90
Layton, Joyce 82, 84, 89
liberal education, importance of 178, 193, 197, 310
Liberal Studies, PLC program 149-52, 291
Liley, Tom 270
Lindsay, Joan, *Picnic at Hanging Rock* 111
Lobban, Allan 177, 184, 205
Loch Long (ship) 11
Loftus, Bill 121, 141, 145, 169, 179, 198-9, 261
    and PLC Council 156-7, 226, 233, 242
London, 1952-54 68, 70-8, 82-6, 87, 88, 90-1
    1958-59 100-3, 108-9

Index

Luly, Lexie   47–8, 347
Lyman, Reverend   249
Lynch, Lizzie   22
Macaulay, Robert Wilson   48–9
Mackay, Fred   140
Mackay, William Morton   246, *Fig. 50*, 248, 342–5, 347, 352, 366
Mackinnon, Alison   152
MacKinnon, Ian   184
MacLeod, Neil   139, 140–2
Macmillan, Helen   161, 322
Macmillan, John Thomson   161–2, 204
MacPherson, Margaret   112
Macrae, Donald   144–5, 165
Mahlab, Eve   188, *Fig. 55*
Mallesons (PLC solicitors)   5–6, 161, 188, 189, 217, 240
Malvern Star bicycle   25, 37
Mao Tse Tung, death   153, 342
Martin, Jean   152
Maslen, Geoff (*Age* journalist)   296, 342, 347, 354
Mason, Marion   328–9
Mathers, Jim   142
McAnally, Graham   184
McArthur, John   137, 139, 184, 221–2, 232, 233, 249, 256, 261
McBain, James   33
McCafferty, Sam   142
McCarthy, Wendy   152
McCaughey, Davis   133, 163, 184, 185, 189, 196–7, 198, 271
McColl, Margaret   42
McConchie, Miss   36, 38
McCracken & McCracken (Presbyterian Church solicitors)   175, 188, 189, 235
McCredie, Kathleen   252–3, 304–5, 349
McCulloch, Sir James   33
McGarvie, Richard   144
McInerney, Justice   144
McKinnon, Ken   152
McKnight, Lucinda   300–2
McLachlan, Sylvia   117–8
McLean, Alice   128
McNicoll, David   191
McNie, Ken   348
McPhee, Hilary   95–6
McPherson, Alec   *Fig. 14*
McPherson, Loris   *Fig. 14*
McRae, Don   132
McRae, Ewen   179–80, 226, 350
Medley Hall Council   371
Melba, Dame Nellie *see* Mitchell, Helen
Melbourne, 1878   11–12
Melbourne Girls' Grammar School   105–6, 167
Melbourne Grammar School Council   334, 371
Mence, Olive   120–1
Merritt, David   137–9
Merritt, Mrs   317
Methodist Church, church union vote   139
Methodist Ladies College, Elsternwick   62
Meyer, Eleanor   15, 16, 26
Mill, John Stuart, *On the Subjection of Women*   28–9
Mills, Lady Diana   88
Miscamble, Fay   35
Mitchell, Ethel   184, 195
Mitchell, Frances Isobel *see* Montgomery, Frances
Mitchell, Helen, as PLC foundation pupil   4

Mitchell, James, *A Deepening Roar* 81, 244-6
Mitchell, Roma 160
Mittagong, NSW 58-62
Montgomery, Anne Roberts 45, 52-3, 59
   move to Toorak church 80, 96
Montgomery, Beryl 15-20, 44-5, *Fig. 11*
Montgomery, Elizabeth 17, 35, 40, 44, 53, 59, 63, 86-7, *Fig. 12*
   move to Toorak church 80, 96
Montgomery, Frances 12, 16, 24
Montgomery, Helen 19, 23, 26, 44, 53, 59, 64, 84
   move to Kew church 80, 96
Montgomery, Hugh 11-13
Montgomery, Hugh, Jnr 11, 12, 16, 17, *Fig. 9*
Montgomery, James 12
Montgomery, Joan, 1980
   dismissal attempt xix-xx, 2, 5-8, 147, 217-20, 223, 224, 227, 234, 361
   appointed to Clyde 108-9, 112-13, *Figs 33-4*
   appointed to PLC 123-4, 127-8
   appoints Junior School head 166-7
   appoints PLC Vice Principal 201-3
   as Association of Heads of Independent Girls Schools of Australia President 251-2
   birth 16
   childhood 16-24, *Fig. 9, 12-15*
   as Clyde Principal 111-20, 124, *Figs 35, 37*
   defended by PLC Council 172, 176, 257-8, 259
   defended by PLC staff 219-20, 234, 293, 297, 300, 333-4
   employment in London 69-71
   family 11-18
   farewelled from PLC *Fig. 49*, 349-50, 351
   fruit-picking 57
   homesickness 84-5
   honours and awards 2, 154, 160
   letter-writing 66-7, 75, *Fig. 30*
   love of sport 22, 35, 38-9, 45-6, 98, 117 *see also* cricket; cycling
   and Melbourne Grammar Council 334, 371
   motor accident 112-14
   and Ormond College Council 371
   as PLC Principal xix-xx, 127-32, *Fig. 6*, 148-54, 164-5, 185-6, 192-3, 206-10, *Figs 40, 48, 51*, 263-4, 267-8, 274-6, 278, 292-3
   as PLC student 8, 26-7, 34-50, *Figs 2, 18, 22-5*
   post-retirement *Figs 53-8*, 371-2
   retirement dispute 280-340
   reunion with Bayston and

Index

Northrop   *Fig. 52*, 364–5
support for PLC teachers
   339–40, 341
as teacher   58–62, 95–6,
   Fig. 29
teacher training   5
teaching positions in
   London   71, 82, 83–4,
   90–91, 100, 103
teaching style   95–6
teenage years   25–50,
   Figs 17–18
travel to Europe, 1952–54
   65–92
travel to Europe, 1958–59
   99–110
travels to China   153–4,
   342
and University of
   Melbourne Council   280,
   371
as University of Melbourne
   student   56–7
violin lessons   35–6
Montgomery, L.M., *Anne of
   Green Gables*   23
Montgomery, Margaret   17,
   36, 40, 43, 44, 54–5, 59, 119,
   Fig. 12
   marriage   62–3
Montgomery, Robert   11, 12,
   45
Montgomery, William   12, 13–
   26, 45, 49, *Fig. 11*
   military service   14–15,
      Fig. 10
Moody, Dorothy   249
Moody, Dr   271, 346
Mooroopna, Victoria   13
Moran, Tim   124
Morgan, George   268, 279, 348

Mountain, Edith   106
Murdoch, Dame Elisabeth
   108
Murdoch, Mary   180, 219,
   Fig. 48, 280, 297, 310, 325
   letter to parents   225–6,
      260
   as PLC Council chair   222,
      223, 231, 233, 236, 242,
      244, 258, 259, 260–2
Murdoch, Stuart   *Fig. 48*
Murray, Ian   189, 217, 240,
   283, 308
Murray, Tim   251–2
National Health and Medical
   Research Council   371–2
National Museum of American
   History   xvii
National Reform League   33
National Times, and PLC
   dispute   296–7
Neil, Anne   348
Neilson, Mary   xviii, 27, 37,
   40, 44, 48, 50, 128, *Figs 19–20*
New Zealand, Montgomery
   family in   12–13
newspapers, Montgomery's
   love of   37
Newton, Justice   144
North London Collegiate
   School for Ladies   28
Northrop, Joan   5, 205, 210–11,
   212, *Figs 42, 45, 48*, 296
   as PLC Council member
      240–1, 264–5, 268, 269–70,
      272–4, 276–7, 279, 280,
      290, 297, 310, 325, 344,
      350
Northrop, Ray   5, 121–2, 132,
   135, 212, *Figs 45, 48*, 273–4
   letters to PLC parents

177-9, 200
  as PLC Council member 145-6, 156, 159, 160, 162-3, 165, 166, 169, 171-80, 184, 185, 188, 198, 200, 226
  report to Presbyterian Church 175-6
  reunion with Montgomery and Bayston Fig. 52, 364-5
Notes and News of PLC 235-7, 238-9
Nottman, Miss 36
Numurkah, Victoria 18-24, Figs 14-15
Ogden, Miss 88-9
Ogilvy, Alex 122, 127
Old Collegians, support for Montgomery 284 *see also* former PLC students
Old Collegians' Association 198, 201, 239, 253, 287, 329, 349, 351, 354-5
Old Scotch Collegians 188-9, 199, 204, 205, 212, 248
Olorenshaw, Dorothy 38
Olympic Games, 1956 98
O'Reilly, Winston 184
Ormiston, Bill 211-12, 227
Ormond College 159-60
Ormond College Council 196, 371
Ormsby, Joan 67
Ormsby, Marion 67
Orontes (ship) 109
O'Shea, Bob 180, 183
Otranto (ship) 65-8
Owen, Alec 188
parents, informed of PLC challenge 177-8
  support for Montgomery 242, 243, 253, 258, 284, 287, 290-1, 294-5, 297, 321-2
  survey of views of PLC future 188-90, 194-6, 199-200
Parents' Association 187-90, 194-201, 231, 232, 235
  information evening 195-9, 201, 202
  letter to parents 330-1
  meeting with Corporate Affairs Commissioner 240
  and PLC Council retirement age 238-40, 242
  and Principal's residence 238, 242, 243-4
  public meeting Fig. 47, 303-22, 363-4
  relations with PLC Council 242-3, 259-60, 282-3, 303-22, 325-6, 331-3
  and school newsletter 238-9
  support for Montgomery 242, 245, 259-60, 282-5, 322, 334
Parker, Cynthia 62, 252
Patchwork (student magazine) 27, 35, 37, 38, 39-40, 41, 44, 46, Fig. 19, 210
  tribute to Montgomery 352-3
Paton, Wilfred 120
patriarchal Christianity, Presbyterian belief in 192
Patrick, Janet Mabel *see* Jenny Pring

Index

Pearson, Charles Henry 30, 31, 32–4, 312
Pearsons, Ted 5–8, *Fig. 5*, 184, 217–20, 226–7, 360, 361, 363
  on Bradshaw 362–3
  as Clerk of Presbyterian Assembly 2, 165, 168, 169–71, 174, 175, 179, 200, 203, 211, 253, 361
  as Continuing Presbyterian 3, 141
  as PLC Council member 222, 233, 249, 264, 268
  and Scotch College Council 246, 342–3
Perkins, John 139–40
Phillips, John 323–5
Pike, Eileen 94
PLC *see* Presbyterian Ladies' College
polio outbreak, 1937 25
Potter, Miss 209
Potter, Philip 162
Powell, Ruby 112, 117, 120, 123, 128, 160, *Fig. 38,* 285
Presbyterian Assembly, Property Commission 4, 5, 134–5,142–3, 147–1, 154–6, 159–61, 299–300, 368
  PLC legal challenge 161–5, 173–86, 188, 195–6, 203, 204–5, 206, 210–13, 215, 254
    media coverage 190–9
Presbyterian Church of Australia 1, 98, 132
Presbyterian Church of Australia Act 1900 132
  1971 134
Presbyterian Church of Victoria 2, 29, 30, 155, 184
  interference in PLC 168–71, 199, 258–9
  internal dissent 258–9, 260, 282
  rejects schools' incorporation 179
Presbyterian Church of Victoria Special Commission 179–80, 257, 260, 323, 350, 367–70
Presbyterian Church of Victoria Trust, challenges anti-unionists 143–4, 146, 147
Presbyterian Ladies' College xviii, 111, 135
  awarded to Continuing Presbyterians 159–62
  building appeal 200, 277–8, 284–5
  building program 277, 312
  centenary 148–9, *Fig. 40*
  ecumenical ethos 358
  foundation 4, 27, 29, 30–1, 156, 311–12
  Presbytery visitation 137–9
  Principal's residence, plans for 31, 238, 239, 242, 243–4
  school orchestra 36, 38
  as separate legal entity 215, 216, 229, 231–2, 238, 254–5, 312, 313
  staff resignations 341, 354
  staff support for Montgomery 219–20, 234, 293, 297, 300, 333–4, 341
  statement of aims 193–4

395

Presbyterian Ladies' College
Council   120–3, 161, 166,
170–1, 173, 179–81, 200, 210,
212
  1982 tensions   264–85
  appoints Montgomery
    120–3
  appointment of
    Montgomery's successor
    336–7, 339, 342–5, 347
  bulletin to parents   332–4,
    336, 339–40
  dismissal attempt   203–4
  Executive and Finance
    Committee   224, 265,
    266, 268, 270
  newsletter to parents   266–
    7
  post-1980 settlement   221–
    7, 230–3, 240–1, 249–50,
    255–7, 260–2, 313–14,
    324–5, 368–9
  proposed constitution
    215–16
  purged of conservative
    Presbyterians   347, 350
  push for Montgomery's
    retirement   280–5, 369,
    370–1
  relations with Parents'
    Association   188–9, 242–
    3, 259–60, 282–3, 303–22,
    325–6, 331–3
  retirement age   224, 231–2,
    238–40, 273–4
  and school newsletter
    236–7
  submission to Presbyterian
    Property Commission
    154–7, 160
  support for Montgomery
    176, 257–8
  writ filed against   211–12
Presbyterian Ladies' College
  Parents' Association *see*
  Parents' Association
Presbyterian schism, 1974   3,
  139–42, 143, 145, 359
Presbyterian schools, seek
  independence   163, 174,
  176–9, 182, 183–4, 190, 197,
  198–200, 204–5, 215
Presbyterian Schools Bill   201,
  206, 210, 217
Presbyterian Trusts Act Bill
  201, 206, 215
Presbyterians, plan to
  dominate PLC Council   254–
  6
Pring, Jenny   148, 149, 152,
  Fig. 41, 276, 294, 346
Pring, Jim   318
Pringle, Alice, appointment as
  Clyde Principal   124
Pringle, Grant   124
Pritchard, Mrs J   348
Pritchard, Norman   257, 259,
  347, 350, 370–1
Queen Elizabeth II, 1977 visit
  to Australia   78–9
  coronation   73, 75–7 *see
    also* coronation festivities
A Queen is Crowned
  (documentary)   78
Queen Mary, funeral
  procession   73–5
Queen Salote   76–7
Queen's College for Ladies,
  London   28
Ramsay, Tom   318
Rayner, Mark   320, 321
reading, influence on

Index

Montgomery 23, 37, 39
Rechner, Alison *Fig. 48*
Rechner, Russell 236, *Fig. 48*, 249–50, 264, 280, 297, 310, 326, 347–8, 350
Reid, Elizabeth 152
Reid, M.O., *The Ladies Came to Stay* 111
Reilly, Graham (*Age* journalist) 331–2
religious education,
  Continuing Presbyterians' view 229–30, 266–7, 290, 294–5, 298, 307, 315, 329–30, 359, 366, 367–8
    and Presbyterian Ladies' College 265, 266, 301, 312, 313, 315–16, 317–18, 353–4, 366
Rentoul, Annie 8–9
Rentoul, Yvonne 318
Roberts, Dame Joan 121
Robertson, John 72
Rodell, Susanna 296–7
Rodwell, Helen 352
Roff, Philip 244–8, 254
Roosevelt, Eleanor xvii–xviii, 27
Ross, Dorothy 62, 105–6
Rothberg, Adele 38
Royal Concert, Festival Hall 85–6
Royle, John *Fig. 48*
Royle, Pam, and Building Appeal Committee 277, 284, 293–4
  letter to parents 194–5
  letter to Victorian Attorney-General 200, 201
  letters to PLC Council 230–1, 242–3
  letters to Premier and Legislative Assembly 201, 206
  and Parents' Association meeting 303, 307–8, 317, 321, 322
  as Parents' Association President 187-2, 196, 232, 235, 238–9, 242, *Fig. 48*, 263, 282–5, 300, 325
Russell, Ray 179, 221, 223
Ryan, Susan 152
Sandbach, Margaret 198, 296, 320–1
Sandberg, Catherine 62
Saulwick, Irving 188, 199
Schieblich, Frank 35–6
school community, newsletter 235
  representation on PLC Council 215–16, 236–7, 241, 269, 280, 297–8, 303, 310–11, 331
school principals, support for Montgomery 252–3, 302, 304–5
schoolgirl friendships 42–3
Schools Commission 152
Scotch College 4, 13, 26, 51, 135, 159, 244–8, 343
  capitulation in legal proceedings 212
  parents' survey 199–200
  Principal 244–8, 254, 343
Scotch College Council 1, 160, 177, 205, 240, 245–8, 257, 259
Scots' Church 39–40, 221, 257, 350, 370
Scott, Susan 300

Searby, Richard 205, 210
sectarianism, in Numurkah 19
Seifert, Deborah 150
Sergeant, Delys 271
Shaw, Brian 210
Shaw, Leila, *The Way We Were* 39
Skaubryn (ship) 99–100
Smith, Harry 331
Smith, Kat 76
Society for the Settlement of British Women Overseas 88
Souvestre, Marie xviii
Spain, travels in 87–8, 106–7
sport, Montgomery's love of 22, 35, 38–9, 45–6, 98, 117
St Hilda's College, Oxford 28
St Margaret's School Council 371
Stanton, John 271, 279
Starke, Justice 144
Stevens, Bert 163, 183–4, 190, 197, 248, 326
Stevens, Geoff 142
Stewart, Ruth 207–10
Stone, Warren 304
Storey, Haddon 174, 175, 176, 182, 184, 200, 327
Stratford, June 167–9, 176, 181, 198, *Fig. 44*, 342
Stratherne Presbyterian Girls' Grammar School 26, 52, 135
Stubs, Alan 282, 287, 291, 297, 299, 300, 303, 338–9
Sturt craft centre, Mittagong 60
Summers, Anne 152
Sun (newspaper), and Montgomery's appointment to Clyde *Fig. 34*

Swanton, Robert 55, 56, 70, 80, 81, 136
Tait, George 31, 33, 34
Teale, Bruce 320
Templestowe High School selection committee 335–6
ten Brink, Annie 116
Thomas, Bob 139–40, 145
Thompson, Helen 11
Thomson, Barbara 279
Tindale, Evelyn 2, 6–8, 117, 123, 202–3, 218–20, 234, 322, 349
  tribute to Montgomery 353–4
  as Vice Principal *Figs 6, 8*, 258, 336, 342, 345–6
Tintern Grammar School 85, 89, 90, 93–6
Toorak Presbyterian Church 96
Torsch, Daniela 152
Tregenza, John 32, 33
Turnball, Val 62, 65, 67, 68, *Fig. 25*
United Kingdom, travels in 68–70, 81, 82, 90, 101, 106, *Figs 25–6, 30–32*
Uniting Church in Australia, Assembly 184
  commitment to women's equality 192
  establishment 2–3, 4, 133, 162
  schools, as incorporated companies 228–9
  Victorian Synod 184
University of Melbourne 50, 56–7
  opens to women 4–5
University of Melbourne

Index

Council 280, 371
Victorian Attorney-General *see also* Kennan, Jim; Storey, Haddon
  proposed as umpire in PLC Council dispute 316–17, 318, 320, 321, 325, 330, 331
Victorian Corporate Affairs Commissioner 240, 330
Victorian government, and PLC dispute 174–6, 182, 184, 204–6, 316–17, 326–8
Waddell, Ian 221, 222, 249–50
Wade, Jan 240, 330
Walker, Hilary 234
Walker, Jenny 321–2
Walsh, Katie 21–2
Walter and Eliza Hall Institute Human Ethics Committee 372
Ward, Elizabeth 360
Warr, Anne 279, 337
Washington, Miss 34
Waters, Mary 252
Watson, Alan 96
Watson, Marsha 274–6
Webster, Peter 184
Welsh Girls' School, Middlesex 100–1, 105

West, Winifred 58, 59–61
Wiesen Cook, Blanche *see* Cook, Blanche Wiesen
Wilkinson, Nora Jo 46–7, 129, *Fig. 21*, 187, 354–5
Wilson, David 321
Wilson, Sir Samuel 33
Winifred West Schools Limited 60
Winneke, Lady 148, *Fig. 40*
Winneke, Sir Henry 148, 162, *Fig. 40*
Wolstenholme, Elizabeth 30
women elders, Presbyterians objection to 192
women's equality, Uniting Church commitment to 192
Wong, Amy 127
Wood, Constance 85, 88, 89, 90, 93–4, 98, 106, 123
Wood, D'Arcy 162
Woodleigh School Council 371
World War I 14–15
World War II, outbreak 38
  rationing 40
Wykes, Olive *see* Mence, Olive
Yule, George 160

www.ingramcontent.com/pod-product-compliance
Lightning Source LLC
Chambersburg PA
CBHW020313010526
44107CB00054B/1821